The Reign of the Lumber Barons

THE SECRET HISTORY OF SANTA CRUZ COUNTY SERIES
Edited by Derek R. Whaley

This series brings to light long out-of-print books, dusty manuscripts, and other lost material documenting the history of the county from pre-colonial times to the present.

The History of Rancho Soquel Augmentation
The Tragedy of Martina Castro by Ronald G. Powell
The Reign of the Lumber Barons by Ronald G. Powell
The Shadow of Loma Prieta by Ronald G. Powell

Ronald G. Powell

The Reign of the Lumber Barons

Part Two of the History of
Rancho Soquel Augmentation

Edited by Derek R. Whaley

First published in 2021 by
ZAYANTE PUBLISHING
Santa Cruz, California, USA

www.zayantepublishing.com

© 2021 Zayante Publishing

Designed by Derek R. Whaley
Cover and layout: Derek R. Whaley
Printed in the United States of America.

The moral right of the authors has been asserted.

Material from this book courtesy the Ronald G. Powell Collection, Special Collections, McHenry Library, University of California, Santa Cruz.

Front: Portrait of Frederick A. Hihn, from the Aptos History Museum

Back: Workers at the Loma Prieta millpond, 1890s, from the Porter Family Collection, Santa Cruz Museum of Art & History; Hihn mill crew celebrating 143,000 board feet of lumber cut in one day, August 14, 1888, from the Aptos History Museum

All rights reserved. Without limiting the rights under copyright reserved above, no part of this publication may be reproduced, stored or introduced into a retrieval system, or transmitted, in any form or by any means (electronic, mechanical, photocopying, recording or otherwise), without the prior written permission of the copyright owner.

ISBN 978-1-953609-41-0 (printed book)
ISBN 978-1-953609-42-7 (ebook)

In memory of the hundreds of
Chinese laborers who built railroads
into the Santa Cruz Mountains,
without whom none of this history
would have been possible.

Contents

Introduction by Derek R. Whaley ix

The Reign of the Lumber Barons
    Chapter 1: The Call of the Wild 3
    Chapter 2: Redwood Logging in the
        Santa Cruz Mountains 53
    Chapter 3: The Hidden Hand 83
    Chapter 4: The Luck of Roaring Camp . . . 151
    Chapter 5: The Gilded Age 243
    Chapter 6: Life in the Woods 301
    Chapter 7: The Turn of the Screw 363

Notes 421
Select Bibliography 433
Glossary of Logging Terms 437
Index 467

INTRODUCTION
by Derek R. Whaley

Growing up in the Santa Cruz Mountains, I was surrounded by the redwood forest every day. I went to school in Felton, spent my summers at the Forest Lakes pool, hiked through Henry Cowell Redwoods State Park, and rode the Roaring Camp steam train up Bear Mountain. I took for granted the verdant paradise that I lived in—it was just normal. I never wondered why there was a massive, sawed-off redwood stump behind my house. I never asked questions about the history of the San Lorenzo Valley. It wasn't even until my first job at Round Table Pizza in Felton that I realized Santa Cruz County *had* its own history. School never taught local history and I never sought it out.

The truth is, history is everywhere in Santa Cruz County. The Santa Cruz Beach Boardwalk with its grandiose rotunda ballroom and palatial former bathhouse still dominates the Santa Cruz Main Beach. Smokestacks of the now-abandoned Santa Cruz Portland Cement Company plant still tower over Davenport. Both of these structures were completed in 1907, well over a century ago. Meanwhile, Capitola below the iconic Southern Pacific Railroad bridge across Soquel Creek, still feels like a nineteenth-cen-

Introduction

tury summer resort. In Watsonville, old packing houses and freezing plants still line Beach Road and Walker Street, harkening back to a time when all the county's produce went out by rail. But nowhere does the present more directly collide with the past than along the Aptos Creek Fire Road and the myriad trails of The Forest of Nisene Marks State Park.

The park may be named after a woman who briefly owned the property in the mid-twentieth century, but the park's history began over a century earlier, when María Martina Castro Cota Lodge Depeaux was deeded the land by the Mexican government as an augmentation to her small Rancho Soquel in 1844. The massive Shoquel Augmentation, as American authorities labeled it in the 1850s, came to occupy nearly a tenth of the total land in Santa Cruz County. It extended from the peak of Loma Prieta in the southeast to Laguna del Sargento in the north to the hills above Soquel and Aptos in the southwest, creating a massive, trapezoidal rancho encompassing approximately 32,702 acres. Martina Castro was unable to hold onto it, though. Due to deception, fraud, misfortune, and her own mistakes, the entire property slipped through her fingers and fell into the hands of others. This tale is told in its entirety in the first book of this series, *The Tragedy of Martina Castro: Part One of the History of Rancho Soquel Augmentation*.

The people who acquired the Augmentation were initially her children and their spouses, but most of it was soon sold to settlers, investors, and entrepreneurs. Many of these people formed companies and partnerships to harvest the valuable old-growth redwood trees that blanketed the hillsides. Over time, larger and more ambitious companies formed such as the Watsonville Mill & Lumber Company, Grover & Company, the Loma Prieta Lumber Company, and the F. A. Hihn Company. Between 1884 and 1902, they systematically deforested the Aptos, Corralitos, and Valencia Creek watersheds. While the destruction would take another seventy years to complete, what began as a vast untamed wilderness became a wasteland of broken trees and overgrown underbrush interrupted by rural farms and orchards.

Ron Powell saw something in the Santa Cruz Mountains that I did not when I was young. He didn't just see the forest or the trees—he saw a forgotten history. He looked at the massive stumps with sockets drilled into their sides and wondered what they meant. He explored the deep gashes cut into hillsides, asking who cut them and why. He investigated the fills and bridge debris along gullies and creeks, searching for clues as to their purposes. And then he began to research, and he didn't stop until he saw the end of his life approaching. Powell died in 2010 having never published his monumental history of the Augmentation. Instead, he left an unedited first draft for the University of California, Santa Cruz's (UCSC) website, where it was available for a decade before a systemx refresh erased its existence. Ever since, hard copies of the material have sat in McHenry Library's offsite storage, while digital copies have remained in the possession of the former map librarian, Stanley D. Stevens. It was Stevens who made me aware of Powell and his unpublished magnum opus.

Powell was never one to hoard his research discoveries but rather sought to share them with the public. In a Letter of Gift dated March 7, 1998, he specified that: "the materials included in this gift shall be identified as the Ronald Powell Collection and when used and/or copied for research purposes, reference to this source will be included as an acknowledgment." A second document dated June 15, 2005 stated Powell's condition for the use of his research: "All my books and photos are designed for public use and may be copied and reproduced in any medium with the stipulation that acknowledgment is given to the source: The Ronald G. Powell Collection." The photos are the product of Powell's hobby as an amateur photographer. From the 1960s through the 1990s, he took thousands of photographs throughout Northern California of state parks and historical sites. He donated these, too, to UCSC. The Online Archive of California (OAC) includes a collection guide (https://oac.cdlib.org/findaid/ark:/13030/kt-9779s2tn). While these photographs are not included in this text, they are available upon request from the McHenry Library.

Although Powell was a thorough and proficient researcher, he was not a classically trained historian nor was he infallible in his approach. Indeed, he held most historians in such high regard that he accepted their findings without question and often copied their research verbatim into his own work. A consequence of this is that he sometimes copied from bad sources, none more ubiquitous in this book than Estelle Latta's *Controversial Mark Hopkins: The Great Swindle of American History*. Latta argued that two men named Mark Hopkins lived in Sacramento at the same time in the

Introduction

1850s and that their individual stories were conflated due to the machinations of one of their wives, Mary Hopkins. The problem with this narrative is that it is almost entirely wrong and several historians have since debunked it outright. The real Mary Hopkins succeeded her deceased husband on the board of the Southern Pacific Railroad, and she and her adopted son, Timothy Hopkins, owned a large tract of land within the Augmentation. Timothy also later became president of the Loma Prieta Lumber Company. Thus, these individuals are important to the history of the Augmentation, but Latta's interpretation is generally incorrect. To correct this problem all references to Latta's book have been removed or replaced with more reliable sources. A similar approach has been taken with other less reliable or problematic sources.

More problematic, Powell decided to do away with citations entirely midway through writing his manuscript. He stated in a preface to his bibliography that he did this

> *because of the abundance of ambiguous information found in published articles and books and arrived at through interviews conducted by both others earlier and myself. Also, during many exploratory hikes beginning in 1978 conducted throughout the Soquel Augmentation Ranch...plus surrounding territory in Eureka Canyon, San Lorenzo Valley, in sections of Scotts Valley as well as along Los Gatos Creek, I discovered physical evidence that contradicted accepted history. Whenever evidence was discovered by any means that differed from that accepted, it is so stated how my assumption or 'guess' was arrived at.*

The primary problem with this approach is that the majority of information in his manuscript dated after the point where he abandoned citations—from 1884 in context—is still based on outside sources. He addressed this fact by including in-text citations in many instances, but I still had to reconnect the dots in scores of cases to properly attribute the sources of Powell's information.

More generally, Powell made some interesting narrative choices in compiling the information for his manuscript. His intense interest in local railroading matters led him to copy extensively from Rick Hamman's *California Central Coast Railways*, even when the subject matter was not directly related to the history of the Augmentation or Frederick A. Hihn—nominally the two primary subjects of his manuscript. To streamline the text and stay on topic, I have removed all mention of railroads in the San Lorenzo Valley, the Central Pacific Railroad, and the Southern Pacific Railroad, except where they appear as part of a quote. Meanwhile, wherever Hamman or any other author is directly copied, I have replaced the text with an original source or, if that was not possible, paraphrased the source and added additional citations.

The original premise of Powell's work was a history of the Soquel ranchos and Frederick Hihn. However, once Martina Castro's relationship with Rancho Soquel was severed in the 1850s, Powell moved away from it as a focal point in his story. Similarly, he distanced himself from Hihn shortly after noting the completion of the Santa Cruz Railroad in 1876. To compensate for this, he decided to rely on Hamman to fill in the details of what Hihn was doing for the final four decades of his life. But this was a mistake. The story that is told in this book is of the lumber barons who rose to the challenge of harvesting the forests of the Augmentation. Hihn was one of those men but Hamman wasn't focused on Hihn's industrial pursuits, only his railroads. Therefore, to correct this oversight, I have substantially expanded the social history sections of Hihn's large mill on Valencia Creek, adding dozens of articles from the *Santa Cruz Sentinel* and *Santa Cruz Surf* showcasing day-to-day life in a lumber town in the Santa Cruz Mountains. Although it does not do the story justice since the Valencia Creek railway is still grossly under-researched in comparison to most other railroads in the county, it goes a long way toward fleshing out the story of the mill and its adjacent village.

As with *The Tragedy of Martina Castro*, this book is organized chronologically in an unorthodox style more reminiscent of medieval chronicles than modern histories. But this technique creates a uniquely fluid story where different plots intersect, merge, and diverge organically just as they happened. The history is only lightly interpreted, with much of the actual analysis left to the reader. Powell did not want to impose his ideas on readers—he wanted them to come to their own conclusions using the evidence

Introduction

he provided. In that spirit, I have avoided needless interpreting wherever possible and I have left spelling errors and strange grammar in primary source quotes unless clarity is absolutely necessary.

Structuring this book into seven chapters was my own invention to break up the story into thematic units. Chapter 2 is notable in that it is a thorough examination of logging practices in the Santa Cruz Mountains based on three separate documents produced or compiled by Powell. At the end of the book is also a comprehensive glossary of logging terms. All of the maps included in this book were created by Powell to illustrate his arguments. All dollar amounts are contemporary and have not been converted to account for inflation. Powell had originally converted all contemporary U.S. dollar amounts to 1991 values, but the ease of finding inflation calculators online now renders these unnecessary. Unlike the first book in this series, this book does not end conclusively—*The Reign of the Lumber Barons* is very much the first half of a two-part story.

Thanks goes to Ron Powell for compiling this important history and to Stan Stevens for bringing it to my attention. Much thanks also to Dr. Kara Kennedy and Dr. Lindsay Breach for once more proofreading the entire book.

This book begins in the earliest days of redwood logging in the Santa Cruz Mountains, where the imposing forests along Corralitos, Valencia, Soquel, and Aptos Creeks still hosted grizzly bears, and wildcat roars still echoed across hollow canyons. Although Martina Castro's lawsuit had settled claims in the Augmentation, few of those property owners had actually taken possession of their lands. Even the bravest settler dared not venture too far into the twilit woods for fear of losing their way. Ultimately, it took reckless ambition, a patent disregard for the environment, and a tremendous amount of money from Bay Area elite to turn this millennia-old sylvan paradise into a clear-cut wasteland in less than twenty years. Behold the advent of the lumber barons!

Derek R. Whaley
August 22, 2021

The Reign of
the Lumber Barons

CHAPTER 1

~

The Call of the Wild

Logging begins on Corralitos Creek

In 1862, John Bernard Brown of Taswell County, Illinois, built a small sawmill on Rancho Corralitos. Brown was born in 1832 and crossed the Great Plains in 1853 to try his hand at mining in the Sierra Nevada. In 1858, he gave up the pick and moved to the Pajaro Valley where he became involved in the lumber industry along Corralitos Creek. The rural community, located about six and a half miles northwest of Watsonville, was surrounded by mountain slopes covered with the southernmost section of coast redwoods in the Santa Cruz Mountains. The close proximity of these timber tracts to Watsonville and the Pajaro Valley made them an ideal place to begin the first significant commercial logging operation in Santa Cruz County.

Brown, however, was not the first person to cut timber along the creek. Pruett Sinclair and Jones Hoy, two farmers, were the first to erect a small sawmill along Corralitos Creek in 1853. Over the next decade, they helped develop the town of Corralitos. By 1861, the town consisted of two general stores, a livery and blacksmith shop, a schoolhouse, twenty dwellings, and several additional homes under construction. A total of three mills operated along the creek by this time, drawing lumbermen and their families to the village.

Brown moved to take over the nascent lumber industry and recruited former state assemblyman James L. Halstead, Newman Sanborn, and William Williamson as partners. The company, incorporated as Brown, Williamson & Company, erected a second mill further up Corralitos Creek, but both mills quickly reached capacity and the partners were unable to keep up with demand. This led them to build a third, larger mill in the hope that it would resolve the problem, at least temporarily, but demand quickly increased to meet the new supply.[1]

New investors join John Brown in logging operations along Corralitos Creek

In need of additional financing in order to continue to satisfy customer demands, Brown, Williamson & Company invited Charles E. Ford and Lucius Sanborn to join as investors in December 1863.

Ford was born in New Brunswick, New Jersey, on January 23, 1824. At the age of fourteen, his father died and Ford went to work in a dry goods store in Newark. At eighteen, he opened his own drug store and was allowed the title "doctor," as was often the case with druggists at the time. After he opened this store, he purchased two more, both located in New York City. But the thought of gold enticed him to California. He arrived in San Francisco on July 31, 1849 and immediately went to the Gold Country, but he soon became sick and returned to New Jersey to recuperate. In 1850, he returned to California. Avoiding the trap of the gold fields, Ford opened a mercantile store on Jackson Street in San Francisco. From some of his customers, he heard stories of the rich Pajaro Valley to the south. He eventually decided to move to Watsonville to try his hand at farming. Like so many at the time, Ford planted potatoes, making money until the bottom dropped out of the market. He then left farming and opened a mercantile store at the corner of Main and Wall Streets in 1852. The success of the company eventually led him to hire Lucius Sanborn as a bookkeeper in 1865.

Sanborn was born in Maine around 1824 and moved to California in 1849, settling in the Pajaro Valley along with three of his brothers, Alvin, Newman, and William. His success working with Ford was such that he soon became a full partner and the business ran as Ford & Sanborn for fourteen years, until Sanborn retired and sold his interest back to Ford. Sanborn had previously operated as a successful blacksmith in Santa Cruz and was interested in the growing lumber industry, likely through his brother Newman, who was one of Brown's business partners.

It is unclear what the relationship between Sanborn and Ford was prior to their partnership, but the two men both joined Brown's logging business at the same time. When Newman died in 1868, Sanborn helped promote his brother Alvin to the board of directors. Despite this influx of new investor money and further expansions to the company's facilities on Corralitos Creek, the timber firm still struggled to keep up with demand.[2]

The Grover family purchases stumping rights in the Augmentation

The Grovers of Machias, Maine were an old family well known for its grist- and lumbermills. This tradition would continue when the family relocated to the West Coast in the mid-nineteenth century. Elijah Grover and his wife, Hadassah Bean, had several children, among whom were James Lyman (born 1822), Elijah Whitney (born 1828), Stephen Frealon (born 1830), and Jarvis Hilliard (born 1833).

In 1848, Whitney left his family, which was suffering heavily from a typhoid epidemic, and traveled to California to join in the Gold Rush. The journey took eight months around Cape Horn and, once on the West Coast, he staked a claim at French Camp in the Sierra Foothills. In 1850, Whitney invited his three brothers to join him in his hunt for gold. They promptly left Maine and took a ship for Panama, crossing the isthmus and arriving in San Francisco by the end of December.

The brothers reunited at Whitney's claim but quickly split up again to pursue different dreams. Hilliard moved to Stockton while James, with his young son, Dwight William, and his wife, Sarah Ann Steward, petitioned for government land in the San Joaquin Valley to build a farm. Stephen and

Whitney, meanwhile, joined a party of six other men and became some of the first white men to explore the Yosemite Valley in 1852. Two of their party were killed fighting Native Americans and the remaining six left, although they briefly returned to bury their comrades.

The encounter in Yosemite convinced Stephen and Whitney to seek safer pastures. Stephen was hired by Wells, Fargo & Company to run express coaches between Angeles Camp and Stockton. But this became tiresome and Stephen convinced Whitney and Hilliard to join him in an expedition to the coast. After a short while, the brothers decided to settle in Santa Cruz County, likely due to the abundance of redwood trees that could be cut for profit. But times were difficult. Hilliard died on September 30, 1865 leaving Stephen and Whitney without enough cash to finance the building of a sawmill. It is probably at this point that James, Dwight, and Sarah were drawn into the plan. Even so, Stephen and Whitney were forced to take on Luther Elsmore and James Linscott as financial partners to fund the purchase of the mill and timber claims.

With their support, the Grovers approached Guadalupe and Joseph Averon and negotiated a takeover of Joel Bates' derelict mill on December 8, 1865. Along with this purchase, the family acquired a 1/27 claim in the Augmentation. The family also purchased from the Averons stumpage rights to 500 acres in Tract 7. This deal allowed for the Grovers to cut all the timber on the land without purchasing the property itself. The agreement for the land was set at $53.82 per acre, an amount that eventually netted the Averons $26,910 when it was paid in full on September 27, 1882. For an unknown reason, Whitney never appeared on any of the agreements despite being active in the milling operations. Also on December 8, a separate agreement was reached with the heirs of Joel Bates, specifically Louis P. Bates, Rebecca Bates, Abbie Bates, Aura R. Bates, Martha B. Packer and Charles W. Packer. They agreed to sell to the Grovers the 330 acres that composed the unlogged portion of Tract 4, as well as the sawmill and all of its machinery and support structures.

For the first few years it operated, the 15,000-board-feet capacity mill remained at its original location beside its millpond. Both Elsmore and Linscott, soon after joining in the partnership, withdrew from the logging industry completely. Linscott eventually became the county superintendent

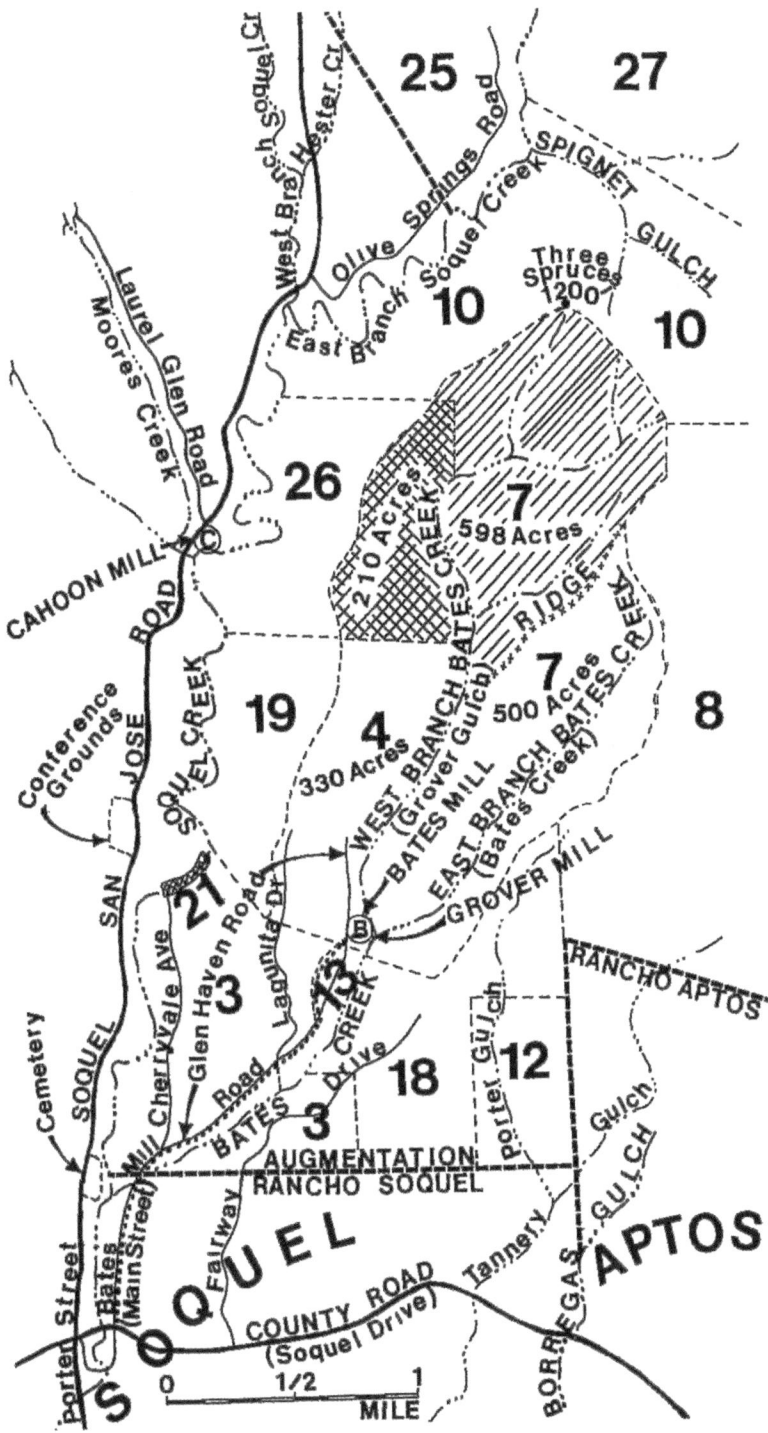

FIGURE 1.1 TRACTS 4 AND 7 IN THE AUGMENTATION

of schools while Elsmore transitioned to other businesses.

Phyllis B. Patten, who lived there as a child, gave a description of the Grover family's first mill. She remembers the mill site as a cluster of cabins built on rough boards and battens (floorings). There was a two-story company store, corrals for the livestock, and a skid road that led up along Grover Gulch Creek and a second one up Bates Creek, both heading into the forest. She remembers watching teams of eight to twelve oxen pulling trains of eight to fourteen logs from the forest to the millpond for soaking and sorting. At its peak, the mill employed up to sixty men who were paid $1.50 a day. They worked six days a week from 6 a.m. to 6 p.m. If the mill worker ate and slept at the logging camp, which most did, 50¢ a day was deducted from their wages. Because the mill workers and loggers in the forest had to live either within the logging camp or in temporary camps in the forest and were reliant on the company for food and sustenance, they often were in debt to the company.[3]

James Dougherty arrives from the East and joins his brother William in San José

William Patrick Dougherty, born in 1832, left Ireland with his younger brother, James, and settled in Missouri. Wanting more adventure, William headed west, settling in the Santa Clara Valley in 1858. He first tried farming but ended up turning to the large redwood trees that dominated the Santa Cruz Mountains, cutting and selling them at a small scale to local firms.

After serving in the Union Army during the Civil War, James Dougherty headed west to join his brother William in San José in late 1865. The brothers were able to quickly establish themselves as leaders in the lumber industry in the Santa Cruz Mountains and began expanding their operations deeper into the foothills above Los Gatos.[4]

Frederick Hihn pens letter to the *Sentinel* promoting a railroad

On January 6, 1866, Frederick A. Hihn penned a letter to the editor of the *Santa Cruz Weekly Sentinel* entitled "The Necessity of a Railroad—How and Where Can It Be Built?" It reads:

> EDITOR SENTINEL.—Many of the leading men of Watsonville and Santa Cruz have, for some time, tried to devise means to connect various points of our county by a railroad to San Francisco, but up to the present time, nothing has been accomplished. Three different routes have been spoken of, but, owing to the many difficulties which would have to be encountered to build a road across the mountains in the northern and middle portion of our county, the route from San Jose up the valley to Gilroy, and thence along the Pajaro river to Watsonville, seems to be the most feasible and the most likely to pay, because it would run nearly all the way through fertile land where no good shipping facilities can be had. The road might be extended to the town of Santa Cruz, but, although desirable, it is very doubtful whether that portion of the road could be made to pay even running expenses. We have a large amount of freight, but can ship much cheaper by water than by rail. To the Pajaro valley this road has become a necessity. While the people in our neighborhood have no immediate, direct interest in a railroad ending at Watsonville, no one will deny that it would be very convenient to be even within nineteen miles from the terminus. Feeling interested in the enterprise I propose to start the ball rolling by suggesting a plan:
>
> Let the interested parties raise a sufficient amount of money to pay for grading the road and to purchase the necessary ties, the iron to be bought on credit, giving mortgage bonds as security; the road, when finished, to be delivered to the San Jose Railroad Company, they agreeing to carry freight and passengers at a stipulated price, using their own rolling stock, to keep the road in repair, to pay the interest on the mortgage bonds, and after the first or second year, to set aside five or ten per cent of the gross receipts for the gradual redemption of the mortgage bonds.
>
> So far as I can ascertain, it has cost for grading, ties, depots and laying down the track on the San Jose railroad from

$10,000 to $14,000 per mile. The distance from San Jose to Watsonville is said not to be more than forty-five miles, and as the road would run nearly all the way through level land, with the exception of say five miles of steep hillsides between Gilroy and Watsonville, the expense of grading, etc., would not be more, perhaps even less than on the San Jose road.—The necessary timber for the ties would also be at a convenient distance. But, taking the highest estimate the road would cost, exclusive of iron and rolling stock, $600,000. This amount should be raised as follows:

San Jose Railroad Company	$150,000
Citizens of Santa Clara County	250,000
" Monterey County	100,000
" Santa Cruz County	100,000
Total	$600,000

But the people of this county could raise $200,000 if needed, particularly as the money would be payable in installments within a term of three years, and even that sum would not be one-third of the amount of the direct benefit to be derived by the building of the road. There are 10,000 acres of land in Pajaro valley which would be increased in value,

$30, per acre, making			$300,000
10,000 acres	"	$15, "	150,000
10,000	"	$5, "	50,000
Real Estate in Watsonville			50,000
The remainder of the country would surely be benefited			100,000
Total			$650,000

The people of Pajaro valley, and of the county generally, should act at once. Let there be a railroad meeting in Watsonville.   F. A. HIHN.

The railroad of which Hihn speaks was the San Francisco & San Jose Railroad, incorporated on August 18, 1860 to link the two named cities. Trains first operated along the entire line on September 14, 1863, and the Bay Area erupted in railroad fever, although very little resulted from this excitement initially. On December 2, 1865, the company incorporated a subsidiary, the Southern Pacific Railroad, with which the directors hoped to continue its main line south from San José to Gilroy and beyond, eventually crossing into the San Joaquin Valley and Sierra Nevada where it could meet up with the Atlantic & Pacific Railroad near the Nevada border. The United States Congress had passed an act commissioning the construction of an Atlantic & Pacific Railroad on July 27, 1866. It established that a transcontinental railroad would run from St. Louis to San Francisco following the coast north from Los Angeles. The fact that this proposed transcontinental line would pass within an easy reach of Santa Cruz County motivated local entrepreneurs such as Frederick Hihn.[5]

Meeting held in Santa Cruz to plan a county railroad

The first official meeting concerning the construction of a railroad within Santa Cruz County was held in Watsonville on the evening of February 3, 1866. During the meeting, Frederick Hihn outlined his plan for building a railroad between Watsonville and San Jose and its associated costs, which totaled $861,930. None in attendance opposed the idea but some did not want county bonds to help pay for the project. A Railroad Committee was formed at the end of the meeting to investigate further issues with constructing a railroad line and work out how to fund such a route.[6]

Highland Center, Skyland, and Hotel Miltonmont on the Summit

Around 1867, a man surnamed Dodge leased land from Lyman J. Burrell along the western end of Skyland Ridge off Stetson Road in Tract 15 and along the western side of Tract 20 in the Augmentation. He built a large home which he surrounded with a vineyard, and he soon built a small winery. Not long afterwards, other settlers began to move into the area and called it Highland Center.

Around the same time just to the north, Judge George Miller purchased four acres of land and began subdividing it. He named his subdivision

Skyland, possibly because it was slightly higher in elevation than nearby Highland. Most of the people Miller attracted to Skyland were from the Santa Clara Valley, San José in particular, and wanted a summer vacation home in the mountains. Around 1880, Miller built a small hotel for his frequent visitors, which became known as Hotel Miltonmont. The building was located near the junction of Miller Road and Miller Cutoff just off the Soquel Turnpike. The popularity of the area was such that a post office was established on April 18, 1893. Highland Center, meanwhile, became subsumed into Skyland and the name was translocated elsewhere.

Although Miller never intended to use the hotel for commercial purposes, his son Anson took it over and ran it as a roadside hostelry for many decades. By the end of 1910, however, when the post office shut its doors, business was flagging. The Miller family continued to own the land until 1930, when the Tre Monte Corporation bought the property and converted the hotel for use as a mental health hospital. This facility operated until around 1959, when the old hotel became a private residence.[7]

The California Coast Railroad forms a joint stock company

Plans to build a railroad from Gilroy to Watsonville were finalized during the week of June 16, 1867, when Nathaniel W. Chittenden, Charles Ford, Alvin Sanborn, Augustine W. Blair, Thomas Donato Alexander, and Frederick Hihn, alongside several smaller investors, combined their forces to finance the formation of the California Coast Railroad Company.[8]

Construction begins on the Santa Clara & Pajaro Valley Railroad

With the Southern Pacific Railroad incorporated, the directors of the San Francisco & San José Railroad felt that it was time to move forward with their plans to build a transcontinental railroad across the southern United States. The first step was the incorporation of the Santa Clara & Pajaro Valley Railroad on January 2, 1868, which would link San José and Gilroy together via thirty miles of track. Construction began on April 21.

The start of the Southern Pacific project attracted the attention of the Big Four—Leland Stanford, Collis Huntington, Mark Hopkins, and Charles Crocker—who jointly controlled the Central Pacific Railroad, which built the western end of the first transcontinental railroad. In mid-1868, the Big Four bought a controlling interest in the San Francisco & San Jose Railroad in an attempt to eliminate a potential competitor and eventually establish a transcontinental line not reliant on the Union Pacific Railroad, which controlled the eastern end of the existing transcontinental route. As a result, the Atlantic & Pacific Railroad was forced to seek a partner elsewhere. Suddenly, the Bay Area was dominated by the Central Pacific Railroad and its subsidiaries. Meanwhile, Santa Cruz County capitalists saw the likelihood that their county would sit along a transcontinental railroad disappear and they began petitioning the Big Four for railroad access.

As scheduled, the Santa Clara & Pajaro Railroad route between San José and Gilroy was completed on March 13, 1869, bringing rail one step closer to Santa Cruz County.[9]

Land transfer by James Phillips to James and Stephen Grover

On July 29, 1869, James B. Phillips sold half of his interest in Tract 27 in the Augmentation to James Grover. Until this date, the sawmill on the property had remained inactive. Immediately after buying a stake, Grover began refurbishing the facility. Due to a debt that Phillips owed to James How, he agreed on August 29 to transfer all of his profits from the mill and property to How until the debt was fully paid. For the next seven months, the facility operated as the Phillips & Grover Mill.

Despite the successful reopening of the mill in late 1869, Phillips was unable to make sufficient profit to repay the debt that he owed to How and was forced to sell his remaining half interest in the mill to Grover's brother Stephen on February 5, 1870. With the sale of the land and mill, the facility passed entirely into the hands of the Grover family.[10]

Frederick Hihn advertises "Homes for a Thousand Families"

On July 29, 1869, Frederick Hihn took out two advertisements in *The Pajaronian* promoting his "Homes for a Thousand Families" program.

He wrote:

> F. A. Hihn, Esq., with his usual enterprise and liberality has thrown into market an immense tract of first class land, situated in the county of Santa Cruz. Six thousand acres of fine farming land and six hundred lots, are offered to those who desire homes, at most liberal rates. Those of limited means can ask for no easier terms on which to purchase good land, than ten years *to pay the principal, with only* eight per cent *interest per annum. Probably there is no county in California that offers more enticing inducements to the farmer or any other class. See adv.*

The advertisement in question included a hefty mix of perks and enticements:

HOMES FOR
1,000 FAMILIES!
IN THE
COUNTY OF SANTA CRUZ,
CELEBRATED FOR
The Best Climate in the World,
GOOD SCHOOLS,
Its Thrifty Population,
Manufactories, Productions.
EXPORTS—*Grain, Flour, Fruit, Wines, Lumber, Wood, Lime, Powder, Fuse, Paper, Glue, Butter, Cheese, Live Stock, Meats, Eggs, etc.*
Value of Annual Exports, $5,000,000
FOR SALE
600 TOWN LOTS *in the prosperous Towns of* SANTA CRUZ *and* SOQUEL, *at from $100 to $500.*
6,000 ACRES OF LAND, SUITABLE FOR
Grain-growing, Dairies, Orchards, and Vineyards, at from $1 to $100 per acre.
TERMS OF SALE—*Purchase price payable in U.S.*

> *Currency, in ten equal yearly payments, with EIGHT per*
> *cent. interest per annum.*
> *For further particulars, address*
> *F. A. HIHN, Santa Cruz.*

The locations of the 6,000 acres of land mentioned are not named specifically, but it can be assumed that they were located within Rancho Soquel and the Augmentation, of which Hihn owned 865.857 acres and 15,441 acres respectively.

At this time, Hihn had not yet settled on the name 'Capitola' for the property at the mouth of Soquel Creek. However, the name was already circulating in newspapers. Derived from the main character in the book *The Hidden Hand* by E. D. E. N. Southworth, *Capitola* became a popular traveling play that reached peak fame in the Bay Area in the early 1870s. Meanwhile, Capitola was also the name of a beloved racehorse—undoubtedly named after the character—in the same years. It was only on June 18, 1874 that Capitola was permanently chosen as the name of the camp.[11]

Frederick Hihn accepts candidacy for State Assembly

Before the Democratic Party Convention was held in Santa Cruz on August 7, 1869, twenty-eight businessmen had signed an endorsement for Frederick Hihn as their candidate for the California State Assembly, even though Hihn claimed no party affiliation. Among his supporters were Elihu Anthony, John Porter, Benjamin Nichols, Benjamin Porter, and Samuel Drennan. The other Democrats in attendance at the convention consented and Hihn was nominated.

In an interview with a *Sentinel* reporter on August 10, Hihn said: "Believing that I can be of service to our county, I have accepted the above call, and present myself to you as an Independent Candidate for Member of Assembly—pledging myself to you that, if elected, I will guard the interests of our county and State to the best of my ability."

On August 24, 1869, Charles Osgood Cummings, the editor-in-chief of *The Pajaronian*, strongly endorsed the candidacy of Frederick Hihn, which he published in a letter included in the August 28 issue:

As the election approaches, the interest in the election of the People's Ticket increases here; still, the friends of the "Slate," who desire to prostitute the County Government to their own selfish ends, for the next two years, are prolific with low-flung slander against F. A. Hihn, the recognized champion of the people in the present contest. We will notice but one, however, for the baseness of the attack disarms the force of the slander. Mr. Hihn is accused of opposing Free Schools. This is refreshing to us here in this little town. No one has stood forward with more zeal and interest in the advancement of our School System here than F. A. Hihn. When the funds were exhausted, he went down into his own pocket for money, while his present slanderers skulked behind their duty. Why, bless us, one would think they owned the whole Free School System, to hear their talk. Time rolls on, with two members of our Board of Trustees here impotent for any good whatever, the School funds now being basely mis spent. The people demanded a hearing—a showing of accounts. They could not get it. The public Schools were getting to be a "pet" institution—taxes were levied, and paid by the liberal population here—Hihn among the number—and those taxes were as liberally spent in the interest of the Trust as above referred to. The people, Hihn among the number, opposed any further outlay of money until the Trustees accounted for past moneys. Another large School Tax was levied. The people, Hihn among the number, asked the privilege of knowing where the money was going. They were refused notice. They resisted the collection of the tax until another election could be held for Trustees. This was done, and one not in the ring was elected. Then the delinquent taxes were all paid without a murmur. Out of this trial for right comes this slander.

Among those who approved the squandering of School money, are many supporters of the Red Ticket. Why not slander them? But it is too late now to influence the Republican or Democratic voter of this county by these groundless slanders against Hihn. He has always been in the first rank of progress and improvement in this county, and is there today. He numbers more warm friends in both parties than any man in our midst; and hence, those who sit in their dingy offices here in Santa Cruz, and level their shafts of slander at such a prominent mark, find it necessary to do so by sending their candidate for Sheriff ahead, loaded with their malice, in order to shelter their cowardly heads from the merited rebuke of the people.[12]

Frederick Hihn's opponent speaks out against him

Frederick Hihn's Republican opponent in the State Assembly race, C. K. Ercanbrack, wrote a letter to *The Pajaronian* on August 16, 1869, but the newspaper chose not to print the letter until the day before the election on September 2. Ercanbrack was attempting to win over the wavering Republicans of Watsonville:

Having been nominated as your Candidate for the office of Assemblyman at the Primary elections held in the various precincts of the county, on the 17th day of July 1869—having received a large majority of your votes as nominee for said office, and knowing that the most determined efforts are being made by a few pretended friends of the Republican party, who have formed a coalition with the Democratic party, to defeat me at the coming election, I consider it my duty now, for the first time since the opening of the canvass to address a few words to you. I sought your suffrages in an open and fair manner, at the late Primary election, and received the handsome majority of one hundred and fifty votes. Since that result was made known, certain Republicans who worked hard at the primaries to defeat me, have issued a "call" to F. A. Hihn, to run as an Independent candidate. This call was presented to the late Democratic Convention held in Santa Cruz. This body, in their published minutes use the following language:
"The Democratic Convention, having considered the call of Messrs. Anthony, Kirby, Porter and others, naming you as

an Independent candidate for member of Assembly, decided to endorse said call."

Mr. Hihn was called before this Democratic Convention, and, proving satisfactory, was thus endorsed, and became, to all intents and purposes the candidate for the Democratic party. But it is urged that the Convention endorse the "call," but not the man. This must be intended as a sugar-coated pill for Republicans but not for Democrats. Let Democrats once believe Mr. Hihn, and how many of their votes would he get? Endorse a "call" upon a man to come out for an office without endorsing the man! As George Francis Train would say, "Glory be to tweedledum, hallelujah to tweedledee." I, then, as the Republican candidate, solicit the suffrages of the people of Santa Cruz county and am opposed by the candidate of the Democratic party, F. A. Hihn. It is true they call their ticket the "People's Ticket," but some persons would like to be informed, when the Democratic party became the "People." If Mr. Hihn has not been endorsed by the Democratic party, and if he does not expect to be elected chiefly by democratic votes (if elected at all), let him enter a fair and square denial.

But not merely as the candidate of the Republican party, do I solicit your votes. I know that I have an honest purpose to do my full duty, if elected, and I believe that I have the ability to be of some service to the County and State of my adoption. If elected, I pledge to you, that I will endeavor to labor for the best interests of our County and State.[13]

Frederick Hihn elected to State Assembly for 6th District

On September 4, 1869, the *Sentinel* reported the results of the election of the previous day. It revealed that Frederick Hihn beat C. K. Ercanbrack 945 to 677 in the race for the State Assemblyman for California's 6th District. The *Daily Alta California* extolled the virtues of Hihn on August 28:

> *Mr. F. A. Hihn, of Santa Cruz county, has accepted his nomination as an independent candidate for the Assembly. Santa Cruz is fortunate in the probability of being represented by a*

> *gentleman so well suited in ability and social standing as Mr. Hihn. A Legislature composed of such men as he could be relied upon for honest and intelligent service in promoting the general welfare, and protecting the State from the raids upon her treasury so constantly attempted.*

The *Sentinel*'s editor added his own comment following the election:

> *Mr. Hihn is our Legislator elect. If the prophesies of those who opposed him can be taken for future history, he will be the next State Senator from this District. We will see what we will see!*[14]

Frederick Hihn proposes a railroad for Santa Cruz County

On October 2, 1869, a meeting was held in the courthouse in Santa Cruz, presided over by Jacob Parsons of Soquel, in which Frederick Hihn made a formal proposal to incorporate a railroad to operate within Santa Cruz County. His paper read:

> *"Proposition for the county of Santa Cruz to aid the construction of a Railroad from the town of Santa Cruz, up the San Lorenzo river for fifteen miles, and from the town of Santa Cruz through Soquel and Watsonville to the southern boundary of the county, with a branch up the Soquel creek for ten miles, by the issuance of county bonds, bearing eight per cent, interest per annum, and payable within twenty years, to the amount of six thousand dollars per mile, upon the construction of each five miles of such road, with a good iron tee rail; such bonds to constitute a first-mortgage on such road. The interest on said bonds to be paid by the county for the first ten years. Such road to be taxed the same as other property, but not to be assessed at less than eight thousand dollars per mile, and all taxes collected therefrom to be used towards the payment of the interest on said bonds. At the expiration of ten years such additional sum shall be*

annually collected from said road, which added to said taxes will be sufficient to pay the interest, and one-tenth part of the principal of said bonds."

Mr. Hihn then stating that while the above proposition had been drawn up for the purpose of bringing the subject of railroads before the people, with the view of obtaining county aid, for the benefit of every part of the county, as far as practicable, read the following statement for the purpose of showing that a railroad, even if built in one end of the county, only would result to the benefit of the whole county, and therefore deserved county aid.

Pajaro township, including town of Watsonville, has a territory of 10 square miles, or, in acres..........................64,000
Deduct for waste land, acres..................................14,000
Total..50,000

Present assessable value, $4 per acre, making a total of $200,000, which at two per cent, yields now a County tax of $4,000.

It is generally admitted that the value of this land would be double, if connected by railroad with Gilroy, yielding thus an additional tax of $4,000.

The interest on the bonds for ten miles of railroad from Watsonville to the center line of county at the rate of $6,000 bonds per mile, would amount annually to $4,800.
Deduct tax derived from railroad..........................$2,400
Balance int. to be paid by county...........................$2,400
Increase of county tax on real estate in Pajaro township by construction of railroad.............................$4,000
Annual net gain by county..................................$1,600
Without counting the increase of personal property and improvement in real estate, or the increase of value of property in all other parts of the county.

Col. Heath moved an amendment. Discussion pro and con and paper laid on the table. R. C. Kirby moved that a Committee of seven be appointed, to report two weeks from *to-night in this house, on the plans of constructing a railroad, and that the Chair appoint such Committee. The motion was carried, and the following named gentlemen placed on said Committee:*

S. L. Bennett, San Lorenzo; A. Pray, Sr., L. Heath, Santa Cruz; B. Porter, Dr. Fagan, Soquel; Dr. Ford, B. A. Barney, Watsonville. By motion F. A. Hihn added to Committee.[15]

Railroad Committee holds first public meeting

A week after Frederick Hihn's proposal, the first meeting of the Railroad Committee met on October 9, 1869 to discuss the various aspects of building and operating a railroad in Santa Cruz County. Because of the complexity and length of the article published in the *Sentinel*, it has been rearranged and shortened for the sake of clarity.

The committee members almost unanimously agreed that a railroad was an absolute necessity to promote the town and maintain local industries. The only disagreement was regarding the routes and the best means of building a route that would connect with the San Francisco and San Jose Railroad in the Bay Area.

The majority of the people at the meeting advocated for the construction of a main trunk line from Santa Cruz via Soquel and Watsonville to Gilroy. Meanwhile, a minority favored a route up the San Lorenzo Valley via Felton and then over the mountains to Belmont or Redwood City. Surveyors also found that a more affordable potential railroad route could go up Soquel Creek and through the mountains to Los Gatos Creek, cutting the distance to San Jose significantly, although this option was not considered seriously at the meeting.

The committee elected Eben Bennett as chairman to oversee the engineering aspects of the routes and have the various survey teams report back at the next meeting. Bennett had come to Santa Cruz in 1866 where he operated at lime kiln in Felton. His toll road to Santa Cruz, which later became Highway 9, opened in 1868. Bennett sent two teams of surveyors to inspect the two favored routes and compiled the following conclusions from their reports:

SANTA CRUZ TO SAN FRANCISCO
VIA FELTON AND TIN CAN RANCH
Assigned to Dr. Spencer and Alexander McPherson

A previous preliminary report had determined that the divide at the top of the San Lorenzo Valley near Tin Can Ranch would be at approximately 2,000 feet elevation and require a substantial tunnel of approximately 1,700 feet. However, any substantial railroad project in the San Lorenzo Valley would greatly benefit the area by opening it up to settlement. It would also bring it into direct communication with San Francisco since the route would bypass San José and go straight north from the other side of the range. This would mean that goods could be shipped more directly to market at a cheaper rate than the other two routes under consideration.

SANTA CRUZ TO SAN JOSÉ
VIA SOQUEL AND LOS GATOS CREEK
Previously examined by Thomas W. Wright

Wright had determined several years earlier that the divide at the top of Soquel Creek was at 1,430 feet elevation and a tunnel could reduce that elevation to as low as 600 feet if a mile-long tunnel were bored under the ridge. This would make the distance between Santa Cruz and San José about 31 miles, which would make it the shortest route to the San Francisco and San José Railroad.

SANTA CRUZ TO SAN JOSÉ
VIA WATSONVILLE AND GILROY
Assigned to Mr. Black

This route has the benefit that it would hit all of the major population centers in Santa Cruz County, including Soquel, Aptos, and Watsonville, as well as Pajaro. It also would in effect act as an extension of the current Santa Clara and Pajaro Valley Railroad route to Gilroy and could potentially become part of the planned Southern Pacific Railroad. All of these elements made it more important as a corridor of commerce than the two alternative routes. Its potential for expansion was also greater, with it eventually extending south to the Salinas Valley, where it could tap sources of grain, wool, dairy, and other industries. In addition, it would be easier to convince south county residents to support the route and potentially still lead to the route's expansion north through the San Lorenzo Valley or along the coast, where it could become a mainline thoroughfare.

In the end, those present at the meeting were nearly unanimous in their support for a track between Santa Cruz and San José via any of the proposed routes and agreed to a subscriber bonus of between $150,000 and $200,000 for its construction. However, attendees were mostly opposed to any branch lines in the first round of construction, although a small minority argued that building branch lines first could attract outside investors into building the more expensive main line without as heavy a cost to the county and its residents.[16]

Land sold by Benjamin Cahoon for the erection of Mountain School

On October 20, 1869, Benjamin Cahoon formally deeded to the Trustees of the Mountain School District a small parcel of land for a school along the west side of the Soquel Turnpike (today's Soquel San Jose Road). Plans for the erection of the school began in April when a notice of an assessment was announced for inclusion in the next local election. In June, it was decided that the school would be located a quarter mile from Cahoon's mill, suggesting Cahoon had already agreed to the land sale by that time. The final location of Mountain School was a half mile north of Laurel Glen Road on School Creek Road. The schoolhouse was completed in the fall of 1870 with an inaugural class of thirty-five students under the discerning eye of Miss Lulu Hall of Soquel.[17]

Railroad Committee submits report concerning the route of the county's proposed railroad

Following three weeks of surveys, research, and debates, the report of the Railroad Committee was submitted for consideration by the public on October 23, 1869. The report recommended that a railroad be built from Santa Cruz through Soquel to Watsonville and then continue an additional ten miles to the county line east of Chittenden. This would mean that railroad crews working from Gilroy would only have to build ten miles of track to connect with the Santa Cruz line. Frederick Hihn estimated several costs for building and maintaining the route, as well as the potential income from freight, passenger service, and other revenue sources. Those in attendance at the meeting accepted his statistics as fair and reflected more than a passing knowledge of railroad matters.

The committee recommended

> *that the county of Santa Cruz aid the construction of said railroad from the town of Santa Cruz by the way of Watsonville to the southwestern line of said county, to the amount of $10,000 per mile, in the bonds of said county, bearing interest at the rate of eight per cent per annum and payable within ten years from the issuance thereof. Said bonds to be issued upon the construction and completion of each five miles of said railroad.*
>
> *Provided. That four thousand dollars ($4,000) per mile, in bonds, shall be withheld on the road from the eastern line of the county to Watsonville until the railroad is constructed to a point at least ten miles westerly from the said town of Watsonville, when the said four thousand dollars per mile shall be paid to the company who shall have constructed said last mentioned ten miles of railroad. Such bonds to constitute a first-mortgage on said road.*
>
> *Provided. That on the road from the southeastern line of the county to Watsonville an additional amount of four thousand dollars per mile may be borrowed by the company owning said road, and to be secured jointly with the amount received from the county as first-mortgage bonds on said road.*
>
> *The interest on said bonds to be paid by the county for the first ten years. All taxes assessed on, and collected from said road, to be used toward the payment of the interest on such bonds. At the expiration of ten years such additional*

sum shall be annually collected by the county, from said road, which, added to the taxes, will be sufficient to pay the interest and one-tenth part of the principal of said bonds.[18]

Watsonville responds to the Railroad Committee's report

The editor of *The Pajaronian*, having insufficient space in his October 23, 1869 summary of the Railroad Committee's report to comment on the proceedings, took the opportunity in the November 4 issue to make some observations on the matter:

> *The proposed railroad, as stated in the report, will commence at Santa Cruz, go to Watsonville, via Soquel, and from Watsonville to the county line, ten miles toward Gilroy. The estimates made by Mr. Hihn, in regard to the cost of the road, amount of freight, travel, etc., are very fair, and show more than a passing knowledge of railroad matters. The report of the railroad Committee, however, is open to a great deal of criticism...*
>
> *...it will be seen that the 20 miles of road from this place to Santa Cruz, will receive $10,000 per mile, while from here to the county line, $4,000 of the bonds are to be withheld, leaving us only $6,000 per mile for the 10 miles! What is that for? No one with any idea of justice will vote in favor of such a proposition. It looks to us as though a touch of coercion is to be tried on at this end of the county. We will not charge any man in Santa Cruz with enmity to the interests of Watsonville, but will say that the Committee have doubtless made a mistake in regard to the proposed appropriation of county bonds, and before further action is taken in the matter we would advise them to make proper corrections. After the ten miles of road are completed, however, from Watsonville to the county line, the $4,000 withheld shall be paid* to the Company *who constructs the aforesaid ten miles of road, the county taking a mortgage thereon. What good, we would like to know, would $4,000 per mile do us after ten miles of road is completed. There would still be ten miles more to construct be-*

fore we reached Gilroy. To sum up this question of county aid, it stands thus: The citizens of the Pajaro Valley desire a road to Gilroy, twenty miles in length. To aid us in this venture certain astute individuals at the County Seat propose that the county give us for the first ten miles the sum of $60,000 to start with, then take a mortgage on the road for $40,000! This operation will effectually knock the remaining ten miles of road to Gilroy higher than Gilroy's kite; for moneyed men, of whom we expect aid, will not touch a road on which there is a prior mortgage.

At the same time the citizens of Santa Cruz desire a road from Watsonville to Santa Cruz, and the aforesaid astute individuals propose to obtain aid from the county to the amount of $200,000, but say nothing about withholding two-thirds of the amount until the road is completed. They take the turkey and give us the crow, or give us the crow, and they take the turkey. The least that could be done under the circumstances would be to give us the full $10,000 per mile withholding nothing.

The proper way for the county to act in the matter is to take stock in the 30 miles of road to the amount of $300,000, the same as Los Angeles, Santa Clara, San Joaquin and other counties have done. If the county intends to aid in the construction of a road let it do it in a businesslike way. Take stock in the road or loan its credit to each mile alike, or do nothing. By taking stock as we propose the county would have a controlling interest in the road and would be amply secured.[19]

Letter from Frederick Hihn concerning railroad matters

With railroad matters heating up and an impending conflict over differing priorities between Santa Cruz and Watsonville, Frederick Hihn chimed in on December 16, 1869 in a letter in *The Pajaronian*, writing:

> In Railroad matters I have yet done nothing; that is to say I have not introduced any bill, nor shall I before next month, for the following reasons: It is proposed to have the State aid the construction of Railroads to the extent of, say $5,000

per mile, survey and location to be approved by a Board of Commissioners. Furthermore, Mr. C. Maclay, Senator from Santa Clara, has introduced a bill, of which, I have not got the insight yet, proposing the granting of a franchise for a Railroad through the counties of San Mateo, Santa Clara, Santa Cruz and Monterey. Besides this it is proposed to extend the road from Gilroy, south, via Salinas, by the San Jose and San Francisco Railroad Company, if sufficient aid is granted. All these projects will develop themselves within a few weeks; and by that time it may also be possible that the conflicting interests of our county will come to some better understanding. I get all kinds of letters on this subject. Every writer seems to be sure, unless his views are adopted, we will have no Railroad at all.[20]

Frederick Hihn confers with railroad leaders in Watsonville

On December 29, 1869, during his journey home from Sacramento, Frederick Hihn met with the leading railroad men in Watsonville to discuss the bill that he planned to submit to the California State Assembly early the next year. The group, after much discussion, finally agreed on the terms of the bill, which *The Pajaronian* reported the next day, arguing that "we think [it] will be satisfactory to all parties, when it is known that the present proposed bill will decrease the amount of county aid to the extent of nearly $200,000." The newspaper explains:

> *It is proposed in the new plan that the county aid in the construction of a main trunk road from the eastern line of the county to Santa Cruz, to the amount of $7,000 per mile. The Soquel branch is ignored, entirely, but the county shall aid the construction of a road ten miles long up the San Lorenzo river, to the extent of $2,000 per mile. The amount of aid by the county, according to the above plan, is not large—hardly more than one-half by the former plan. We shall probably see a copy of the bill before our next issue, when we can speak more at length on the subject.*[21]

The Burrell Schoolhouse on the Summit

The Summit School District was established around 1870 with a single room of a private home on Schultheis Lagoon near the crossroads of Summit Road and the Santa Cruz Gap Turnpike (Old Santa Cruz Highway) just to the east of today's Highway 17. The lagoon was a favorite spot in which to pass away the noon hour paddling around on half-submerged logs, as recalled by E. H. Chase (*née* Loomis). The school was eventually moved to a permanent location a half mile down the turnpike towards Los Gatos. This new structure was built by Edward Martin and is a private residence today.

The second school on the Summit opened shortly afterwards on land donated by Lyman Burrell near the boundary of Santa Clara and Santa Cruz Counties. To this day, the school district bears his name. In 1889, the schoolhouse burned down during a brush fire that consumed much of the Summit area. The building was rebuilt by local residents in 1890, and then on July 4th of the same year, it was given the first flagpole of any school in the mountains. The school was also the first school to have a bell in the area. The second structure is currently located on the south side of Summit Road at a slight southwest angle from Loma Prieta Avenue and is now a private residence that has been refurbished and surrounded with grapevines.[22]

California Southern Railroad Company formed

The management of the Central Pacific Railroad Company, known as the Big Four, began to take notice of profits that were available in both Santa Cruz and Monterey Counties. To realize these profits, they established a subsidiary on January 22, 1870: the California Southern Railroad Company. With this, they planned to construct a 45-mile line from Gilroy to Salinas via Watsonville. The estimated cost was set at $1,500,000. Charles Mayne, Peter Donohue, Richard P. Hammond, H. M. Newhall, and N. S. Sweeny were appointed directors.[23]

Frederick Hihn introduces Railroad Bill A.B. 264 in the State Assembly

In late January 1870, Assemblyman Frederick Hihn introduced Railroad Bill A.B. 264 to the California State Assembly for consideration. The primary goal of the bill was to permit Santa Cruz County to use county funds to partially finance the construction of a railroad within its boundaries. Such a resolution required both an act of the California government and a positive vote from the people of the county. In addition, the bill revealed several important features of the proposed route.

Section 3 is the most relevant part of the bill and outlines the county's funding scheme. It also notes that branch lines would receive county funds at a rate of $2,000 per three miles built and operable. There were conditions, though. The priority was to build a branch line up the San Lorenzo River to Felton, for which over half the maximum amount was earmarked. The next priority was a branch line up Soquel Creek of a minimum of six miles in length. Construction on both branches would have to begin within a year from June 1, 1870, dependent on a positive vote for county funding.

In addition to his plans for building a railroad from Watsonville along the coast, Hihn had also been instrumental in campaigning for a route up the San Lorenzo Valley. The railroad bill merged his two campaigns into one and added a Soquel route as well. Unsurprisingly, these lines would all greatly benefit Hihn, who owned large tracts of land around Felton and along Soquel Creek.[24]

Frederick Hihn adds California Southern Railroad to his bill

Realizing the potential benefit his scheme could gain from partnering with Southern Pacific, Frederick Hihn added the California Southern Railroad to his railroad bill on March 5, 1870. The California Southern was incorporated by the Big Four as a subsidiary entrusted with the task of connecting Gilroy with Salinas via Watsonville.[25]

The Pajaronian objects to the railroad bill while Frederick Hihn amends the bill again

On March 24, 1870, the editor of *The Pajaronian*, Charles Cummings, published a scathing objection to Frederick Hihn's railroad bill. The primary target of his ire was the proposed funding provided for the Soquel branch, which would directly benefit Hihn but provide little benefit to the county or its residents.

The same day and likely the cause of Cummings' concern, an amendment to the railroad bill was published in which, if either the San Lorenzo branch or the Soquel branch failed to be constructed within the prescribed timeframes but construction commenced within the two years following, the county board of supervisors would have the power to approve the release of tax dollars according to the previous terms at their discretion.[26]

Frederick Hihn's Railroad Bill rejected by State Assembly

Around April 1870, Frederick Hihn's railroad aid bill was rejected by the California State Assembly. Without government funding, there simply was not enough money to build the line along any of the proposed routes. Southern Pacific, meanwhile, continued with its plans for a railroad from Gilroy to Salinas, consolidating the California Southern in the process and running the line as its new main trunk. Yet the Big Four were in the midst of legal trouble with the United States government and decided that the more costly and less lucrative route to Santa Cruz would have to be shelved for the time being.[27]

Big Four reveals plans for Southern Pacific Railroad

During mid-summer 1870, the Atlantic & Pacific Railroad Company requested Congress to ask the Big Four if they intended to honor their commitment to extend their lines to the California border, where they could join the Atlantic & Pacific line. The original agreement for such a route had been made with the previous owner of Southern Pacific and the

Big Four were not fond of working with rivals. The Atlantic & Pacific's management also wanted to more clearly define the relationship between the Central Pacific and Southern Pacific Railroads, which by this point were owned by the same syndicate.

At a public hearing, the Big Four clarified that the two railroads were one and the same. Indeed, over subsequent years, Southern Pacific management carefully and slowly migrated over components of the Central Pacific Railroad and ensured that nearly all new lines and related operations were firmly associated with Southern Pacific. The goal of this was to eventually phase out Central Pacific entirely, although this was not accomplished functionally until April 1, 1885 or legally until June 30, 1959.

Shortly after this hearing, the California State Legislature passed a new bill that granted the right to build and finance roadways and railroads to counties without requiring legislative approval.[28]

Chase family purchases land from James Taylor

Stephen "Si" Hall Chase and Josiah "Joseph" W. Chase had first moved to the Santa Cruz Mountains around 1860, where they quickly established themselves within the lumber industry. In 1863, they opened the first commercial lumber mill in the Summit area. Over a six-year period, the cousins harvested most of the surrounding tracts and finally relocated their mill to Los Gatos Creek in 1867. They tasked Joseph's younger brother, Foster Chase, with managing the new mill.

In 1871, the mill burned to the ground. The surrounding tracts still had enough timber to make rebuilding viable, and Joseph added to that stock by purchasing land from James Taylor above the Schultheis Ranch in Santa Clara County. This property was located on the Soquel Turnpike so felled logs could be skidded down to the mill on Los Gatos Creek. This provided the mill with a source of timber for two more years.[29]

Agreement between Charles Olive and James and Stephen Grover concerning Tract 27 in the Augmentation

By 1871, James and Stephen Grover were looking for new tracts to harvest. They operated a smaller mill on Bates Creek but it was unable to keep their lumberyards fully stocked. On March 22, 1871, the Grovers made an agreement with Charles Wesley Olive regarding land in the Augmentation. Olive was born in Maine in 1841. He moved to Santa Cruz County at some point in the 1860s and began running a shingle mill along the San Lorenzo River. This business grew into one of the earliest successful lumber mills in the county. Olive agreed to take possession of the Grovers' half of Tract 27 as well as the sawmill, in exchange for which the Grovers would receive 700,000 board feet of lumber from Olive's mill on the San Lorenzo River.[30]

James Cunningham opens a store in Felton

Sometime in 1871, James Francis Cunningham joined Hubbard W. McKoy in opening a general store in Felton. Shortly afterwards, Cunningham's brother Jeremiah joined in the venture. The brothers had fought together in a Maine Union regiment during the Civil War and arrived in Santa Cruz County sometime in the mid- to late-1860s. After opening the store, the brothers became interested in the local logging industry. They soon purchased several small parcels of timberland along the San Lorenzo River north of Felton and built a small sawmill to process the timber from the properties.[31]

Corralitos Lumber Company founded

Probably in the spring of 1871, Dickamon Allen Rider of Bennington, Vermont, founded the Corralitos Lumber Company alongside Augustus Lemuel Chandler, a future California state senator. Rider (sometimes spelled Ryder) was born on December 17, 1832 in Bennington, Vermont. He arrived in California via Panama around 1852 and briefly ran a ferry service over the Feather River in Sutter County. He became a miner in Grass Valley for a few years but, after making little progress, moved to Truckee where he opened his first lumber mill. Not long afterwards, he became aware of the redwood forests of Santa Cruz County and relocated to a property along Corralitos Creek in Eureka Canyon. From the mid-1860s, Rider began to buy property from throughout the watershed, including

Tract 11 in the Augmentation from Frederick Hihn. Very little is known about Rider's logging operation, but a report in the *Sentinel* for the year 1873 stated that the company cut 2,225,000 board feet of lumber, 500,000 shingles, 20,000 posts, 125,000 clapboards, and 250,000 pickets.[32]

Frederick Hihn discusses potential railroad between Santa Cruz and Santa Clara Counties

In an article published in the *Sentinel* on May 13, 1871, it was revealed that Frederick Hihn and Richard C. Kirby had left Santa Cruz to meet with the president of the San Jose & Santa Clara Railroad Company, Samuel Addison Bishop, and his assistant, W. J. Lewis, near the Summit. The four men spent the week discussing potential routes for a railroad to cross the Santa Cruz Mountains into Santa Cruz County from the Santa Clara Valley.[33]

Frederick Hihn's term in state assembly ends

In September 1871, Frederick Hihn's term as state assemblyman for California's 6th District came to an end. A year earlier, on April 7, 1870, *The Pajaronian* editor Charles Cummings gave his assessment of Hihn's impact on political matters to date:

> *The* Sentinel *of last week publishes Mr. Hihn's Record! and says that during the short time he has been there he has "introduced* twenty-six *Bills, one Concurrent Resolution, and a Memorial to Congress!" Great Hevings* [sic]*, how ink and paper have been wasted! We cannot see the necessity of trying to prove that Mr. Hihn is a man of talent, or that he has earned his money. The people can judge for themselves as to whether he has acted honestly or not. It strikes us as not being in good taste. It looks like anticipation of an adverse judgement. On railroad matters we have not been hand in hand with him, but have never questioned his industry, and furthermore think he has done as well as any member which*

composed the late Legislature. Out of 26 bills introduced by Mr. Hihn, we would like to ask the Sentinel, how many have now upon them Governor Haight's signature?[34]

Storm damages Soquel Turnpike

On October 28, 1871, the *Sentinel* reported that the Soquel Road over the mountains was in very poor condition and in need of repair. Stagecoach drivers decided to use alternative routes through the winter since the old turnpike would likely be impassable.[35]

Santa Cruz & Watsonville Railroad Company incorporates

On January 18, 1872, the Santa Cruz & Watsonville Railroad Company was incorporated. Its investors planned to build a 20-mile-long standard-gauge route between the two named cities with a connection with the Southern Pacific Railroad's line at Pajaro. The directors included Frederick Hihn (president), David Tuthill (secretary), Elihu Anthony, W. F. Peabody, Titus Hale, and Samuel A. Bartlett.[36]

Patchen Post Office established

Over the decades, many resorts sprang up along the ridge of the Santa Cruz Mountains localized in clusters that eventually emerged as small rural hamlets, with schools, stores, and post offices marking their significance. The earliest of these was the settlement of Patchen, once centered at the junction of Mountain Charley Road and the Santa Cruz Gap Turnpike (Old Santa Cruz Highway). The first post office on the Summit was established on March 28, 1872 on the ranch of Josiah S. Fowler.

The Fowler family had moved to the Summit a few years earlier when Jacob Fowler purchased 240 acres in order to ranch and grow fruits. Prior to 1872, Jacob sold the land to his son, Josiah, who planted 40 acres of orchards and parceled off 30 acres elsewhere to be used by settlers. It was due to the influx of settlers to his land and the surrounding area that he petitioned the government for a post office in 1872.

The Call of the Wild 1872

Curiously, the new post office was not named after Fowler or, indeed, anybody on the Summit. In fact, the name 'Patchen' still remains a mystery. John Young, while researching the history of the Summit area, came across several stories from locals claiming to know the origin of the name. One suggestion was that an old man—possibly Jacob prior to his death in 1875—was stitching clothing on the porch of his home when the postal inspector stopped by. When the inspector asked what he was doing, the old man replied 'patchin.'" The more likely explanation, however, is that the post office was named after a popular racehorse from the period, 'George M. Patchen.' In any case, the spelling—Patchen or Patchin—was debated well into the twentieth century but finally settled on the former.

The Fowler property was the first home of the post office, but no formal structure was built initially to support the service. Until the erection of a second, larger home on the Fowler property in 1876, mail was deposited into a hollow tree and locals were responsible for sorting the mail themselves. Meanwhile, Josiah married Abbie A. Proseus in 1882 and built an even larger home, named Laddick, in 1884. However, by this point, the post office had moved elsewhere.

The Patchen post office had a permanence problem for most of its existence. It had a tendency to move to the home of whoever chose to be postmaster at any particular time. Around 1878, the postmaster became D. C. Feely, whose house was about half a mile north of Fowler's on the Santa Cruz Gap Turnpike. His death made him briefly notorious when his entire fortune of $40,000 went to the Socialist Party. After Feely, the next postmaster around 1880 was Joshua White, who owned the White & Gibson house halfway between Mountain Charley Road and Summit Road along the Santa Cruz Gap Turnpike. In 1882, the post office moved one final time to the Edgemont Hotel, run by L. N. Scott. The post office closed in 1925.

Because of the remoteness of the area, the hotels around Patchen were not heavily advertised in newspapers and little is known about them. However, a description by Skyland Realty on February 6, 1906 gives a glimpse at life at the Anchorage, which was located next door to Edgemont:

Spend your vacation in the Santa Cruz Mountains. The Anchorage is the place to rest and recuperate. Situated mid-

way between San Jose and Santa Cruz on the Soquel Road. Beautiful new rustic cottages, well furnished for housekeeping. Cottages stand on a fine open plateau, surrounded by hundreds of acres of beautiful redwood, madrone and oak timber. Splendid walks and drives through the woods. The best of spring water piped to each cottage. Altitude is 1,900 feet. Public hall and church adjoin the place. Long distance telephone near. Hunting, fishing, croquet, tennis, shooting gallery, swimming pool and other amusements. Branch store will be opened for benefit of guests. Butcher calls three times a week. Rural mail delivery. Horses boarded. Magnificent camping grounds at a nominal rental. Entirely under new management. Trains met at Alma. Write in advance for accommodations. Address 'The Anchorage, Wrights, Santa Clara County, California.'

Patchen was not just a post office, though. The small community hosted the Patchen Social Club, as well, which eventually became the Santa Cruz Mountain Improvement Club when it merged with a local floral society. Their headquarters was the Summit Opera House, built through a joint stock venture run by Volney Averill and Charles Aiken. This community hall hosted traveling road shows, neighborhood socials, musical events, and community theatre programs led by Shakespearean drama coach Charles Wildinson. The building survived until the early 1940s, when it was dismantled and the lumber repurposed to build a new structure in Laurel.

The legacy of Patchen lives on through a geographic name that is as poorly named as it is ahistorical. Patchen Pass, as it appears on maps, is an artificial cut made through the Santa Cruz Mountains beneath Summit Road to allow for the passage of Highway 17. When the United States Geologic Survey set about naming the artificial gap through the mountains, they settled on two options: Cuesta de los Gatos (Wildcat Ridge) or Patchen Pass. The first reflected the history of the area and accurately described the location as it had been described over the past century. However, it did not describe the specific location in question. The second implied a passage between the mountains and was favored by the local historical associations and the board of supervisors of Santa Cruz and Santa

Clara Counties. Thus, the latter name was adopted.

The problem with calling the passage Patchen Pass is that the location is two miles south of the original location of the Patchen post office and seems to acknowledge a settlement that barely was. In addition, an artificial cut through the mountains hardly qualifies as a pass, which is generally natural, but more accurately describes a gap, which is narrower and can be artificial. In fact, the passage in question is indeed identical to Santa Cruz Gap, which was the point where the Santa Cruz Gap Turnpike met Mountain Charley's turnpike to Santa Cruz. Why the various parties involved in the naming decided to invent a name rather than adopt the historical name for the passage is unknown but displays a general lack of knowledge of the history of the Summit area.[37]

Soquel Turnpike's condition after winter's storms

The predictions of the October 1871 *Sentinel* proved true. On March 30, 1872, the newspaper reported that several bridges and roads needed repair after they were washed away or damaged during the winter's storms. The Soquel Turnpike was impassable and required considerable work before travel to Lexington along Los Gatos Creek could resume.[38]

A verbal promise by Leland Stanford concerning the Santa Cruz & Watsonville Railroad

After he returned from San Francisco, Frederick Hihn reported that Leland Stanford of the Big Four had given him a verbal promise that, after he visited Santa Cruz, he would have a preliminary survey done for a railroad route between Pajaro and Santa Cruz. By this point, the county had approved a $100,000 subsidy for the railroad, which was causing consternation with Charles Cummings of *The Pajaronian*, who, in an editorial published on April 11, 1872, expressed his feeling that the funds were unnecessary since the Southern Pacific could build the road without taxpayer expense. Cummings was also upset with Hihn, whom he accused of claiming victory for the railroad despite having only a verbal guarantee.[39]

Repairs completed along Soquel Turnpike

On April 29, 1872, the *Sentinel* announced that all repairs were completed along the Soquel Turnpike and that the stage would resume its

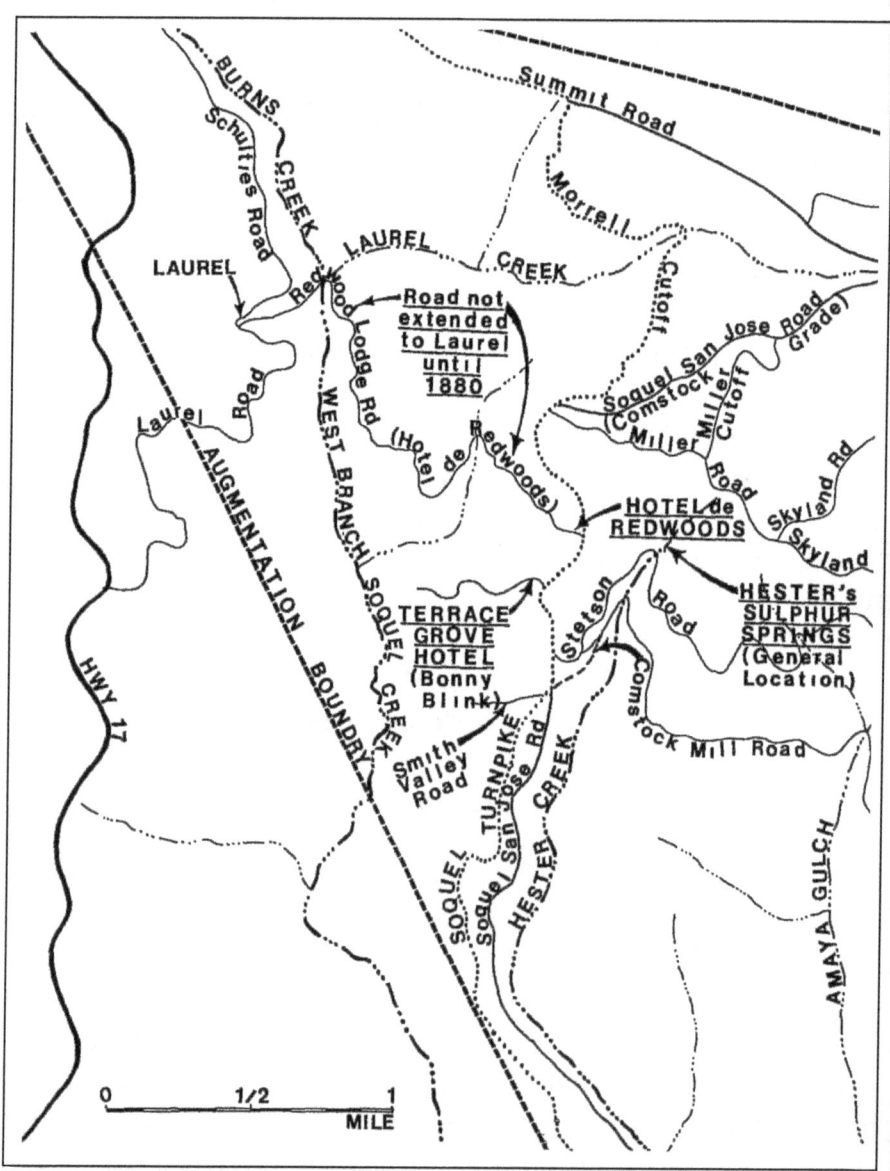

FIGURE 1.2 RESORTS ALONG THE SOQUEL TURNPIKE

standard service of shuttling passengers between Soquel and San José on alternate days.

The article also announced the reopening of the Hotel de Redwoods under the new management of Edwin Bowker, to be heralded with a grand gala celebration. The redwoods-themed hotel was situated about nine miles north of Soquel at the intersection of the Soquel Turnpike and the road to Hester's Sulphur Springs resort. Both the hotel and springs opened in 1860 and immediately became popular tourist sites. Over the following decade, the entire area became associated with the Hotel de Redwoods and a community developed there, with a general store and post office opening in the 1870s.[40]

Frederick Hihn's road to Spanish Ranch and beyond

On May 11, 1872, the *Sentinel* reported that Frederick Hihn had "just completed a new road, finely graded, up the middle fork of Soquel creek, from the old Kentuck Saw-mill at the Hinckley creek junction." The origin of the name of this mill is a mystery but it refers to the water-powered mill built by Roger Gibson Hinckley and his son-in-law, John Lafayette Shelby, who subsequently sold it to Richard Savage. Savage, in turn, lost the mill to Benjamin Cahoon, who later sold it to James Phillips. During the Shoquel Augmentation partitioning suit, the property was designated Tract 27 and by 1872 had passed into the hands of the Grover family. Today, the middle fork is the East Branch of Soquel Creek. The article continues:

> *[the road] will compare with any first-class road in the county. The road is on the south-east side of the creek, and extends up into the mountains in the direction of Loma Prieta for many miles, nearly to the settlement made by Peter Warner and Mr. String, two years ago. There is a fine body of arable land in that direction, and no end to the amount of first-class timber, such as redwood, fir, laurel, tan-bark and other oak, madrona, and all the different varieties of wood (including hazel for hoop-poles) usually found along streams and hillsides, in the Santa Cruz mountains. The new road has been*

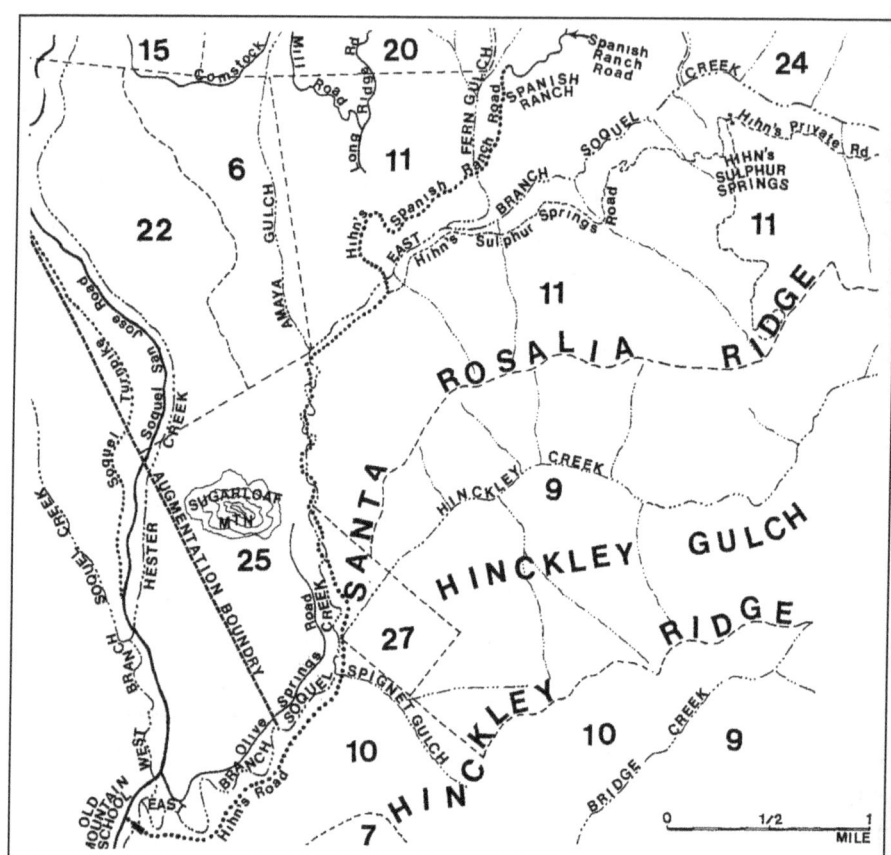

FIGURE 1.3 HIHN'S ROADS ALONG THE EAST BRANCH OF SOQUEL CREEK

built at great expense, and will open up a large district of country, desirable for grazing land and for agricultural purposes.

The road began on the Soquel Turnpike opposite the original location of Mountain School about a half mile north of Laurel Glen Road. It crossed Soquel Creek on a wooden bridge and continued north along the east side of the creek and then continued up the East Branch, passing Spignet Gulch and Hinckley Creek. Just north of here, the road essentially became the creek bed and forded the creek no fewer than twenty-four times. After the last crossing east of Amaya Gulch, it climbed above the creek and continued over Asbury Gulch (now Amaya Gulch) and reached the broad expanse of Spanish Ranch. This area was the pastureland and agricultural land mentioned in the article.[41]

Charles Olive cancels agreement with the Grovers concerning Tract 27 in the Augmentation

Wanting to return to Sonoma County, Charles Olive approached the Grover brothers on May 18, 1872 to ask that his agreement with them be cancelled. An equitable agreement was reached wherein the Grovers reclaimed full custody of their sawmill and facilities, as well as the remaining uncut timber on Tract 27 in the Augmentation. Olive, meanwhile, passed control of his lumber company onto his son, George, and left for Sonoma.[42]

Land transfer from Rafael Castro to Claus Spreckels in Rancho Aptos

Breaking with his tendency to hoard property, Rafael Castro, owner of Rancho Aptos, sold 2,390 acres of his Mexican land grant to sugar magnate Claus Spreckels on July 16, 1872.

Spreckels was a newcomer to Santa Cruz County. He was born on July 9, 1828, in Lamstedt in the Kingdom of Hanover (now in Germany). When he was a boy, he worked as a poor farmer but fled the country in 1846 for the United States. Within only a few years, the young Spreckels repaid the price of his passage across the Atlantic Ocean and then bought the grocery store in which he worked in Charleston, South Carolina. In 1852, he married his childhood love, Anna Christina Mangels, who worked at the time as a maid in New York City. Spreckels sold his store in 1855 and moved to New York, where he bought a larger grocery store. However, in 1856 he made the fateful decision to move to San Francisco to take over a grocery store run by his brother, Peter, at the same time selling his New York store to his brother-in-law, Claus Mangels, who would also later become a large landowner in Santa Cruz County.

In San Francisco, Spreckels, his brother, and eventually Mangels became interested in the sugar industry. They helped found the Bay Sugar Refinery in 1863 but none of them really understood the process involved. Therefore, Spreckels returned to New York, quickly learned the technical details necessary to process sugarcane into sugar, and then promptly bought the bankrupted United States Refinery and had its machinery shipped to San Francisco. Although the Bay Sugar Refinery was almost immediately profitable, the board of directors was a cautious group and Spreckels was anxious to expand. He decided to sell his stake in the company in 1865 and returned to Germany to work at a beet sugar refinery in order to learn more details of the industry.

When Spreckels returned to California in 1867, he founded the California Sugar Refinery using sugarcane imported from around the Pacific. His reputation as the Sugar King of California only grew from there. Spreckels likely viewed Santa Cruz more as a vacation getaway than a business venture when he bought the land in Aptos in 1872, but he soon saw other potential benefits to his newly-acquired property and almost immediately began experimenting with sugar beets. It was for this reason that he became involved in Santa Cruz County railroad and political matters.[43]

Santa Cruz & Watsonville Railroad— standard or narrow-gauge?

On August 1, 1872, a letter to the editor in *The Pajaronian* questioned plans for the Santa Cruz Railroad project:

> *We hear a rumor to the effect that a narrow gauge railroad is seriously contemplated from this place to Santa Cruz. We have no opposing words to utter—but if it will pay to build a narrow gauge, why will it not pay to build a broad gauge, thereby saving an important item in regard to handling freight? We do not know, as yet, who project [sic] the movement, and can only learn that it is proposed to vote a subsidy of 5 per cent. on the taxable property of the county in and of the road. Mr. Hihn, as one of the principal moneyed men of the county, probably has something to do in the matter. If the plan, after being made public, is a feasible one, and is calculated to benefit all the people of the county, we shall take great pleasure in advocating the construction of the road. Otherwise, we shall fight it, as we did the last subsidy swindle.*[44]

Railroad meeting held concerning Santa Cruz & Watsonville Railroad

On August 28, 1872, a meeting was held to induce the Atlantic & Pacific Railroad Company to construct its road down the coast through Santa Cruz County.

> *On motion, J[osiah] S[amuel] Green was elected Chairman and Roger Conant, Sec'y. The Chairman of the meeting stated that the object of the meeting was to devise some plan to obtain a railroad through this section of the country along the coast and to correspond with other parties along the route on the subject....*
>
> *Col. Heath—I move that an Executive Committee of five be appointed, consisting of A[masa] Pray, Sr., Wm. Cooper, D[avid] Tuthill, E[dward] Briody, R[ichard] C. Kirby and J[ohn] N[elson] Besse, to take charge of this matter.*
>
> *Mr. Kirby, Mr. Hihn and Mr. Anthony, advocated the construction of the road from Santa Cruz to Watsonville, and in favor of petitioning the Board of Supervisors to increase the subsidy from $100,000 to $250,000, and also the taking of stock by the people, and also to change the road from a Broad to a Narrow Gauge.*
>
> *Mr. [Benjamin Parke] Kooser and Col. Heath spoke in opposition to this plan, and in favor of getting the co-operation of the Atlantic and Pacific Co., to build a road down the coast.... On motion, the chairman, J. S. Green, was added to the committee. The committee were instructed to correspond with committees in other sections, as to right of way, and to appoint such special committees as might be deemed necessary to secure subscriptions &c.*[45]

Land transfer from the Grovers to Frederick Waterman concerning Tract 27 in the Augmentation

When Charles Olive cancelled his agreement with the Grovers in May

1872, he left them short of about 250,000 board feet of lumber. Although they had the facilities to process such an amount, they decided to search for a new buyer to do the job for them. They found such a person in Frederick H. Waterman, who owned several mills in the San Lorenzo Valley. The Grovers agreed on September 2, 1872 to take no payment for the land, in exchange for which Waterman would fulfill the open contract within a set period of time.[46]

Letter from Frederick Hihn to Railroad Committee

On September 4, 1872, Frederick Hihn wrote a letter to the Railroad Committee that the proposed line between Watsonville and Santa Cruz must be narrow gauge and must be built and financed using county resources. He wrote:

> *To the Committee on Railroads:—The Atlantic and Pacific R. R. Co. having changed their route, and the owners of the Southern Pacific Railroad Co. not complying with their promises to build a wide gauge Railroad, from Santa Cruz to Watsonville, we are forced to conclude that if we want a railroad we must build it ourselves. A wide gauge railroad from Santa Cruz connecting with the Southern Pacific Railroad, near Watsonville cannot be built for less than $25,000 per mile, or, say $500,000. In addition to the subsidy granted for this purpose, amounting to $100,000, the further sum of $400,000 would have to be raised by private subscription and loans. This is impossible.*
>
> *We must therefore build a cheaper road; a narrow gauge (3 foot wide) Railroad can be built from the Pajaro depot to Santa Cruz, for $12,500 per mile, with equipment, or, say $250,000, and can be continued along the coast to the northern line of our county, without equipment, at a cost of 12,500 per mile, or, say $250,000 more. The utmost amount of private subscription for any railroad now obtainable in this county, and from non-residents interested, is $100,000. The balance must be raised by county aid and by loans. In order to*

> get county aid, we must make it the interest of every tax payer to grant such aid. It is therefore proposed that a company be organized to build a narrow gauge Railroad, commencing on the line of the Southern Pacific Railroad, near the Pajaro river, and running thence along or near the survey of the Atlantic and Pacific Railroad, along or near the coast to the Northern Boundary line of our county, a distance of 40 miles. That county aid be solicited to the amount of $6,000 per mile, such aid to be in lieu of the subsidy already granted. That subscriptions to the stock of said company be solicited from every person interested in this county. That the right of way and necessary depot grounds be secured, and that the citizens of all the coast counties from San Francisco to San Diego, be invited to organize like companies in their respective counties, in order to secure the construction of a 3 foot gauge Railroad from San Francisco along or near the coast, to the southern line of the State.
>
> Santa Cruz county should certainly take the initiative in such a movement, because if even partially successful, or in other words, if we should only secure the construction of such a railroad from Watsonville to Santa Cruz, it would be of an immense benefit to the county at large, by the development and opening of the varied resources of more than three-fourths of our county, and by the large increase of taxable value. But it is reasonable to expect that if a narrow gauge Railroad constructed from Watsonville to Santa Cruz should prove a financial success, of which there is hardly any doubt, the means would not long be wanted to extend the road both North and South, and thereby the permanent prosperity of our county would be secured.

The next week, on September 19, *The Pajaronian* lampooned Hihn's statements, surmising "we 'are forced to conclude,' from what we know of Hihn and his railroad operations heretofore, that the Southern Pacific Railroad Company never promised to build a road from Santa Cruz to Watsonville."[47]

Railroad route between Pajaro and Santa Cruz resurveyed

Following a Railroad Committee meeting on September 4, 1872, surveyors were sent to examine the route first proposed by the Atlantic & Pacific Railroad. The goal was to have the new survey completed by the November 8 election. Surveying began on October 14 and concluded on October 25.[48]

Countywide election favors building railroad— Board of Supervisors votes to begin construction

Santa Cruz County went to vote on Tuesday, November 5, 1872 and among the items on the ballot was a referendum on a narrow-gauge railroad between Watsonville and Santa Cruz. In the end, only Pajaro voted against the measure. The final breakdown by precinct printed in *The Pajaronian* was as follows:

> Santa Cruz: YES 587 to NO 36
> Soquel: 133 to 55
> Scott's Valley: 38 to 21
> New Years (North County): 41 to 9
> San Lorenzo 87 to 16
> Corralitos: 41 to 9
> Pajaro: 13 to 395

With the successful vote for the railroad, the Board of Supervisors voted unanimously to not only begin construction of the railroad, but to subsidize it.[49]

Leland Stanford announces the Southern Pacific Railroad will build a railroad from Pajaro to Santa Cruz

Leland Stanford, member of the Big Four and recent governor of California, made a surprise visit to Santa Cruz on November 18, 1872. His mission was

The Call of the Wild 1872 – 1873

to look into the feasibility of building a standard-gauge railroad from Pajaro to Santa Cruz. After three weeks of no further word on the matter, surveyors sent out by Stanford and Company suddenly arrived in the county in mid-December and investigated the proposed work through to mid-January. The newspaper speculated that construction could begin within a month and was optimistic that it could be fully operational by July 4, 1873. However, six weeks after the survey was completed, the Crédit Mobilier scandal drew in Stanford. All major Southern Pacific projects not already under construction were put on hold as the Big Four defended themselves before an angry public.[50]

Frederick Hihn announces plan for the Santa Cruz & Watsonville Railroad

Speaking as the president of the Santa Cruz & Watsonville Railroad, Frederick Hihn stated on May 24, 1873 that the company intended to build a narrow gauge across the length of the county along a direct line on or near the coast, with priority given to the Pajaro to Santa Cruz section. The total length of the road would be about forty miles from the Monterey County line to the San Mateo County line, twenty from Pajaro to Santa Cruz. The total stock subscriptions were set at $150,000, or 1,500 stocks of $100 each. The remaining funds would be provided by the $100,000 county subsidy and a floating debt of $50,000.[51]

The Santa Cruz Railroad Company is incorporated

On June 3, 1873, the Santa Cruz Railroad Company registered its articles of incorporation. The Board of Directors, all to serve on the board for the first year, were Claus Spreckels of San Francisco, and from Santa Cruz County, Frederick Hihn, Benjamin Porter, John Nelson Beese, David Tuthill, Amasa Pray, and Titus Hale.

The Capital Stock of the company was set at $1,000,000 to be divided into shares of $100 each. The initial subscription was claimed to be $40,000, paid for each of the estimated 40 miles of the extent of the road, from Pajaro Station to the northern county line just beyond Waddell Creek at the southern boundary of Rancho Año Nuevo. The stockholders were listed as follows with their purchased shares following:

Frederick A. Hihn 200
Claus Spreckels 100
Titus Hale 30
Benjamin F. Porter 15
Amasa Pray 10
Joseph Boston 5
John Nelson Besse 5
Samuel Drennan 5
John Werner 3
Jacob F. Kron 2
William Effey 2
David Tuthill 5
John L. McLaughlin 5
George E. Logan 5
Ellery Willis 2

While Richard Kirby was listed in the articles of incorporation, he was not a stockholder.

The articles were filed with the county clerk on June 16 and certified by the California Secretary of State on June 18. The certificate states that the company was being formed for the constructing, conducting, and maintaining of an iron railroad in Monterey and Santa Cruz counties.

On August 4, the Board of Supervisors voted unanimously to enter into a contract with the new railroad, agreeing to contribute $6,000 per mile toward its construction. Initial grading of the line from the Pajaro River by Chinese work crews began on August 14.[52]

The Panic of 1873

Following eight years of economic growth, a crisis led to a prolonged depression beginning on September 18, 1873. On this day, Jay Cooke & Company, which funded the construction of the Northern Pacific

Railroad, collapsed. This caused a land and securities speculation bubble to pop, which then led to a devaluation of the United States dollar. By the end of the year, over 5,000 businesses had failed across the county. Another 5,000 closed over the next five years before the economy finally rebounded around 1879.[53]

The Chase family expands its logging operations to Hester Creek and the San Lorenzo Valley

Near the end of 1873, the Chase family's mill on Los Gatos Creek shut down and the machinery was relocated to Hester Creek on Tract 14 in the Augmentation. For the next decade, Foster Chase ran this mill as the primary facility of the Chase family. Meanwhile, Joseph and Stephen Chase erected a smaller mill on Bear Creek northeast of the town of Boulder Creek in the San Lorenzo Valley. In addition to cutting lumber, their mills produced fruit boxes, drying trays, doors, sashes, and splitstuff.[54]

Watsonville grants right-of-way for the Santa Cruz Railroad

On March 6, 1874, the town of Watsonville granted a right-of-way along any throughfare except Main Street to the Santa Cruz Railroad. The next day, Frederick Hihn, president of the railroad, returned from a trip to San Francisco with enough rails to lay the first four miles of track. These rails were purchased from the Sutro Tunnel Company.[55]

Bank of Watsonville organized by local businessmen led by Charles Ford and John Porter

Two of Watsonville's prominent businessmen, Charles Ford and John Porter, alongside Godfrey M. Bockius, Thomas Walker, Charles Lewis Thomas, Charles Moss, and John Nelson Besse, came together on May 11, 1874 to form the town's first bank, appropriately named the Bank of Watsonville. Ford was elected president and the other six men became the bank's first directors.[56]

Santa Cruz Railroad stockholders hold meeting in Santa Cruz

The first annual meeting of the stockholders of the Santa Cruz Railroad Company met on June 6, 1874. Frederick Hihn, as president, presented the balances for the year, showing that around $40,000 had been received while $35,000 had been expended. He anticipated that the first fifteen miles of track would be completed by the end of the year and that negotiations were ongoing with a New York firm to supply the remaining rails needed for the job. He further reported that the Pacific Bridge Company had been hired to install the bridge over Soquel Creek at a cost of $6,500, while plans for the bridge over the San Lorenzo River had been finalized.[57]

Camp Capitola opens

On June 18, 1874, Frederick Hihn formally opened Camp Capitola to the public. A grand gala ball was held to celebrate. In the announcement published in the *Sentinel*, it noted that a "fine new Pavilion with good dancing floor has been erected, sufficiently large to accommodate ten sets." Samuel Alonzo Hall was given charge of the new establishment and was largely responsible for its expansion and upkeep.[58]

CHAPTER 2

~

Redwood Logging in the Santa Cruz Mountains

The operations at and within a sawmill did not consist simply of pushing a log in one end and getting lumber out from the other. It took many people and several concurrent operations to produce quality wood products. There were people working in the forest cutting down trees. There were other people moving logs to the millpond. There were the millpond workers sorting the logs and fishing out sinkers. There were people trimming and edging lumber before it could be stacked by grade and size. And all of these people needed support, from cooks and mess assistants to planners, store clerks, and management. Everybody was necessary and all played a role in getting wood products to the customers.

This chapter is an attempt to enlighten readers about the methods used, problems and difficulties faced, and the solutions found to reach, cut down, and produce wood products in the Santa Cruz Mountains between 1852 and 1942. To date, no work has been produced from within Santa Cruz County that provides a historical assessment of lumbering practices in the county, specifically in the Augmentation. Therefore, in order to compile this chapter, outside sources had to be used extensively, many of which are based on circumstances and conditions that differ slightly from this county. As a result, much of the material has been interpreted to conform to conditions and situations as they existed in the county.

Three local sources were found that provided important material for this chapter. The first are conversations with Bob Lincoln, who was once closely associated with the Big Creek Lumber Company and the Monterey Bay Redwood Company. The second are the memoirs of Bert Stoodley, which provide a wealth of information concerning the local splitstuff industry. And the third is the Big Creek Lumber Company's Catalog & Price Guide, published in 1981. This catalog includes short articles concerning many aspects of the lumber industry's history in the Santa Cruz Mountains from the earliest days, as well as interviews with old-timers conducted by Bernard Woods Mattingley. Mattingley, who knew little of local history, conducted most of his interviews in the 1960s and focused primarily on former Loma Prieta Lumber Company employees, including Michael Bergazzi, Bernard Klink, Bud Pasha, John B. Wikkerink, Clarence Strock, Teck B. Cathey, and Bert Stoodley.

Meanwhile, the majority of the technical data in this chapter came from outside sources, such as "Logging with Ox Teams: An Epoch in Ingenuity," published by the Mendocino County Historical Society; Frank M. Stranger, "Sawmills in the Redwoods: Logging on the San Francisco Peninsula, 1849-1967," published by the San Mateo County Historical Association; and Dean Walter F. McCulloch, "Woods Words: A Comprehensive Dictionary of Loggers Terms," published by the Oregon Historical Society. In addition to these, I relied on the findings of my own exploratory hikes that I made within and around the Augmentation over a period of some 25 plus years. A detailed Glossary of Logging Terms is provided at the back of this book for further reference.

Logging in the Forest

Timber fallers, sometimes called choppers or, incorrectly, cutters, were considered the *prima donnas* of the forest. In the rough terrain of the Santa Cruz Mountains, great skill accompanied with courage was required to bring down the giants of the forest. The goal of the faller and his partner was to bring down a large redwood with the least amount of damage to its brittle, valuable trunk. One mistake or miscalculation in judgment could reduce the tree to a useless pile of splinters. Both tree and terrain presented problems and dangers. Large dead branches caught up in the eaves—nicknamed 'widow-makers'—could be shaken loose by the vibrations caused by an axe and fall on a faller. A tree may not fall where planned or fall earlier than expected. And then there were all the obstacles presented by the steep, difficult terrain. Any mishap or miscalculation could cause great bodily harm or even death.

A year or two before any area was logged, cruisers were sent in to make a plan for what was going to be logged and where. They would make a crude map showing where the main groves were located, where overhead cabling could be installed, and where roads would be needed to get logs out of an area and to a mill. Usually, cruisers would divide an area into smaller sections ranging from 10 to no more than 50 acres, although everything was dependent on terrain and property boundaries. They would then estimate the potential timber yield for each section using a cruiser's stick, which was a long stick marked with graduations for measuring a tree's height, diameter, and volume. Other information, such as the amount of tan oak and fir trees, would also be gathered. This information would be bundled in a report that would be given to the owner or lumber company, or a potential buyer.

Once a section was entered but before any redwood could be cut, the area where trees were to be felled had to be prepared. The ground was levelled, which involved removing all rocks and boulders, then it was covered with branches from other felled trees in order to provide the tree with the softest bed possible to fall on. This was necessary because an immense amount of the tree's finest trunk sections could be ruined if it broke in two or if part of the trunk shattered. While an area was being prepared for felling, shake makers sought out trees that would have the best chance of producing quality shakes and shingles. If a tree had the outward appearance of being a good candidate, a cut would be made through the bark and a chip removed. If the chip appeared to have the quality necessary to produce shakes or shingles, the tree was marked. But if the chip indicated that the tree was of inferior quality, it would be felled later and cut into lumber. As

The Reign of the Lumber Barons

a final step in the preparation of an area for felling, peelers were sent in to remove bark from nearby tan oak trees. This ensured that the valuable tan oak bark with its tannic acid used in leather tanning was protected from any damage caused by a falling tree.

It sometimes took three to four days to prepare and fell a tree. After the tree was on the ground, it would either be cut up into manageable sections and taken to a nearby mill or would be processed on site. In both cases, peelers usually came to strip the bark off the tree before moving the log to a more convenient location. The log could then be dragged or otherwise transported to a mill to cut into lumber or splitstuff. If a skid road was not available or practical, a piece maker would cut out shingle and shake bolts for transport by mule. If the log was processed on site, piece workers would carefully cut off shakes. Shingles required a portable shingle-making mill, so the piece maker would cut shingle bolts and send them a short distance to the mill for final cutting into shingles. Once all the best wood was used, the remainder would be turned into other splitstuff, such as posts and grape stakes. The poorest quality wood was turned into cords of firewood.

After the tan oaks were debarked and the shake and shingle trees felled and cut, fallers then moved in to cut the larger, lumber-producing redwood trees. Work usually began at the lower elevations and then continued up the sides of a gulch. After the bed was prepared for felling, the head faller would size up the tree by sight. Sometimes he would check the lean of the tree by holding an axe by the handle between two fingers so that it acted as a plumb bob. If a faller doubted or questioned a tree's falling angle, he would call in his boss for advice and instructions. Most fallers also had an assistant unless the size of a tree made one unnecessary.

Because lumber made from the flared base of a redwood tree was considered poor, it was common practice in the days of hand timber felling to cut above the base, sometimes eight feet or more above the ground, although this was much more common in the forests farther north. This often meant working atop 2' x 6' pieces of lumber called springboards, which were notched into the sides of the tree. For larger trees, two springboards were required, one on either side.

Once the direction of the tree's fall was decided and the bed made, fallers started making the undercut on the side of the tree that it was going to fall towards. This was accomplished by sawing approximately one-third of the distance through the tree with a falling saw. When this first cut was completed, the area either above or below the cut was chipped out with axes.

When the undercut was completed, the fallers moved around to the other side of the tree to start the back cut. They began by removing a band of bark with their axes, which made it easier to pull their saws through the trunk. The back cut was started slightly higher than the undercut on the opposite side. When the saw cutting the back cut was well buried into the trunk, fallers would drive wedges made of tool steel into the cut using sledge hammers. The number of wedges used depended on the diameter of the tree—sometimes as many as ten were needed. The wedges helped establish the direction of the tree's fall. Sawing then resumed until the saw was within six inches of the undercut, or until the tree began talking to them.

A talking tree was the sound of wood breaking and stretching as the tree began to lean. If the tree was in a particularly dangerous spot, each time the tree talked, the fallers would jump from their springboards and scurry for cover, usually behind other trees, if they were available. In gulches, fallers usually planned to have the tree fall against the nearest side, which would mean it would fall the shortest possible distance before hitting the ground. In these cases, the fallers were usually on springboards high above the ground and would have to be extra careful when fleeing from a talking tree. If a tree didn't fall after talking, the fallers would have to climb back up to their springboards, drive their wedges deeper, and saw some more until the tree talked again. This process might repeat itself several times before the tree finally let go. If the tree was less than ten feet in diameter, it could be cut by most teams in one day. If it was more than ten feet, it would usually take more than a day.

When a tree finally began to go, fallers would yell out a warning, although others could usually hear the creaks and groans of the falling tree, which often sounded like a rusty hinge opening. As the top of the tree gained momentum, a loud swooshing sound was followed by the earth-shaking, albeit muffled, impact of the tree hitting the ground.

There were two main methods of felling a redwood tree, depending on the terrain. If the area that the tree was to fall on was level between the tree's base and the point where its top was to come to rest, then the tree

The Reign of the Lumber Barons

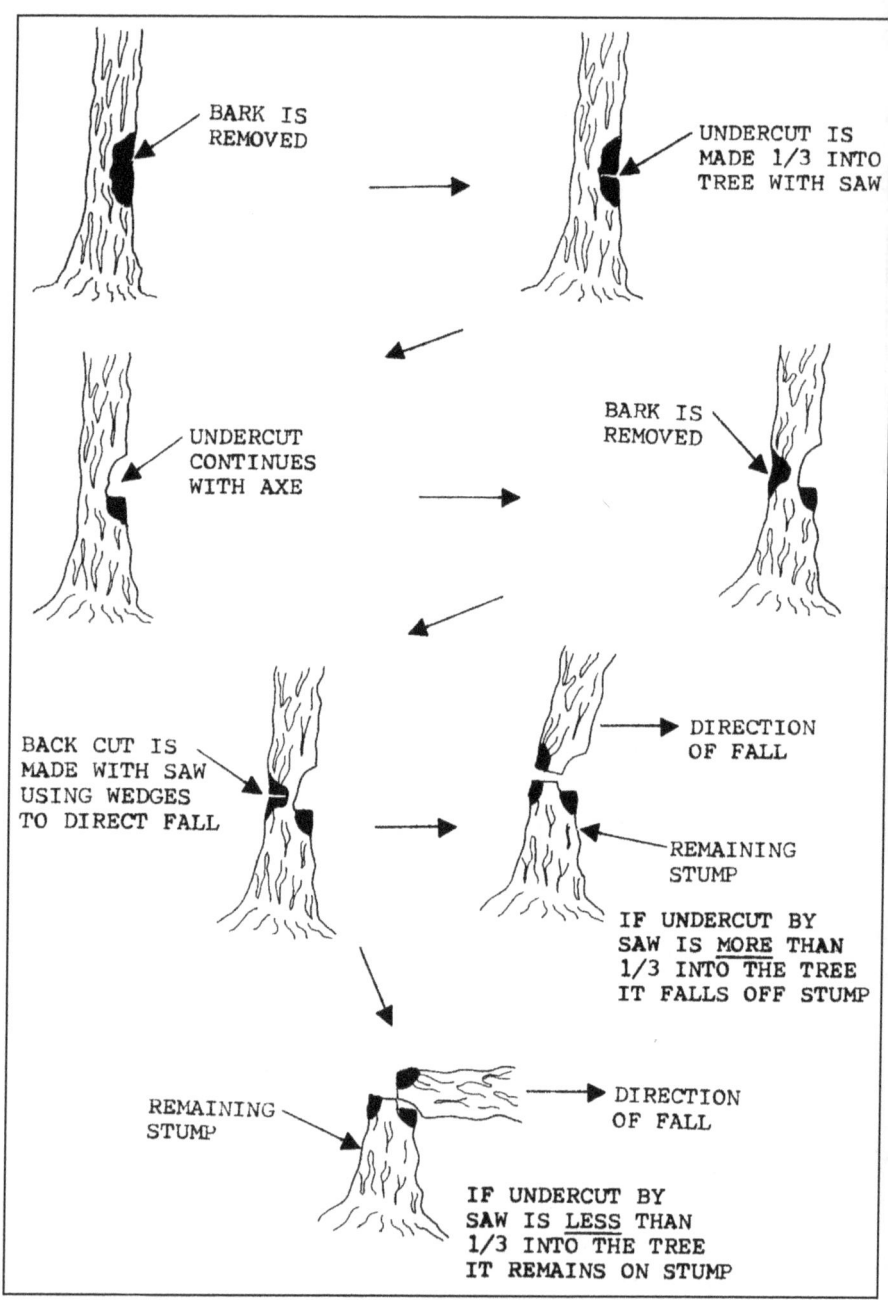

FIGURES 2.1-2 DIFFERENT METHODS OF FELLING REDWOOD TREES IN THE SANTA CRUZ MOUNTAINS

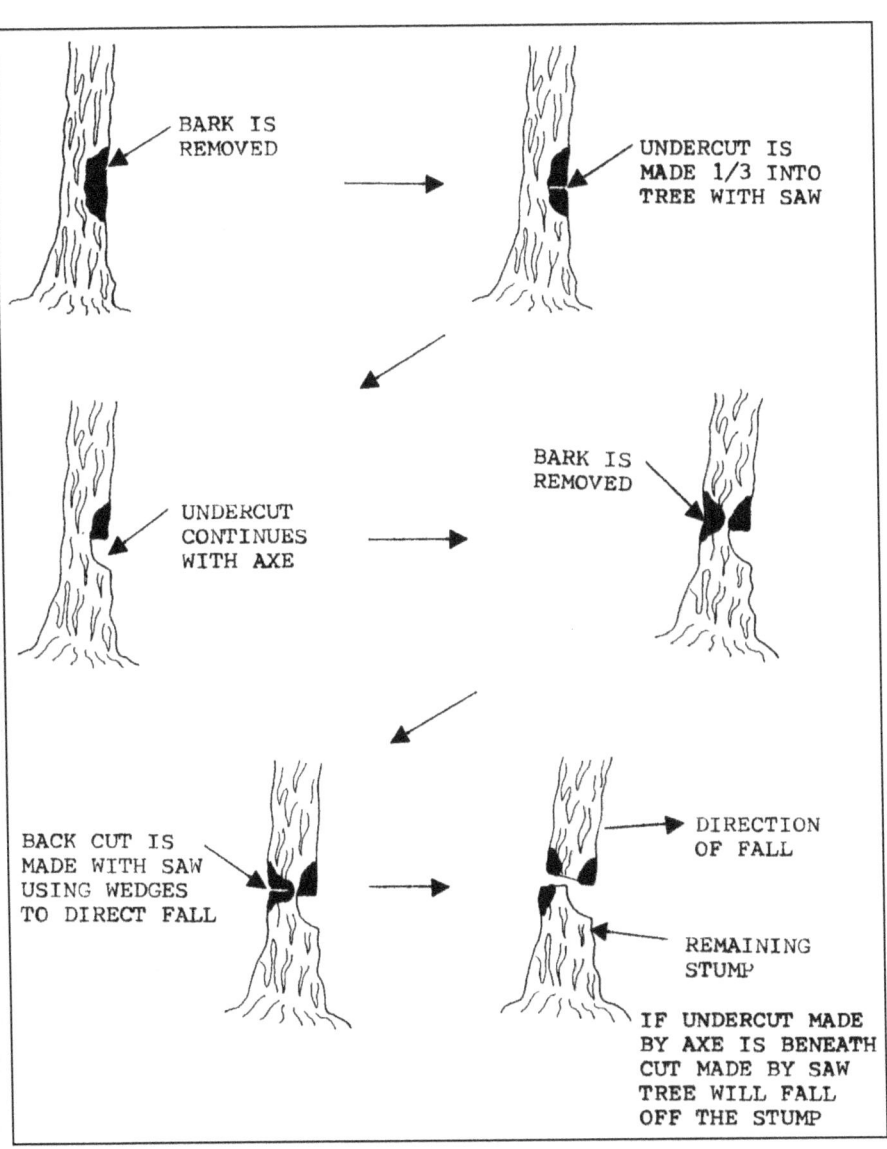

would be cut in such a way that it would fall off its stump and come to rest completely on the ground. In contrast, if there was a depression within close proximity to the tree's base, then the tree would be felled so that its base remained on the stump. This ensured that it remained relatively flat and would not break into multiple pieces upon hitting the uneven ground. These different types of felling could be achieved based on how the undercut was made. A shallow undercut allowed the tree to remain on the stump, while a deep undercut allowed it to slide off.

After a tree was on the ground and there were no other trees nearby in the process of being cut, the tree was prepared for cutting. Based on photographs taken between 1883 and 1898 along Aptos Creek, it appears that the Loma Prieta Lumber Company had peelers strip the bark from trees on site. This helped keep a mill's saws clean and in working condition. It also reduced the amount of space needed to store bark debris at the mill site. However, during the company's operations on Bridge Creek between 1917 and 1923, the bark was left on trees before they were taken to the mill. This was likely due to a change in sawing technology that occurred some time around the turn of the century. The Monterey Bay Redwood Company, which operated in the Augmentation from 1925, also did not peel the bark before delivering trees to the mill.

Peelers were responsible for removing branches from trees and, if necessary, removing the bark using long steel poles. Even if the mill could process trees with bark, peelers were still needed to debark trees that were to be used for splitstuff. If the tree was cut down in spring or early summer and the sap was high up in the tree, the bark would probably come off with ease. But if the falling occurred in the winter, when most trees were felled, then the sap was set. In this case, peeling was miserable and hours could be spent on one big tree. After all of the trees in an area had been cut and peeled, they were left to dry out. Many of the Loma Prieta Lumber Company mill's workers worked as peelers and fallers during the winter months to supplement their wages.

In late winter or early spring, before the forest had a chance to dry out from the winter weather, buckers and piece workers entered the area to cut trees into splitstuff and logs of various lengths. Lengths depended on a tree's characteristics. A tree could be cut into a number of varying lengths, although the standard lengths were 16, 24, 32, and 40 feet. If a tree was marked for use as a telegraph pole, which was 60 feet long, it was cut into a length that allowed it to be turned into a pole at a pole-making facility. After the felled trees were cut, crews set fire to the worked over forest to rid it of the trash left behind. Along with the branches and bark, all recent vegetation was destroyed by the fire. This freed up the area of obstacles for the next phase of harvesting lumber.

With the area cleared of felled trees and other obstacles, other piece workers began searching for trees that for one reason or another had been left standing. These were trees that usually were growing in precarious locations, such as in narrow gulches. To cut and process these, men with special talents and qualifications were brought in. Because of the difficult terrain in the Santa Cruz Mountains, returning to an area that was already cleared was impractical; therefore, this second round of inspection was essential to ensure that all saleable timber was removed before moving on. Meanwhile, road builders were busy putting in the necessary skid roads and overhead lines needed to move the logs to the milling facilities.

Moving the Logs

In the earliest days of redwood logging in the Santa Cruz Mountains, lumber was cut on site. The first rudimentary mills were saw pits. Once a tree was felled on the ground, it was stripped of its limbs and bark and then cut into its desired lengths. Then, a pit was dug either directly under the log or close by. If it was close by, then the log was first dragged or rolled over the pit. At this point, one man would go into the pit and another would climb atop the log and they would alternate pulling a long saw through the log in a process called whipsawing. Two men could cut about 100 feet of square redwood beams a day. This process, however, only worked with small and mid-sized trees—larger trees were too difficult to handle, so were ignored.

The earliest known saw pit operation in Santa Cruz County was run by José Amesti around 1832 in Eureka Canyon at the confluence of Rider and Corralitos Creeks. Rafael Castro also operated saw pits on Rancho Aptos at around the same time. Prior to this, redwood trees held little interest for local residents because the Spanish and Mexican settlers were more familiar with using adobe and tile in constructing their homes and buildings. The only high quality wood that was needed in these structures was for roof beams.

As Americans began to arrive in the Santa Cruz area en masse in the 1840s, they brought with them an intense interest in the redwoods, especially their commercial value. Peter Lassen built the first powered sawmill

The Reign of the Lumber Barons

in Santa Cruz County in 1841 at the confluence of Zayante and Bean Creeks on land owned by Isaac Graham. The first larger redwoods to feel the faller's axe were those that grew along creek beds. Piece workers would cut the logs up so that they could eventually be floated to the mill once the adjacent creek levels were high enough, usually in the winter months. However, these easy to reach and process trees were soon all cut and more inventive ways had to be found to transport logs to mills for cutting.

The solution was to bring in animals to drag the logs to the the millpond. In the early days, logs were pulled by horses, mules, or oxen—whichever was available. While oxen proved the best, horses and mules were often used in tandem to similar effect. However, as the demand for lumber increased, larger teams were required to haul increasing amounts of logs to millponds in smaller timeframes. One innovation to address this was the creation of skid roads to make dragging logs more efficient. With a skid road, a bull team could lead a train of several large logs from the cutting grounds to a landing or millpond with only marginal difficulty, moving at a speed of about two miles per hour.

Oxen were male cows that were castrated shortly after reaching maturity. This put them into contrast with steers, which were castrated when they were calves. The extra muscle and bulk an ox had, especially around the neck, allowed them to better endure the strain of pulling thousands of pounds of logs through the forest. However, training oxen and then attempting to control them on a skid road was not the easiest job in the world. A full train of logs could contain up to 57,000 board feet of lumber and weigh over 600 tons. Control was achieved mostly through voice commands and the use of either a goad or bull whip. The four commands used by a bull driver were "haw" and "gee" for turning, and "go" and "whoa" for starting and stopping. If a team ignored the driver, there was no way to stop it. It is said that the vocabulary of the bull driver was legendary and that the air of the canyons was filled with the smoke of their curses.

The training of oxen was both difficult and time-consuming. The leaders and wheelers (last oxen in a yoke) were the most difficult to train, usually taking many months of learning to work together and obey commands. Anyone who attempted to control a bull team earned every penny of their pay. Caring for and maintaining oxen were also difficult. Ox hooves wore down to the point where it was necessary that they be shod. Two-piece shoes, designed especially for their cloven hooves, were made by blacksmiths. When an ox needed shodding, he did not take kindly to having his legs handled. Therefore, heavy timber stocks with windlass straps that could be tightened were anchored in the ground. The ox was driven into the stock and then the straps were tightened until the animal was lifted clear of the ground. With the ox in this position, the blacksmith could nail the new shoes on in relative safety.

Once the oxen were trained, they could haul logs. Skid roads were usually steep dirt roads lined crossways with sticks of wood spaced from four to five feet apart. Skid roads were built with as gradual a grade as possible in order to reduce the chance of runaway logs and also reduce the strain on oxen climbing up the roads. If a steep incline was encountered, the road builders would extend the road in order to reduce the grade. If a skid road was only intended to be used for a few months, almost any kind of wood could be used for the skids. For longer-term roads, oak or madrone was preferred, although redwood suckers hewed down to the heartwood with all the sapwood removed could be used if well greased. Roads of oak, madrone, and redwood could last several years if properly maintained. Skids were sometimes notched in the center in order to keep logs on the road.

The rugged terrain of the Santa Cruz Mountains meant that traditional skidding was not always possible. Sometimes logs had to be pulled across skids suspended over a creek or gulch like rungs on a ladder. Their descent would be controlled with a nearby donkey engine, or the logs would simply be allowed to slide on the skids until they reached the bottom of the incline.

Once all of the logs were assembled on a main skid road, which usually followed a major creek or stream, new difficulties were encountered. Many times, in a narrow canyon or gulch, the road became so narrow that it would have to cross through the creek, often repeatedly. In some cases, there were points that were so narrow that a yoke of oxen could not pass, and so a donkey engine would take over to drag the logs through the gap. A skid road bridging a creek was often constructed using long logs assembled in an X-shape with skids mounted atop them. The important point to emphasize is that logging crews would do whatever it took to get the logs to the sawmill. Each obstacle was approached with determination and solved

The Reign of the Lumber Barons

in a way that was practical in the circumstances.

Donkey engines went a long way toward making logging in the Santa Cruz Mountains more efficient. A donkey engine is a wood-burning boiler set atop a wooden platform on logs that uses steam power to turn one or more drums with cables wound around them, controlled via a series of gears, brakes, and levers. The drums and their cable are controlled like winches or hoists that can be used to pull a log or a train of logs across the ground or through the air. Most of the donkey engines used in the Santa Cruz Mountains were of the two-drum variety that have a cable called a main line mounted on one drum. This can be up to a mile and a quarter in length. On the second drum, a smaller, lighter cable called a back line is mounted. This is usually twice as long as the main line and is used to pull the main, heavier line to its destination. From the 1880s through to the 1930s, donkey engines were a vital piece of machinery in nearly all logging operations in the Santa Cruz Mountains.

Use of the pre-patented donkey engine in Santa Cruz County can be traced back to the late 1860s. This machine consisted of a small platform and a wood burning boiler along with a single drum that was sitting vertical, not horizontal like the later models. This vertical spool, called a capstan, held a short cable and lacked a back line and brakes. It also was not very mobile. After the engine was anchored, the cable was hauled out to a log and attached to it. Then the boiler was fired up and the log would begin its drag to the engine. With no brakes to stop the return, the boiler had to be shut down to avoid the log crashing into the machine.

The first patented donkey engine in the county was purchased by Frederick Hihn for use by the Valencia Creek mill in the late 1880s. Because operating it was difficult and complicated compared to the earlier engines, Hihn brought down from Mendocino County two donkey engineers, the Seagrave brothers, to train his employees. Being a generous man at times, Hihn opened the training to all interested persons. It was this newer style of donkey engine that truly accelerated the denuding of the forests of the Santa Cruz Mountains.

The patented engine, called a yarder donkey, had several different uses. Smaller engines were primarily used to arrange logs on a skid road. Once this was done, a second larger engine pulled the load down the skid road to a set location. When the logs reached the location, the lines were detached, the engine was turned around, the back and main lines were placed around either a stump or tree, and it pulled itself to the next location. When that location was reached, the engine would be turned again and the entire operation would be repeated until the logs reached their final destination, either a landing or the millpond. This system, though more complex than using oxen, was far more efficient and could bring logs to a millpond quicker and more safely than when using animals to haul the logs. Yarder donkeys could also be used in more creative ways, such as to haul logs up or down an embankment or across a gulch.

One constant problem with all forms of donkey engines was their insatiable need for water. During a day's operation, one engine could steam away hundreds of gallons of water. This problem was especially acute when the engine was operating some distance from a water source. Another problem was the weight of the cable. When a main line was fully extended, it could pull more weight than a team of oxen. But as the line wound around its drum, the weight of the drum increased, reducing the pulling power of the engine.

Despite these problems, donkey engines worked side-by-side with oxen teams throughout the late 1800s. From 1890 to 1898, they were used almost exclusively along the headwaters of Aptos Creek, although oxen were used elsewhere in the Augmentation. The first time in Santa Cruz County that oxen were completely abandoned in favor of donkey engines was when the Loma Prieta Lumber Company relocated to Hinckley Gulch in 1900. For this operation, the company purchased a massive donkey engine measuring 60 feet in length, 10 feet in width, with a boiler almost 16 feet high with its smokestack. This engine and others of the same type were used across the county into the 1920s. Meanwhile, the use of oxen in logging in Santa Cruz County was entirely phased out by 1910.

Turning Logs into Lumber

The first mechanical sawmills in California were quite crude facilities. They consisted of a frame (like a window) that could be raised and lowered via a crank shaft, through which logs were pulled. Through the frame, the logs

The Reign of the Lumber Barons

FIGURE 2.3 LUMBERMEN WORKING USING A PIT SAW

were cut with one or more straight saws. Cant hooks and crowbars kept the log in place during cutting. The saw blades were moved by hand via a hand crank or by a mechanical ratchet connected to a power source. A combination of manpower and waterpower ran all mills in the county until small steam engines became available in the 1850s.

The best recorded waterpower operation in Santa Cruz County was that of Roger Hinckley and John Shelby along Hinckley Creek in the Augmentation during the late 1850s. To supply water to their mill with sufficient force, they tapped a natural spring high up on Hinckley Ridge and built a mill race—a small flume—to their mill located just to the north. Because a slope of Santa Rosalia Ridge blocked a direct route to the mill, Hinckley and Shelby dug a tunnel through the ridge so that the race could continue without turning and losing speed. As the race approached the mill, the channel narrowed gradually, increasing the velocity of the water in the channel. Thus, by the time the water struck the wheel that ran the machinery of the mill, the force of the water had achieved substantial power. Similar techniques were adopted by other mills in the Santa Cruz Mountains, although this style of milling declined as the steam engine became more practical.

There was a natural evolution from pit saws to the saws used in mechanical operations. Many pit sawyers used a sash or frame saw, which was simply a saw surrounded by a measured frame that helped standardize lumber cut sizes and made sawing slightly easier since the saw was less likely to wander. This problem of wandering saws became an even bigger issue with mechanical saws, where the speed at which they cut made it impossible to quickly correct for a suddenly turned log. Thus, similar-style frames were used even with mechanical saws. To achieve even further control, logs were mounted on moveable frames called ratchets, which would pull the log into the saw to be cut. Once the slab or cant was sawed off, the ratchet would return to the other side of the saw and be rotated and sent through again. This process would repeat until the log was cut into lumber.

Every successful invention made automating the sawmill easier, but

FIGURE 2.4 A MODEL OF AN EARLY WATER-POWERED SAWMILL, BUILT FOR THE SAN MATEO COUNTY HISTORICAL MUSEUM BY E. L. OAKS

mills in California faced several challenges that took years to resolve. For example, ratchets were useful but came with their own difficulties. Many different types of timber dogs and mechanical clamps were invented, most with the goal of making it easy to accurately mount and secure the log to the ratchet. But this process of trial and error took decades. Meanwhile, the idea of gang mills—several saws working simultaneously in a frame—were attempted to increase the efficiency of cutting lumber. A frame of twenty-six saws operating in the 1850s was the largest to ever operate in the vicinity of San Francisco. It could completely cut a small, squared log with a single cut, producing twenty-seven boards of equal width. Later, muley saws were brought in to achieve the same goal without the need for a frame. These saws operated independently and were held in place by bearings located along each end.

The greatest change in milling in California began with the introduction of the steam engine. The first engine in California appeared around 1835 but they did not enter widespread use until the early 1860s. Steam engines reduced a mill's dependence on water, which could be difficult to find in sufficient quantity during the dry summer months. Initially, steam-powered mills operated much the same as water-powered mills, but the introduction of the circular saw revolutionized the industry by replacing the inefficient straight saw with a large, many-toothed steel disk. When the circular saw was first introduced, it was considered too radical for many to accept.

There were two major concerns regarding the practicability of using circular saws. The first stemmed from the fact that with the outer rim of the saw so far from the source of power in the shaft, there would be a great loss of power. It was found, however, that this disadvantage could be more than overcome by running the saw at a greatly increased speed. By doubling the speed, for instance, the depth of the bite of the saw could be reduced by one half and still cut as much wood, and if the speed was tripled or quadrupled, there was a net gain in work done with practically no increase in cost. The second concern was more practical. In order to cut a log three feet in diameter, which was not large for the redwoods, a saw of more than six feet was required. The solution to this problem was using two saws, one below and one above. To prevent filling the cut with sawdust, the two blades revolved in opposite directions. Logs that were too large for this treatment were split in half using wedges or blasted apart, although dynamite damaged the wood causing a loss in profit.

In the long run, the circular saw proved that it could turn out more lumber at less cost than gang mills. By 1882, ninety-five percent of the lumber mills on the Pacific Coast cut their logs with circular saws. However, gang saws were not entirely abandoned. They were still used well into the twentieth century for certain types of lumber because they could cut with less waste produced. Circular saws, for strength, must be made of thick sheets of steel, whereas gang mill saws could be much thinner, thereby reducing the percentage of wood that went into the sawdust heap. The invention of detachable teeth for circular saws made this final point worse. While being able to remove a saw's teeth to sharpen or replace them greatly prolonged the life of what were quite expensive tools, thereby reducing costs, the broad teeth further increased the width of the saw leading to even more loss of wood to sawdust.

A compromise between the gang mill and the circular saw was the band saw, which first appeared in Santa Cruz County at the Monte Vista mill on Aptos Creek in 1884 and soon came into widespread use among the larger lumber mills. The band saw consisted of a long continuous blade that revolved around two broad wheels, called a band rig. This meant that the saw's width was narrower than a circular saw's and could benefit from most of the other improvements introduced by the circular saw. However, band rigs were more expensive and complex to operate, meaning only the better funded operations could afford them.

Only with the advent of steam-powered engines could the giant redwoods of the Santa Cruz Mountains be efficiently cut, and this did not begin in earnest until the 1870s. The maneuverability and flexibility of donkey engines synchronized perfectly with the efficiency of the circular and band saws to allow lumber mills to reach every corner of the county. Lumber mills by their very nature were meant to be temporary and somewhat portable. A mill was usually built using timbers, boards, and shakes either cut at the site or brought over from a previous mill. Belts for drives were made from the hides of retired oxen, which were butchered to feed the crew. Even tramway and railroad tracks were reused when they were no longer needed at their current locations.

The Reign of the Lumber Barons

The only part of a mill that could not be moved was the millpond. Lumber mills were usually built near a creek, and a dam was erected across the creek, usually upstream of the mill, to form a millpond. Millponds were where logs could be sorted, soaked, and stored before being moved to the

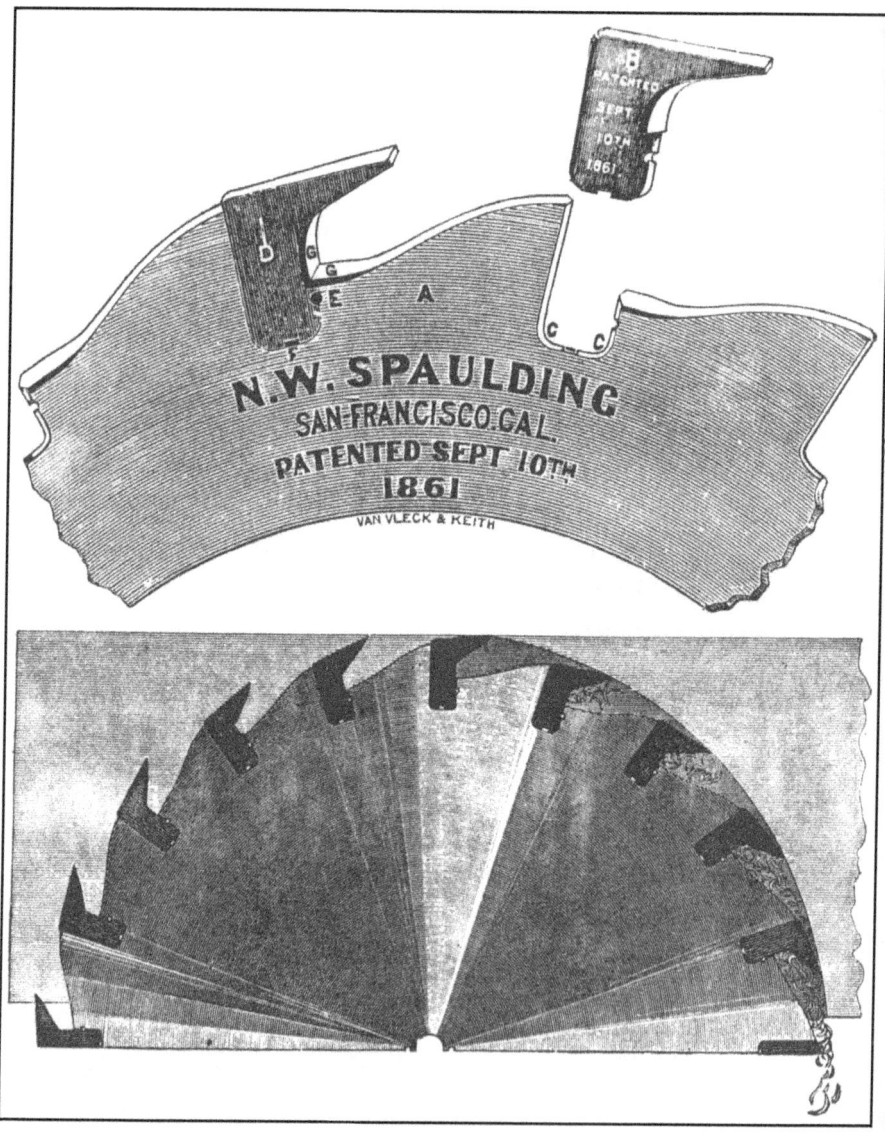

FIGURE 2.5 SAWS WITH DETACHABLE TEETH, INVENTED BY N. W. SPAULDING OF THE PACIFIC SAW MANUFACTURING COMPANY OF SAN FRANCISCO

mill to be cut. The dams of millponds were usually piles of logs tightly stacked across the creek with a spillway on the mill side. Mills usually had a ramp into the pond to make dragging heavy, soaked logs into the mill easier. Logs were soaked through primarily for the benefit of the sawblades, which could overheat if the wood were dry, potentially catching the sawdust or log on fire. After cutting, lumber was set out in tall stacks beside the mill to dry out and await shipment.

Prior to the opening of the Monte Vista mill in 1884, all of the mills in Santa Cruz County were classed as small-to-medium mills, with headrigs consisting of two 4- to 5-foot diameter circular saws. The Monte Vista mill, in contrast, had two 50-foot-long continuous band saws that revolved around 8-foot-diameter wheels. It also had several circular saws to cut products such as railroad crossties. Frederick Hihn also likely installed band saws in his Valencia Creek mill around the same time. Although the configuration of his mills on Valencia Creek and Gold Gulch is not known with certainty, his mill on Laurel Creek in the early 1900s operated using a band rig with two 9-foot-diameter wheels and a 60-foot-long continuous band saw. This machinery left the county around 1913 but returned in 1924 and was used by the Monterey Bay Redwood Company at Olive Springs until 1942.

The main components that made up the inside of a steam-powered sawmill were: the headrig, on which the primary saws were mounted; a carriage to hold the log; tracks for the carriage, which enabled the carriage to move both back and forth and side to side; an edger with a set of smaller saws; and a trimmer, also with a set of smaller saws. Before the log could be cut into lumber, it had to be squared up. To accomplish this, a log was pulled from the millpond, put on the carriage, and dogged (tied down). A bull wheel—a belt-driven gear—was mounted on one end of the log. This would turn the log three times as each side of the log was cut off until only a large square post remained. The removed slabs of wood would either end up in the burn pile or be sold for various uses. The person who tied down the log was called the dogger, while the person who controlled the carriage and set the amount to be cut off from the log was the ratchet setter. Meanwhile, the person who controlled the speed of the carriage and determined the thickness of a cant was the sawyer. Because the noise in the mill was so loud, the sawyer communicated his commands to the ratchet setter via hand signals.

The Reign of the Lumber Barons

FIGURE 2.6 AN UP-TO-DATE LUMBER MILL OF THE 1870s.
NOTE THAT THE RATCHET SETTER RIDES THE CARRIAGE BACK AND FORTH
WITH THE LOG, SHIFTING IT OVER WITH LEVERS FOR EACH NEW CUT.
HANDLING OF LOGS ON THE GROUND IS STILL DONE WITH CANT HOOKS.

During the early days, with so many trees available for harvesting, deeper cuts were made to remove from the finished product the white streaks of sapwood. Sapwood is the outer layers of a tree which are rich in sap between the bark and the heartwood. Most mills removed the sapwood because their competitors were doing it and because it presented to customers a clean redwood face. But this practice resulted in a loss of yield amounting to as much as twenty-five percent. By the 1900s, this loss was reduced to seventeen percent because of improvements to saws and new uses for sapwood.

When a cant was cut off a squared log, it was sent to the edgerman, who used his edger machine and its three-to-five moveable saws to shape it to the appropriate dimensions. Most of the cants were not standard sizes of lumber, so the edgerman would cut off smaller boards from the cant. For example, a cant measuring 2 inches by 48 inches could produce twelve 2x4s. After passing through the edger, boards went to the trimmerman, who removed boards with broken ends, bark, and large knots, and then trimmed them until they were all the desired size and shape.

The success of a sawmill depended heavily on the knowledge, ability, and skill of the sawyer, edgerman, and trimmerman, but other people also provided support. In addition to assistants to all of the above, lumberjacks were essential. After trimming, boards were loaded onto tramcars and carted out by hand to the drying yard for sorting and stacking according to size and grade. This task was done by lumberjacks, who used various sizes of jacks to lift lumber from tramcars to lumber piles or to move lumber around a yard. Lumberjacks were versatile and worked both in mill yards and at company lumber yards across the county. For many, they were the blue-collar face of a lumber company since they were one of the few workers who appeared in public by helping customers load lumber onto wagons at company lumber yards.

Getting Lumber to Market

Until the introduction of the gasoline-powered truck in the early 1920s, getting lumber from a mill to the public marketplace could be quite difficult. Some operations such as the Loma Prieta Lumber Company, the F. A. Hihn Company, and the Santa Clara Valley Mill & Lumber Company had direct access to the railroad at most of their mills, so they could relatively easily ship their goods directly to San José and San Francisco. But most other mills had to settle for shipping out lumber via large wagons with trailers.

These special lumber wagons often carried 3,000-4,000 board feet of lumber and were pulled by teams of eight or more horses. The wagon driver frequently sat astride the near wheeler—the left horse nearest the wagon—and controlled the team by use of a jerkline. When a steep uphill grade was encountered, the trailer would be unhitched, and the team would haul the main wagon to the top of the grade first and then return for the trailer. On steep downgrades, the wheels of the wagon would be locked using metal shoes or chains and the wagon would be dragged like a sled. Two wagons meeting each other on a tight narrow road could spell disaster, so Hames bells were strung atop the collars of the lead horses as a warning signal. Drivers would use pullouts set up at regular intervals to listen for an oncoming team before continuing down the road. Each team had a unique set of bells to let the drivers know who was approaching.

During the summer, roads became so dry that fine powdery dust would literally flow before the wheels of a wagon. Great clouds of dust rolled above teams and coated everything along the way. In contrast, during the late autumn and winter, after the rains came, the roads became an impassable quagmire. Wagons could not move and mills shut down, allowing the horses much needed rest.

Shingles and Shakes

Shake and shingle mills were the lifeblood of many redwood logging operations. Running year-round from small mobile mills on hillsides, they were more versatile than lumber mills and did not require heavy machinery or millponds to operate. They produced what their name implies: shakes and shingles, used on the roofs and sides of buildings to provide extra protection from the elements. Shingles were produced from the choicest portion of redwood trees, between the base and the point where the upper branches began. Shakes, meanwhile, could include some sapwood and were, as a result, split into two different quality grades, the lower of which included up to an inch of sapwood.

Shakes and shingles began life as felled redwood trees. After a tree was stripped of its bark and branches and cut into manageable sections, the log was brought into a mill. Logs used for shakes and shingles were cut into four-foot lengths and then cut lengthwise into four sections. A bolting saw then cut these into three smaller pieces of a set height and width, thereby producing shake and shingle bolts. After shingle and shake bolts were removed from the tree, the remainder of the tree, if large enough, was cut into lumber, while the leftovers were turned into splitstuff.

Until the 1860s, shakes and shingles were virtually identical products except for their lengths and grades. Shakes were 36 inches long while shingles were 16 inches. Otherwise, they were both about a quarter inch thick and 6 inches wide. For most of history, shakes and shingles were split rather than sawed, and the softer redwood wood lent itself well to this process. Sawyers would saw bolts of the appropriate size and use a froe—a straight blade about 10 inches long with a handle at a right angle—to peel off the desired products. To cut the shakes and shingles off the bolt, the blade of the froe was placed about a quarter inch from the edge of the bolt and gently hammered to make the split. However, the split only went about two-thirds down the length of the bolt, leaving the shake or shingle attached. Once all of the cuts were made, the bolt was tied together using hay rope, the predecessor of bailing wire. After the bolts were sold and taken to where they would be used, workers pulled off the shakes and shingles by hand before nailing them into place.

The Industrial Revolution sparked hundreds of inventions related to customizing and optimizing shake and shingle production. Many were focused on profitably making shingles with tapered edges, which were in high demand. After much experimentation, it was determined that the best way of accomplishing this was by using a single vertically mounted circular saw in a fashion akin to a spinning wheel. A sawyer would place a bolt in a frame and slowly push it into the spinning saw, controlled by their foot. After the shingle was cut, the bolt would be pulled back and tilted at a set angle. The sawyer would then push the bolt back into the saw to make another cut at a different angle than the first. This process produced bolts split into shingles with tapered edges.

Over time, this new system of cutting shingles was automated through the use of water and steam power. A sawyer placed a bolt in an automated

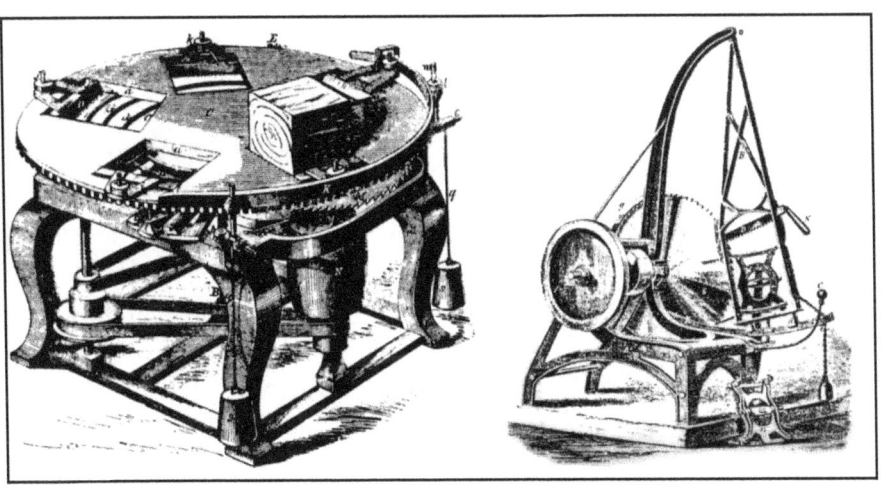

Figure 2.7 Two different types of shingle cutters patented in 1858

The Reign of the Lumber Barons

clamp and a machine then quickly processed the bolt. Shingles then fell off on the opposite side of the machine, where a trimmerman would straighten their edges and drop them down a chute to a packer. Packers were the most nimble-fingered of the crew. They stacked the shingles in proper order—two hundred to a bundle—and nailed up the bundle before stacking it for shipment. Shake and shingle mill operators were usually paid as piece workers and a fast crew who worked well together could make good money. However, the demand for tapered shingles meant that shingle mills, unlike shake mills, required machinery and so were, by necessity, less mobile.

After shingle cutting was mechanized, the thickness of shingles could be controlled much more closely. Tapered shingles usually varied on their thick side from 3/8th to 7/16th inch before narrowing to a point. However, sawing the shingle bolts led to a loss of wood to sawdust, so bolts grew from 16 inches long to 18 inches to compensate for the loss. The other dimensions of a bolt continued to vary based on the desired size of the shingles.

Specialized shingle and shake mills in Santa Cruz County appeared on the scene relatively late, although many multipurpose sawmills produced shingles and shakes as part of their operations. In the Augmentation, the first and largest-scale shingle mill was built by the Pacific Improvement Company at Molino on Tract 8 in 1884. The second mill was built by Hihn around 1888 on Spignet Gulch within Tract 10. Hihn only operated

FIGURE 2.8 ADVERTISEMENT FOR AN EARLY TYPE OF FULLY-AUTOMATED SHINGLE-MAKING MACHINE, 1876

this remote mill for about two years before deciding that the shingles and shakes produced there were of insufficient quality. He did not open another dedicated shingle mill until around 1908, when he built three near the headwaters of the East Branch of Soquel Creek on Tract 11. The products cut here were shipped to Watsonville via Eureka Canyon. Meanwhile, the Loma Prieta Lumber Company operated three shake mills along Hinckley Gulch from 1900 to 1906. These were considered unique by A. C. Bassett since most shakes were cut further to the north near Davenport. Throughout this time, both Hihn and the Loma Prieta Lumber Company also cut shingles and shakes at their lumber mills as a part of their overall operations.

Splitstuff, Tanbark, and the Pack Mule

Splitstuff is a catch-all term used for wood products cut using simple hand tools. Depending on the time and circumstances, it covered different products of varying quality and type. By its broadest definition, it encompassed shake and shingle bolts, shakes and shingles cut in the forest, grape stakes, pickets, fence and corral posts, and railroad crossties. It also encompassed cordwood and rough-cut firewood. Indeed, the volume of splitstuff products brought out of the forests of the Santa Cruz Mountains far surpassed the amount of lumber and encompassed nearly half of the total volume of wood cut.

The reason why so much splitstuff was produced in the mountains is simple: not everything cut can or should be turned into lumber. Added to this was the difficulty of getting logs out of some rugged areas. Sometimes it was just easier to cut up a tree on site and turn it into splitstuff. Some smaller companies even focused on producing splitstuff exclusively, since it did not require an expensive mill. This applied especially to areas where there was no room for a mill, or the surrounding timberland was insufficient to justify building a mill. While splitstuff appeared rough when compared to milled products, it performed its intended purpose. Splitstuff was cut by piece makers—literally people paid by the piece, or rather the amount of splitstuff they produced. Thus, before it was sent out by mule, splitstuff was counted to ensure that the worker got paid correctly.

The production of splitstuff was often performed alongside the peeling of tanbark in areas too remote to effectively log or where logging crews had not yet reached. Tanoak trees (*Notholithocarpus densiflorus*) are a native California plant that attracted Spanish, Mexican, and American immigrants to the Santa Cruz Mountains. Like most oaks, the tanoak bark produces tannic acid, although it does so in higher quantities than its old-world relatives. Tannic acid is the key resource needed to tan leather. The abundance of tanoak in California during the Mexican period led to a thriving leather industry across the state, especially along the Central Coast. Until the 1910s, almost any tanbark was accepted at tanneries without inspection, which allowed the tanbark industry to thrive.

Before an area was logged, peelers were sent in to peel the bark off any tanoak trees. Tanoak sap dries from the top down and the bark can only be removed when the sap is still liquid. This means that most peeling was done in the spring and early summer, when the sap was up. It was also younger trees that were usually peeled since they had a higher quantity of sap and were therefore easier to peel. Most tanoak trees would have one 4-foot ring of bark removed, but some could have two rings, which was as high as a peeler could possibly reach by climbing on the back of their horse or mule. Peeling the bark made tanoak trees vulnerable to fire, but they could recover and grow a new ring within a few years.

A felled tanoak tree could sometimes produce up to five rings of bark. When it was felled, a peeler scored the tree at four-foot intervals that could be up to an inch deep. These were then pulled off the tree in large sheets and then curled into a loose roll that was slowly tightened. The rolls were left to dry for a year before they were packed out of the forest for shipment on mules.

Just like cutting splitstuff, peeling tanbark was a relatively cheap investment with a good return. A peeler only needed an axe, a spud (a peeling bar), and a sturdy horse to do their job. Similarly, piece makers used a combination of saws, axes, wedges, sledgehammers, and muscle power to make their products. Indeed, piece makers and tanbark peelers were often one and the same. Many, even if employed by a larger firm, lived on the land where they worked and built their own cabins to live in while doing their work. And they relied heavily on hardy pack mules to haul their products to market.

Mules rarely carried their loads all the way to the city. In most cases, they delivered the splitstuff and tanbark to a landing where they were transferred to a railroad or a wagon. Packers would carefully load the mules at the harvesting site and send them on their way down the trail to the landing. The people who carved out these crude paths were called trail makers, while those who unloaded the mules at landings were called dump men. A normal mule train was composed of one saddle animal and five laden pack mules.

The packer was usually the owner of the mules and understood each animal's maximum capacity and their idiosyncrasies. Since mules are not particularly large animals, they could rarely carry more than 700 pounds on their backs. In fact, it was mule saddles that restricted the length of splitstuff products and tanbark rolls. Any product cut in the forest had to be small enough to fit on the back of a well-laden mule. However, it also had to be at least four feet long because that was the space between the hooks that held a mule's load in place. Mule saddles were contrived so that they would not chafe a mule's back. They had four hooks, two on either side, which were spaced in such a way to balance a load of splitstuff or tanbark while travelling. However, this restricted how much and the types of products that could be cut in the forest.

Heavier splitstuff operations such as those producing bolts or crossties required two packers, or rather a packer and an assistant. One would hold the hooks in place while the other would carefully load the mule, being careful not to cause an imbalance. Meanwhile, heavy fence and corral posts were loaded alternately on each side to keep the weight balanced. Usually, loads were secured with rawhide thongs cut from the side of latigo leather, which was specially prepared by the tanners. As the thongs would wear out and have to be replaced, the packer usually bought the leather in a large piece, called a side, and cut strips as needed.

Trail makers had the sometimes-difficult job of finding pathways between these splitstuff and tanbark camps and the landings. They had to understand how steep a trail the mule could travel and how wide it needed to be to avoid the load or hooks becoming snagged. In some circumstances, trail makers would even need to construct crude bridges to bypass deep gullies.

As soon as a mule was loaded with splitstuff or tanbark at a camp, it was sent down the trail to the landing unaided. Mules are generally intelligent animals. They do not loiter on their journey but hurry excitedly to their

The Reign of the Lumber Barons

destination to be relieved of their loads. At the landing, the dump man unloaded each mule as it arrived and piled the material carefully for measuring and counting. Once so relieved, mules rested beside the landing until the packer arrived to take them back. Mules traveled in tandem on the return trip, fastened together with ropes and led by the packer on the saddle horse.

A water barrel was always kept at the landing. When the barrel needed refilling, a mule would be led over to the nearest water source where bags would be filled. The filled bags would then be slung on the hooks on either side of the mule's saddle and the mule would return to the landing to refill the barrel. Mules would receive a regular supply of rolled barley throughout the day to supplement their twice daily rations of wild oat hay, given to them in the morning and in the evening. If there was no feeding trough at the landing, a packer would place a feed bag filled with grain over the nose of a mule. The mule could quickly consume all the grain in the bag by reaching to the ground and occasionally shaking its head.

Consuming raw barley can cause a mule's mouth to become sore, so it was essential that the oats were rolled prior to being used as feed. At Opal west of Capitola, the Loma Prieta Lumber Company built a rolled barley mill to address the issue of feeding the dozens of mules that operated along Hinckley Creek from 1901 to 1917. It consisted of a large building containing a boiler, engine, large tank for steaming the grain, and rollers that flattened and partly ground the grain. A charge of barley was placed in the tank, where steam from the boiler saturated the grains. The grains were then taken by a conveyor to heavy rollers, which broke down the barley into a more manageable size. The rolled barley was then stacked and stored in a nearby barn until it was needed.

The hay and barley were purchased from farms in the Salinas Valley. The general manager was responsible for tracking down quality feed. He sought good quality hay and barley that were plump and not shriveled. He also avoided in earnest any hint of feed that had mixed with the spiny, invasive tocalote weed (*Centaurea melitensis*), which could injure mules and horses. Most of the time, the manager purchased grain from the Salinas Valley Mill Company, which maintained relatively high standards, but he also sometimes worked with the Southern Pacific Mill & Warehouse Company, which later merged with the Salinas firm.

Although most people who worked in the splitstuff and tanbark business were independent contractors, lumber mills would hire them and their animals on occasion to assist in clearing out an area. The rates for their services varied. Around 1900, a single pack mule in the Santa Cruz Mountains cost about $1.00 per day and a horse with a train of five mules about $2.00. The mill may also have needed extra workers to help with the operation: a dump man cost about $2.00 a day, a trail maker $2.50, and a packer $3.00. The mill was always responsible for providing the grain and hay for the horses and mules.

Chapter 3

~

The Hidden Hand

Brad Morrell returns to the lumber industry

After helping his brother on the Summit for approximately seven years, Brad Morrell yearned to return to the lumber industry. In 1874, he purchased from M. W. Whittle land that was located about two miles north of the confluence of Boulder and Bear Creeks and the San Lorenzo River. Whittle was a stockholder in the San Lorenzo Flume & Transportation Company, incorporated August 26, 1874, and with his purchase, Morrell was contracted to produce the material to build the new flume from his so-called Flume Mill. Construction began shortly after the mill was erected and he continued to operate it for the next year.[59]

Land transfer from Frederick Waterman to the Heaton family and partners

On September 3, 1874, Frederick Waterman sold the 126 acres he owned in Tract 27 of the Augmentation to Hiram Heaton, his wife, and their partners, H. P. Parkinson, E. G. Spencer, Frank Kenyor, Charles H. Waterman, P. B. Fagan, Charles H. Parker, H. Simpkins, and Charles W. Thomas.[60]

Santa Cruz Railroad stockholders hold another meeting in Santa Cruz

Only three months after its first annual meeting, the Santa Cruz Railroad's board of directors called together a second meeting of stockholders in a closed session intended to hasten completion of the line. On the evening of September 5, 1874, Frederick Hihn outlined the financial position of the company, stating that the cost of the easements and real estate, equipment, and fencing amounted to $306,000, which was to be provided via the county subsidy ($110,000), subscriptions ($100,000), and loans ($96,000). The remainder Hihn hoped to reduce or find alternative means of funding.

Hihn had originally intended to construct the first five miles of track—thereby securing the initial $30,000 of the subsidy—east from the San Lorenzo River toward Soquel. However, after work began, graders realized that more bridges, cuts, and fills were required along this section than had been surveyed. With these obstacles, it was unlikely that the railroad would be completed by the end of 1875, as planned.

Hihn did have some more positive news, however. The iron rails that he had procured for the line were found at a lower price and higher quality than anticipated. Furthermore, Hihn had been able to reduce the projected loan amount to $65,000 by offering shares to stockholders at the reduced cost of $60 each. If the 1,100 shares on offer were not all taken up by stockholders then they could be sold to the public at the same rate or higher, up to their face value of $100.[61]

Santa Cruz Railroad's first locomotive arrives and construction continues

Weighing in at just five tons, the first locomotive to operate on the Santa Cruz Railroad line, 'Betsy Jane,' arrived at Pajaro on October 17, 1874 before crossing the Pajaro River and entering Watsonville. By this point, grading was completed to the Rancho San Andreas schoolhouse while construction on the Soquel Creek bridge was ongoing. The locomotive was hauled by wagon down the county road to the vicinity of Camp Capitola, where it entered service. 'Betsy Jane' was used in the construction of the line to haul material to the two ends-of-track. It also led excursion trains over completed sections of the route, usually for promotional purposes except in the final year when regular, albeit infrequent, service began.

Within Rancho Aptos, the Nichols mill, run by brothers Benjamin Cahoon, Samuel Meritt, and Wiel Schemerhorn Nichols, began producing lumber for use on the line, with their first commission being material for the construction of the railroad bridge over Aptos Creek. The felling crews operated under the direction of James Holcraft.

Work on all of the bridges progressed rapidly. By October 31, all of the smaller bridges between the San Lorenzo River and Aptos were completed and the trestlework on the Soquel Creek bridge was in the process of being installed. Grading along this fifteen-mile stretch was also nearing completion, with only a section between the river and Seabright still requiring work. The first load of rails had also arrived from the East Coast aboard the steamship *Arizona* via Panama and San Francisco. The contractors decided to delay installing the rails until enough had arrived to lay ten miles at one time.[62]

Letter in the *Sentinel* concerning the Santa Cruz Railroad

On November 21, 1874, Benjamin P. Kooser, editor-in-chief of the *Sentinel*, published the following letter simply signed "Los Gringo" in his newspaper. It reveals much concerning the ongoing conflict between Santa Cruz and Watsonville.

> *As there is a scarcity of other local matter, and as it seems to be quite fashionable, I propose to write "Railroad" a little now—that the road between Santa Cruz and Pajaro is soon to be completed. What I can write will not make much difference any way but may do to fill up with. I now say that I have been considerably surprised at the spirit of opposition manifested by at least a portion of the people of Watsonville to*

this enterprise. *As I live about half way between the two towns of Santa Cruz and Watsonville, and not being interested in the road to the amount of a dollar, I think I can look upon the matter without prejudice.*

Of the two places, Watsonville will undoubtedly derive the greater benefit from the completion of this road. The people of Santa Cruz, to be sure, will be benefited to a degree; if they did not expect to be, they would not take such an interest in the enterprise.

Santa Cruz is a manufacturing town, and what her people want is a market for their manufactured articles—especially lumber—and a cheap mode of reaching that market. These wants are tolerably well supplied at present, but the completion of the railroad will, of course, be an advantage in this respect. The growth and prosperity of Watsonville mainly depend upon the agricultural resources of the country around the town, and what the people want is a market for their farm produce, and a cheap manner of reaching that market; these wants the Railroad will supply to a dot. Freight can then be taken to San Francisco by the way of Santa Cruz, for at least a dollar less on the ton than the present prices.

Watsonville also requires a considerable amount of the article manufactured at Santa Cruz—such as timber, lumber, lime, fencing, leather, powder—all of which has to be hauled over a rough wagon-road, at a high rate of freight. Perhaps I should make a present exception to firewood, lumber and fencing, a small amount of which comes from the Coralitos [sic] district, but which supply is very limited, and will give out entirely in a few years, when all of the lumber will have to come from Santa Cruz. And I would ask if it is not cheaper and better to have the lumber delivered in Watsonville at a dollar or a dollar and a half freight, than to pay six or seven dollars, the present prices.

And again. Before six years more roll around, it will require the whole surplus product of the Pajaro Valley to supply the Santa Cruz market. Now, I know that some of the big farmers of that fertile district will look at this with surprise, and mutter something about my being crazy, but let us look at the matter a little. Six years ago, all of the surplus produce raised in the vicinity of Soquel, was shipped from that landing to San Francisco for a market. Three years later, all of that produce found a ready market in Santa Cruz, and at a price considerably above what could be realized in the city. Three years ago, the farmers in the vicinity of Aptos, San Andreas and Corralitos, shipped their produce to San Francisco, from the Aptos or Miller's Landing [Manresa Beach]. *Last year all of this grain, potatoes, etc., found a market in Santa Cruz, and at a price sufficiently above the San Francisco prices to pay the farmers for hauling a distance of twenty miles. And yet this did not near supply the market; a large number of teams were engaged in hauling grain and hay from Salinas and Castroville, and even Hollister, and nearly every teamster from Moss' Landing brought from one hundred to one thousand sacks of grain, for the Santa Cruz merchants. Now, if the Pajaronian can find a ready market for his farm produce in Santa Cruz, at a price equal to that he would receive in San Francisco, and save the price of the freight, is he not largely the gainer by the Railroad? And if the Santa Cruzan can get his needed supplies from Watsonville, at the same rate he could get them at Salinas or San Francisco, and save freight, is he not the gainer also? It looks to me so. Why is it then that any oppose this enterprise?*

And another thing. Hollister is going to build a Railroad to the seacoast. The people of the Pajaro Valley should see to it that this road does not go by the way of Salinas to Monterey. Properly speaking, Watsonville has no Railroad yet and if the Santa Cruz road passed them on one side, and the Hollister road on the other, they will be left out in the cold. But this the people will not allow, if they consult their own interests. With these Railroads, and with the many other advantages, Watsonville will, in a few years, be classed among the leading cities of this State.[63]

Storms damage the Santa Cruz Railroad

Abnormal amounts of rain during the week of November 28, 1874 damaged several parts of the Santa Cruz Railroad's right-of-way leading to a four-week delay in construction to make repairs.[64]

An excursion on the Santa Cruz Railroad to Soquel

On December 8, 1874, a group of reporters for the *Sentinel* joined an excursion along the Santa Cruz Railroad. They wrote the following in the next issue of the newspaper:

> *The little engine glided away quietly with but little "fuss and bother" so common with our big swelled-head railroads, and "all went merry as a marriage belle." The heavy rains of last month, although they did unsettle things for a short time, served to make the road bed more solid, and we found the track much smoother than one could reasonably expect, of work that had been pushed through so rapidly in so short a time. As we neared Soquel the engine slackened speed and we gently dropped down the grade to the substantial bridge where Santa Cruz and Soquel shook hands with a cheer and a—tiger in perspective. Again the bell rang, and away we went winding around the bluff, through deep cuts, until just ahead we found a long 40 foot deep cut, literally alive with Chinese.... Here we were brought to a halt, for John Chinaman said no farther just now.... With one parting glance "over the hills and far away," we proposed to return....*
>
> *The scenery and atmosphere were so exhilarating, our trip back was enlivened with songs, jokes, lively repartees and pleasant squibs, while all returned, delighted, with nothing to mar the enjoyment of the occasion, or cause a regret....*[65]

Jared and Smith Comstock settle on the Augmentation

In 1867, Jared and Smith Comstock from Norwich, Connecticut arrived in Santa Cruz County. They lingered in the county for seven years before they finally accumulated enough money to purchase around 1,180 acres from William L. Dickinson on December 15, 1874. The land was located within Tracts 15, 20, and 22 of the Augmentation. Soon after the deed was signed, the Comstock brothers built their first sawmill along Hester Creek just north of Montecito Springs at the foot of Blackberry Grade. This mill would later be sold in the 1890s, after which it was known as the Franch & Miracle shingle mill.

Over the subsequent eight years, the Comstocks expanded their operations to other sites within the Augmentation. Their second mill was to the north of the first. To reach it, they extended a short, twisting wagon road from the Soquel Turnpike which was and still is named Comstock Mill Road. This mill burned to the ground in about 1884.

During the period that the Comstock brothers logged along Hester Creek, they acquired acreage within Frederick Hihn's Tract 11 and built a small sawmill. Because the market for lumber was more lucrative in the Santa Clara Valley, the Comstocks began shipping their products there. To reach the valley, the lumber had to travel up the narrow, steep dirt Long Ridge Road and then continue along the twisting forerunner of today's Stetson Road until reaching the Soquel Turnpike. While this route fulfilled its purpose, it was inefficient and dangerous. As a result, the Comstock

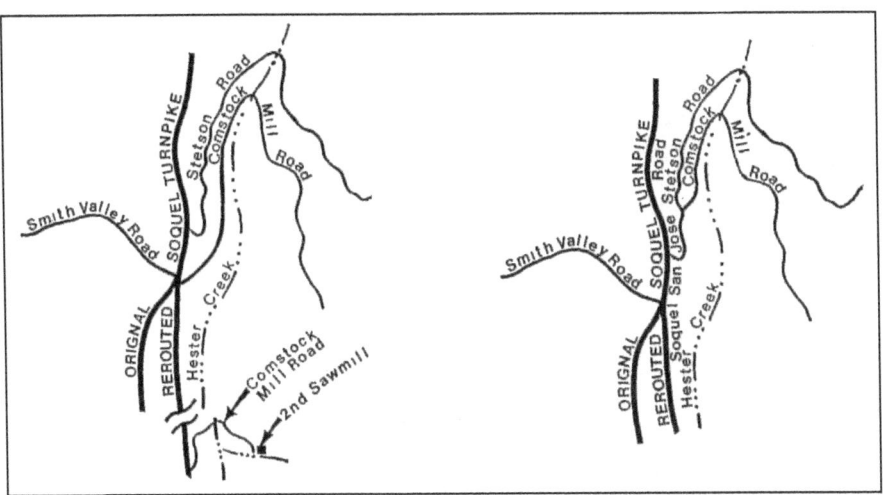

FIGURE 3.1 SOQUEL TURNPIKE REALIGNMENT FOR COMSTOCK MILL

brothers extended Comstock Mill Road to reach their third mill.

Getting lumber to the Santa Clara Valley, however, still required a steep and precarious climb over the Soquel Turnpike, which had an espe-

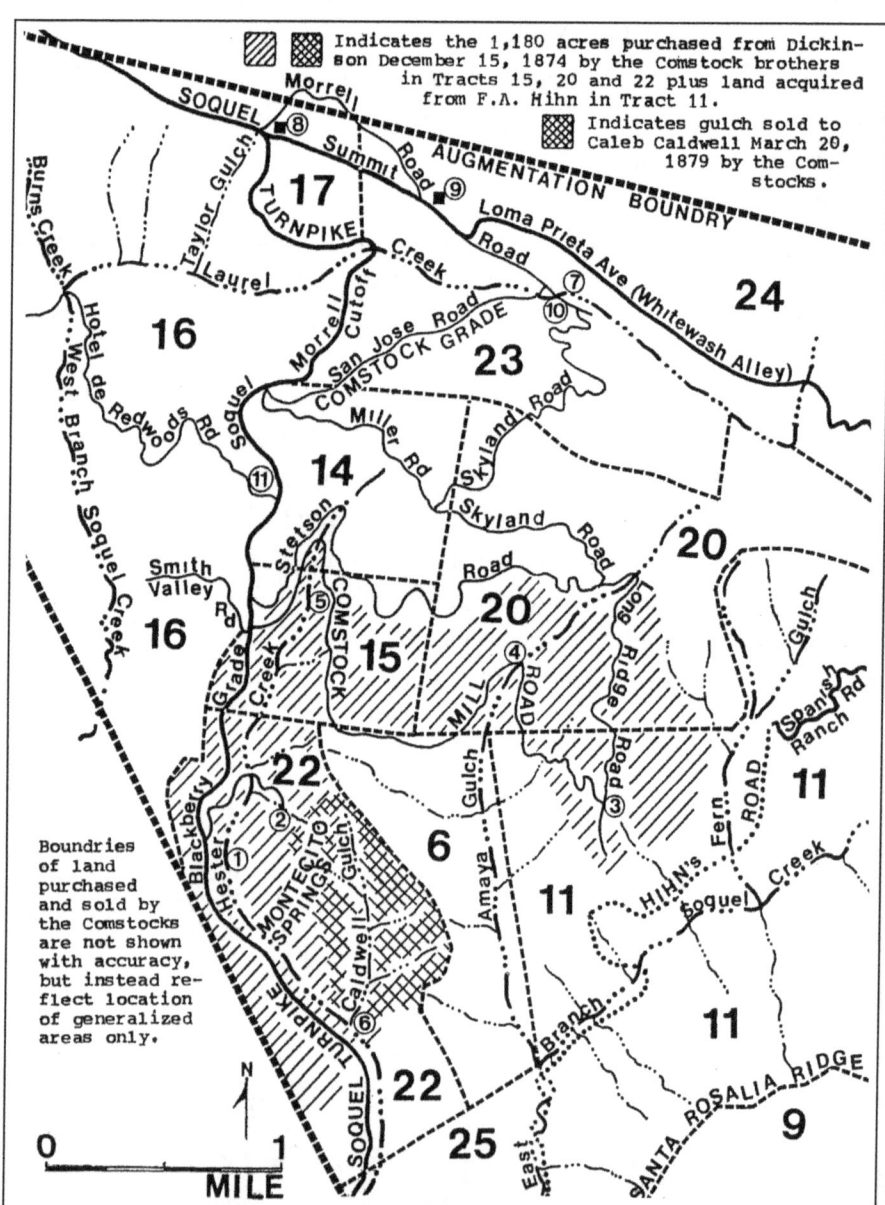

FIGURE 3.2 THE COMSTOCK BROTHERS' LAND WITHIN THE AUGMENTATION

cially dangerous section near the top known today as the Morrell Cutoff. To bypass this, the Comstocks cut a new, safer route around the cutoff. As soon as it was completed, it became a popular alternative to the hair-raising original route and became known as the Comstock Grade. After the grade was completed, the brothers could easily haul their lumber to the valley.

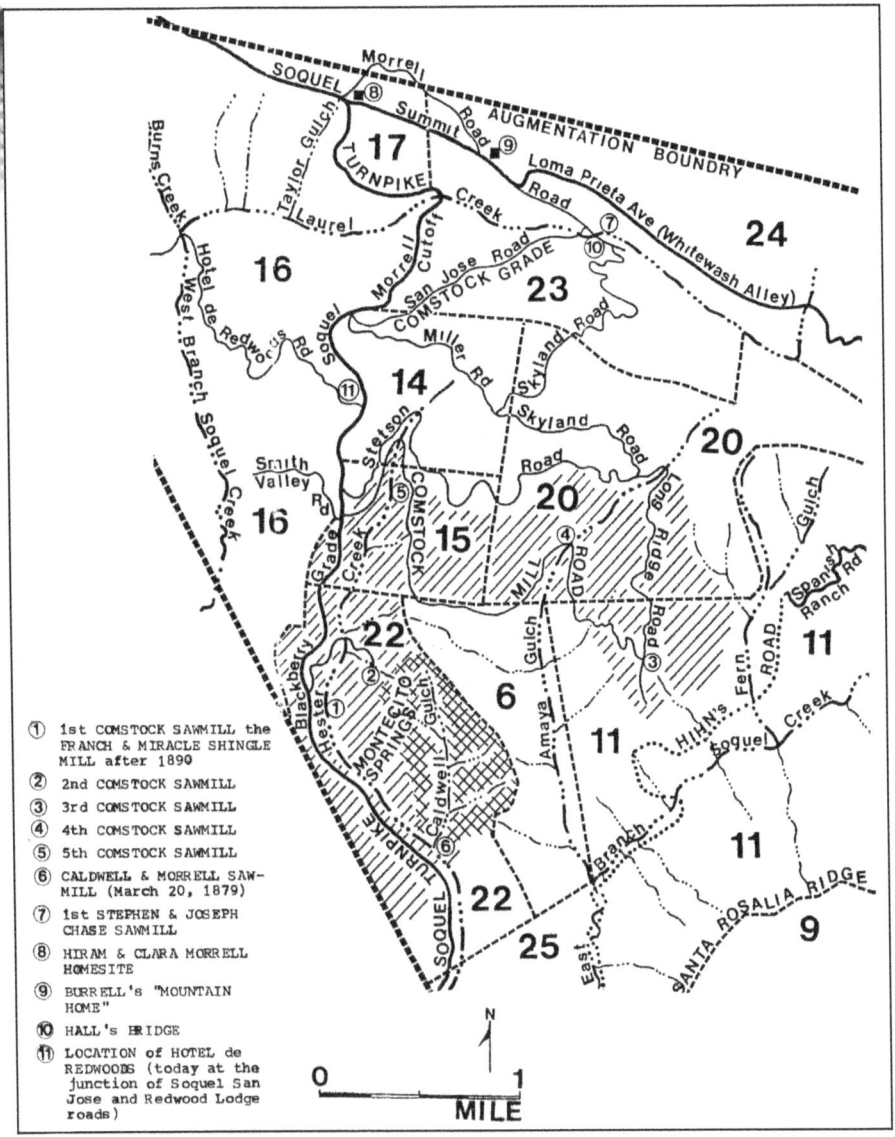

FIGURE 3.3 LOCATIONS OF VARIOUS MILLS WITHIN THE AUGMENTATION

The new route did have one accidental victim: Hiram Morrell. The increased traffic over the ridge led to an excess of dust in the air that wagons kicked up as they passed his homestead. As a solution, Morrell once more build a road on the Summit, this one to send wagons away from his home and around it to the north along what is now called Morrell Road. For several years, the Comstock Grade and Morrell Road together served as the main route across the Summit from the Soquel Turnpike to the Santa Cruz Gap Turnpike, which led to San José.

When the land within the vicinity of their third sawmill was stripped of its timber, the Comstock brothers moved up to the point where Comstock Mill Road crosses Amaya Gulch. When this area was logged, their fifth and final mill in the Augmentation was built just below their road on Hester Creek. After all of their Augmentation tracts were cleared, Jared Comstock moved to Boulder Creek where he build a mill on Big Basin Way. He died there on October 21, 1889 at the age of 41 leaving behind a wife and two children. Smith, meanwhile, moved to Fresno and later Visalia, where he also ran a mill above Badger. He ran for sheriff of Tulare County in 1896 and, after losing, moved to Mexico to mine. However, when there he discovered he had cancer and returned to Visalia, where he died on March 29, 1901 at the age of 58. He left a wife and three daughters.[66]

A. C. Bassett promoted to superintendent of the Southern Pacific Railroad's Northern Division

Almeron Cornelius Bassett, born in Chicago in 1838, began his career working as an employee of a cross-country telegraph company. While working in this role, he was discovered by the Southern Pacific Railroad and hired as the assistant superintendent of the company in 1871. In April 1875, following a reorganization of the company's lines, Bassett was appointed superintendent of the newly created Northern Division, which encompassed the whole of the trackage in the Bay Area and Monterey Bay. Bassett was known to have an honest and agreeable personality and became one of the railroad's most respected and trusted employees.[67]

Frederick Hihn offers manufacturers land at favorable terms

An article that appeared in the *Sentinel* on March 20, 1875 stated:

> TO MANUFACTURERS
> FOR SALE!
> On Favorable Terms
> GOOD LOCATIONS!
> for
> FACTORIES!
> in
> Santa Cruz and Soquel
> and vicinity
>
> Santa Cruz County offers more advantages for the location of Factories than any other county in the State. It is already a
> Manufacturing Center.
>
> List of Factories now in successful operation:
> One Powder Mill, one Fuse Factory, five Lime Works, one Beet Sugar Mill, (being built), three Flouring Mills, eight Tanneries, one Glue Factory, one Soap Factory, twenty-two sawmills, 4 Shingle Mills, two Foundries. For particulars, address F. A. HIHN, Santa Cruz.[68]

Santa Cruz Railroad construction continues

The *Sentinel* reported on May 1, 1875 that:

> The S. C. R. R.'s bridge is now completed, and the engine is busy ballasting the road bed along the bay, and hauling ties up Chestnut street. They have a gang at work, laying ties and rails as fast as they can be brought to the front. They have track now laid to Rincon St. Cars will be running to the beach and Aptos, as soon as they can make the necessary

arrangements to accommodate them to the work of farther construction. Due notice will be given as soon as time tables can be arranged.

Two weeks later, on May 15, the paper published a follow-up article noting that:

By the 1st of September it is the intention of the Santa Cruz R. R. Co. to have their road completed to its connection with the Southern Pacific, and trains running. The delay that has embarrassed them was occasioned by lack of timber to build the trestle work over the gulches below Aptos. They have now overcome that difficulty and as soon as that work is done they can push the road right along, and by the date mentioned they expect to have it done.

The same issue included the following timetable for the Santa Cruz Railroad:

On May 15, Saturday the train will leave Santa Cruz at 9 A.M. and at 1, 7 and 9 P.M....and at Aptos it will leave at 10 A.M. and at 3 and 5 P.M.
On May 16, Sunday it will leave Santa Cruz at 1 and 3:10 P.M....and at Aptos it will leave at 6 A.M. and 2:30 and 5 P.M.
Fare for the round trip is 50 cents.

With the impending start of regular passenger service for both the Santa Cruz Railroad and the Santa Cruz & Felton Railroad, the *Sentinel* announced that it would begin printing newspapers daily.[69]

Opening of the Santa Cruz Railroad celebrated early

The opening celebration for the Santa Cruz Railroad, which was conducted prior to the completion of the route partially to attract new investors and partially to deflect attention from the Santa Cruz & Felton Railroad, happened on May 16, 1875 to great fanfare. The *Sentinel* provided an extensive summary of the events, which is included below. The original summary also included an excessively long list of VIPs as well as an overly detailed description of Claus Spreckels' new Aptos Hotel.

Great Event of the Season!

―――

Formal Opening of the S. C. N. G. R. R. to Aptos.

―――

Inauguration Ball, and Reception at Hon. Claus Spreckels' Aptos Hotel.

―――

The Event Honored by the Presence of his Excellency Romualdo Pacheco and Lady and Members of His Military Household, Gen. J. M. Schofield, U. S. A., Commander of the Pacific Coast Department, Gen. L. H. Foote, Col. Eddy, U. S. A., and others

―――

The dispatches bringing us word of the culmination of three events of great importance in quick succession or connection, we dispatched our Faber No. 2 to see how it was, and here is his report of what he saw and heard.

THE RAILROAD EXCURSION, Was inaugurated quietly, yet considerable enthusiasm was manifested; vast crowds gathering about the little engine and four cars, that were loaded to their utmost capacity, nearly an hour before the time set for starting; while those who could not find seats or standing room, yielded gracefully to the force of circumstances, resolved to bide their time. Promptly on time the bell rang, and away went the little engine with its living freight, as light as a feather, while cheer on cheer rent the air, and hats, fans and handkerchiefs waved adieu to the crowd of upturned faces and loved ones all along the line * * *

Being too busy in the office on Saturday, we failed to connect with the noon train, but succeeded in getting a foothold on the 7 P. M. train by being 15 minutes ahead of time. Promptly to time the bell tapped, and away we went with the speed of a grey hound and found ourselves in Aptos on time for the fray, with a half hour to spare for introductions. We had the pleasure of meeting not only Governor Pacheco and his staff, but a cordial shake of the hand by that prince of good landlords, Geo. A. Bromley and lady, who looks as fresh, hale and hearty as in years gone by.

THE INAUGURATION SERVICES Were opened with a grand banquet, at which His Excellency Romualdo Pacheco, Col. Spreckels' honored guest was chairman, and did the honors of the occasion, occupying the head of the table, while Colonel Spreckels sat at the foot. Gov. Pacheco's staff and their lady friends occupied the right hand left respectively. After doing ample justice to the good things provided, the first toast was given by Gov. Pacheco in a near address:—"Mine Host Claus Spreckels," to which Col. Spreckels responded by proposing the health of Governor Pacheco and lady. Toasts were then given and responded to by Gen. J. M. Schofield, U. S. A., Adjunct Gen. L. H. Foote, Col. Eddy, Chief of Governor's Staff, Col. Whidington, Col. McArthur, Col. Harney, Mr. Eckles, Treasurer of San Francisco, Mr. Rosenbaum and others, which occupied the time until the arrival of the delegation from Santa Cruz, embracing our most prominent citizens with their ladies and friends from Watsonville, Soquel and other places. Two hundred names were registered in a brief hour's time. Following are the names of some of the visitors, embracing those already named. Santa Cruz furnishing the majority, and Watsonville, Soquel and Aptos having their quota of representatives. San Francisco, Sacramento and Stockton contribute to the mass, and some of the first men in the State have left their autographs on the register....

The Ball was opened by a Grand March, Gov. Pacheco and lady leading the procession followed by Gen. Schofield and lady, Gen. Foote, Col. Eddy and their ladies, &c. Music was furnished by a Santa Cruz Quintette of violins and horns which harmonized delightfully in the spacious Club Rooms. This building is a beautiful specimen of architecture, 75x115 feet, containing two bowling alleys, a Reading Room 20x24 feet, Billiard Room 24x34 feet, 2 Card Rooms, 10x20. The Bowling Alley, lighted by ten double burners, was transformed for the time being into a Bar, where was dispensed Cappleman's choicest brands of native and imported liquors.

The happy revelers literally "danced all night, till broad daylight, and went home with the girls in the morning," the party not breaking up till half past four A. M. A splendid supper was had at 12 o'clock. The Dining Room being of limited capacity, only 25x60 feet, the tables had to be set three separate times. At the second table a vast deal of amusement was created by the frantic efforts to get what they wanted in the shortest possible time, seeming to think the train was about to leave and they would not get enough. The irrepressible Bromley attempted to get in a toast—rising to explain, and bringing forward the name of Mr. Spreckels in a piquant little speech—but was compelled to subside with "I remain yours most truly," amidst deafening cheers. After supper and a few more dances the number of participants began to diminish and at the close in the morning only fifteen couples remained to take part in the last dance. These the spirit of the entertainment seemed to hold tenaciously, for while the brave little Band worked persistently on "Home, sweet home," the merry dancers held on their way, to the measure of the last waltz played. Finally the musicians in desperation ended with a grand discord and crash that closed the scene.

Did space permit we should be glad to give some of the private notes taken, of the salient features of the occasion, and the actors in the little drama. Nothing occurred to mar the enjoyment and pleasure of all present.[70]

Land transfer from Frederick Hihn to Guadalupe and Centonia Bernal

On or about June 12, 1875, Frederick Hihn purchased 108.646 acres of land in Rancho Aptos from Guadalupe and Centonia Bernal. He wanted this land for the construction, operation, and maintenance of the Santa Cruz Railroad, although he would later use it as a staging area for his mills along

Trout Gulch and Valencia Creek.

Trout Gulch was named after Emmanuel T. Trout, who had been born in New York on April 25, 1824. Trout arrived in Branciforte in 1847 and then moved to the Aptos area, settling near the headwaters of Ricardo Gulch, which was later associated with him. Little else is known about Trout himself.

The original name for Trout Gulch—Ricardo Gulch—came from Jean Richard Fourcade, a son-in-law of Martina Castro via his marriage to her daughter Luisa Cota. He adopted the Spanish name Ricardo Juan when he settled in the Branciforte area around 1842. The Juan home was located within the gulch and was named after Ricardo.

In the Hihn Record Book, there is a copy of an agreement between Hihn and Charles Cummings dated November 17, 1887 that mentions Trout Ranch. The ranch is mentioned again in an agreement between Hihn and William Ball dated June 5, 1890, which states the "old Trout house South of the Vineyard and the field of said house containing six to seven acres, and the field between the vineyard and the last mentioned house and extending westerly to the Loma Prieta road." This description definitely places the Trout house near the headwaters of Trout Gulch.

During my research, I came across a map that was commissioned by Hihn in which R. R. McLeod and A. T. Herrmann surveyed the boundary between Aptos and Valencia Creeks because of a conflict between the F. A. Hihn Company and the Loma Prieta Lumber Company. The map shows a ranch exactly as described in the aforementioned deeds with a log house and barn, grazing fields, corn field, vineyard, orchard, and bean field all clearly visible. The property is identified as a 'Ranchita' or 'Ranchito' on several other maps. A trip three and a half miles up Trout Gulch Road will take one to the former site of the Trout Ranch, located on the left side of the road.[71]

Progress continues on the Santa Cruz Railroad

In a meeting held on June 12, 1875, the Santa Cruz Railroad's officers announced that the company needed an additional $70,000 to complete the line. While the company had enough money to build the final six miles of the route, it did not have enough funds to pay staff and run the line. A total of 3,613 shares valued at $100 each remained unsold, causing this deficit. To encourage investment, management offered 2,027 of these shares to current stockholders at a cut rate of $25 each. Another 1,200 were offered to the public at $50 each. To set an example, both Frederick Hihn and Claus Spreckels purchased $15,000 worth of stock to help keep the company afloat.

Despite the financial difficulties, construction continued apace with ballasting, grading, and trestle work ongoing over the gulches and creeks southeast of Aptos. By the end of July, the track was in the heart of Rancho San Andrés, where 135 Chinese workers and their foremen were busy grading and building bridges. Two bridges, one small and one quite substantial, were required to reach San Andreas Road and the schoolhouse there, but both were completed by the end of the month. The rights-of-way for three miles beyond that point were also secured and crews were actively grading to the outskirts of Watsonville.

Meanwhile, construction of the rolling stock for the company had begun in Santa Cruz. The wheels for the company's locomotives were all set to be cast at foundries downtown and several cars were under construction at the railroad depot on Park Street (Union Street).

The final decision regarding the route through Watsonville had still not been made by this time. One group campaigned for it to pass directly through town, while another was pushing for it to bypass downtown a half mile to the south. The *Sentinel* speculated that the line would go through the town pending a final decision by the Board of Directors. This left the fate of the final mile to Pajaro Station in the wind until funding was secured and the political rivalry between Watsonville and Santa Cruz resolved.[72]

Brad Morrell relocates to a new mill north of the Flume Mill

When his contract with the San Lorenzo Flume & Transportation Company was fulfilled in late 1875, Brad Morrell purchased another mill half of a mile north of the Flume Mill on the San Lorenzo River, which he operated for the next two seasons until the difficult economic situation of the late 1870s forced him to shut down operations.[73]

Agreement between Benjamin Porter and the Grover family concerning stumpage rights in Tract 7 in the Augmentation

On October 9, 1875, Stephen and his brother James Grover, as well as the latter's son Dwight William, purchased stumpage rights from Benjamin Porter to the upper 598 acres of Tract 7 in the Augmentation. These rights allowed the Grovers to harvest the timber within Porter's land in exchange for a small upfront payment and $20,000 to be paid at a later date. At the time, it was estimated that 17,940,000 board feet of standing timber grew on the upper part of Tract 7 along either side of what would become known as Grover Gulch. On the same day, the Grovers also purchased Tract 4 from the Joel Bates estate—another 10,000,000 board feet of lumber were thought to be available from this land.[74]

Charles Ford predicts the future of logging in Eureka Canyon

Charles Ford was a visionary in many ways, but was not overly eager to expand the logging operations of Brown, Williamson & Company. In 1876, he asked for a prospectus regarding the viability of long-term logging up Eureka Canyon. The narrow, densely-wooded canyon on the west branch of Corralitos Creek was named after the Eureka Mill Company, founded by James Austin Linscott of Maine. Linscott had built his first mill in Santa Cruz County on Scott Creek on the North Coast in 1872, but the next year he moved to Corralitos, where he harvested timber for eleven years via his Eureka mill, Clipper mill, and Eureka shingle mill, all located along the main creek.

Ford received an estimate that the timber tracts to which the group could obtain stumpage rights could last ten years if the maximum annual output was set at ten million board feet. Ford's group of investors were satisfied with these findings and began the process of acquiring rights to logging in Eureka Canyon.[75]

The South Pacific Coast Railroad Company is incorporated

Although the Santa Cruz Railroad was nearing completion and the Santa

Cruz & Felton Railroad was a done fact by early 1876, other transportation prospectors still sought entry into Santa Cruz County. The bolder plans called for a coastal railroad between San Francisco and Santa Cruz. But a more realistic plan was formulated by the Santa Clara Valley Railroad, which reincorporated on October 6, 1875 to construct a narrow-gauge railroad from Potrero Point in Alameda County to Santa Cruz, with branch lines to Saratoga and the New Almaden quicksilver mines, a total of fifty-five miles of track. Construction began almost immediately between Alviso and Dumbarton Point when the same winter storm that severely damaged the Santa Cruz Railroad decimated the Santa Clara Valley Railroad, leaving only a partially graded right-of-way behind. The route was all but abandoned and the company fell into abeyance, awaiting new capital and a resurgence of local interest.

After two months of patiently waiting, the board of directors found a new source of income from James G. Fair, a Comstock Lode millionaire who had a vision for a narrow-gauge network across California that could displace Southern Pacific's transportation monopoly. Fair turned to the defunct Santa Clara Valley Railroad because that line had already secured much of the required right-of-way and had surveyed most of the remainder of the route. He brought on as a partner Alfred E. Davis, who would manage the day-to-day affairs of the railroad as president. On March 24, 1876, Davis reincorporated the firm a second time, renaming it the South Pacific Coast Railroad Company, with largely the same aims as its predecessor.

The new company was almost entirely owned by Fair and Davis and had an initial capital stock of $1,000,000. By July 1, six miles of the narrow-gauge route between Dumbarton Point (Newark) and Alviso were already done, with 250 men working on continuing the line to Santa Clara. The company anticipated that the completed route from San Francisco and Santa Cruz, including a paddle-wheeler ride between the city and Newark, would take less than four hours, which at the time was an impossible feat via rail or any other means.[76]

The Santa Cruz Railroad begins operations

A year after the opening celebrations and five months after the scheduled date to begin regular freight and passenger service, the Santa Cruz Railroad finally completed its entire 21.2-mile length between downtown Santa Cruz and the line's junction with the Southern Pacific Railroad at Pajaro. Devastating winter rains in December and January saw multiple fills washed away leading to four months of hard labor to recover from the damage. The first regular train finally left Pajaro on the morning of Sunday, May 7, 1876.

The first complete timetable for the railroad was published in the *Sentinel* on June 17:

TRAINS LEAVE
Santa Cruz	9:30 A.M.
Soquel	9:50 A.M.
Aptos	10:20 A.M.
Leonard's	10:30 A.M.
San Andres	10:40 A.M.
Martin's	11:00 A.M.
Watsonville	11:15 A.M.

Connecting with the Southern Pacific
up train at Pajaro at 12 M. [*sic*]

LEAVE
Pajaro on arrival of Southern Pacific
down train

Watsonville	2:05 P.M.
Martin's	2:15 P.M.
San Andres	2:30 P.M.
Leonard's	2:50 P.M.
Aptos	3:10 P.M.
Soquel	3:30 P.M.
Santa Cruz	4:00 P.M.

An Express Train
Leaves Pajaro every Saturday evening after
arrival of Southern Pacific Express

Train, arriving at	
Aptos	8:15 P.M.
Soquel	8:40 P.M.
Santa Cruz	9:00 P.M.
Leaves Santa Cruz every Monday morning at	4:00 A.M.
Soquel	4:20 A.M.
Aptos	4:45 A.M.
Arriving at Pajaro	5:50 A.M.

During the final days of construction, word reached the investors in the Santa Cruz Railroad that the South Pacific Coast Railroad had begun construction. The speed at which the railroad was being graded caused great concern among them, rightly fearing that a route through the Santa Cruz Mountains to Santa Cruz would make their own line almost entirely redundant.[77]

Santa Cruz County's highest taxpayers

On July 15, 1876, the *Sentinel* published a list of 296 companies and individuals who paid taxes in excess of $5,000 annually. While the California Powder Company topped the list with a value of $134,769, Frederick Hihn was assessed at $109,383, making his the fourth most valuable firm in Santa Cruz County, just ahead of Claus Spreckels at $95,055. Meanwhile, Thomas and Carmel Fallon, who owned large tracts in the Augmentation, were valued at $54,740—ninth place. Other firms and people on the list who operated in the Augmentation included Benjamin and George Porter (21st place at $38,404), the Grovers (67th place at $15,261), the Santa Clara Valley Mill and Lumber Company (98th place at $11,605), and Charles "Mountain Charlie" McKiernan (125th place at $9,823).[78]

Santa Cruz Railroad's freight depot completed in Watsonville

On August 5, 1876, the *Sentinel* reported that construction of the freight depot at Watsonville was completed. That same day, the corporate offices for the railroad were moved to purpose-built rooms upstairs above the Santa Cruz Park Street depot across from the Pacific Ocean House. The newspaper reported that the offices were "commodious and appear to be well arranged." The previous Tuesday, August 1, the board of directors of the company rode over the entirety of the route and found everything to their satisfaction. Following the tour, they chose the new board and reelected Frederick Hihn as president.[79]

Road under construction to Tract 11 in the Augmentation

After a four-year delay, Frederick Hihn finally turned his attention to the natural sulfur springs in Tract 11 in the Augmentation, where he hoped to build a resort. On August 5, 1876, the *Sentinel* reported that construction had begun on a road along the East Branch of Soquel Creek to reach his planned resort.[80]

Letter critical of Frederick Hihn published in *The Pajaronian*

In an editorial published in *The Pajaronian* on December 7, 1876, editor-in-chief Charles Cummings wrote:

> *The history of the Santa Cruz Narrow Gauge Railroad, compiled from the columns of the* Pajaronian, *would be entertaining. F. A. Hihn is the central figure and all through, correctly represented with his hands in the pockets of the tax payers, which latter class of long enduring and suffering humanity of this county have been drawn upon to build the above road. In addition to the heavy debt assured by this county for the benefit of the Narrow Gauge Fraud, the people of Watsonville paid $6,000 to induce Hihn to run the road into the town of Watsonville, instead of two miles below. Now, this man, whose god is money, and who seems to be devoid of all consideration for his fellow man, issues a writ of mandamus commanding that the Board of Supervisors of Santa Cruz County, "issue to the Santa Cruz Railroad Company bonds to the amount of $14,178," for construction of the rail-*

road from the point two and 365-1000 miles distant from the town of Watsonville, into said town, and for which change in the route the people of this place have already paid $6,000, as stated.

By some, Hihn is called a man of enterprise; perhaps he is, but the people have supplied the money for every enterprise he has engaged in, and it looks to us that the people will pay the $14,178 now demanded by this small railroad king.[81]

The matter of the South Pacific Coast Railroad's route through the Santa Cruz Mountains

Construction of the South Pacific Coast Railroad continued without a break from mid-1876, but the route beyond San José to Los Gatos and through the Santa Cruz Mountains to Santa Cruz remained unclear at first. Initial surveys had focused on a Saratoga Gap route, which would have seen the railroad climb up the grade southwest of Saratoga until reaching a point where it could tunnel through the ridge and arrive near the headwaters of the San Lorenzo River, from which point it would continue down the valley through Boulder Creek, Felton, and eventually Santa Cruz. There were many problems with this route, though. An extremely long tunnel would be required to overcome the ridge and dozens of bridges over the river and creeks, some in precarious locations, would be needed, and some of the curves would be dangerously sharp.

As an alternative, a route up Los Gatos Creek was chosen by the railroad. This required several more tunnels, but these were considerably shorter than the one demanded by the Saratoga Gap. This route also catered to more industries including the Santa Clara Valley Mill & Lumber Company's sawmill beyond Lexington and dozens of small farms and orchards in the foothills. Far up Los Gatos Creek, a tunnel was carved through the mountain and into the Augmentation at the headwaters of the West Branch of Soquel Creek. This gave Frederick Hihn access to the railroad since some of his most remote timber tracts were located nearby. From this spot—called Highland—the railroad passed into another tunnel and into the Bean Creek valley at Glenwood, from which point it continued through a small tunnel into the San Lorenzo Valley. Just south of Felton it linked up with the existing Santa Cruz & Felton Railroad's right-of-way

Highland proved an important piece in Hihn's puzzle, even if it did not factor into his mathematics originally. Soon after the Augmentation was partitioned in 1863, he began selling and leasing stumpage rights for those sections that were too difficult or too expensive to harvest, focusing instead on sections on the southern side of the Augmentation closer to Soquel and Aptos. Sections near the Summit that were able to sustain farms or ranches were sold, but Hihn hesitated to sell all of his timber tracts in the area and held onto some. Thus, when the South Pacific Coast Railroad expressed interest in running its line through part of his property at the top of the Augmentation, Hihn knew he had made the right choice.

The name Highland was likely borrowed from nearby Highland Center, which by the mid-1870s had become subsumed into Skyland. In any case, it was an appropriate name for the highest point on the railroad line and it soon became the construction site for two mile-long tunnels that flanked the settlement on either side. The railroad operated a small mill in the area to produce timbers to support the tunnels and bridges and crossties for the roadbeds. It also cut splitstuff for fencing, firewood, and other construction-related needs. While Chinese workers were Highland's original residents, others soon moved into the area once the railroad began formal operations in May 1880. A school opened in 1882 and a post office soon after. Thomas W. Wright, the Santa Cruz County Surveyor, drew a new map of the area in late 1880 or early 1881 and used a California laurel tree as a boundary marker. Shortly afterwards, locals began to call the settlement Laurel and the name stuck. By 1887, the name Highland had been translocated a second time to a site two miles to the east and the railroad rechristened its highest elevation station Laurel.[82]

Land transfer from Thomas Fallon to Carmel Fallon concerning Tract 9 in the Augmentation

The relationship between Thomas Fallon and his wife, Carmel Cota, was never on the best terms. Carmel shared traits with her mother, Martina Castro, in that she was quick to temper, jealous of her husband, and at-

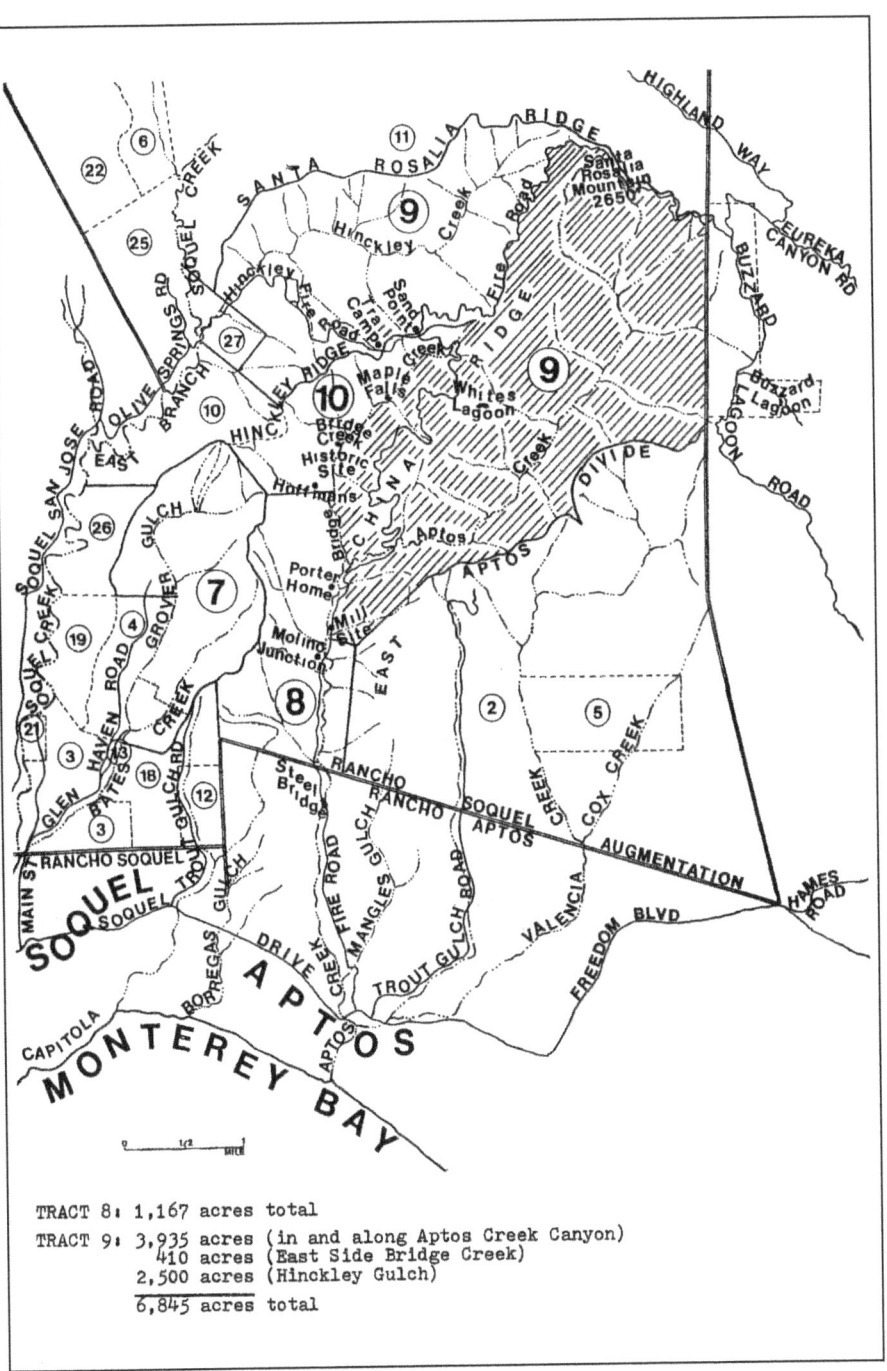

TRACT 8: 1,167 acres total
TRACT 9: 3,935 acres (in and along Aptos Creek Canyon)
410 acres (East Side Bridge Creek)
2,500 acres (Hinckley Gulch)
6,845 acres total

FIGURE 3.4 FALLON FAMILY PROPERTY WITHIN THE AUGMENTATION

tempted to possess him totally. In her case, this was a more significant problem due to Thomas's well-known roving eye and attraction to and by the ladies. He was a handsome and charming man, and never hid his interest in the opposite sex.

By December 7, 1876, things had gone too far, and Carmel filed for divorce. Interestingly, during the case Thomas accused his wife of attempting to murder him, a charge that District Judge David Belden thoroughly dismissed. Carmel, meanwhile, accused her husband of adultery. Both charges were later stricken from the record in an attempt by judicial revisionists to clear the record on Fallon and the Castro family. Judge Belden ruled on January 4, 1877 in favor of Carmel, bringing an end to one of the most highly publicized trials in the state.

As part of the divorce settlement, on January 30, Thomas was forced to renounce the land that he had obtained on behalf of his wife within the Augmentation, transferring 6,845 acres within Tract 9 to Carmel. This effectively put an end to logging activities in this section for the time being. He was allowed to retain the 124 acres that he owned on his own behalf in Tract 8 and in the vicinity of Buzzard Lagoon. On February 3, Carmel was also awarded $30,000 in gold, the family's home at the intersection of 3rd Street and Minnie Street in San Francisco, and custody of their children, unless they objected.[83]

Benjamin Nichols opens Nichols Iron & Magnesia Springs

Frederick Hihn was not the only property owner in the Aptos region interested in operating a resort. At some point in 1877, Benjamin Nichols or one of his employees discovered a mineral-rich spring two hundred yards from the Nichols home. Allen Collins recounted that

> *a natural spring oozed out of the ridge into Valencia Creek. It didn't take long to learn that this water had "magical medicinal qualities;" it was a "cure-all" and a "life-extender," but mostly it was a laxative! The Nichols dug out the spring, shoring up a cave maybe 20 feet back into the ridge. There was a facade at the entrance, and a dip-trough at the back. Then*

> *Aptos Mineral Spring was advertised broadly and became famous. People came in droves, from all over the country, for jugs of the "goodie"—it was grand and glorious, fearful and wonderful! Remains of the structures can be seen today, if you negotiate the steep bank, but the spring dried up when the freeway was cut through the ridge behind it in 1948.*

The first advertisement for Nichols Iron & Magnesium Springs appeared in the *Sentinel* on May 18, 1878, and noted that the springs were a quarter mile from the Aptos Hotel and 500 yards from the railroad depot, thereby making it equidistant to Santa Cruz and Watsonville. At the time, Nichols was selling the water exclusively from his home and via Hazels' Drug Store at a cost of 25¢ per gallon. He offered to ship the spring water to any address provided to him.[84]

The Montgomery family on the Summit

In 1877, David Harvey Montgomery arrived in California from Scotland and settled in the Summit area of the Santa Cruz Mountains. He purchased a sizeable section of land from Lyman Burrell in Tract 24 of the Augmentation. It was situated between Highland Way and Loma Prieta Avenue near the end of the Soquel Turnpike (Soquel San Jose Road). Montgomery continued to cultivate his land until 1904, when he sold the property to a Japanese-run company.

During the years that he managed the land, Montgomery expanded and improved upon the roads that existed on the Summit. At the time, Summit Road was called Morrell Road and ended at Loma Prieta Avenue, which served as the main route east. Montgomery built an extension of Morrell Road that led to his house. The Comstock brothers soon afterwards used this new route as a bypass for the Soquel Turnpike. Traffic quickly increased as the Comstock Grade became a more popular road than the actual turnpike. But people wishing to head east along the Summit still had to backtrack once they reached Loma Prieta Avenue. Montgomery rectified this by building a short cut through his land that became known as the Old Montgomery Road, which no longer exists today. This short section of road

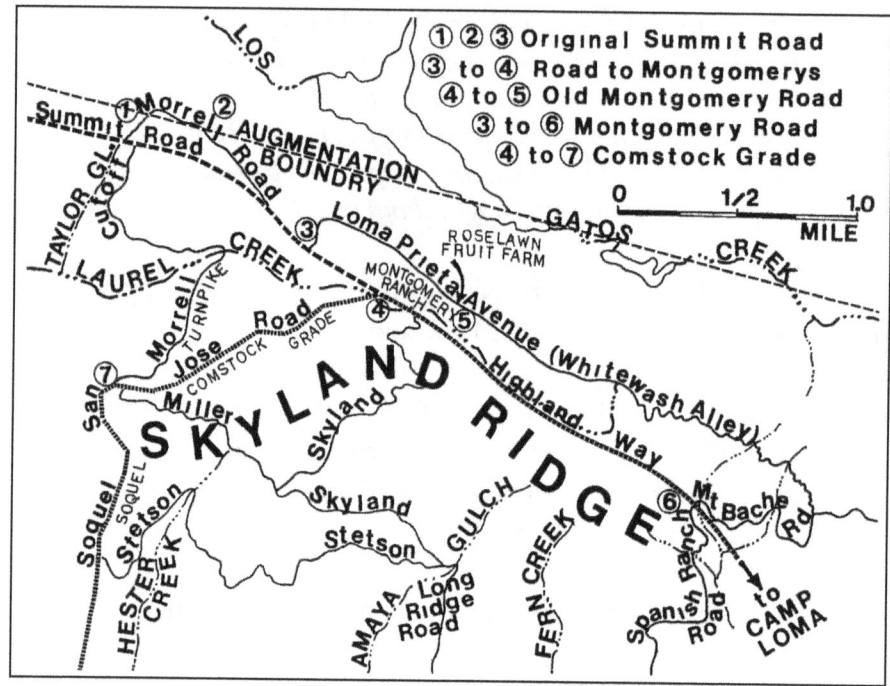

FIGURE 3.5 ROADS IN THE SUMMIT AREA

connected the Comstock Grade with Loma Prieta Avenue to the north. Montgomery never charged for the use of this cutoff but wished travelers a joyful trip along a road lined with many flowers. Over subsequent decades, the road to the Montgomery house was extended ever further east along the ridgeline until eventually reaching the other end of Loma Prieta Avenue at Mt. Bache Road. This new road, now called Highland Way, was originally called Montgomery Road.[85]

Thomas Fallon files suit against Hiram Heaton over an unpaid debt

Because of an unpaid debt, Thomas Fallon brought suit against Hiram Heaton, his wife Ellen, and their partners, H. P. Parkinson, E. G. Spenser, Frank Kenyon, Charles H. Waterman, P. B. Fagen, Charles Parker, Amelia J. Whittaker, Charles H. Simpkins, and Charles W. Thomas on July 17, 1877. The Third District Court ruled in Fallon's favor and ordered that several properties, including 126 acres of Tract 27 in the Augmentation and mentioned in the suit, be sold at auction to repay the debt. The 14 acres left of Tract 27 remained with Frederick Waterman, who had sold the rest to the Heatons and their partners in 1874.[86]

Land transfer from Roger Hinckley and John Shelby to Frederick Hihn concerning Tract 25 in the Augmentation

On November 28, 1877, the Roger Hinckley estate and Hinckley's son-in-law John Shelby sold Tract 25 in the Augmentation, encompassing 853 acres, to Frederick Hihn. The property did not have an abundance of timber but included all of Sugarloaf Mountain and its natural springs, giving Hihn water rights over a large section of the Soquel Creek watershed. Hihn hoped to acquire control over most of the watershed in order to put together a water company that could supply the residents in and around Camp Capitola, as well as other projects in the area. The only substantial section of the watershed he did not control was Tract 26, owned by Lucy Cahoon, the daughter of the late Benjamin Cahoon.[87]

The Watsonville Mill & Lumber Company is incorporated

Between 1868 and 1869, the State of California issued patents to timber land along Corralitos Creek in Eureka Canyon to the following men, all investors in Brown, Williamson & Company:

Charles Ford and Lucius Sanborn (640 acres)
James L. Halstead (160 acres)
Lucius Sanborn (160 acres)
Newman Sanborn (320 acres)
William Williamson (160 acres)
Alvin Sanborn (80 acres)

During the week of December 15, 1877, Ford, Lucius and Alvin Sanborn, Halstead, and John Brown incorporated the Watsonville Mill & Lumber Company. Within a short time, the company under the leadership

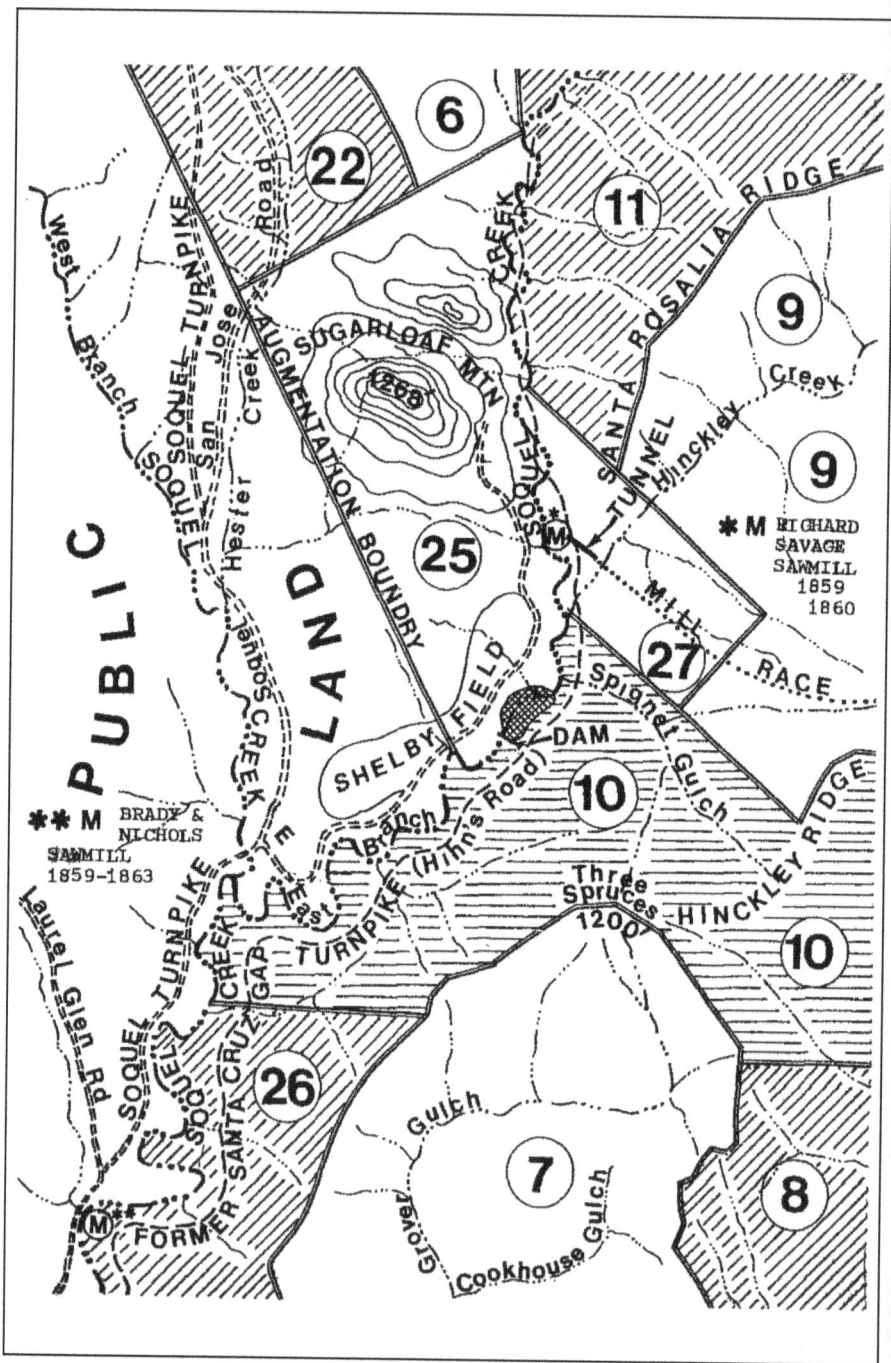

FIGURE 3.6 TRACT 25 IN THE AUGMENTATION

of Ford became the largest producer of lumber south of San Francisco. For the next thirty years, the company logged within Eureka Canyon then sold the land for homes and businesses.[88]

Land transfer from Frederick Hihn to Fred Loomis

On March 13, 1878, Alvirus "Fred" Loomis purchased 15 acres from Frederick Hihn that were located within Tract 16 of the Augmentation along the south side of the Summit Road about three quarters of a mile to the east of the road's junction with the Santa Cruz Gap Turnpike (Old Santa Cruz Highway). Loomis moved onto the land in about 1882 and began constructing the Summit Hotel. The complex took five years to build and when it opened, it immediately became popular. Patrons visited from throughout the Bay Area and beyond, with most arriving via the Southern Pacific Railroad station at Wright's. Besides featuring the usual walking trails and gardens for guests to enjoy, the hotel also had a croquet field, horses for hire, and other amenities. In 1891, Fred sold the hotel to A. N. Nichols, who continued to operate the facility until 1910 when it was converted into a private residence.

Mark Hopkins dies

In the early morning of March 29, 1878, Central Pacific Railroad treasurer Mark Hopkins died in Yuma, Arizona. He was one of the Big Four who helped build the first transcontinental railroad, but he lived a quiet life and avoided the spotlight whenever possible. His mansion in San Francisco was built for his wife, Mary, and his de facto adopted son and heir, Timothy, both of whom would go on to leave a major impact on Santa Cruz County.[89]

Hiram Heaton auctions his property to repay his debt to Thomas Fallon

On March 30, 1878, Hiram Heaton and his partners auctioned 126 acres in Tract 27 in the Augmentation to the highest bidder in order to repay their debt to Thomas Fallon. The winner of the auction was Fallon, whose ex-wife

1878 — The Reign of the Lumber Barons

Carmel bid $25,000 for the property on his behalf. With this acquisition, the combined holdings of the Fallons came to constitute nearly a quarter of

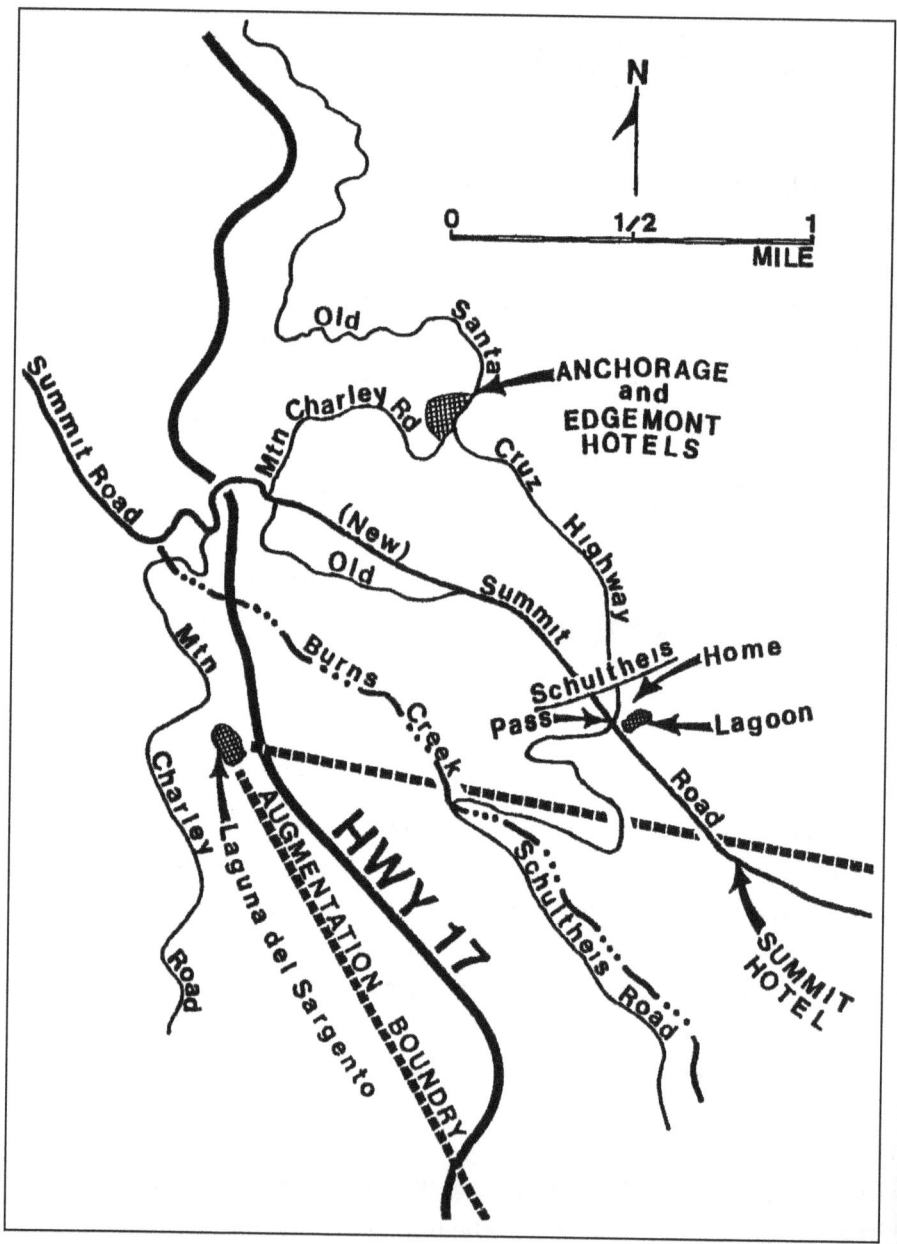

FIGURE 3.7 EARLY RESORTS IN THE SUMMIT AREA

the total land within the Augmentation. Frederick Hihn, in contrast, owned approximately forty-three percent of the former Mexican rancho.[90]

Brad Morrell relocates to Bean Creek

Following the economic crisis that led to him selling his mill north of Boulder Creek, Brad Morrell relocated to Bean Creek in 1878, where he was contracted to cut timber for Charles McKiernan. McKiernan's mill was located just to the north of the town of Glenwood.[91]

The Chase family expands operations

Even as the Chase family continued to operate mills along Hester Creek and in the San Lorenzo Valley, they built a third mill on the Summit in 1878. This small mill was located approximately a mile and a quarter west of the top of the Soquel Turnpike. It was the family's first mill that was capable of direct shipment to the Santa Clara Valley and its erection prompted the company to finally build a planing mill in San José. Over the next seven years, the Chase family's lumber operations expanded to become one of the largest in the Summit area.[92]

Grovers relocate mill to upper Tract 7 of the Augmentation

As the available timber for lumber within the lower 500 acres of Tract 7 and in Tract 4 in the Augmentation decreased, the Grovers decided to move operations to the upper 598 acres of Tract 7 in August 1878. They decided to move their mill a mile and a half up Bates Creek along its western tributary, which became known as Grover Gulch. The location chosen for the mill was in a wide clearing at the bottom of a horseshoe bend where another tributary fed into Grover Gulch. While the old, relocated mill was going to continue cutting lumber and railroad crossties, the Grovers also planned to build a new, smaller mill on the site to cut sixty-foot telegraph poles.

This pair of mills required a large workforce and its remoteness meant everyone had to live on site. Thus, worker bunkhouses and cabins, a cookhouse with an attached dining room, and a company store were all built in the basin at the confluence of the two creeks. A corral for mules and oxen was also nearby for hauling logs to the millpond. Most of these structures were located on the hillsides to the northeast, which became known as Cookhouse Gulch for this reason.

The mills, meanwhile, were set upon a massive platform suspended over the the creek just below the millpond's outlet. The platform was so large that even the lumber drying stacks and storage yard were elevated. Many of the pilings used to support this platform still exist today. The Grovers also expanded the older mill to increase output by adding a second headrig and boiler. This allowed it to produce around 30,000 board feet of lumber per day.

The increased capacity of the mill paired with the new ability to produce telegraph poles meant that a new shipping solution had to be found to get products to the railroad at Capitola. As a result, the Grovers extended a two-mile-long wood rail tramway from the mill down Grover Gulch to Bates Creek. The tramway began running down the east side of the gulch but crossed midway to the old mill site at the confluence of Bates Creek. From there, it continued along the west side of Bates Creek, utilizing several skid roads in the process, until reaching a shingle mill near the southern boundary of the Augmentation. The southern portions of this tramway, which were exceptionally narrow in parts, became Prescott Road after the tramway was removed. The modern-day junction of Prescott Road and Glen Haven Road marks the former site of the shingle mill. From the shingle mill, wagons hauled the timber, crossties, poles, and splitstuff to local lumber yards or to Soquel Wharf for shipment.

Because the wagon road north of the old mill site was too narrow, another route had to be found to access the mill in Grover Gulch. The solution was a short road that left Glen Haven Road about halfway between Pampas Lane and Timberview Drive. This road crossed Grover Gulch and joined the tramway on the east side at a point where the gulch was wide enough to allow both the tramway and wagon access up to the mill. The short bypass became known as Slab Alley because it was lined with slabs—exterior and curved sections of logs that have been cut off during squaring—with their arched sides facing up toward the sky. Several commented that the road was so rough that traveling on it at a fair speed could shake the false teeth right out of the wearer's mouth![93]

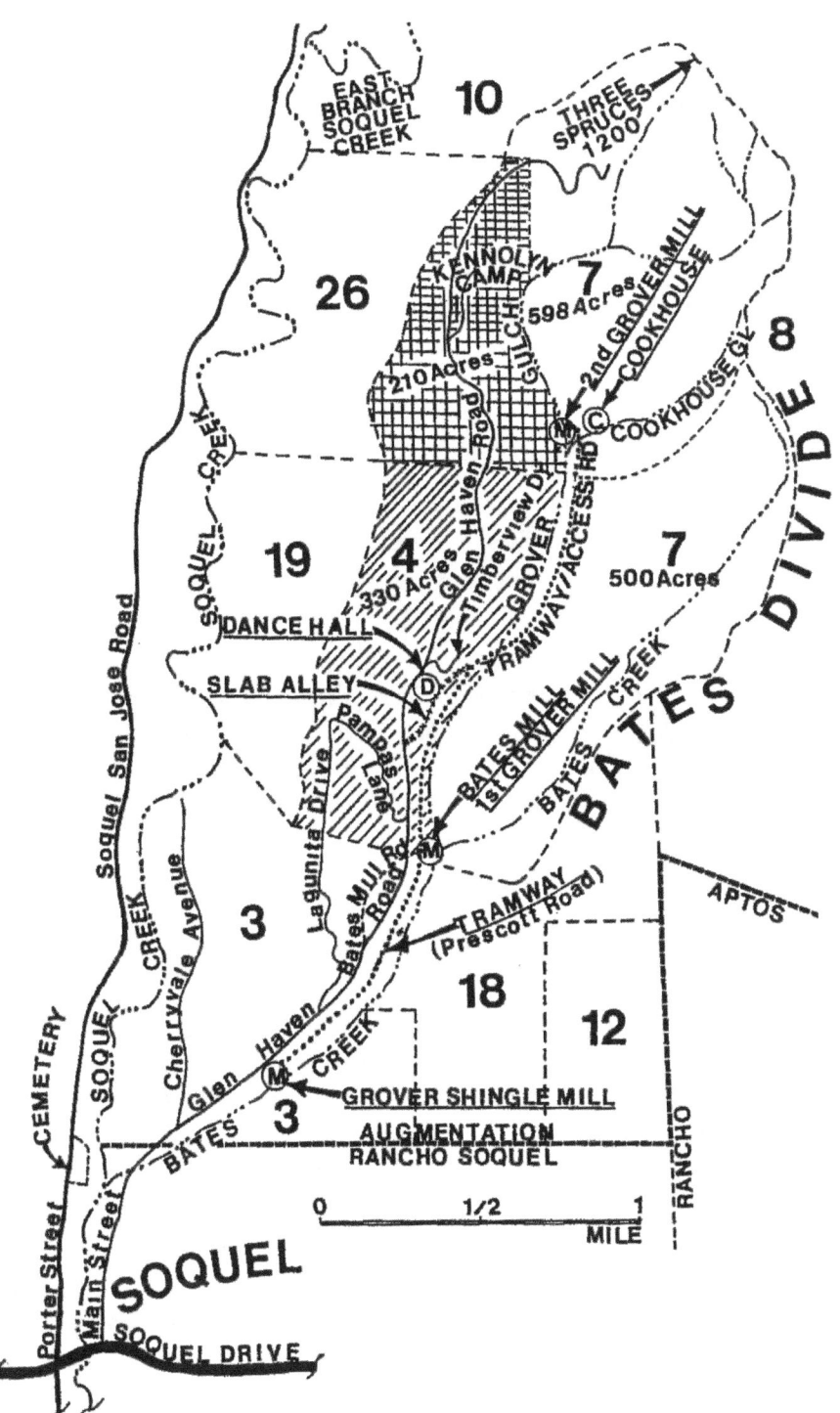

FIGURE 3.8 TRACTS 4 AND 7 IN THE AUGMENTATION

Frederick Hihn opens Hihn's Sulphur Springs in Tract 11 of the Augmentation

After Frederick Hihn completed his road beyond the Spanish Ranch, he turned his attention to a natural sulfur spring that was located along the south side of the East Branch of Soquel Creek a short distance to the east of his new road. At the time, it was popularly assumed that bathing in sulfur-infused water had curative effects. He planned to surround the spring with a campground, which quickly evolved into a major resort.

On August 15, 1878, the *Pajaronian* announced the opening of Hihn's Sulphur Springs "for the accommodation of the afflicted and ailing." It added that the "place already has a reputation as a health resort and we now expect to see it more generally patronized." However, the route to the resort was not easy. An article in the August 28, 1880 issue of the *Sentinel* explained:

> *Hihn's Sulphur Spring is on the Soquel Augmentation ranch, about fifteen miles from Santa Cruz. To reach it you go to Soquel, and follow the Soquel creek on the left to and across the bridge above Cahoon's, and then take the new road to the right over the hill and follow its circuitous windings till the Soquel creek is again reached, which is crossed no less than nineteen times before you reach your destination. The road is one of the wildest that can be imagined, and has to be traveled to be appreciated. For a long distance you travel in the narrow bed of the creek, with high straight mountains on both sides. You have to pick your way with great care or your wagon will be smashed against the huge boulders that lie in the creek. After you have passed the creek the road leads up the side of a steep mountain, you, the meanwhile, passing a signboard reading, 'This path leads to Loma Prieta,' which we learned was eight miles higher up the mountains. After thus traveling a considerable distance we come to a clearing on the side of the mountain, and we are at Hihn's Sulphur Spring Camp, where we find R. H. Hall, Geo. C. Stevens, L. E. Hihn, J. R. Patterson and E. S. West, encamped. When we left Santa Cruz Sunday morning the sky was overcast with*

> *a fog almost akin to rain, but at the camp the sun was shining brightly and the air was warm and dry. The campers were taken entirely by surprise by our party, which consisted of J. D. Chace and wife, Mrs. R. H. Hall, Elbert Austin and wife, and C. W. Waldron and wife, excepting the chief cook and major domo of the camp, J. R. Patterson, who beforehand had been warned of the approach of the visitors, and had made preparations for their visit. The surprise of the visit to the rest was complete. Such a hurrying of the campers to fix their toilettes you never saw, and the only white shirt in the party was possessed by Mr. Hall, and he was asked to divide. The gentlemanly campers, however, apologized to the ladies for not being better prepared to receive them. Their apologies were accepted, and the visiting party prepared to make themselves at home. An excellent dinner was prepared* a la *camp style, with all the accessories, and with sharpened appetites the party sat down to a meal that was fit for the gods. After dinner a pleasant conversation was carried on till late in the afternoon, when the visitors returned home without accident, with the well wishes of the campers and an invitation to come every Sunday.*
>
> *The camp has been in existence over six weeks, and it is contemplated to keep it up longer—for over a month at least.*
> *W.*

In subsequent years, Hihn added a nine-room house and a large barn, and put 70 acres of land under cultivation. By the mid-1880s, he also erected a large hotel complete with guest cottages that stretched from the springs to the top of Santa Rosalia Ridge. Recreational facilities were also available to guests.

On July 8, 1888, it was announced in the *Sentinel* that the resort would go by a new name, Precioso Sulphur Springs. This reflected a change in management, although Hihn retained ownership of the land. The article, which was attempting to recruit a lessee for the resort, noted that seventy percent of the property was under cultivation and that both hot and cold baths were available to visitors. Hihn still touted the benefits of the sulfur baths in the advertisement, noting that this place was "unsurpassed for healthfulness, mountain scenery and fine climate. It is the paradise of campers. The spring has superior curing, health-giving and invigorating qualities, as man will attest who have been benefited by it." After three years, Hihn leased the resort to H. Fine for $250 effective August 1, 1891. People came from far and near to enjoy the benefits of the resort, which remained operating into the 1920s.

The facilities were located around the 1,440-foot elevation level about a half mile south of the East Branch of Soquel Creek's 900-foot elevation. The main access road coming up from Olive Springs was called Hihn's Sulphur Springs Road. At the turnoff to the resort there was a locked gate installed to restrict unwanted wagon traffic. Another gate on the opposite side of the resort sat along Highland Way at today's Camp Loma. For many years, this eastern road was known simply as Hihn's Private Road and provided a route for visitors traveling from the Pajaro Valley. Once in the springs, a journey of a mile heading south brought a person to the top of Santa Rosalia Ridge at about 2,200 feet in elevation.[94]

Partnership formed between Benjamin Porter and George Porter

On March 17, 1879, Benjamin and George Porter formed a partnership through which they combined their assets, debts, and properties in Santa Cruz County and then divided them equally between each other. Both cousins owned several properties in Rancho Soquel and the Augmentation, with Benjamin Porter originally owning Lots I, L, N, R, and S, and George Porter owning Lot M and Tract 12. They also together bought 121 acres in Tract 18 from Frederick Hihn. In the end, the cousins had amassed nearly 750 acres of contiguous land in the area.[95]

Land transfer from Jered and Seth Comstock to Caleb Caldwell concerning Tract 22 in the Augmentation

On March 20, 1879, Jered and Seth Comstock sold about 160 acres of Tract 22 in the Augmentation to Caleb Caldwell. It seems that at the time of the

The Hidden Hand   1879

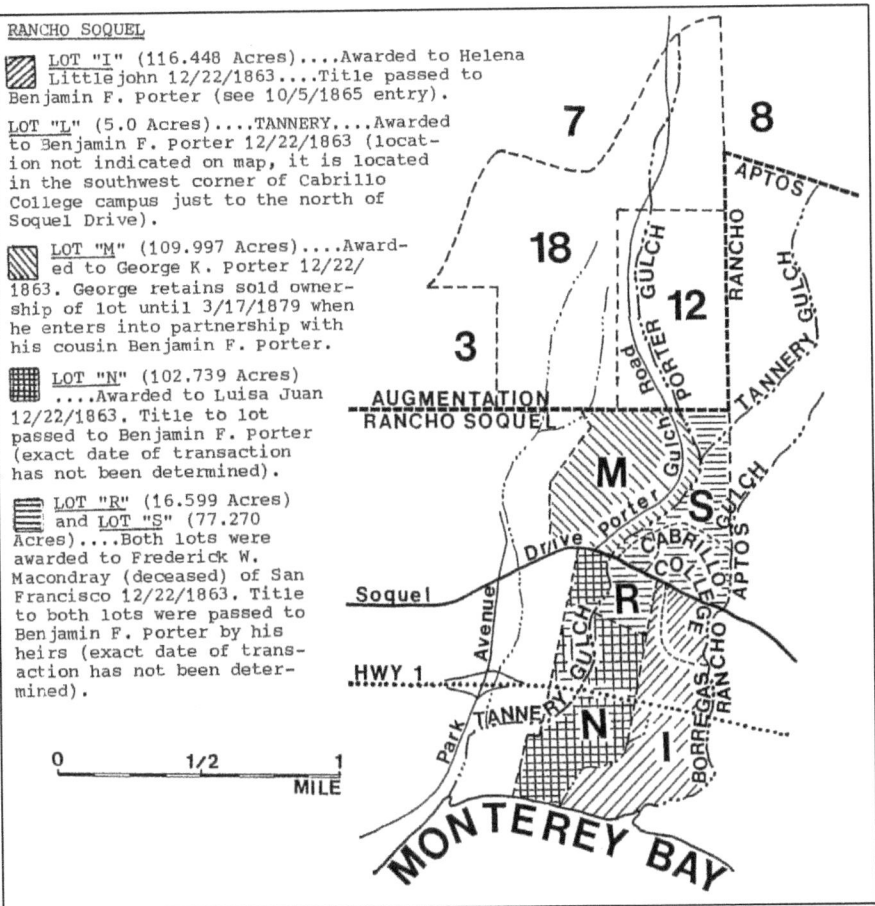

FIGURE 3.9 PORTER FAMILY LANDS IN RANCHO SOQUEL

sale, Caldwell was in partnership with Brad Morrell because shortly after the sale, Morrell built a sawmill at the confluence of Caldwell Gulch and Hester Creek.[96]

Confidence in Santa Cruz Railroad slumps

As it became apparent that the South Pacific Coast Railroad Company was more than a rumor, the bright future of the Santa Cruz Railroad Company began to dim. The shorter route between San Francisco and Santa Cruz offered by the South Pacific Coast meant a loss of revenue from passengers and freight traveling between the two points or anywhere in between. This left the Santa Cruz Railroad as essentially a freight hauler between Santa Cruz and Pajaro with only limited passenger appeal, mostly for locals. Management was justifiably worried and began to pull out of their investment before the light winked out entirely.

Frederick Hihn and the railroad's management made sure to maintain a rosy facade publicly. The railroad invested heavily in repairing damage to its line from the 1875-1876 winter storms and continued to do so through subsequent winters, which regularly damaged sections of track. By the time the line fully opened in 1876, nearly $600,000 had been spent, twice what analysts had predicted. Nonetheless, in April 1878, as the South Pacific Coast began cutting its way through the Santa Cruz Mountains, the Santa Cruz Railroad levied a $10 assessment on its shares in a desperate attempt to recoup costs and shore up the company's finances. The bid failed and only Hihn had paid the assessment by June 15. Worse, the courts became involved, suspending bond sales when they suspected the company was acting dishonestly. It was luck more than anything that kept the company afloat throughout the end of 1878. In the financial earnings statement for the year, it was revealed that the railroad had made less than $10,000 in 1878 and was over $275,000 in debt.

Hihn alone financed the railroad throughout 1879, as the South Pacific Coast slowly approached completion of its line to Santa Cruz. He paid most bills out of pocket and the railroad would have made a decent return for the year if not for the burden of debt hanging over it. Nonetheless, the writing was on the wall for the Santa Cruz Railroad in the summer of 1879.[97]

Frederick Hihn's wealth evaluated

Frederick Hihn was a wealthy man by the standards of the day and the County Assessment Roll released on July 19, 1879 made that clear. His properties alone were evaluated at $114,122, an increase of $5,000 since 1876. Meanwhile, his investment in the California Beet Sugar Company at Soquel earned him an additional $20,005.[98]

The South Pacific Coast Railroad crosses the San Lorenzo River

On September 6, 1879, a train crossed the bridge over the San Lorenzo River south of Big Trees for the first time. Since the route through the Santa Cruz Mountains was not yet connected, the train was from the Santa Cruz & Felton Railroad, which had been leased to the South Pacific Coast Railroad earlier that year. With the completion of the bridge, construction north to Highland could continue at a quicker pace, thereby expediting the demise of the financially enfeebled Santa Cruz Railroad.[99]

Land transfer from Lyman Burrell to Henry Hite concerning Tract 24 in the Augmentation

On December 15, 1879, Henry Hite purchased 26 acres in Tract 24 in the Augmentation from Lyman Burrell. The property was located along the southern side of Loma Prieta Avenue.[100]

The Watsonville Mill & Lumber Company surpasses its production schedule

By the spring of 1880, after all the timber was cut for the year, the directors of the Watsonville Mill & Lumber Company realized that it would run out of profitable timber well before 1886, as had been anticipated. The company had at least three sawmills operating in Eureka Canyon producing over 15,000,000 board feet of lumber annually. They also had several shingle mills operating, each producing over 40,000 shakes and shingles every day. The directors realized that new timber tracts had to be found to harvest if the company was to remain in business. A short-term solution to this problem was the purchase of the Corralitos Lumber Company in mid-April 1880. This gave the company the remainder of the harvestable timber within Eureka Canyon. But more drastic measures would need to be taken to ensure the long-term profitability of the firm.[101]

The South Pacific Coast Railroad is completed

In late March 1880, the tunnel under the summit of the Santa Cruz Mountains was finally bored through and limited freight operations along the entire line between Dunbarton Point and Santa Cruz began on April 11, with scheduled service starting in May.

The completion of the line began a long period of prosperity in the Summit region that lasted into the 1910s, with thousands of vacationers

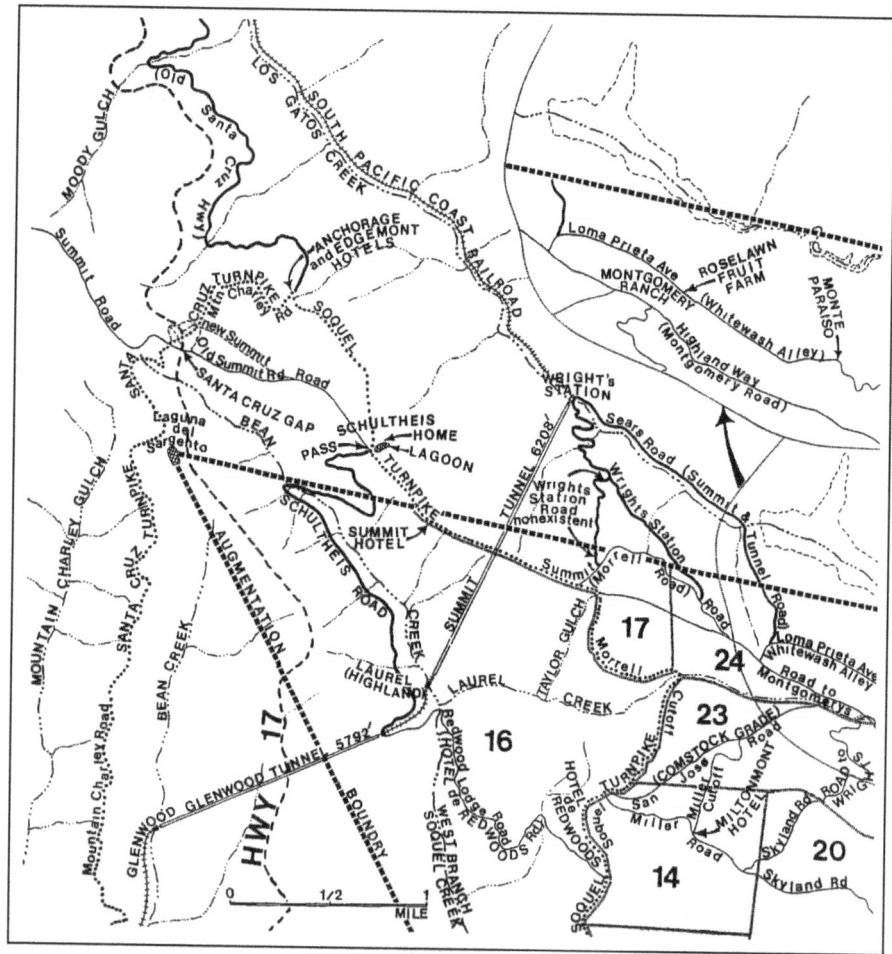

FIGURE 3.10 THE SOUTH PACIFIC COAST RAILROAD'S ROUTE THROUGH THE SUMMIT AREA

visiting each summer. Campers traveled by railroad to stations in the mountains, where they would be picked up by hotel buggies and transported to the various resorts that dotted the hills. Many men went to San Francisco and San José during the week to conduct business and then returned to the various resorts on weekends to relax. Most families paid around $7.00 a week for room and board at a mountain resort, although the amounts varied widely depending on the level of accommodation. Dances were held at many resorts for the amusement of visitors and locals alike.

From 1878 to 1880, Wright's Station served as the southern end of the main line of the railroad. To continue beyond this point, passengers had to transfer to waiting stagecoaches and wagons, which would cross the Summit and take them either to Felton, where they could continue their train journey, or Soquel via the turnpike. Similarly, vehicles departed from these locations to take passengers to the railroad at Wright's. But Wright's did not originally have a link to the Summit. The earliest road climbed up above the tunnel's northern portal via several switchbacks before turning up a light grade to the south (today's Wrights Station Road), where it eventually met the original Summit Road (now Morrill Road). Not long afterwards, a steeper grade was built that connected directly with the Soquel Turnpike. This road no longer exists. A third route popularly known as Tunnel & Summit Road was also built that followed the east bank of Los Gatos Creek for a mile east from Wright's. It then crossed the creek where Austrian Dam is today and headed up a steep gulch before reaching Loma Prieta Avenue near its junction with Summit Road. Today, the portion of the route that follows Los Gatos Creek is Cathermola Road, which is almost entirely owned by the San Jose Water Company and is off-limits to the public. A remnant of the upper part of the road survives as Locust Road.[102]

Warren Porter is hired by the Bank of Watsonville

Fannie Cummings, the wife of John Porter, gave birth to Warren Reynolds Porter on March 30, 1861. At the time, John served as sheriff of Santa Cruz County, although he left shortly afterwards under questionable circumstances. After an unremarkable childhood, Warren attended Saint Augustine College in Benicia, from which he graduated in June 1880. Soon afterwards, he was hired as a bookkeeper for the Bank of Watsonville, which his father and Charles Ford had organized in 1874.[103]

Land transfer from Thomas Fallon to Frederick Waterman concerning Tract 27 in the Augmentation

On August 27, 1880, Thomas Fallon sold the 126 acres in the Augmentation that he had won in his suit against Hiram Heaton to Frederick Waterman. This transaction gave Waterman complete control over all of Tract 27.[104]

Agreement between Frederick Hihn, John Schultheis, Enoch Ellis, Volney Averill, and Santa Cruz County concerning roads to Highland

In the months prior to the completion of the South Pacific Coast Railroad, Frederick Hihn approached property owners in the Highland area to discuss the access roads through their lands in order to allow wagons and other vehicles to travel from Highland to the surrounding resorts and industrial sites. Hihn wanted direct routes from Summit Road, Glenwood, and Hotel de Redwoods to Highland's railroad station, and he hired former county surveyor Mansel Vardman Bennett to find these routes. Bennett submitted his survey in September 1880. Shortly afterwards, an agreement was reached between John Martin Schultheis, Enoch C. Ellis, and Volney Averill, as well as with the Santa Cruz County Board of Supervisors, which follows:

> *We the undersigned herewith grant to the County of Santa Cruz and to Frederick A. Hihn the right to construct maintain and operate a wagon road forty feet wide from the Soquel Turnpike near the north side of the John Martin Schultheis Lagoon and thence southerly to Elbon and Houck's Mill near the east end of tunnel No. 3 on the South Pacific Coast Railroad substantially on the line of survey as made by M. V. Bennett in the month of September 1880.*

The first section of road that the agreement authorized the county to

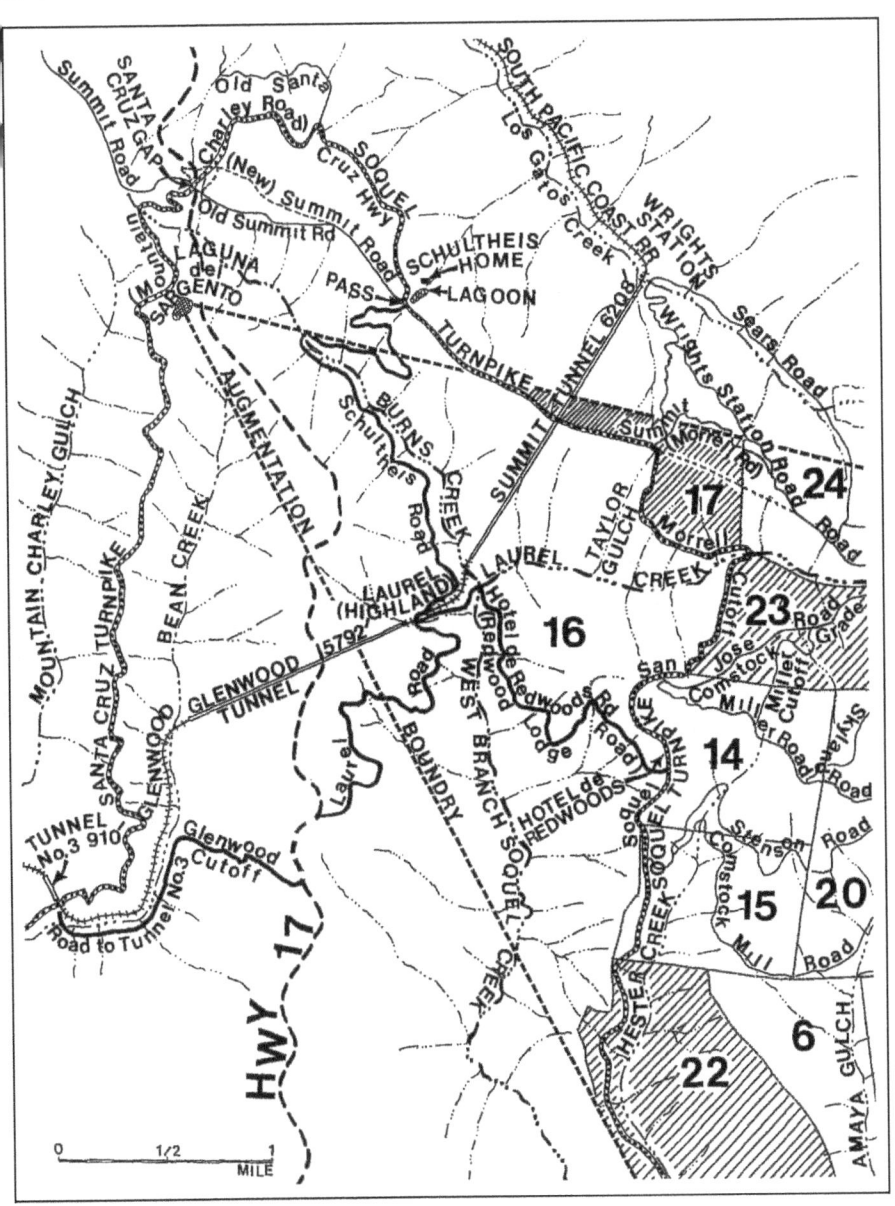

Figure 3.11 New roads in the Summit area

build was the narrow, twisting 3.4 miles from Summit Road to Highland that followed along the west bank of Burns Creek. Over a short distance, the road dropped 700 feet in elevation—from 1,600 at the Summit to 900 feet at Laurel. This route was named Schultheis Road after the owner, but the spelling has since become corrupted to Schulties Road. The lagoon mentioned in the agreement was once located at the northeast corner of the intersection of the Old Santa Cruz Highway and Summit Road but has since been filled.

The second road in the agreement stretched to the west from Highland to Glenwood via a 2.3-mile-long road since named Laurel Road. While today's Laurel Road reaches Highway 17 just north of a hill, the original road went to the south of that hill, reaching Highway 17 directly across from Glenwood Cutoff, which served as the final 0.7-mile-long leg of the road from Highland to Glenwood. The full 3.2-mile-long route reached a top elevation of 1,200 feet but both ends were at 900 feet above sea level.

The last road in the agreement connected Highland to Hotel de Redwoods via a 2.2-mile-long meandering route that roughly followed the east bank of the West Branch of Soquel Creek. Hotel de Redwoods, a popular resort on the Soquel Turnpike, made a logical destination for the road since it provided railroad access via transfer wagons for vacationers staying at the hotel. The road remains today as Redwood Lodge Road.[105]

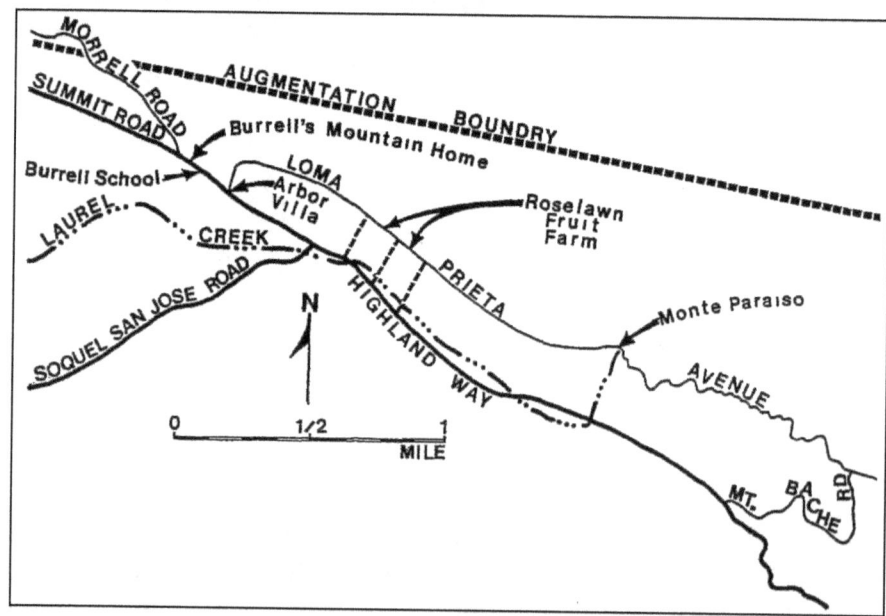

FIGURE 3.12 HOMES IN THE SUMMIT AREA

Land transfer from Lyman Burrell to Josephine McCrackin concerning Tract 24 in the Augmentation

On October 22, 1880, when Josephine Womper McCrackin (*née* Clifford) purchased 26 acres in Tract 24 in the Augmentation from Lyman Burrell, she became one of the first single women to live on the Summit. On her land, she built her home far to the east on Loma Prieta Avenue at the headwaters of Laurel Creek. She named her estate Monte Paraiso ('mountain paradise' in Spanish). McCrackin soon became famous through both her literary achievements and her push to save the redwoods, specifically those of Big Basin.[106]

Storm severely damages Santa Cruz Railroad leading the company to declare bankruptcy

On January 21, 1881, it began to rain heavily, causing extensive damage to Santa Cruz Railroad's line in a number of locations. This damage only added to the company's financial problems brought on primarily by the South Pacific Railroad's reaching Santa Cruz the previous May. Since that time, only one regular train had run each direction daily to cut costs.

Five days after the storm, the railroad stopped all service along its line in order to assess the damage and make repairs. But the bad news kept coming when the next day, January 27, another heavy rain washed away a section of the trestle viaduct along the beach beside the San Lorenzo River. With no money left to make repairs, the company declared bankruptcy.

Frederick Hihn, desperate to avoid shutting down the project he had championed for over a decade, attempted to levy a $10 per share assessment on March 28. But a month later, on April 27, the investors gathering for a final meeting of the Santa Cruz Railroad refused to pay the levy. The railroad was officially defunct and passed to its creditors.

On May 4, the following article appeared in the *Santa Cruz Weekly Courier*:

> *The Santa Cruz Railroad was an enterprise conceived, constructed and carried on, in its early history, with much*

popular enthusiasm. The people of the upper portion of the county in particular fancied that the one thing lacking was a railroad. Outside capital was appealed to in vain, even when tempted by a subsidy, and for the interest and public spirit of Frederick A. Hihn, supported by subscriptions from the greater portion of the men of means in the community at that time, it would have remained unbuilt to this day. The people of Santa Cruz, especially stockholders in the railroad, do not need to be informed that as a financial investment it proved from the beginning a disastrous failure. It was worse than a white elephant in the hands of its owners and managers. The problem of building and operating 20 miles of independent railroad, alongside of water competition for freight, and both steamship and stage competition for passengers, has never been successfully solved. Mr. Hihn was plucky and persistent, and when the South Pacific Coast Railroad seemed likely to absorb the lion's share of the limited business to be done, he still kept the road equipped and running, and advanced his own money to supply the deficiencies of delinquent assessments. The violence of the elements last winter was more than a match for his patient investments, and when the bridge across the San Lorenzo River went out to sea, it was the death knell of the Santa Cruz Railroad.

The collapse of the Santa Cruz Railroad did not necessarily mean a closure of the line between Pajaro and Santa Cruz. But the question remained: who would take it over? It ultimately fell to Southern Pacific, which had toyed with the idea of building such a line since the 1860s. Shortly after the above article was published, the Pacific Improvement Company purchased the delinquent stocks of the line on the Southern Pacific's behalf and immediately set to work making repairs.

All of Southern Pacific's maintenance crew chiefs came to inspect the line and assess its potential. A. C. Bassett, the general superintendent for the railroad, declared that the route could resume operations within a month. And this his team achieved, with the line reopening to through traffic on June 4. Soon afterwards, Bassett declared that the entire route

The Hidden Hand   1881

would soon be standard-gauged, thereby making it competitive against the South Pacific Coast Railroad since freight would not have to be transferred between cars of incompatible gauges. Bassett also hinted that the railroad line would be continued up the coast to San Francisco at a later point in time, which would place Santa Cruz on the map as a waypoint along a major thoroughfare.

More importantly, with the Santa Cruz Railroad now in capable hands and well-funded, Hihn and other local businesspeople could finally trust in the line and make it profitable to them. Hihn had made sure that the railroad passed through Aptos so that it would be near his vast timber tracts in the Augmentation. With Southern Pacific now in control, it was only a matter of time until the railroad made harvesting these tracts a whole lot easier.[107]

Dickamon Rider sells company and creates new company

Throughout the late 1870s, the Watsonville Mill & Lumber Company operated on the east side of Eureka Canyon Road and the Corralitos Lumber Company logged the timber to the west of the road. But the latter company had less timberland overall and, in 1880, Dickamon Rider decided to cut his losses and sell the Corralitos Lumber Company to his competitor. Early the next year, he created a partnership with his son, Homer Merchant Rider, under the name D. A. Rider & Son. For this new venture, he purchased a tract of 900 acres at the northern end of Corralitos Creek above Shingle Mill Gulch. To reach this area, the family built what is now called Buzzard Lagoon Road off of their old mill road (Rider Road). Buzzard Lagoon is a small natural lake that sits just outside the easternmost limit of the Augmentation and is located 1,900 feet above sea level. The origin of the name remains unknown.

Beyond the lagoon, the road was extended until it reached the eastern end of Highland Way. For the first five years, the Riders operated a lumber mill at the top of Eureka Canyon. In 1886, it was relocated 1.5 miles to the north, to the headwaters of Corralitos Creek. This location gave them easy access to Loma Prieta Avenue and Summit Road, which meant they could haul lumber straight to the Santa Clara Valley. As a final note, Eureka Canyon Road was not completed beyond Grizzly Flat at the top

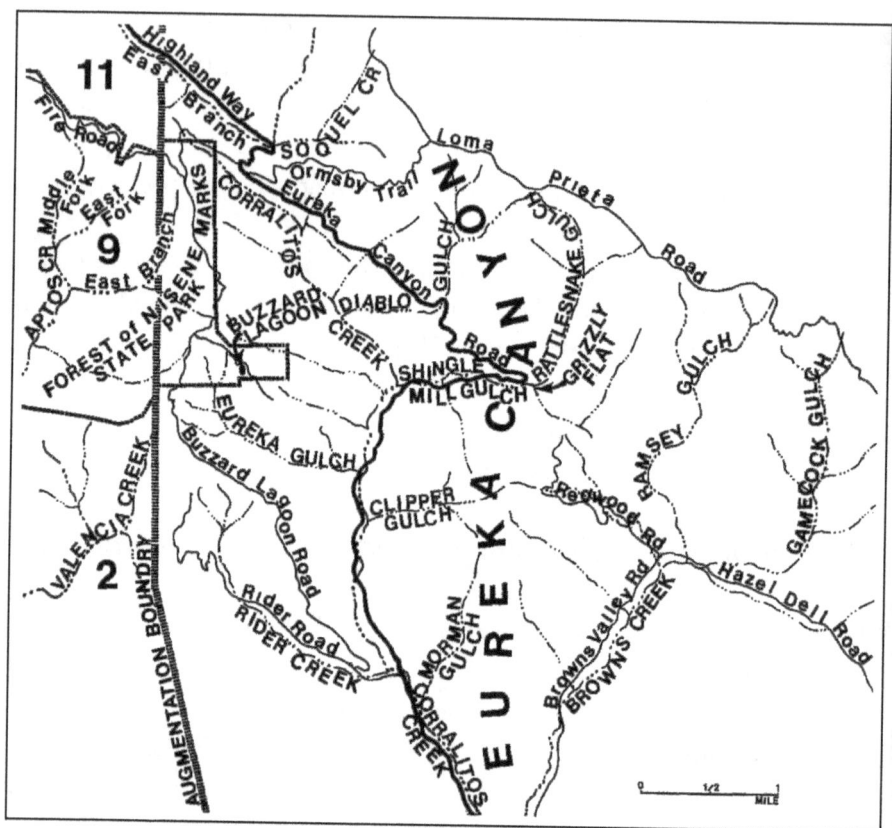

FIGURE 3.13 EUREKA CANYON AND THE EASTERN SUMMIT AREA

of Shingle Mill Gulch until the mid-1910s. Meanwhile, Highland Way operated as a private road until the 1930s, when the county finally took over its maintenance.[108]

Agreement between Carmel Fallon and John Porter, William Dougherty, Alvin Sanborn, and John Brown concerning Tract 9 of the Augmentation

The Watsonville Mill & Lumber Company was the single largest redwood logging operation south of San Francisco throughout the 1870s. However, its once-vast timber tracts in Eureka Canyon were almost spent by 1881. Kent Devereaux explains:

> *By 1880, the state of California, and Santa Cruz County especially, was in the midst of a lumber boom that was rapidly diminishing the coastal redwood forests. Whereas in 1858 the output of 10-million board feet of lumber was from but a total of only 10 sawmills, by 1880 the number of mills had more than doubled and the annual output had risen to over 40-million board feet. Lumber production in Santa Cruz County exceeded all other California counties with the exception of Humboldt, and Southern Pacific's Pajaro station claimed to ship more timber than any other point in the state. Clearly, if logging continued at such a feverish pace it would not be long before the hillsides of the Santa Cruz mountains were devoid of timber. As 1880 approached, most of the virgin stands of redwood blanketing the slopes near Watsonville had been cleared. Now the lumber men turned northward, to the untouched woods hidden within the many canyons of the Santa Cruz mountains above Aptos and farther up into the San Lorenzo Valley.*

Management was rightly worried that they would be unable to secure new, profitable tracts, and were eager to find a practical solution. The divorce of Carmel and Thomas Fallon provided just such an opportunity.

Fallon had spent years maintaining a small toll road through the heavily forested Tracts 8 and 9 of the Augmentation. However, the divorce split the lands between him and his wife, granting the latter the substantially larger Tract 9 along with its tax liability. With the toll road now bisected, that source of income was curtailed, and Carmel needed to find a new means of paying her annual property taxes. As a result, she turned to the Watsonville Mill & Lumber Company to find a mutual solution to their problems.

No written records survive that provide insight into the initial negotiations between Carmel and the lumber magnates. The primary sticking point, however, was likely over whether she would sell her land outright or only sell the stumpage rights to the timber company. The property had been assessed as encompassing between 6,000 and 7,000 acres (the final number was 6,845 acres), but the Watsonville Mill & Lumber Company was unsure precisely what this included. Therefore, it sent in surveyors to determine the composition of the forest, the types of terrain and natural obstacles, the likely forms of transportation that would be required to extract the timber, and the estimated lumber yield for the property. In hindsight, it is clear that the lumber company had already made its decision regardless of the costs.

Lumber companies at this time were not overly concerned with having a sound financial footing. The sheer number of old-growth redwood trees still standing meant that most companies viewed them as a near infinite resource. Thus, land ownership was often avoided in favor of leasing the land and buying stumpage rights. Once land was under its control, a company would erect a mill, cut and process the timber, and then move on to the next tract. Due to the increased cost of cutting remote trees, strands would often survive in corners of properties. After the lumber company left, the landowner or someone new would take over the property for another use or, if the land was too rugged, it would be left to regenerate.

As a result of these practices, large companies gave little thought to the financing of their next venture. Instead, they were more committed to their present operation and in satisfying themselves, their backers, and stockholders. When it came time to move on to a new tract, necessary financing for the move would be acquired through whatever means necessary. This was precisely the situation faced by the Watsonville Mill & Lumber Company in 1881, when it wished to acquire control of Carmel Fallon's timberlands in the Augmentation: the company did not have the necessary funds. It needed outside help.

Over the previous decade, William and James Dougherty had amassed a small lumber empire in the Santa Cruz Mountains. Following the absorption of several smaller companies, they had incorporated the Santa Clara Valley Mill & Lumber Company on January 13, 1873. It slowly came to dominate the Santa Clara Valley lumber scene even as the brothers continued to expand their operations deeper into Santa Cruz County. By 1881, they owned vast tracts along Zayante Creek, where they had their largest mill operating off of a spur of the South Pacific Coast Railroad.

The success of the Santa Clara Valley Mill & Lumber Company attracted the attention of Charles Ford of the Watsonville firm. Ford had already succeeded in pulling his old Bank of Watsonville partner John Porter into his plans, but he needed the backing of a larger, more impressive firm to secure the necessary funds to buy Fallon's land and the necessary capital to begin operations within the Augmentation. Thus, he turned to William Dougherty, who eagerly joined in the new venture.

The final piece in the puzzle of how to acquire and harvest Tract 9 was the matter of transportation. The Southern Pacific Railroad had just entered the Santa Cruz scene earlier in the year through its acquisition of the Santa Cruz Railroad, and it was eager to turn a profit from its new line. While standard-gauging the track between Santa Cruz and Pajaro would give it an edge in the county, it would by no means eliminate the competition with the South Pacific Coast Railroad. The latter's route through the mountains gave it substantially more access to profitable timberlands while also providing passengers a faster, more direct route from San Francisco with more interesting waypoints along the way, such as Welch's Big Trees Grove.

Southern Pacific felt that it needed equally appealing destinations to attract passengers, while at the same time required more industrial customers to increase daily revenue. One option it considered was building Frederick

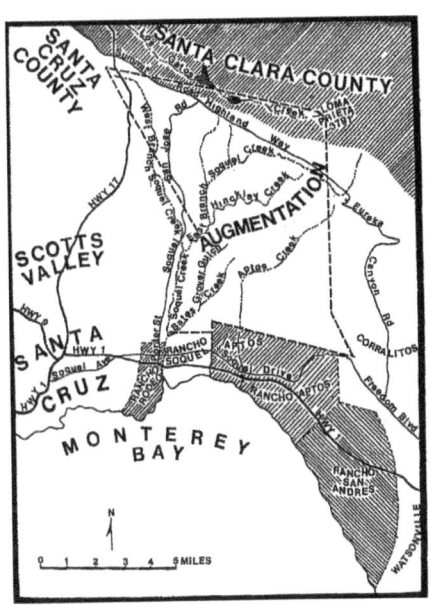
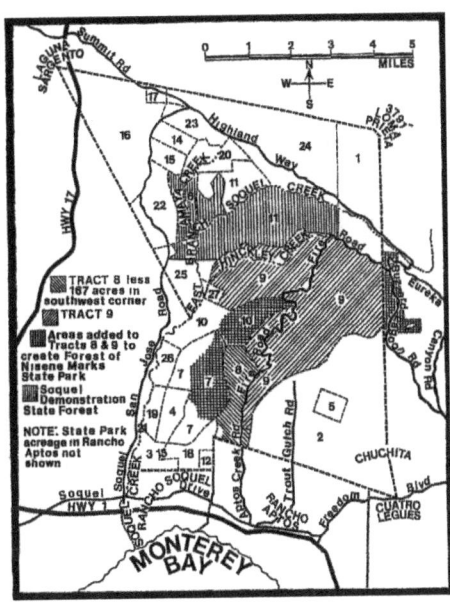

FIGURE 3.14 LOCATION OF RANCHO SOQUEL AND THE AUGMENTATION

FIGURE 3.15 TRACTS 8 AND 9 IN THE AUGMENTATION

Hihn's planned branch line up Soquel Creek. This would give the railroad access to Hihn's timberland at the top of the Augmentation and also potentially allow for the construction of a Big Trees resort of its own, with a hotel and other recreational facilities. However, the surviving members of the Big Four did not especially like Hihn after his campaign against them during his term in the state assembly. Thus, Southern Pacific turned to the Watsonville Mill & Lumber Company as an alternative.

It is not known precisely through which means Southern Pacific got pulled into Ford's ambitious scheme for the Augmentation. One possibility is that it was through Porter's friendship with attorney Thomas Benton Bishop, sometime lawyer for the Big Four in San Francisco. Another possibility is a chance meeting between Ford or Porter and A. C. Bassett, who would soon take control of the Santa Cruz Railroad for Southern Pacific. In any case, the two parties met and quickly came to an agreement and got to work realizing their vision.

Soon, the Pacific Improvement Company, Southern Pacific's construction arm, sent surveyors into the Augmentation to see if it was practical and economically justified to build a railroad from Aptos to Tract 9. They estimated that 3.7 miles of track would be required to reach the property, including six bridges, three of which at over 200 feet in length. Once within the tract, another 1.3 miles of track would be needed to reach an area where a suitable mill could be erected for processing the timber in the tract. This second segment of track would need another eight bridges, with two more exceeding 200 feet in length. Aptos Creek would be crossed a total of four times, with the other bridges crossing feeder streams and gulches. The surveyors' final conclusion was that the line could be built and operated effectively, but at considerable cost.

There were several other problems that could not be ignored before they could commit to building the line up Aptos Creek. First, they had to receive permission to cross Hihn and Claus Spreckels' land in Rancho Aptos. Then, once the Augmentation boundary was reached, they had to cross Thomas Fallon's Tract 8. Despite bad blood, Hihn, as well as Spreckels, gave permission to cross their land with a 100-foot-wide right-of-way, and Fallon also agreed to a 60-foot-wide route through his land. The Pacific Improvement Company agreed to build the surveyed route, which left as the final matter the issue of Carmel Fallon's land itself.

Porter, Dougherty, Brown, and Alvin Sanborn approached Fallon at her home in San Francisco on June 16, 1881 to formalize the details of the agreement. Fallon agreed to sell stumpage rights for 4,345 acres of her land—the land along Aptos and Bridge Creeks—to the four partners in exchange for $5,000 upfront, with an additional payment of $10,000 by January 1, 1883 and $15,000 annually for the three years following. Fallon would also receive seven percent interest per year for the amount not yet paid. Each partner would, in turn, own a claim to one quarter of the stumpage rights, with fifty percent controlled by the Watsonville Mill & Lumber Company through its agents, Brown and Sanborn. A third party, J. R. Whitney, agreed to loan to the partners $10,000 for the purchase, with a repayment set at seven percent due by June 1, 1885.

The four partners agreed more generally to take immediate possession of the land and begin operations as soon as possible. Permission was granted to build roads through the property and erect mills, as necessary, for the purpose of manufacturing lumber. The partners agreed to denude exactly 1,000 acres of timberland each year. If less or more than that amount was harvested in a single year, the next year's payment would come due immediately, including the interest that would have been due had it been paid on schedule. If this stipulation was not upheld, the agreement would be deemed void. Fallon reserved a right to enter and inspect her land unannounced and immediately expel the company if she found it had violated any terms.

Although at first glance, these terms seemed reasonable, they proved impossible to uphold. The task of harvesting 1,000 acres annually at any mill would be difficult, and at a mill that required extensive roadwork and the construction of a railroad, not yet built, even more so. In reality, the task of harvesting 1,000 acres of timberland in a year would amount to harvesting nearly the entire output from all of the county's other mills combined. In the end, the company managed to harvest an average of 255 acres annually over a period of seventeen years.

Shortly after the agreement with Fallon was signed, Brown transferred his quarter interest in Tract 9 to Sanborn. This made Sanborn the sole representative of the Watsonville Mill & Lumber Company in the partnership, although he retained a controlling interest among the three.

Brown retired as director of the milling company on August 7, 1882, passing leadership to Sanborn, and Sanborn did not reveal his ownership of Brown's interest until August 19.[109]

Frederick Hihn enters the lumber industry

What motivated Frederick Hihn to enter the lumber production and sales industry? It seems reasonable to assume that the agreement between Carmel Fallon and the Watsonville Mill & Lumber Company had something to do with it. After all, here was a man at the age of fifty-four, a resident of the county for some thirty years, whose various entrepreneurial pursuits and investments had placed him near the top of Santa Cruz County's list of heaviest taxpayers. Not only was he among the richest in the county, but he had far more wealth than the Watsonville Mill & Lumber Company. And he owned approximately 15,837 acres within the Augmentation, which included timber tracts capable of producing more than 400 million board feet of lumber.

What did Hihn fear the most when he heard of the planned logging activity in the Augmentation? Was he afraid of a loss of influence in Aptos, since large amounts of material and supplies would pass through the town from the mill? When considered today, it seems more likely that Hihn was less afraid and more maneuvering. With Hihn's substantial power in the Aptos–Soquel region, the buyers of Fallon's stumpage rights may have actually been acting aggressively to secure a foothold in a contested area. That would explain why they agreed to near-impossible terms with Fallon. They would agree to anything to secure the timberland and work out the details later, once they inevitably failed to uphold their end of the original agreement.

Another factor in Hihn's entry into the lumber scene may have been Southern Pacific's refusal to extend a branch line up the East Branch of Soquel Creek. Although there is little primary evidence for this failed negotiation between Hihn and the railroad, several later statements suggest that the proposal was rejected. A lack of railroad service to his timber tracts put him at a serious disadvantage compared to the Aptos Creek mill, which would soon have its own dedicated branch line. The solution he found was to shift his focus to timber closer to Aptos and build a mill at the bottom of Trout Gulch. Thus, even as construction began on the Aptos Creek road and railroad, Hihn began arrangements to open his own lumber mill a short distance from Aptos Station, where he could ship lumber out to market quickly and efficiently without the high overhead of a railroad line.

Land transfer from Frederick Hihn to Jered Comstock concerning Tract 11 in the Augmentation

On July 21, 1881, Jered Comstock purchased 50 acres in Tract 11 in the Augmentation from Frederick Hihn for $2,500, with the option to purchase the rest of the timberland in the adjacent Tracts 6 and 20 within the following week. Comstock did not exercise this option.[110]

Agreement between Alvin Sanborn, A. C. Bassett, and Nicholas Smith concerning Tract 9 in the Augmentation

On October 8, 1881, a final step was taken to complete the compact made in June regarding plans to harvest the timber within Tract 9 of the Augmentation. Alvin Sanborn, representing the Watsonville Mill & Lumber Company, met at the law office of Thomas Bishop in San Francisco to sign a document ceding one-fifth of his stumpage rights in Tract 9 to the Southern Pacific Railroad. The two agents for the company, A. C. Bassett, superintendent of the Coast Division of the Southern Pacific Railroad, and Captain Nicholas T. Smith, treasurer for the Pacific Improvement Company, were not physically present at the meeting, so Bishop signed the agreement on their behalf. This transaction in effect gave to Southern Pacific one-tenth of the total stumpage rights sold in Tract 9, which amounted to about 108.6 acres. This land was not in fact intended to be used for logging; rather, it was to secure a right-of-way for the planned railroad through the Augmentation. Although the agreement was put into effect almost immediately, it was not filed until August 7, 1882.

At the time of this agreement, Bishop and Smith were still newcomers to the Santa Cruz logging scene. Bishop was born in Providence, Rhode Island in 1841 and attended Brown University from 1860 to 1863. He moved to San Francisco where he quickly rose through the ranks of the local legal firms. It was during his time at Bishop, Wheeler & Hoefler that he became the general counsel for the Central Pacific and Southern Pacific Railroads, a position he retained until his death in 1906. At some point in the late 1870s, Bishop became friends with John Porter and the two participated in several financial ventures together, both in Santa Cruz County and elsewhere. This relationship likely led to the Watsonville Mill & Lumber Company inviting Southern Pacific into its plans. Less is known about Smith except that he was a lifelong friend of Leland Stanford, through which relationship he achieved such a high position within Southern Pacific management.[111]

Land transfer from Henry Hite to Emily Hite concerning Tract 24 in the Augmentation

In October 1881, Henry T. Hite sold half of his land—13 1/2 acres—in Tract 24 in the Augmentation to his mother, Emily J. Hite, for $400. They then combined their properties and planted a fruit orchard under the name Rose Lawn Fruit Farm. They packaged several popular types of fruit and their goods were noted for their quality and fine taste. The *Surf* reported:

> There are some thirteen acres in this farm, ten of which are under cultivation in orchard and some 2000 vines. Mr. Hite says his prunes are the best paying crop, the grapes tho' fine bringing but poor prices. There is a well of fine water on the place close to the snug looking, old fashioned cottage built some thirteen years ago.... Mr. Hite has the only "cannery" seen so far on these mountains. This is a modest building 16x20, fitted with appliances for canning the excellent fruit (peaches especially) grown on the farm. As the highly colored and attractive label on the can says: "The fruit contained in this can was grown on the summit of the Santa Cruz mountains and put in the orchard where grown; consequently the fruit is left to ripen, as it naturally should, on the tree." Using the best sugar and the greatest care Mr. Hite has established a reputation for first-class goods so that, as he remarked "the brand sells the fruit."

This farm operated until at least February 1899.[112]

Land transfer from Benjamin and George Porter to the Grover family concerning Tract 7 in the Augmentation

On November 4, 1881, Benjamin and George Porter sold the upper 598 acres of Tract 7 in the Augmentation to brothers James and Stephen Grover, as well as their nephew James.[113]

The Meyers and the Loma Prieta German Colony

Judge Andreas Meyer was a prominent citizen in the town of Hadesleben, Denmark, when his son Ernst Emil Meyer was born on January 23, 1843. Ernst attended a polytechnical school and then joined the German Imperial Navy from 1863 to 1864. Afterwards, he became an engineer on the Hamburg-American Steamship Line. During this time, Ernst's eldest brother, Wilhelm, immigrated to San Francisco where he opened a wholesale and florist shop on Geary Street. Ernst joined his brother in business in 1865. His love, Maria Detje, traveled with her sister from Hamburg, Germany, in 1870 to marry Ernst. Their first child, also Ernst Emil, was born September 1, 1874 in San Francisco, while a second son, Arthur, joined the family a few years later. The Meyers settled on 4.5 acres near the entrance of Golden Gate Park and established the Eureka Nursery, while Ernst also established a wholesale business in downtown San José. It was here that Ernst first became interested in the Santa Cruz Mountains.

Meyer and Lyman Burrell became acquainted during several trips that Meyer took into the mountains in the late 1870s. On November 12, 1881, Meyer purchased around 1,400 acres in the Summit area within Tract 24 in the Augmentation from Burrell. The property's boundaries were adjusted on March 25, 1887 in an agreement with Birney James Burrell, son of Lyman Burrell, to account for a surveying error. The result of this was that Meyer deeded 50 acres to Burrell on the northern side of the property and, in return, gained 172 acres on the southern side along the East Branch of Soquel Creek. Shortly after acquiring the property, Meyer subdivided it and sold parcels while also building a home in the mountains. When the last parcel sold in 1884, he relocated his family from San Francisco to

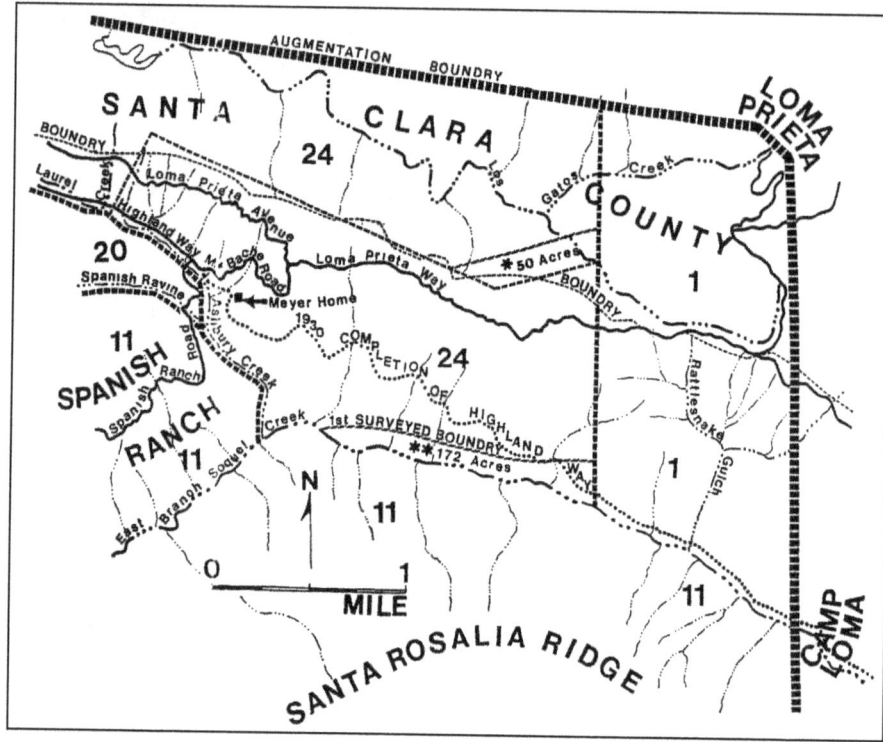

FIGURE 3.16 THE MEYER FAMILY'S PROPERTIES IN THE SUMMIT AREA

the Summit. Their home quickly became known as Mare Vista—Ocean View—but it proved to be much more than simply a scenic overlook.

The Meyer home soon became the envy of the Santa Cruz Mountain community. They installed stained glass windows, the bathrooms were all tile, and there were several fireplaces. They also installed the first gas lighting system along the Summit. Meanwhile, the family's winery quickly gained a reputation for excellence. Meyer recounted in an interview with Phil Francis in 1896 that:

> *Not long after I came here, I found that the deep shaley soil of the ridges were best adapted to both table and wine grapes. We make little, if any, of the sweet wines, as we are not able to compete with the south county growers in that respect, but in the dry wines we have the quality and the market. Buyers and consumers have said that our dry wines are as good as the*

best. However, that is, I know that the buyers always come to us; we never go to the buyers.

The family produced five tons of grapes per acre and their first winery had a capacity of 6,000 gallons. In the late 1890s, the Meyers built a second winery with a 250,000-gallon capacity. This allowed them to make wine from grapes grown on nearby farms and produce a wider range of wines. Indeed, most of the Loma Prieta community contributed grapes to the winery, although some people also had their own smaller wineries.

In August 1900, an extensive article in *The Wide World Magazine* described Mare Vista in substantial detail:

> *The section of the Santa Cruz Mountains herein described overlooks the Santa Clara Valley, and is one of the richest in the entire State, as well as being the most beautiful. Only a few years ago it was virgin forest whose attractions were accidentally observed by a former German naval officer, Mr. E. E. Meyer, who decided to settle there. At that time the slopes were a mass of redwoods, firs, and madrones; and the location selected by Mr. Meyer was one of the most attractive in the whole range, abounding in deep and well-wooded canyons, and provided with a fine water supply.*
>
> *Mr. Meyer is leader in his community, and is highly esteemed and honoured in Santa Clara County.... In fact, if the truth is told, this section of the State seems made up of men and women of remarkable qualities, in which bravery and true heroism appear to predominate. It was after great difficulty that Mr. Meyer established his winery, and then he spent years in waiting for the grapes to grow to maturity. Finally, however, success was assured.*
>
> *Many others followed his example. Mrs. McCrackin... in a letter to the writer says: 'I remember well the enthusiasm with which we drank the first product of the little hand-press, and how proud we were of the first 5,000 gallons of wine which Mr. Meyer made. The hand-press was thrown aside after the first season, and machinery, which I cannot describe*

> except as 'new-fangled,' but of which Mr. Meyer is able, not only to name, but also to construct every bolt, wheel, and rivet, now fills the vast halls and engine-room of the winery. His own wine output has now reached nearly 100,000 gallons, and every season his acreage becomes larger, and some new improvement is introduced in the working machinery.'
>
> Mr. Meyer named his winery the Mare Vista, and today it is one of the best-known in all America. His wine finds its way all over the civilized world. About 500ft. from the winery Mr. Meyer built his home, and reaching away from it are beautiful grounds.... The drives to the house were through natural groves of trees centuries old; groups of laurel, madrones, and firs telling the story of the prodigality of Nature in this country. The winery is a large, two-storied building, with large trees growing to within 100ft. of it. Here was all the valuable machinery, representing quite a large fortune, together with thousands of gallons of wine in all stages of age and development.

Meyer made several improvements to his property over the years. He established the Summit's first telephone service shortly after building his winery, which ran between his home, the winery, and Wright's Station. The service only operated until 1887 due to vandalism by local boys shooting glass insulators on telephone poles with slingshots. The first formal telephone service on the Summit was not organized until 1910 under the guidance of Meyer, Herman Grunsky, and Bob Borello. The three named their company the Santa Cruz Mountain Telephone Company and, as before, its first connection was between Wright's Station and Meyer's home. But around twelve other subscribers also paid for service. Soon, the telephone lines were extended to Ingham's store in the hamlet of Burrell and to Skyland. More lines were extended to Laurel and to the other Summit homes and settlements. By 1934, seven separate lines served the entire Summit community.

At the same time that Meyer was experimenting with telephone service in the 1880s, he had to deal with the problem of rural mail delivery. Postal service to his home proved impossible due to a deep gulch that was

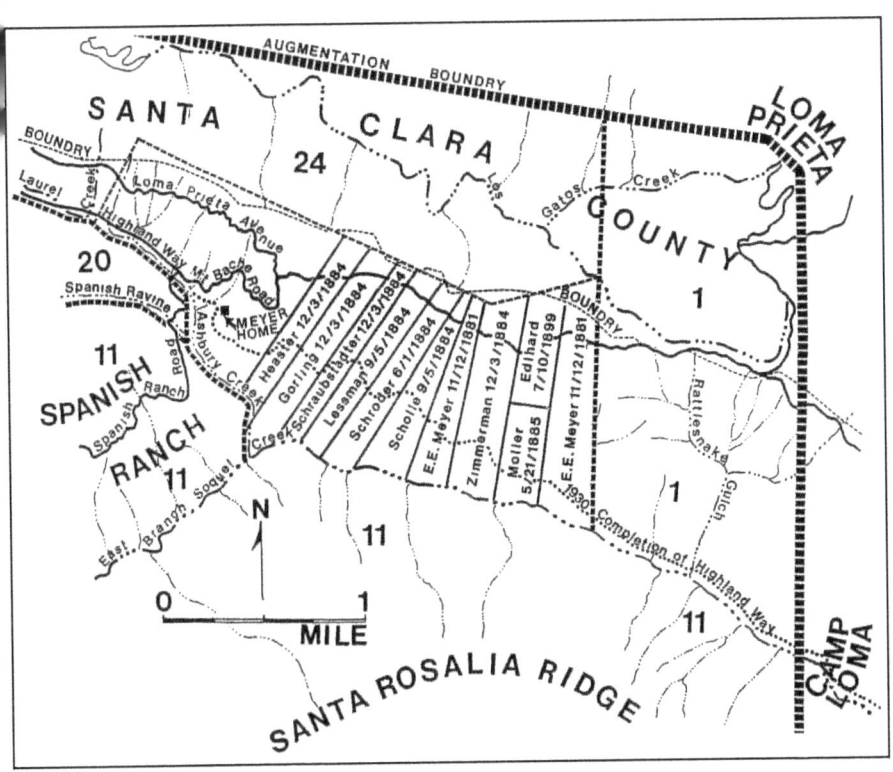

FIGURE 3.17 SUBDIVISIONS OF THE MEYER ESTATE IN THE SUMMIT AREA

too expensive to bridge. Meyer's solution was to rig a pully system across the gulch to a box on Mt. Bache Road where the postal carrier could place the mail. Once delivered, the carrier would shove the box partway into the gulch along the pully, signaling to Meyer that he had mail. After retrieving his mail, he would send the box back to the opposite end to await the next mail delivery.

The Meyers did not keep their newfound mountaintop paradise to themselves. On September 5, 1884, Meyer sold a total of 199 acres to the east of his home to two German immigrants, A. Scholle and Joseph Lessman. Over the next five years, he sold an additional 664 acres to other German families. This eclectic group of artists, musicians, and other professionals were largely seeking peace from the ambitions of the German Empire following the conclusion of the Franco-Prussian War. These new settlers on Meyer's land included:

Scholle, 91 acres, sold September 5, 1884. Corrected February 14, 1885 to address a border dispute.

Lessmain, 108 acres, sold September 5, 1884. Corrected February 14, 1885 to address a border dispute. Lessman later sold his land to Gustav Witzel, a San Francisco businessman, around 1888.

Professor F. Heaster, 120 acres, sold December 3, 1884. He named his home Anita Villa and Vineyard, after his wife.

G. Zimmermann, 126 acres, sold December 3, 1884.

The Gorling family, 80 acres, sold on December 3, 1884. This land was returned to the Meyer family for unknown reasons prior to 1919.

Wilhelm and Lucie Schraubstadter, 109 acres, sold December 3, 1884. Wilhelm was a retired opera singer who won fame on the East Coast and in St. Louis before settling in Santa Cruz County. They named their home Tre Monte.

The Moller family, 84 acres, sold May 21, 1885.

Mr. Schroder, 92 acres, sold June 1, 1885.

Dr. Edmund Goldman, 24 acres, sold October 9, 1888.

Henry H. Woods, 38 acres, sold May 22, 1889. He named his home Lomita.

O. Edlhard, 65 acres, sold July 10, 1889.

After Lessmain sold his property to Witzel around 1888, the latter approached the Schraubstadter family and proposed a partnership in order to form a resort. The result was Mark's Place, which quickly became one of the showpieces of the Summit area. It was located one mile east of the junction of Mt. Bache Road and Loma Prieta Avenue on Loma Prieta Way. The name likely referred to the proprietor of the resort since it later was changed to Herman's Place.

One settler of note was Dr. Goldman. Born in Schotten, Duchy of Schleswig-Holstein, then a part of Denmark, in 1834, Goldman graduated from Heidelberg University and the University of Giessen as a medical doctor. He immigrated to New York where he worked at Bellevue Hospital to complete his postgraduate studies. In the late 1850s, he relocated to New

Orleans, where he began his own medical practice. Due to his successful handling of a yellow fever epidemic in the region, he was elected president of the New Orleans Board of Education. Despite living in the South, he fled north at the start of the Civil War and joined the Union Army as a surgeon. This brought him into contact with several leading military officers of the age, including General William T. Sherman, General Philip H. Sheridan, Admiral David G. Farragut, and General Benjamin F. Butler. During Farragut's siege of Mobile, Alabama in August 1864, Goldman tended to the admiral's wounded.

Shortly after the war ended, Goldman married Amelia Correth, the daughter of a German count who had come to the United States during

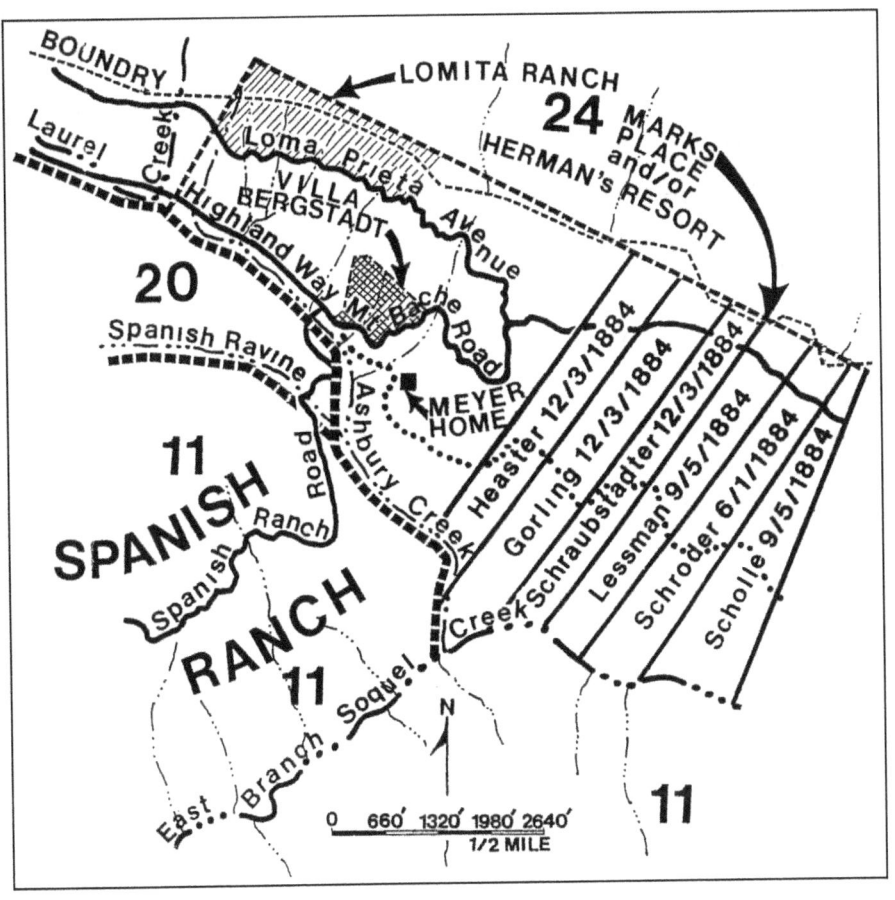

FIGURE 3.18 HOMES AND RESORTS IN THE LOMA PRIETA GERMAN COLONY

the Revolution of 1848. Tragically, Amelia died in childbirth only a year after her marriage. Goldman eventually married Julia Bergstadt, a native of Bremervörde, Duchy of Baden, at Galveston, Texas in 1876. The couple moved to Monterrey, México where Goldman quickly rose in prominence as the family physician of José Evaristo Madero Elizondo, governor of Coahuila de Zaragoza and father of future Mexican president Francisco Modero. While there, Edmund and Julia had two daughters and a son. The poor health conditions in the region finally prompted them to leave in 1887.

The Goldmans initially settled in San José, where the doctor once more set up a medical practice, which he ran for three years. It was during this time that he approached Emil Meyer about purchasing land within the Loma Prieta German Colony on the Summit. Since he did not plan to extensively farm or ranch his land, he only bought a small tract upon which he could build a home and practice medicine. The family moved into Villa Bergstedt, named in memory of Goldman's first wife, in 1890. Goldman tended to all of the residents of the Summit area who suffered any ailment, and he mended broken bones, helped mothers give birth, and generally served the needs of the community.

When he retired, Goldman expanded his house into a convalescence home, which attracted visitors from throughout the Bay Area. He also continued to respond to the urgent medical needs of locals due to a lack of doctors on the Summit. He died in 1910 at the age of seventy-six, with the property remaining in the hands of his wife and children for several more years.[114]

Chapter 4

~

The Luck of Roaring Camp

Loma Prieta Railroad Company incorporated

Following a year of negotiations, planning, and backroom bargaining, the Pacific Improvement Company finally filed articles of incorporation for the Loma Prieta Railroad Company on July 10, 1882. That same day, the Watsonville Mill & Lumber Company announced its plans to erect a substantial milling complex within Tract 9 in the Augmentation. The new facility would include a lumber mill, shake and shingle mill, and box factory. Following the cutting of timber in the immediate vicinity of the mill, a second mill would be built at the end of an extension of the railroad line. Rather than extending the railroad further, skid roads would be used to reach the steep hillsides beyond the second mill.

The new railroad was established as an unambiguous subsidiary of the Southern Pacific Railroad. Central and Southern Pacific president Charles Crocker assumed the presidency of the Loma Prieta Railroad, while the parent company's treasurer, N. T. Smith, and secretary, Joseph Lewis Willcutt, both assumed the same roles as well. Coast Division superintendent A. C.

Bassett was named vice president. Alvin Sanborn was also given a director position, although it came with no additional roles.

While neither company mentioned it at the time, the two firms had agreed not to log the southern part of Tract 9 until all of the timber to the north was depleted. This would allow for a large hotel to be erected among the redwoods, to be accompanied by recreational facilities. The hope of the two companies was that this resort could rival and draw traffic away from Welch's Big Trees in Felton.

Over the next few months, advertisements appeared in several Bay Area newspapers, especially in the North Bay, seeking experienced loggers and pieceworkers to join the crews along Aptos Creek. A possible incentive to attract workers was an offer of stock in the company. This may explain how Bassett, Timothy Hopkins, and other individuals who would later become major investors first became involved with the company financially at around this time.[115]

Agreement between Alvin Sanborn and John Brown filed and recorded

On August 7, 1882, John Brown retired as director of the Watsonville Mill & Lumber Company. This retirement activated the agreement signed between himself and Alvin Sanborn the previous year whereby Sanborn would receive title to all of Brown's rights within the company. The title was finally filed with the county on August 19, giving Sanborn majority control over Tract 9 in the Augmentation.[116]

Land transfer from Guadalupe and Joseph Averon to Grover & Company concerning Tract 7 in the Augmentation

After operating as a family partnership for nearly two decades, the Grovers finally decided in the fall of 1882 to incorporate as Grover & Company. The decision seems to have been primarily procedural. In its first known corporate transaction, the company purchased stumpage rights within Tract 7 of the Augmentation by finally paying $26,910 to Guadalupe Lodge and Joseph Averon on September 27. The original agreement with the couple had been made on December 8, 1865. The company added to this stumpage rights to 598 acres purchased from Benjamin and George Porter in November 1881, and 330 acres in Tract 4 purchased from the Joel Bates estate also on December 8, 1865. Together, these tracts constituted a significant section of timberland available for Grover & Company to exploit.[117]

Agreement between Thomas Fallon and the Loma Prieta Railroad concerning Tract 8 in the Augmentation

Work on the Loma Prieta Railroad could not begin until an easement was allowed through Thomas Fallon's Tract 8 in the Augmentation. He finally agreed to a 60-foot-wide right-of-way through his property on October 2, 1882. Part of this right-of-way followed the abandoned Fallon Wagon Road, built in 1866, and the proposed route of a railroad line surveyed by Thomas W. Wright in 1867.[118]

Land transfer from Claus Spreckels to the Loma Prieta Railroad concerning land in Rancho Aptos

In a deed signed on October 11, 1882, Claus Spreckels granted an easement through his property to the Loma Prieta Railroad with a 100-foot-wide right-of-way for a length of approximately 2.2 miles from 745 feet north of the county road (Soquel Drive) to the southern boundary of the Augmentation.[119]

Land transfer from Frederick Hihn to the Loma Prieta Railroad concerning land in Rancho Aptos

The third and final easement that was required in order to build the Loma Prieta Railroad was through Frederick Hihn's land in Rancho Aptos. Only 145 feet of land had to be crossed just north of the county road (Soquel Drive). On October 12, 1882, Hihn granted a 100-foot-wide right-of-way, same as Claus Spreckels, but required the easement to be fenced on both sides. A small portion of this fence survives on the creek side of Aptos Creek Road.[120]

The Santa Cruz Railroad is leased to the Southern Pacific Railroad

On November 10, 1882, the Pacific Improvement Company acquired full ownership of the Santa Cruz Railroad Company and promptly leased it to the Southern Pacific Railroad at a cost of $31,800 annually. Southern Pacific was responsible for paying all taxes, interest, maintenance, and operating costs, in return for which the Pacific Improvement Company was responsible for the payment of the principal cost of the line. With this arrangement finalized and the three sections of right-of-way needed to reach Tract 9 in the Augmentation acquired, work could finally begin on the Loma Prieta Railroad. However, Southern Pacific was still hesitant to begin construction due to the specifics of the agreement made between the Watsonville Mill & Lumber Company and Carmel Fallon. So long as she owned the land, she could make demands upon the lumber company. Any violation of the agreement, therefore, could lead to Fallon revoking the stumpage rights, negating the need for the railroad—a costly possibility. Thus, it was left to the lumber company to resolve the issue of ownership before Southern Pacific would begin construction.[121]

Laurel post office established

Following the 1881 timber season, Brad Morrell left Charles McKiernan's service and returned to the Augmentation where he established a new mill on Tract 16 in the Augmentation on Tateman Gulch along Soquel Creek. It was located about a mile and a half from Highland on the West Branch of Soquel Creek. He leased this land from Frederick Hihn and built a crude road (today's Morrell Mill Road) between the mill and Highland, where he shipped his lumber from the South Pacific Coast Railroad station.

The increased industrial activity in the area prompted a rapid increase in the population of people in the Highland area. By mid-1882, a school was established near the station to support the growing number of children living in the surrounding hills, several of whose fathers worked at the Morrell mill. On November 20, a post office was built across from the station with

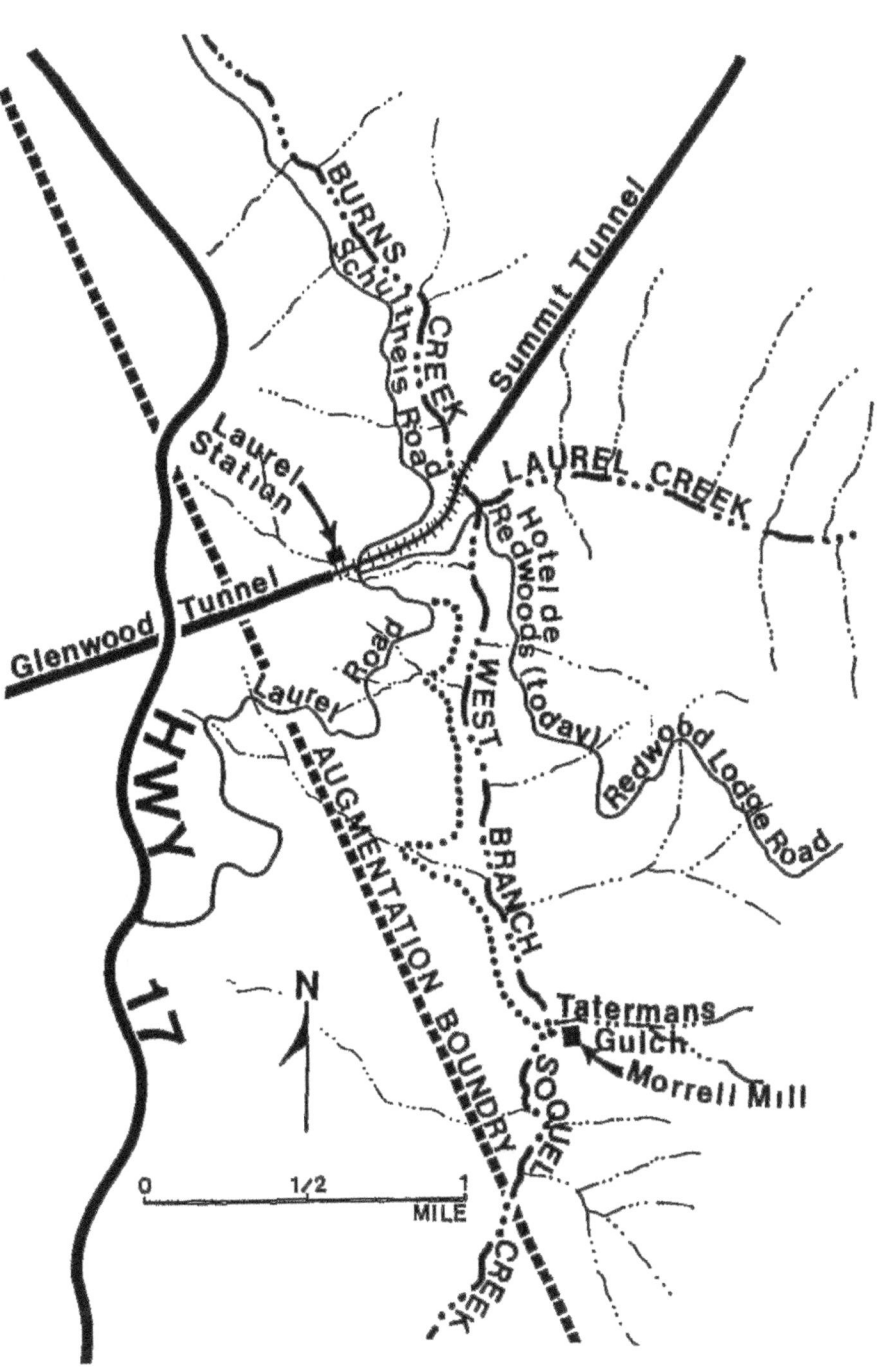

Figure 4.1 Mills along the West Branch of Soquel Creek

William Crichton appointed postmaster. It was likely the postal service that bestowed the name Laurel on the hamlet, with the school adopting the name soon afterwards.

Brad Morrell died a tragic death on July 4, 1903 when a runaway horse trampled him outside Boulder Creek. Hiram Morrell, meanwhile, lived to the age of eighty-nine and died on June 16, 1924 in San José. His son Albert took over the Morrell ranch in the final years of Hiram's life and continued to run it for several more years.[122]

Smallpox scare terrorizes Summit area and vicinity

During the cold winter of 1882–1883, a smallpox outbreak on the Summit led to a panic. Workers including lumbermen were frightened that they would catch the deadly disease and many self-quarantined or restricted their travel to avoid exposure. Everybody was afraid that their neighbors or friends had the disease and would spread it.[123]

Land transfer from Carmel Fallon to Alvin Sanborn, John Porter, and William Dougherty concerning Tract 9 in the Augmentation

On January 10, 1883, two important land transfers were conducted regarding Tract 9 in the Augmentation. In the first, Carmel Fallon sold about 6,845 acres of land to Alvin Sanborn, John Porter, and William Dougherty. The land in question included 3,935 acres along either side of Aptos Creek to its headwaters, approximately 410 acres along the east bank of Bridge Creek to its headwaters, and around 2,500 acres along Hinckley Gulch from its southern boundary with Tract 27 to its headwaters.

With the property finally owned outright, Sanborn, Porter, and Dougherty, along with A. C. Bassett, N. T. Smith, and Thomas Bishop, mortgaged the land in order to pay Fallon a total of $53,000 for the land. The partners took out the loan from the Bank of Watsonville through its representative, Godfrey M. Bockius. The last date for repayment was January 2, 1889 with an interest rate set at seven percent. Although the Watsonville Mill & Lumber Company was now deeply in debt, the purchase of the land resolved the final impediment for the Southern Pacific Railroad and construction on the Loma Prieta Railroad could finally begin.[124]

Land transfer from Frederick Waterman and Charles Parker to John Hacker concerning 126 acres in Tract 27 in the Augmentation

In a deed signed on January 15, 1883, Frederick Waterman and his partner Charles Parker sold Tract 27 in the Augmentation to John C. Hacker.[125]

Land transfer from Edwin Dudgeon to the Watsonville Mill & Lumber Company in Eureka Canyon

On March 22, 1883, Edwin Dudgeon sold 138 acres of land in Eureka Canyon to the Watsonville Mill & Lumber Company. The land spanned two parcels and was located just to the east of the Augmentation and north of Buzzard Lagoon. A road to the land had been built by D. A. Rider & Son in the early 1880s to connect its timber tracts with its mill near the Summit.[126]

Construction of the Loma Prieta Railroad begins from Aptos

As soon as the weather let up for the season, the Southern Pacific Railroad began construction on its Loma Prieta Railroad subsidiary. Construction, which began in April 1883, was complex for many reasons owing to the terrain and the fact that the Santa Cruz Railroad had still not been converted to standard-gauge. Thus, construction crews essentially built a standard-gauge railroad using appropriate crossties and sufficiently heavy rail, but they installed a narrow-gauge railroad as a temporary solution with plans to shift one of the rails to the proper width once the Santa Cruz Railroad's line was upgraded.

A total of 200 Chinese workers were brought to the hills above Aptos to build the line. W. F. Knox of Sacramento served as supervisor of the grading and track laying crews while a Mr. Partridge was in charge of constructing and installing the numerous bridges along the line. Although

1883 The Reign of the Lumber Barons

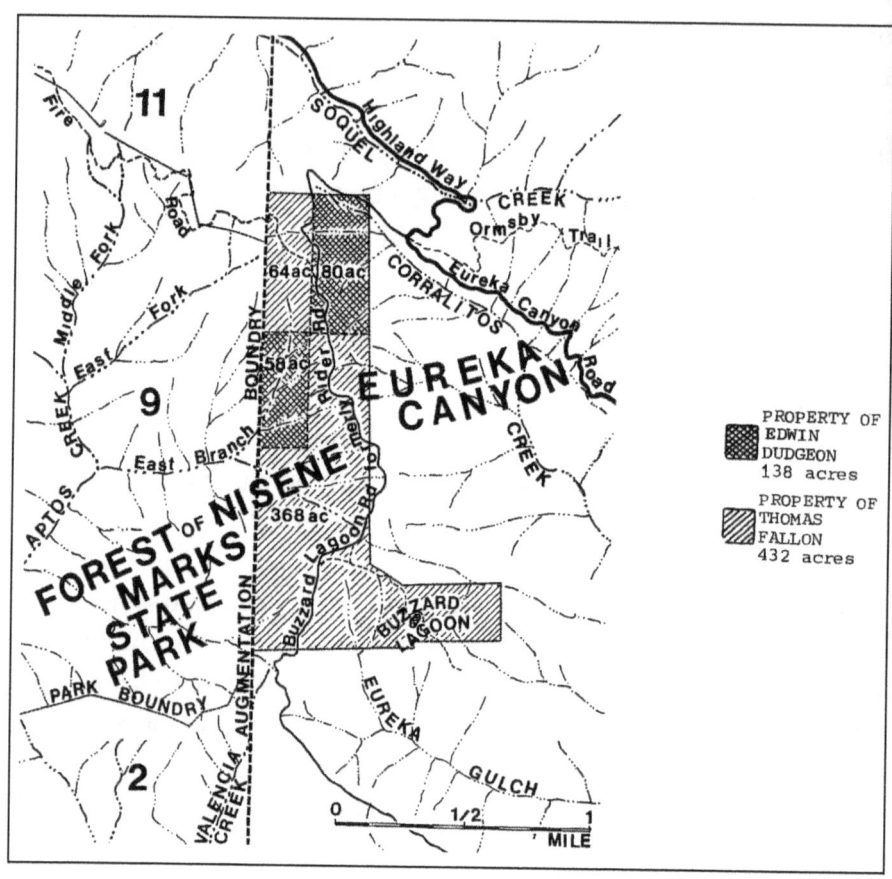

FIGURE 4.2 WATSONVILLE MILL & LUMBER CO. LANDS IN EUREKA CANYON

the railroad was intended to be a terminal route with its primary purpose being the conveyance of lumber from mills in the mountains to Aptos and elsewhere, Southern Pacific ensured that it met all of its exacting standards. The steepness of grades was kept at a minimum, meaning that substantial cuts and fills had to be made across the five miles of the route. The bridgework also had to be exact, with trestle approaches and fills needed to ensure that all substantial spans were exactly 80 feet across. Southern Pacific did not build its fourteen long bridges on site, but rather had redwood trusses prefabricated in Oakland. These were then transported to Aptos Creek and assembled. Construction took over a year to complete due to the technical difficulties grading and bridge

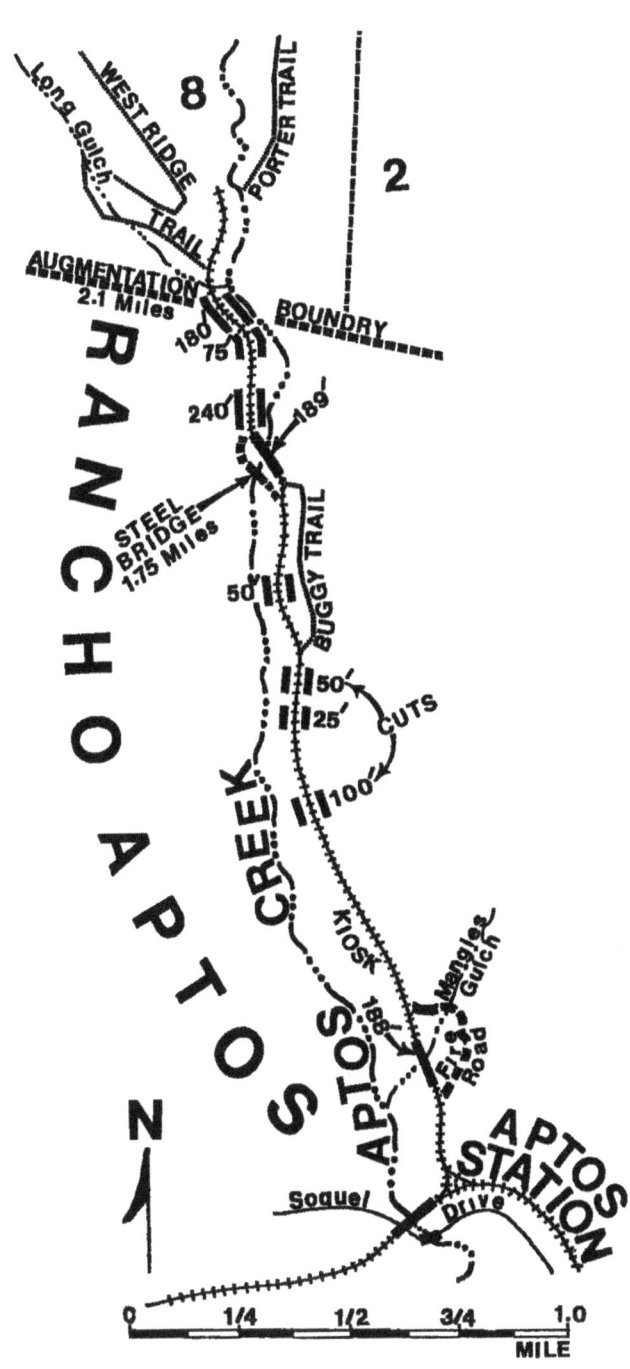

FIGURE 4.3 ROUTE OF THE LOMA PRIETA RAILROAD TO MILE MARKER 2.1

crews encountered along the way.

The ultimate amount that the Loma Prieta Railroad cost the Southern Pacific to build may never be known since most of the company's corporate records were destroyed in the fires following the 1906 San Francisco Earthquake. However, construction costs were divided between the railroad and the Watsonville Mill & Lumber Company. The latter provided the crossties and other wood material required in construction, while Southern Pacific paid for everything else including the wages of the workers. This unequal relationship reflected the railroad's desire to turn a profit on its Santa Cruz Railroad purchase and its hope to displace the South Pacific Coast Railroad monopoly on seasonal tourist travel.

Construction on the track from Aptos to the Augmentation was relatively easy. Today, the route primarily follows the Aptos Creek Fire Road, with minor diversions to address changes in geography and different bridge locations. After passing through Frederick Hihn's property, with the right-of-way fenced on either side, the right-of-way reached its first obstacle, Mangels Gulch, where a 188-foot-long bridge was required. Four cuts were made between the gulch and the next bridge—the first measured 100 feet, followed by a 25-foot cut and two 50-foot cuts. The first bridge across Aptos Creek was located approximately 1.8 miles from Aptos and was just upstream of the modern steel vehicular bridge that crosses the creek. After passing through three more cuts in rapid succession—measuring 240 feet, 75 feet, and 180 feet respectively—the railroad entered Tract 8 of the Augmentation.[127]

Frederick Hihn's mill opens on Trout Gulch

During the two years that the Watsonville Mill & Lumber Company mobilized its resources and connections to begin harvesting timber in the Augmentation, Frederick Hihn was not sitting idle. Indeed, he acted decisively to ensure that he was the first to produce and sell lumber out of Aptos Station. Hihn owned substantial timberland along Trout Gulch and Valencia Creek. To avoid the necessity of building a railroad, as the Watsonville Mill & Lumber Company was doing, he decided instead to build his mill just outside of Aptos near the bottom of Trout Gulch. He

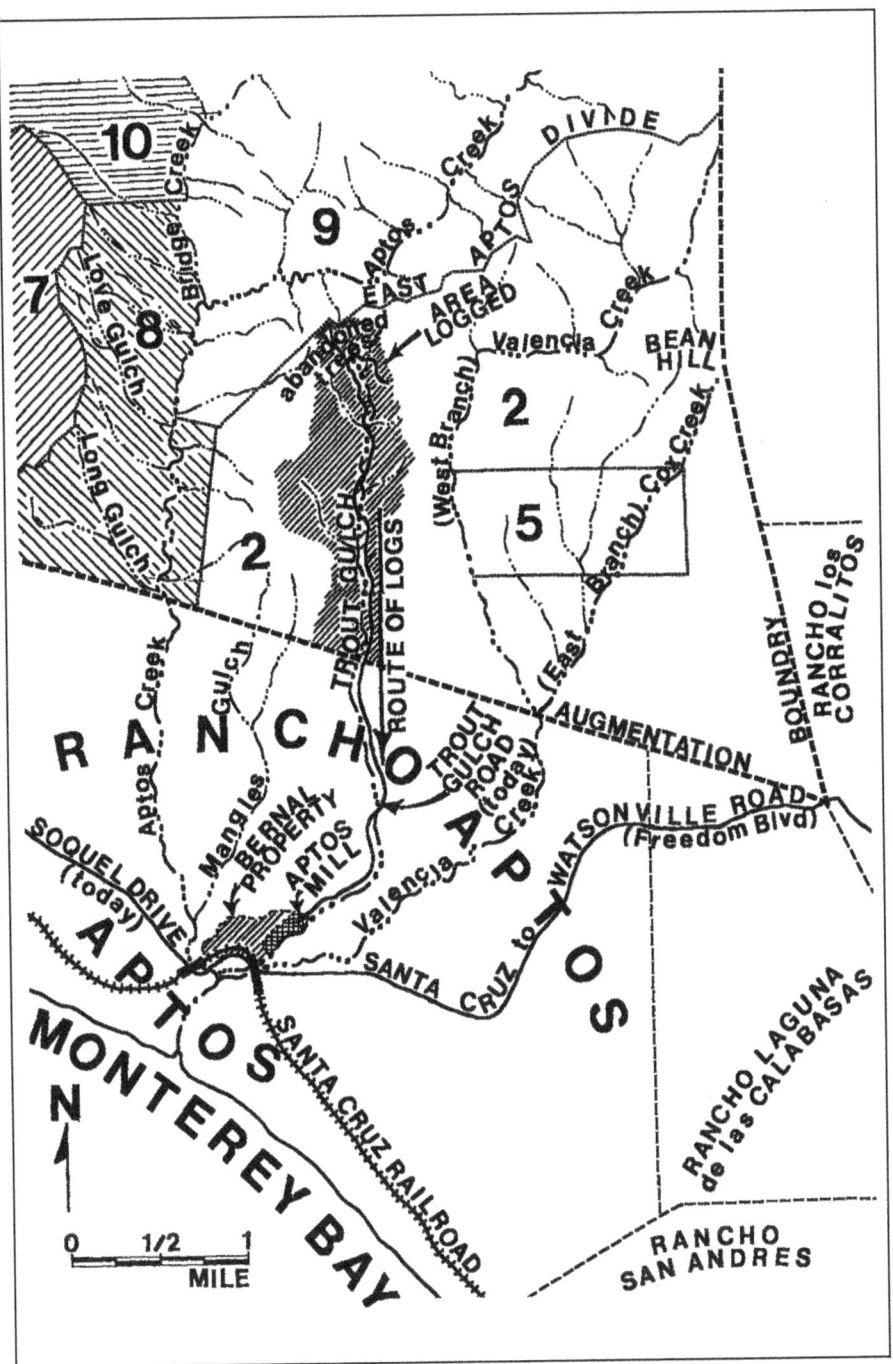

FIGURE 4.4 LOCATION OF HIHN'S TROUT GULCH MILL AND TIMBER TRACT

had purchased this land from the Bernal family in 1875 and it gave him a prime location for such an operation. The mill opened on May 23, 1883. It placed him within direct contact with the Santa Cruz Railroad at Aptos Station, from which spurs were extended to his lumber yard located on land a block from the County Road (Soquel Drive). The timber was a little more difficult to deliver to the mill, but skid roads and mule- and horse-drawn wagons were capable of delivering most of the cut logs to the millpond without encountering substantial difficulties.

A month after the mill opened, the *Surf* reported that:

> *This, the latest enterprise of Mr. F. A. Hihn, is now fully completed, with all the appurtenances thereto, which include cook house, stables, etc., besides the mill proper. The mill has been cutting lumber since May 23d, but the finishing touches have only recently been completed. The modern steam saw mill is a complex affair, as compared with the old water power mills, where a straight perpendicular saw grated its way leisurely through a log, and the 'mill hands' took a fresh quid of tobacco and told a story while the operation was in progress.*
>
> *The Aptos mill has been constructed by Mr. F. W. Cook who has introduced all the latest improvements in saw mill machinery, including the automatic cable feed and a double feed on edger, the latter an invention of his own. Practical mill men pronounce the mill to be the most complete and best arranged of any in the county and it is easy for the observer to perceive that it 'works to a charm' in every detail. Considerable of the machinery from the old sugar-beet works has been utilized in its construction. The mill will be under the management of Mr. Cook, and has a capacity of between thirty and forty thousand feet of lumber per day.*

With his mill operating at full capacity and work on the Watsonville Mill & Lumber Company mill on Aptos Creek not even begun, Hihn suddenly found himself in a position of power and influence within the Santa Cruz County lumber industry.[128]

Agreement between Frederick Hihn and the Watsonville Mill & Lumber Company reached concerning delivery of lumber from Hihn's Aptos Mill

Construction of the railroad stretched the resources of the Watsonville Mill & Lumber Company thin and by June 1, 1883, it was clear that it would not be able to meet its contractual obligations to its customers. With the mills in Eureka Canyon running at full capacity, the lumber firm turned to Frederick Hihn to meet demand. Hihn agreed to sell to the company 200,000 board feet of lumber each month through March 1884, with transportation charges also paid for by the Watsonville company. The only demand Hihn made was that all shipments were carried over the Santa Cruz Railroad line. Through this agreement, Hihn became the primary lumber supplier for his chief competitor, a strange relationship necessitated by construction delays and rapidly depleting timber stocks along Corralitos Creek.[129]

Loma Prieta Railroad enters the Augmentation

By June 1883, construction on the Loma Prieta Railroad had reached Tract 8 at the southern boundary of the Augmentation, 2.1 miles north of Aptos. After crossing Aptos Creek and passing through three cuts, the grading crews reached Long Gulch, which today is marked by the West Ride trailhead in the Forest of Nisene Marks State Park. Graders did not bridge the gulch but rather created their first substantial fill over it after installing a 40-foot-long wooden culvert beneath the right-of-way. Slightly to the north of the gulch, the railroad reached the midway point of the line, marked today by the Mary Easton Picnic Area.

On August 22, the editor-in-chief of the *Sacramento Bee*, J. M. Hawkins, wrote a story for the *Surf* detailing his vacation in the hills above Aptos earlier that month:

>*NEW MOUNTAIN RAILROAD.*
>———
>*Beautiful Scenery About Aptos—*
>*A Magnificent Forest to be Cut Down.*

1883 — The Reign of the Lumber Barons

*The New Road Nearly Completed—
Rumors of the Sale of the Town, Etc., Etc.*

The thousands of people who have enjoyed the sea breezes and the playful surf at Santa Cruz, have also paid a visit to the forest monarchs that tower aloft at Big Tree Station, and driven over the narrow road that leads from the grove to Santa Cruz. It is a charming place, and all about are beautiful ferns and mountain flora. The drive, though not without danger, is a glorious one because of the beautiful scenery. But the grove is about to have a rival claimant for the admiration of the people who got to the seaside. The new claimant lies in the mountains near Aptos, a station eight miles from Santa Cruz, on the narrow-gauge railroad leading to Watsonville or Pajaro, and connecting there with the broad-gauge Southern Pacific line from San Francisco to Monterey—by San Jose. For many years an immense business has been carried on about Watsonville, which has been a supply station for ties, fence posts, and redwood lumber generally, but, to some extent, the timber there has become exhausted and it is necessary to operate upon other forests. The finest one in the State lies along Aptos creek, five or six miles from Aptos, and belongs to the Watsonville Mill and Lumber Company. But the

PACIFIC IMPROVEMENT COMPANY

Or in other words Stanford, Crocker and others of the railroad men, also have an interest in the forest, or at least in opening it up. There are certainly two objects in view. One is to furnish transportation for the lumber which could not be marketed without a railroad up through the mountain canyons. Another is to afford a delightful place for excursions and picnicking parties from Santa Cruz, Monterey, and San Jose. The narrow gauge road from Santa Cruz to Pajaro belongs to the Southern Pacific and is about twenty-one miles long. This is to be changed to the standard gauge within two months, the work having already been commenced under direction of W. F. Knox, of this city. When this is done trains can run from the new forests and transport the lumber to all places and take supplies direct to the south where great quantities are used by the railroad company. The narrow gauge has but little rolling stock, and when the gauge is changed the engines and cars will be sent to be used on a new road in Mexico. Trains can then run from Santa Cruz and Monterey to the forest, which is about twelve miles from the former and forty from the latter. The South Pacific Coast road now gets all of the patronage of the people who go out to see the monarchs and will continue to receive it, the only opposition being the free stage road over the mountains. But this new road will furnish another place of interest to visitors, and doubtless a popular one. It costs but fifty cents to go from Santa Cruz to the Big Trees and return, and the fare to the new resort will not be greater. It is also reported, but whether correctly we cannot say, that the railroad people have purchased nearly all of

THE TOWN OF APTOS,

Which can easily be made a delightful resort, and a rival of Santa Cruz. If it be true that such a transfer has taken place, the town will, ere long, be built up as a feeder for the road. Several months ago, Mr. Knox received orders to construct the road from Aptos to a certain place in the forest. Engineers were long engaged in selecting the route, because it is a precipitous one and has many curves and cuts, so many and so extensive as to make the work difficult, and to require an immense expenditure of money. The place first selected for the terminus is the first spot level and large enough for a sawmill, after the forest is reached, and is five miles from Aptos. It has been determined to extend the road one mile to another level mill site at the foot of a large mountain. At the first site two hundred million feet of redwood lumber can be easily placed at the mill, and more than that amount will be sawed at the second mill. A large force of engineers are now at work locating and determining the curves. The grading for the first five miles has been nearly completed. The track has been laid two miles and a half from Aptos and the construction train runs that far.

TWO HUNDRED CHINESE GRADERS

Are employed. The choppers are Swedes. Cars were the

only vehicles that could be used in the work. Two hundred feet from Aptos the road starts up the narrow canyon of Aptos creek and pursues a winding route. The grade is about 75 feet to the mile, the maximum not over 100 feet, and the five mile terminus is only 300 feet above Aptos. The road was difficult of construction, because it had to be made on the side of the canyon. The first carts had to be hauled up by ropes, and even sure-footed mules could not find ways to get up until paths were dug for them. In many places the road-bed is from fifty to a hundred feet above the creek. There are various places where cuts sixty feet deep have been blasted in the rocky mountains and the sides have been dug out at other places in the sharpest curves. It was impossible to avoid curves by making fills, because to do so the base would have been made so broad that the creek would be dammed completely in times of low water, but when torrents came the filling would be swept away like trash. Down the sides of the canyon pour several smaller streams, over which culverts had to be made. All of these streams abound in mountain trout, and Aptos creek, above the railroad route, is especially blessed with them. The workers had to do a great deal of blasting in the rocks, and thousands of tons of powder were used to clear the route of stumps. At places the trees are so close together that a person may walk over several acres of ground and be

UNABLE TO SEE THE SUN

through the dense mass of branches and foliage above. The trees average six or eight feet in diameter, and some of them are even ten feet thick. The stumps were removed by the use of black powder after an opening had been made below by the use of a half dozen giant powder cartridges. Under the largest stumps eight or ten kegs of powder were exploded, and the fractured pieces left their anchorings and flew away up and down the canyon, large pieces sometimes falling a quarter of a mile away. The noise made by blasting was terrific. Though the work was dangerous, there were but few accidents. All through the redwood forests are oak trees almost limbless, from six to ten inches in circumference and from sixty to eighty feet in height, the bark of which is worth $14 per cord. The Swedes are the choppers engaged in felling trees throughout that section, peeling the bark off in pieces as large around as the tree, and four feet long. Large teams haul the bark down to the tanneries. So far the bark of this forest has not been molested, but in the mountains around Santa Cruz the business is carried on extensively and has proven very profitable. The logs above the new road bed will be lowered on.

"SKID ROADS."

These are made by digging a slope and laying thereon securely tied at intervals of three feet, round sticks of oak, in the center of which a gap or notch is cut about large enough to let a log slide over them continuously without rolling., to the mill below. Sometimes a dozen logs are anchored together and follow one another down the "skids" like the cars of a train. In some places they are hauled down by mules, but at others the "skids" are greased and the logs sometimes go thundering down to the canyons. The writer, recently, when four miles out on the Santa Cruz bay, heard the noise of the giants precipitating themselves to the level far below where they had reared their heads aloft. The waste of the trees, cut for the mill will be chopped or sawed into sizes convenient for engines, stoves, and fire places. The trees that grow in the canyon below the bed of the railroad, and the location of the mill will also, in time, be used. Many of the logs can be raised in sections by means of cables and donkey engines, set upon the mountain side. Portable shingle mills will also be located down in the canyon, and assist in disposing of the timber. Tramways and cars with mules for motive power, will also be constructed at needed places to haul up the wood and shingles to be loaded and sent out away from the fastnesses, where, for thousands of years, the grand trees have been growing, regardless of their future conquest and destruction. A good authority says that were all the trees felled, cut into cordwood, and piled upon the space occupied by the forest, every foot of the ground would be covered eight feet deep. But the noble forest must be sacrificed to the needs of the world. Self-interest will prompt the owners

> *to fell only the larger trees, and leave the others to grow for use in years to come.*

Hawkins mentions several things in his commentary worth expanding upon. The first mill he discusses—later to be named Monte Vista—was located on Aptos Creek about 1.5 miles upstream on the Aptos Creek Trail. The second mill he talks about was never built at the location he states, but a smaller mill three miles north of Monte Vista was eventually constructed. Meanwhile, Hawkins' estimate that well over 400 million board feet of timber would be cut on Tract 9 is a gross exaggeration, although probably through no fault of his own. Approximately 246 million board feet of lumber were eventually cut on the property.

Construction of the line north of the half-way point was more difficult. Two cuts were required measuring 270 and 150 feet in length. Following this, a 135-foot-long bridge was needed to span an unnamed gully. Further along, a 260-foot-long cut was required at a point just beyond the current site of the Porter Family Picnic Area. A 195-foot-long bridge then followed to span another unnamed gully, after which a 180-foot cut completed the road to Love Gulch at the 3.0 mile marker. Up to this point, the route followed the current Aptos Creek Fire Road, but at Love Gulch it continued along the Loma Prieta Grade Trail.

At the time, the gulch was unnamed. It was later named Love Gulch around 1890 after an employee of the Loma Prieta Lumber Company named John Love, who worked as a trimmer for the nearby mill. Where the modern trail takes a brief detour up the gulch, the railroad built a bridge of 95 feet. No further bridges or cuts were required for the next 0.6 miles until the route reached Aptos Creek again in front of the modern Porter House sign. Here, the railroad crossed the creek over a 210-foot-long bridge, the northeastern end of which marked the railroad's entry into Tract 9.

Bert Stoodley, future secretary for the Loma Prieta Lumber Company, recounted in an interview: "after crossing Aptos on a high bridge, it crossed a rather broad flat area in a curve of the creek where the banks fall away vertically for 50 to 60 feet to the creek bottom. A beautiful fringe of trees grew along the margins of the flat and it was here that the Loma Prieta Lumber Company would soon decide to build their little town." Before then, though, Mr. Partridge established a worker village here so his bridge crews would not have to travel all the way from Aptos to work on the railroad line. His workers built several cabins on the site, and these became the first buildings in the future village of Loma Prieta.

The sixth bridge along the Loma Prieta Railroad was completed in August 1883 and bridge-building then paused for grading crews to prepare the final 1.7 miles of track. Partridge used the opportunity to take local reporters on a tour of the first four miles of the line, up to the site of the seventh unconstructed bridge. The *Surf* reported on September 18:

UP THE APTOS.

———

A Forest Paradise Before Its Fall—
The New Lumber Entrepot.

———

A RAMBLE OVER THE NEW RAILROAD.

———

Mementoes of Primeval Days—
Millions for the Lumbermen,
but a Farewell to Fish and Game—
Progress of the Work of Construction.

———

Early in the week, ere it was yet Monday, representatives of the Surf *were sent out to pedestrianate and explore the region of the new railroad up the Aptos Creek. For the past few years Aptos has been a synonym for solitude. Since the closing of the Spreckels' hotel the pulses of its life have been stagnant, save from the incursion of an occasional picnic party and a random passerby. But the incorporation of the Aptos & Loma Prieta R. R. imparted new elixer to the little burg, and now at the Live Oak Hotel and at Arana's is a scene of inspiriting activity. Prospects of the re-opening of the big hotel, and of the enormous lumber traffic that is coming down the canyon, is giving an impetus to everybody. People here talk freely of the erection by the company of a summer hotel in the redwoods, altho' its site is not yet apparent. The Aptos & Loma Prieta R. R. company is but one of many aliases of the Southern Pacific R.*

R. company, but under this name its operations consist of a line of five miles in extent from its junction with the Santa Cruz line at Aptos to the base of the Loma Prieta mountain. With a sharp curve the line leads off from the Santa Cruz road towards the canyon of the Aptos Creek, which it soon enters and follows the stream in close companionship to its destination. To the unpracticed eye there is a few hundred yards near the beginning that appears to be in a straight line, but we apologize to the survey if this is not true. The road soon departs from all semblance of directness, and proceeds up the canyon in a

SERIES OF CURVES

Which would tax the geometric knowledge of any, but an engineer to define. We have followed the devious course of many a Santa Cruz mountain brook with rod and line, but confess the Aptos to be the most crookedest of them all. Across the Spreckels' track the heavy timber has been removed in earlier days, leaving the desolate scenery that marks the path of the woodsman when not followed by the farmer. Here are some redwood stumps that show that there were "giants in those days" among these forests. There are also some fantastic shapes assumed by these trees in their contest with winds and fires, which attract attention. One of these was appropriately dubbed the "dragon tree" by our explorers. The first culvert crossed challenges notice from the substantial, stay-forever manner in which it is built, and this was found to be no exception to all the work on the road. Two miles up, the road crosses the creek at the site of the old "Ben Nichols mill" destroyed by fire years ago. Here a hydraulic ram supplies a water tank. Soon after the primal forest is entered, which never resounded with the axe. Its solitudes were never broken, save with the occasional crack of the sportsman's rifle, until the canyon reverberated with the shrill tones of the "Betsy Jane." [*The construction engine.]

The grading, as would be expected, is a succession of cuts and fills, a point cut through here, and a chasm filled there, closely following the bed of the stream at a moderate altitude above, so as to be out of reach of midwinter freshets. It will *reveal to the traveler the grandeur of the native forest, with its monumental trees, crystalline stream, and invigorating atmosphere, but lacks the sublimity (and the spice of danger which suggests itself) in the San Lorenzo canyon.*

GRAVEN IN STONE.

The picks of the graders on this road have made many revelations of the mysterious workings of Nature in her pre-natal pangs "before the mountains were brought forth." In several cuts wide strata of petrified sea shells are found, in some places taking the form of amorphous rock, and in others simply crumbling sand-stone. These petrifactions consist mainly of the domicils of the defunct clams, yet a variety of other shell formations abound and our prospectors secured several specimens of spiral shape. One day last week a petrified turtle was discovered, but in blasting out the rock it was destroyed. Perhaps the most interesting of these fossils are the birds' eggs which have been quite numerous. These vary in size from that of a pigeon's egg to specimens six inches in length, but all perfect in form. On being broken a different formation is revealed in the yolk and in the "white." Carefully prepared specimens of these are to be forwarded, by Mr. Partridge, the master bridge builder of the road, to the Smithsonian Institute in Washington.

Four miles from Aptos the third bridge is reached, and here the work of the tracklayers is suspended for the present. Here are the "camps" of the mechanics and foremen, a rustic village of no mean pretensions. A hearty hospitality was extended by Mr. Partridge, the bridge builder, to the press pioneers, who partook of a meal that in quantity or quality of the viands, allowed no criticism. It embraced literally the "best the market affords." In passing we are impelled to give expression to the astonishment that is always excited by a visit to a camp like this, when the amount of real comfort is considered which they afford. An upturned stump combines fireplace, mantel and chimney, and the rustic chairs, upholstered by a hatchet, are as restful as the plush-covered appliances of socalled refined life. A Sabbath quiet reigned about the camp. Some were seeking rest-day solace in the pipe of peace, others reading books and papers. From furtive glances at the literature about, we suspect Peck's Bad Boy is a powerful rival of the Bible for campers perusal.

THE LAST MILE.

Beyond this point the road will extend one mile, which has been surveyed, the pathway cleared of trees, and the work of grading commenced. There is a tendency on this mile to steeper grades, and three bridges will be required on this mile, making six in all. The first three, span 210 feet each. At one place on this last mile the road crosses the creek twice and a sharp promentory, all to be covered by one bridge 280 feet in length. The bridges are all made at the company's shops in Oakland, the piers and approaches only being constructed on the spot. Here are two camps of Chinese graders, one of which was being moved from a lower station at the time of visit. The Chinamen know how to make the most of a holiday, and were having a very hilarious time for such sad-faced heathens as they usually appear.

At the terminus of the road is to be located one of those monstrous timber slayers, a modern saw-mill. To-day, the grey squirrels are sporting in the tree-tops, and the speckled trout darting about in the pure waters of the Aptos. To-morrow, the riven bodies of these forest trees will be lumber, and the brook a pool of liquid poison. This is progress. The timber here is mostly redwood, with a per centage of fir and tan-bark oak. The computations of the lumbermen as to the amount "in sight" in this canyon and its tributaries are stupendous, and run into incomprehensible millions. Suffice it to say it will the uninterrupted work of a generation to transform these forests into merchantable lumber.

The climber, who penetrates a short distance beyond the railroad terminus, will be rewarded by a view through the opening of the Loma Prieta, rising in a majestic altitude not seen from any other point of observation. In contemplation of the scene the mind pauses—the consciousness of a sublime silence is borne in upon the soul by every sense. The stillness brings a reverential hush to the spirit; the mighty forest monarchs are lifting their heads hundreds of feet towards the heavens, each a spire from this leafy temple; the atmosphere rises with the sweetness of incense towards the blue vault above; every instinct of nature impels to worship, every impulse of the soul inclines to adoration.[130]

Land transfer from Frederick Hihn to the Loma Prieta Railroad concerning land in Aptos

With the explosion of industrial activity in Aptos, the Southern Pacific Railroad needed additional land in the area for industrial sidings, spurs, and a wye. On October 10, 1883, the company purchased from Frederick Hihn several acres from the formal Bernal family estate. Today, this area is occupied by the commercial buildings on the north side of Soquel Drive near the Bayview Hotel.[131]

Santa Cruz Railroad converted to standard-gauge

After over two years of repairs, rehabilitation, and upgrades, the Southern Pacific Railroad finally completed the standard-gauging of the Santa Cruz Railroad, with the first standard-gauge locomotive arriving in Santa Cruz on November 11, 1883. The *Santa Cruz Courier* reported:

> *The "Jupiter," by a long and loud whistle, as it crossed the trestle at the mouth of the river, Saturday evening, at 8:30 o'clock, bade farewell to the city to which it had been a daily visitor for the past six years. Behind this narrow-gauge Jumbo, with engineer Mynatt in charge, followed an express car, coach and smoker. Faithfully the men worked to get the track ready for the broad-gauge train Sunday, after clearing up the debris of the pioneer railroad to this city. At noon the depot platform and surrounding houses and steps were crowded by men, women and children. At half past twelve the last spike was driven by A. C. Stone and everything seemed ready for the train to make its appearance.... The crowd continues to gather, and as the clock in the railroad office points to two, a strange*

whistle is heard in the distance. Then those on the top of the hill cry out—"HERE SHE COMES!" Smoke is seen curling up in the air and then engine No. 14, (The Red Eagle) with the cars of the S.P.R.R. is in sight. It crossed Locust street safely, and as the curve is reached it stops. Busy hands with hammers are soon at work, and the locomotive is surrounded by the curious in large numbers. The signal is given that all work is ready, and the engine creeps cautiously forward to test the track; the freight cars are switched off; the turntable is tried and found to be in perfect order; the locomotive is coupled on, and at half past two Conductor Garcelon says "all aboard," and the broad gauge starts on her first trip from this city.

The completion of the line did not yet mean the end of the Southern Pacific Railroad's use of narrow-gauge trains in the county. 'Betsy Jane' would continue to be used on the Loma Prieta Railroad as a construction locomotive until the line was completed to the 5.0-mile mark.[132]

Loma Prieta Railroad operational to Tract 9 in the Augmentation

On November 13, 1883, the first 3.7 miles of the Loma Prieta Railroad opened to commercial traffic. For several weeks prior to this, crews had worked to convert the line to standard gauge to match the Santa Cruz Railroad's recently completed gauge. The mile marker location was only a few dozen yards into Tract 9 in the Augmentation but was the site of the worker camp and the future village of Loma Prieta. With the initial work on the line completed, W. F. Knox returned to Sacramento and left the continued work on the line to Mr. Partridge.[133]

Loma Prieta Lumber Company incorporates

The day after the Loma Prieta Railroad opened to traffic, the directors of the Watsonville Mill & Lumber Company incorporated the Loma Prieta Lumber Company on November 14, 1883. The purpose of this wholly

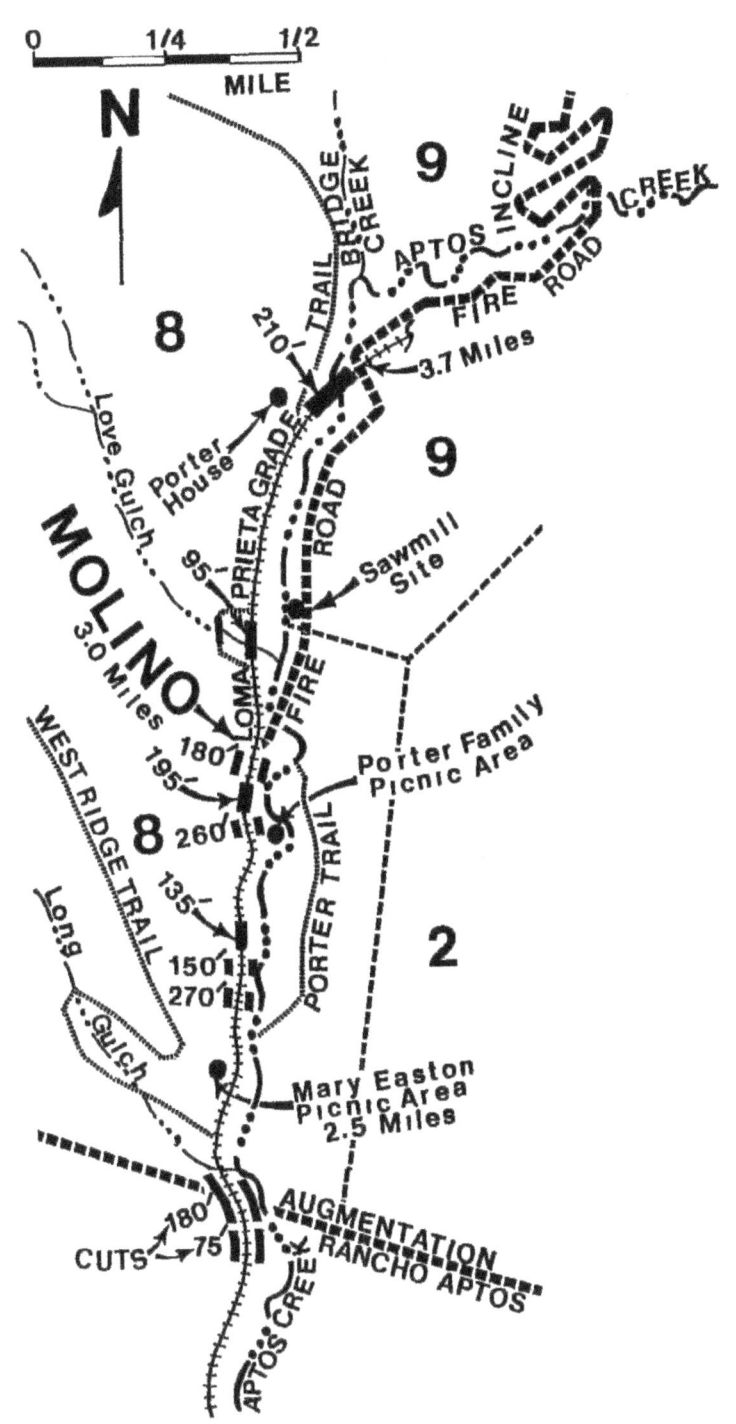

FIGURE 4.5 ROUTE OF THE LOMA PRIETA RAILROAD TO MILE MARKER 3.7

owned subsidiary was to harvest, distribute, and sell timber products produced from its mills in the Augmentation. Two weeks later, on November 26, the Watsonville company announced that it was providing the opportunity for its directors and backers, such a John Porter and William Dougherty, to purchase Loma Prieta Lumber Company stock. The company hoped to raise $500,000 through its first sales, with each stock certificate valued at $100. Most of its initial stocks were purchased by Porter, Dougherty, Alvin Sanborn, Charles Ford, A. C. Bassett, N. T. Smith, Thomas Bishop, and J. A. Linscott, although Linscott shortly after divested himself of his stocks. The actual amount earned through this first offering is unknown, but Bert Stoodley later stated that a record he had found early in his career suggested only $187,000 was gathered at the time.

Not long after incorporation, Warren Porter was hired to serve as head bookkeeper for the Loma Prieta Lumber Company, although he retained his position with the Bank of Watsonville. He operated out of the Watsonville Mill & Lumber Company offices in Watsonville until 1887, when he moved into a new home on Tract 8 in the Augmentation across from the village of Loma Prieta.[134]

Land transfer from Claus Spreckels to Claus Mangels concerning land in Rancho Aptos

On January 4, 1884, Claus Spreckels sold 274 acres of his land in Rancho Aptos to his brother-in-law, Claus Mangels. He would later nearly double the grant when he gifted an additional 266.5 acres. Some of this land included the 100-foot-wide easement that the Pacific Improvement Company had purchased for use by the Loma Prieta Railroad. The land he received from Spreckels soon became known as Mangels Gulch, although he only ever owned the upper portion of the gulch.[135]

Building and Business Review for 1883 published in the *Surf*

On January 5, 1884, the *Surf* published its annual review of building and business activities in Santa Cruz County. Of particular note for the 1883 year is its discussion of the Loma Prieta Railroad and the development of the Aptos area in general. Much of the original text is copied directly from the report of August 3, 1883, but the end of the article adds:

> There were six bridges on the line, three of them of a uniform span of 210 feet. Sites for two lumber mills have been selected, and are now being erected by the Loma Prieta Lumber Co., the successors in interest to the Watsonville Mill and Lumber Company, whose operations have been so extensive for many years in the lower part of the county. The extent of the timber made accessible by this road is almost beyond computation and must afford employment for great numbers of men for many years to come. At places the trees are so close together that a person may walk over several acres of ground and be unable to see the sun through the dense mass of branches and foliage above. The trees average six or eight feet in diameter, and some of them are even ten feet thick. A good authority says that were all the trees felled, cut into cord-wood, and piled upon the space occupied by the forest, every foot of the ground would be covered eight feet deep. At the site of the first mill it is estimated that two hundred million feet of redwood lumber can be easily placed at the mill, and more than that amount will be sawed at the second mill. Portable shingle mills will also be located down in the canyon, and assist in disposing of the timber.
>
> Aside from this enormous development of the lumber industry, the road presages the revival of the Aptos region as a resort, and taken altogether is one of the most important developments of the year in the county. The amount expended by the Southern Pacific Railroad on both lines within the county in 1883, must aggregate in the vicinity of a quarter of a million dollars.[136]

Land transfer from Thomas Fallon to Timothy Hopkins concerning Tract 8 in the Augmentation and land in Eureka Canyon

On January 14, 1884, an ailing Thomas Fallon sold 432 acres of land in

Eureka Canyon to Timothy Hopkins. The land consisted of two parcels located just to the east of the Augmentation and included Buzzard Lagoon. It was accessible via a mill road built by D. A. Rider & Son at the beginning of the 1880s. At the same time, he also sold to Hopkins all 1,167 acres of Tract 8 in the Augmentation. As part of this latter transaction, Hopkins assumed all obligations Fallon had toward the Loma Prieta Railroad regarding its right-of-way through his land. Hopkins purchased this land on behalf of his adopted mother, Mary Hopkins, to whom he transferred both properties on February 21.

The life and legacy of the Hopkins family is one that has been made unnecessarily confusing by Estelle Latta's book *Controversial Mark Hopkins*, published in 1953. In it, she contends that Mark Hopkins, a member of the Central Pacific's Big Four, has been heavily conflated with another Mark Hopkins who resided in Sacramento in the 1860s, and that the former was never married to his wife and first cousin, Mary Sherwood. Overwhelming evidence has now revealed the flaws and leaps in logic in Latta's arguments.

In reality, Sherwood was a loving and loyal wife to Hopkins and the two worked together to build a life of luxury together in Sacramento and San Francisco until Hopkins' death in 1878. The two had married relatively late in life and never had any children together. However, they helped raise the son of their housekeeper, Timothy Nolan, and Sherwood adopted him as an adult in 1879. With a vacancy in Southern Pacific management left by the death of Hopkins, Nolan was quickly appointed treasurer of the railroad company, although he did so as an agent of his mother. Timothy Hopkins, as he was now called, married Sherwood's niece, Mary Kellogg Crittenden, in 1882, firmly imbedding him within his new family.

Sherwood remained a major shareholder in the Central and Southern Pacific Railroads and Timothy used his position as treasurer to advance their agenda. This is likely why he purchased and then transferred land within and just outside the Augmentation. Had Fallon died before selling his land to the railroad, it is highly possible that it would have passed to Carmel Fallon or one of their children, potentially causing complications regarding the right-of-way that passed directly through Tract 8. Control of the land was also vital to ensure the successful construction of a redwood resort on the southern edge of the Augmentation. Thus, with the properly

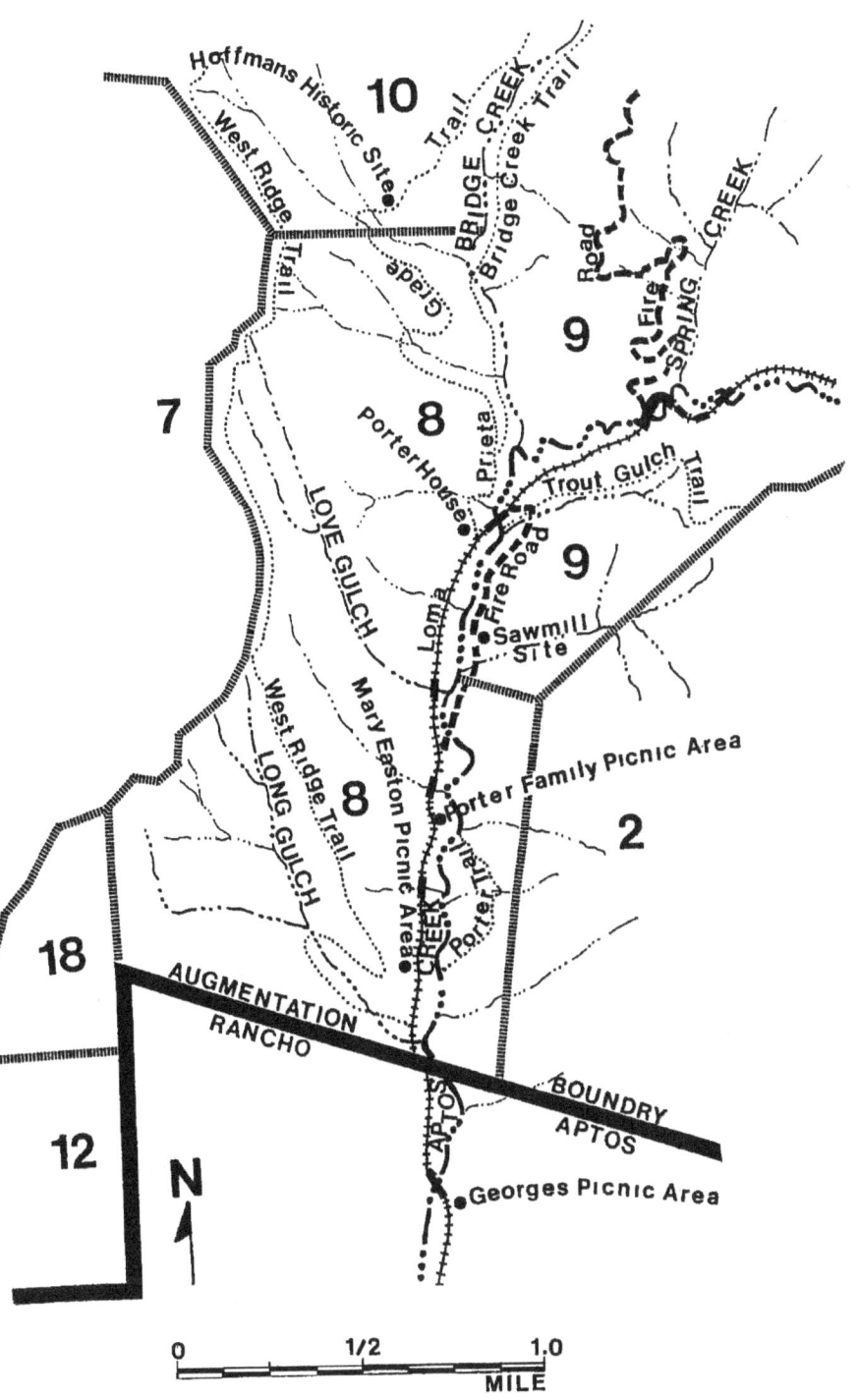

FIGURE 4.6 TRACT 8 IN THE AUGMENTATION

safely in the hands of the Hopkins family, the railroad's continued interest in the Augmentation was assured.[137]

Santa Cruz and Loma Prieta Railroads consolidated into the Pajaro & Santa Cruz Railroad Company

Consolidation was a way of life for railroads in the nineteenth century, and the Big Four had learned early that as soon as progress on a subsidiary had progressed satisfactorily and the liability was sufficiently reduced, it was more fiscally responsible to consolidate. For the Santa Cruz and Loma Prieta Railroads, both wholly owned subsidiaries of the Southern Pacific Railroad, the conditions were finally right on March 6, 1884. Both lines had been standard-gauged the previous year and construction of the Loma Prieta line was progressing gradually on land partially owned by the railroad. Furthermore, the easement problems regarding the approach to Tract 9 in the Augmentation had been resolved via the purchase of the land by the Hopkins. Thus, Southern Pacific management finally decided to consolidate the two railroads into a new subsidiary: the Pajaro & Santa Cruz Railroad Company. The two companies retained some semblance of corporate independence for three more months until June 3, when the final documents were signed eliminating their separate existences.[138]

Loma Prieta Branch completed to Monte Vista and mill construction begins

Following months of construction delays owing to winter weather, construction on the final 1.3 miles of track on the Loma Prieta Branch between the construction site and the mill site was completed on March 14, 1884. Undoubtedly, the impending completion of this section was the final motivating factor in the consolidation of the line into the Pajaro & Santa Cruz Railroad the previous week.

The first half of the route from the construction site to the mill was a fairly straightforward path requiring five cuts of 240 feet, 100 feet, 130 feet, 150 feet, and 120 feet. Just beyond the final cut, the construction crews finally encountered their first substantial obstacle along the route. This far

The Luck of Roaring Camp 1884

up the canyon, Aptos Creek followed a serpentine path that became unavoidable for work crews despite their best efforts. Partridge was faced with a 280-foot-long gap with the creek meandering 60 feet below. In order to span the creek, crews installed a bridge that curved almost ninety degrees to the east to cross the creek twice, with piers installed on a promontory on the west bank of the creek to help support the turn. The *Surf* on October 20, 1906, recounted that "a trestle crosses the creek on a curve, at a bend in the stream, making what surgeons would call a 'compound' crossing, the creek flowing easterly and again westerly under the trestle."

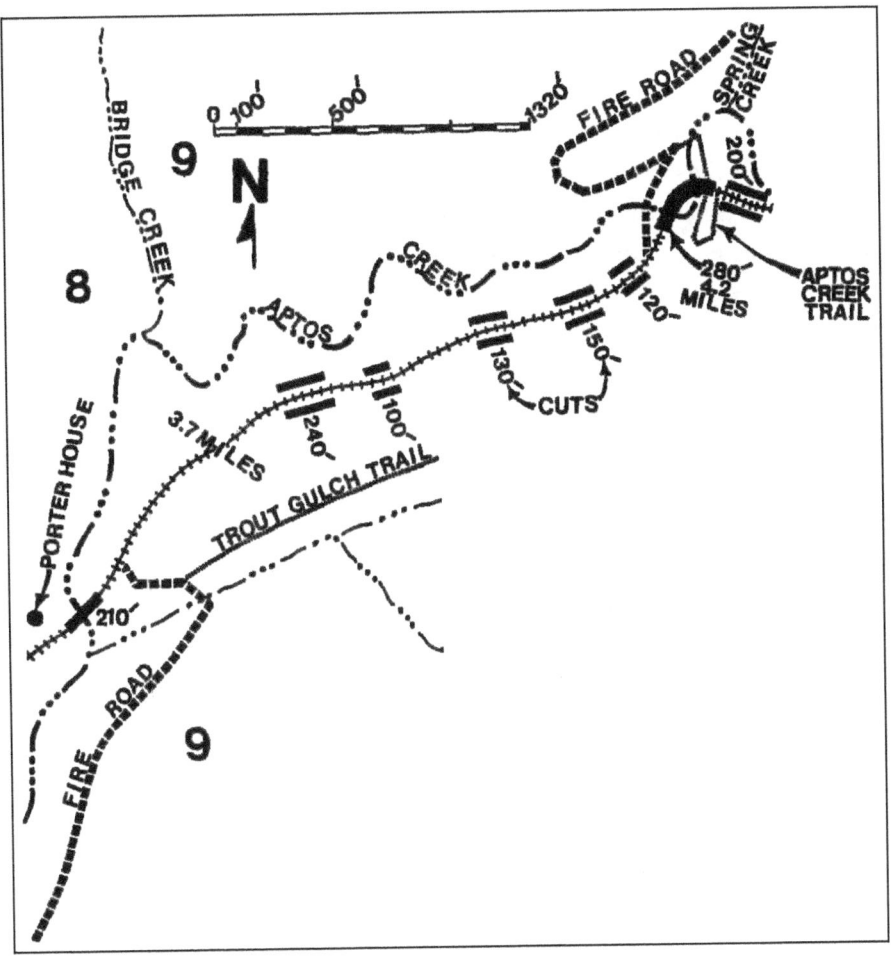

FIGURE 4.7 ROUTE OF THE LOMA PRIETA RAILROAD TO MILE MARKER 4.2

1884 The Reign of the Lumber Barons

Almost immediately beyond this compound bridge, the right-of-way entered a deep 200-foot cut, through which the Aptos Creek Trail passes today. Two short 75-foot-long bridges were then required to cross seasonal streambeds and then the longest cut along the line, measuring 370 feet, was encountered. The northern end of the cut ended at Aptos Creek once again, requiring a 210-foot-long bridge to cross, with a shorter 130-foot-long cut located directly north of it.

The remaining 0.5 miles of the route to the mill site was a much simpler construction project. The tracks ran along the west bank of Aptos Creek along the foot of China Ridge, and only four relatively short bridges measuring 50 feet, 50 feet, 100 feet, and 50 feet—all crossing seasonal streambeds and gullies—were required to reach the end of the line at mile marker 5.0.

As is to be expected, the railroad gradually experienced an increase in elevation the further it approached the end-of-track. The ruling grade for the first 3.7 miles to Tract 9 averaged 67 feet per mile or 1.2%. In contrast, the final 1.3 miles had an average grade of 108 feet per mile or 2%. Neither of these was extraordinary an elevation and they presented few problems for the types of trains that operated in the Augmentation.

With the route completed, construction began immediately on the end-

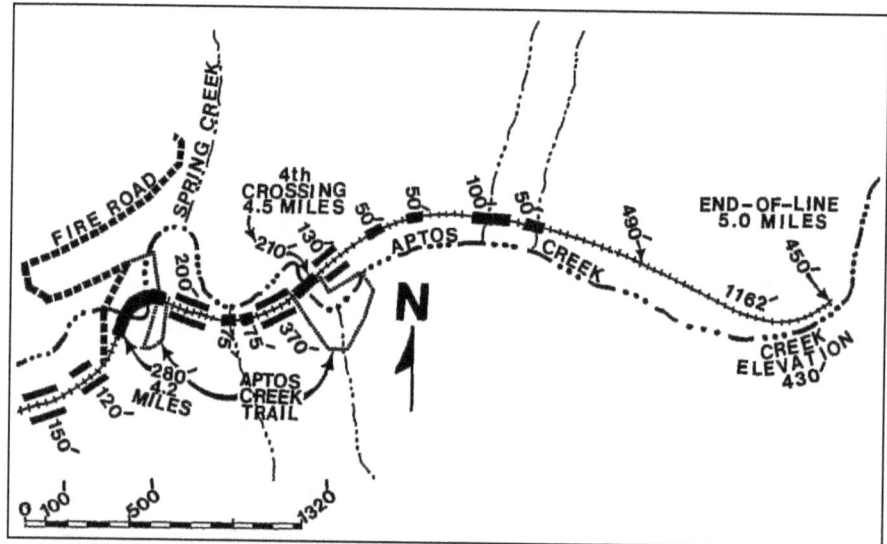

Figure 4.8 Route of the Loma Prieta Railroad to mile marker 5.0

of-track mill that would straddle Aptos Creek from a narrow shelf where the creek shifted its flow from southward to westward. It was here that the railroad encountered its steepest grade—4%—which was required for it to drop the 40 feet from grade level to the elevation of the mill at 450 feet above sea level. The mill, named Monte Vista (Spanish for 'Mountain View'), first fired up its boilers around the beginning of June.

When the mill began production, with its two large headrigs each with its own boiler, it was the largest and most modern lumber mill in the United States, displacing Frederick Hihn's mill, which had briefly held the title. At maximum capacity, the mill could produce 50,000 board feet of lumber daily, although it would rarely achieve this number due to the types of trees cut, the limited size of the millpond, and the capability of the workers. The *Surf* reported on May 13, 1885 that "the outfit was one of the very best, the machinery being high class and costly." The article also noted that the facility included a planing mill, which was unusual for a facility located so

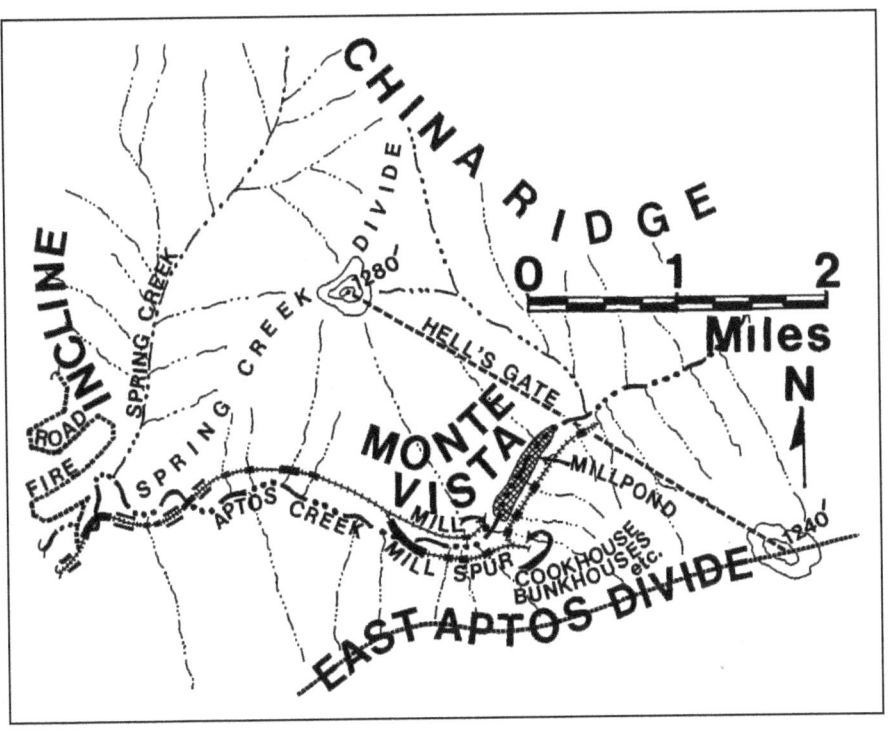

FIGURE 4.9 TRACKAGE IN THE MONTE VISTA MILL AREA

far from a populated area. Over 200 workers lived within the vicinity of the mill in the mill's boarding house or in family cabins located on the hillsides up to a half mile south of the mill. The cookhouse and manager's office were located directly across from the mill on the east bank of the creek.

An early problem the Loma Prieta Lumber Company encountered with this mill was the length of creek bed required for the millpond. Because the canyon was so narrow in this section, the millpond had to extend a good distance upstream from the mill. However, the railroad only accessed the mill from the south, which meant it had no access to the millpond. The solution was to install a track that crossed over to the east bank of Aptos Creek before the steep grade. A long bridge measuring more than 200 feet was required to span the creek here due to the approach angle. Three short bridges then crossed steep gullies, within two of which single-car spurs were installed to collect trees cut from further up the hillsides.

Just beyond the third bridge, the track turned briefly to the east into a relatively flat area where the train could then back up the remaining line beside the millpond. Four more short bridges ran across gullies above the pond before the end of the spur was reached. Logs could be unloaded into the millpond from several locations between these bridges depending on the size of the logs being dumped and the length of the train.

When I first reached and explored this area, the narrow shelves above the site of the millpond were still there to hike. But after the storms of the 1980s, all proof of their existence disappeared. But even earlier, it was impossible to determine how far upstream this spur line went beyond the upper end of the millpond. I would guess that this spur went a good quarter to four-tenths of a mile beyond the sawmill. This would place the end opposite the next major upstream gulch along the canyon's west side, a place that the railroad builders would name "Hell's Gate," because they felt that only the devil himself could have contemplated the continuation of the railroad beyond it.

Even as construction of the railroad to the mill site came to an end, a second operation was underway at the 3.0-mile marker in Tract 8 at a site named Molino (Spanish for 'mill'). The matter of who spearheaded a new shingle mill and narrow-gauge railroad on the east bank of Aptos Creek in Tract 8 remains a mystery. Was it the Hopkins family, who owned the land, or was it the Pacific Improvement Company, which was interested in building a redwood resort somewhere within the property? The novelty of having a redwood resort located directly beside an operating sawmill was surely something that would attract visitors. However, did the recreational value or the lumber output justify the expensive cost of building an internal railroad in exceedingly difficult terrain?

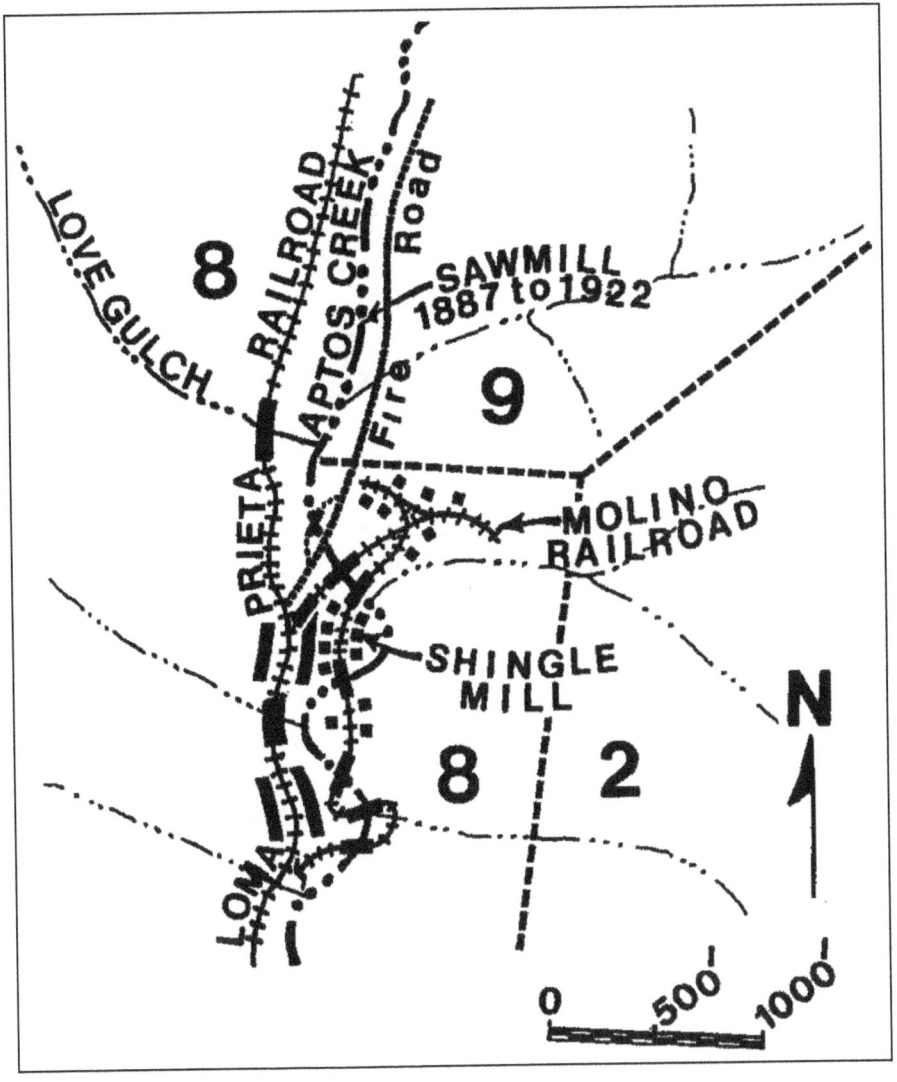

FIGURE 4.10 TRACKAGE IN THE MOLINO SHINGLE MILL AREA

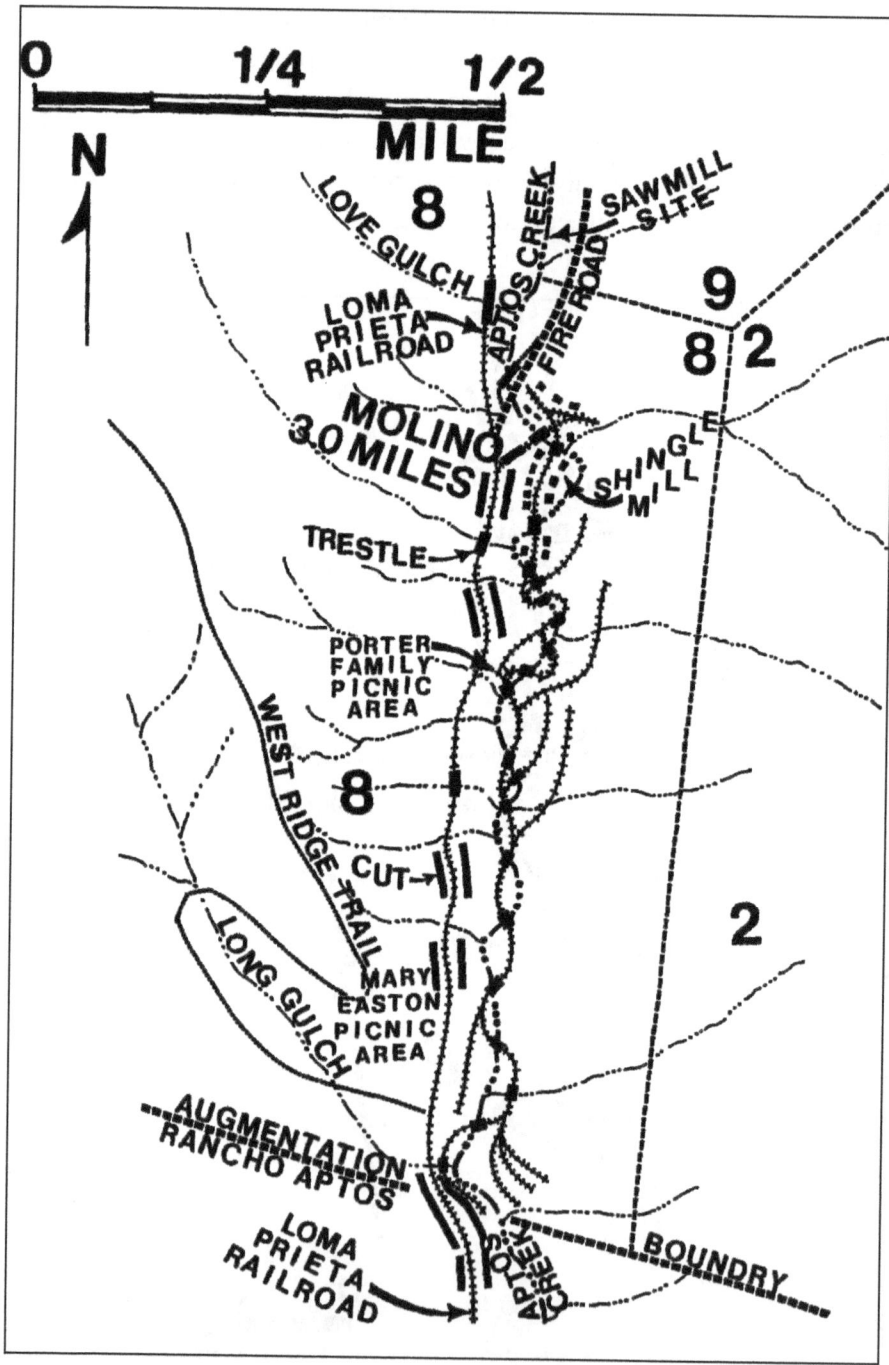

FIGURE 4.11 PRIVATE TRACKAGE SOUTH OF THE MOLINO SHINGLE MILL

Preparation for this new parallel narrow-gauge line began in early 1884 when the main railroad was being standard-gauged. Some of Knox's Chinese laborers were tasked with the job of grading a spur from the cut just north of today's Porter Family Picnic Area to a clearing across Aptos Creek. Meanwhile, Partridge assigned a crew to build a bridge over the creek to access the site. Evidence for this mill is scarce. A photograph taken around 1885 shows the Molino switch with a sign boldly announcing its existence. Three additional photographs exist that show the mill itself. Evidence for the railroad itself is almost entirely anecdotal or derived from my own investigation of the area. However, the right-of-way in many places is clear and there are several remains of bridges still lying in the creek bed just north of the Porter Family Picnic Area.

The narrow-gauge railroad from Molino to the southern boundary of the Augmentation was no straight-forward affair. Two bridges across Aptos Creek were required just to reach the east bank, and then a complex switchback was needed in order to cross the creek a third time at a lower elevation so that the tracks could finally arrive at the mill site. The curves in the switchback were so sharp that no standard-gauge train could have handled them. The track passed directly through the mill site and workers' village on its way south.

As soon as the mill opened, mill crews realized that the steep hillsides to the west, where the main railroad ran, posed an obstacle for getting logs down to the facility. The steepest point proved to be the cut just south of Molino, where even logs hoisted by skylines could not pass over. The solution crews found was to reduce the height of the cut substantially so that logs cabled over from the west could clear it. This indentation is still noticeable, as is a similar indentation on the cut further to the south.

South of the shingle mill and workers' village, the narrow-gauge railroad crossed Aptos Creek for a third time on what would be the start of an odyssey journey to the Augmentation's southern boundary. In under a mile, this little railroad line crossed Aptos Creek at least thirteen more times, crossed two seasonal streams, and built a few more bridges on timber-access spurs. Many of these bridges were between 100 and 150 feet in length, and all but the first two were no more than 15 feet above the level of the creek bed.

I am the first to admit that this description of the Molino shingle mill site and railroad is not accurate on all points. I spent many hours exploring and mapping the mill site and railroad line, and on many occasions I had to rely on guesses and assumptions. I admit to my errors. Therefore, I invite others to explore the mile between Molino and the line's end. But be warned, the storms of 1981-1982 and 1986, plus the heavy rainy winters such as those in the 1997-1998 period, have removed many of the findings I was able to observe. As time passes, future storms will continue to remove many more.

The majority of the larger logs that were harvested south of Molino were brought to this narrow-gauge railroad via skylines, which were able to pass over the Loma Prieta Branch and Aptos Creek without difficulty. Where skylines were not possible, the mill crews relied on oxen and skid roads. Today's Porter Family Picnic Area was originally a log loading facility for this line, where logs brought in via skyline from the west were deposited for loading onto flatcars. As such, the location had at least one spur to park flatcars waiting to be loaded. Further to the south, today's Mary Easton Picnic Area was also a log-loading site where a long spur extended from the narrow-gauge line to run beside the Southern Pacific tracks.[139]

Post Office opens at Loma Prieta

Less than a week after the Loma Prieta Branch was completed, the United States Postal Service opened up an office in the workers' village at the 3.7-mile marker. When the new office opened on March 20, 1884, it went under the name Loma Prieta, a clear reference to the lumber company and railroad, as well as the nearby mountain. The community quickly came to adopt the name, as well.[140]

Agreement between Frederick Hihn and the Watsonville Mill & Lumber Company

Although the new railroad to the Monte Vista mill was now open and the mill itself would open shortly, it would be far too late in the season to satisfy all of the contracts the Watsonville Mill & Lumber Company had pledged to fulfill for 1884. As a result, the company once more approached Frederick Hihn and, on April 1, Hihn agreed to deliver 400,000 board feet of lumber of various grades and types on behalf of his rival. This amount of lumber was twice that of the previous year's contract with Hihn and demonstrates how behind schedule the company was in completing its railroad and mill on Aptos Creek. The agreement included an exclusivity clause restricting Hihn to only sell wood products between April 1, 1884 and March 31, 1885 on behalf of the Loma Prieta Lumber Company, which was a signatory to the agreement.

A Journey to Loma Prieta

On July 16, 1884, a group from the Press Association visited Loma Prieta as part of a tour of the railroads of Santa Cruz County. The *Sentinel* provided a summary of the journey in its July 18 issue:

> *At Aptos the palace car was switched off and left, and the excursionists were put aboard an observation car. With the engine behind them and nothing to obstruct their view they were pushed up the road at a slow speed and over a heavy grade, in two places over a grade of one hundred and twenty feet to the mile.*
>
> *After passing the site of the demolished Nichols shingle-mill, the rails crossing the canyon immediately over the dam, which is in a gorge very narrow, deep and rock-sided, we penetrated the virgin forest. The scene was wild and grand in the extreme, and the air clear and perfectly free of dust. Like a great serpent the road twisted and squirmed through cuts, over trestle-work—in a single instance one trestle crossing the Aptos creek twice—above the flowing waters and along the mountain-side, in some places in the open sun, and in others beneath the shade of great trees. High above on either side were seen logways, wagon roads and pack trails, small mules puffing under large loads of bark coming out*

of the woods. At the shingle-mills there are now 8,000,000 shingles awaiting shipment. The centre of action is at the sawmill, which has been in operation for six weeks. It is turning out from thirty-five to forty thousand feet of lumber per day. From one hundred and fifty to two hundred men are in the employ of the Loma Prieta Co., and only two of them, cooks, are Chinamen. Both steam and cattle are used in delivering logs at the mill. While we were there a steamer, hauling four 4-wheel trucks, on which were loaded ten logs, one monster measuring 7 1/2 x 10 feet across the big end, came puffing into the yard. Superintendent Linscott informed questioners that the average cost of laborers is $2.24 per day and board; that it is expected that the mill will run ten years as now located; that other mills are to be moved to the locality from Corralitos; that the railroad will be extended up the creek by degrees; that they expect to peel two thousand cords of bark the present year; that the timber for milling purposes of the Aptos region will not be exhausted for fifteen or twenty years, and that the timber they are cutting is proving to be very good. As the cars descended the track Mr. Linscott was loudly cheered for the many favors he had extended, and Mr. Bassett, Superintendent of the railroad, who had extended every favor to the excursionists, was stood up against the side of the car by the interviewer. Mr. Bassett said that the Loma Prieta R. R., at present a trifle more than five miles in length, had cost $150,000; that after the rains of last winter it had to practically be rebuilt; that Mr. Crocker built it as a feeder for his main railroads; that they were now in receipt of orders from Philadelphia and Chicago for redwood shingles and redwood lumber; that they expected this demand would grow to large proportions in the East; that redwood lumber from stumps and stump logs was coming largely into demand for furniture and inside house furnishing, and that he hoped that the Loma Prieta R. R. and mills could be kept in operation summer and winter. Mr. Bassett further said that their experience had taught the railroad people that the Santa Cruz redwood is the best timber obtainable for *underground work and bridge covering, and in the matter of fruit and wine he was found to be an enthusiast in favor of the Santa Cruz mountains, having proven his enthusiasm by the purchase of thirty acres of the Fallon home property, high upon the hills, w[h]ere seven acres of vines are now bearing and bringing forth abundantly.*[141]

Alvin Sanborn dies

On September 6, 1884, Alvin Sanborn died following a short illness in Watsonville. The 39-year-old was acting superintendent of the Monte Vista mill and had been instrumental in negotiating the acquisition of Tract 9 from Carmel Fallon and working with the Southern Pacific Railroad in constructing the Loma Prieta line. His funeral was so well attended that it was held in a local skating rink. Following the funeral, a procession of nearly 200 carriages, including representatives from the Watsonville fire companies, the Knights of Honor, and the Ancient Order of United Workmen (AOUW), escorted his casket to the local cemetery.[142]

Aptos mills shut down for the winter

As early winter rains inundated the hills above Aptos in early October 1884, Frederick Hihn and the Loma Prieta Lumber Company shut their mills down for the year. Closing mills for the winter months was required since wet soil made it easy for rocks to become lodged in felled and dragged trees. These rocks could later damage a headrig's saw blades, increasing costs and also making operation of the machinery more dangerous for workers.

While the two mills along Aptos Creek planned to reopen the next year, Hihn used the closure as an opportunity to relocate his mill three miles up Valencia Creek at its confluence with Cox Creek, just within the confines of the Augmentation. His crews erected a 60 by 100 foot sawmill and planned to dam the creek to the north to create a large millpond as soon as the winter weather subsided. All of the machinery to operate the mill would come directly from his former mill at the bottom of Trout Gulch outside Aptos.[143]

Land transfer from the Watsonville Mill & Lumber Company to the Loma Prieta Lumber Company

On the last day of 1884, a deed was signed by representatives of the Watsonville Mill & Lumber Company transferring all of the land in Tract 9 in the Augmentation to the Loma Prieta Lumber Company. This was likely done for legal and fiscal reasons, since it was the latter company that was actually operating within the property, but the deed also transferred all liabilities from the former company to the latter. This helped protect the Watsonville Mill & Lumber Company from risk, but it also largely divested it from the company it had helped found.

A good year expected by all

Great things were on the horizon in the winter of 1884-1885. Redwood fallers were operating across the Augmentation, chopping down trees that would later be brought to the Loma Prieta Lumber Company mill at Monte Vista or to Frederick Hihn's new mill on Valencia Creek. While the Monte Vista, Molino, and Eureka Canyon mills were all quiet during the winter months, Hihn's crews were busy moving equipment and building materials to the confluence of Valencia and Cox Creeks to erect the new facility, scheduled to open in the spring.

Meanwhile, sometime near the beginning of 1885, Thomas Bishop, attorney for the Southern Pacific Railroad, was elected president of the Watsonville Mill & Lumber Company. This change in leadership reflected the degree to which the railroad company maintained an interest in the lumber company's operations in the Augmentation.

The allure of the Santa Cruz Mountains and Aptos area attracted attention from newspapers as far afield as New York, where *The Spirit of the Times* recounted the following, as abridged by the *Sentinel* on June 12, 1885:

> *Aptos is situated on a bluff overlooking the magnificent Bay of Monterey—about eight miles from Santa Cruz, and on the line of the Southern Pacific Railroad. In beauty of location it can hardly be excelled, and as a healthful place of resort it*

is not surpassed by any locality on the Pacific coast. Whether Spanish or Indian, certain knowledge escapes us. Indeed, whether Aptos or Autos, some dispute. But the explanation that Aptos is Indian for the "Meeting of the Waters," satisfies both poetry and history, and may as well stand. Aptos and its immediate vicinity combine more unusual and more varied attractions than any other upon the whole coast. Its climate, by the united testimony of tourists, railroad builders, transient boarders at all seasons, and the oldest residents, comes nearest perfection. Two romantic creeks here meet each other and the sea. Up the beds, along the banks, through the woods or over the flanking hills of either or both of these creeks, fisher, hunter, botanist, geologist, tourist or artist may roam at will, sure to find such varied attraction and rewards as will yield the amplest dividends of solid satisfaction and soundest health. Will you have a splendid surrounding panorama of hill, forest, field, shore, bay and sea? Stand upon the pier's end and it is yours. Will you fish? The pier gives safe and clean accommodation and yields an excellent catch. Will you row? The smooth, safe bay invites your shortest effort, or offers an all day pull, even to Monterey. Will you bathe? A smooth, hard, nicely sloping beach, and a gently breaking surf invite, detain and reward you. If you choose fresh *water bathing, just cross the beach, within a hundred yards, the Lagoon formed by the meeting of the two creeks, awaits you. Here you or your children may wade, or bathe, or boat in warmer water, and in perfect safety. Perhaps you'll drive or ride? Both north and south the smooth beach stretches for miles between the tumbling surf and the sharp bluffs. Friends at Camp Capitola, at Brighton, or even at Santa Cruz, if you wish as long a trip, can easily visit along the beach, or if the fields, the groves, the hills, the forests or the mountains attract you, numerous highways and connecting trails conduct you anywhither. The gentlest walk for the most delicate invalid or the sturdiest, Loma Prieta, mountain climb for the stoutest tourist, with every imaginable variety and dimension of intermediate walk, tramp or climb, you here may choose from. To these add the strolls along the bluff, the views from the Hotel Plateau, the charming outlook from Prospect Knoll, the Rustic Bridge which leads to Prospect Knoll, the Ville Terrace with the broad bay panorama continually unfolded thence; the hill-side trail from hotel to village, winding among the Giant Redwoods which here make their only sally to the sea for a hundred miles or more, both north and south; or, if you tire of sea-side and sea-air, you may roll or stroll up the new Loma Prieta Railroad, winding along the picturesque banks of Aptos Creek for five good miles, straight away from the sea, into the very heart of the hills. By a delightful, easy grade you may wind back through charming forests, cross romantic tributary creeks over massive bridges, free, at any point to clamber down to the escorting creek; stroll off into the flanking forests, explore the seductive side-creeks, investigate the mysteries of shake or shingle making, study the geology of the petromorphic formations along the cuts, sketch or photograph a still more charming view at each successive turn; and, finally, at the Lumber Mills and camp, you may see how conquering man ruthlessly lays low the very pillars of "God's First Temples," that he may transform them into the material for pigmy human habitations. Loma Prieta..., Monte Vista, White's Lagoon, Buzzard Lagoon, Hihn's Mills, the Sulphur Springs, Soquel Creek, and the ever-challenging peak of Loma Prieta, over-topping Mount Diablo by nearly two hundred feet, certainly present attractions enough to detain and delight you for a full month of solid satisfaction.*[144]

Agreement between Frederick Hihn and the Watsonville Mill & Lumber Company ends

After two years of Frederick Hihn fulfilling lumber contracts on behalf of the Watsonville Mill & Lumber Company due to delays in the construction of its mill on Aptos Creek, the arrangement between the two firms finally came to an end on the last day of March 1885. With the Monte Vista mill now fully operational, the Watsonville company could not fulfill its own contracts without the need for subcontractors.

The Luck of Roaring Camp 1885

Mills throughout county prepare for new season

By mid-May 1885, the rain had subsided sufficiently to begin firing up the boilers at the mills in the Augmentation. The Monte Vista, Molino, and Eureka Canyon mills all began operating on May 11, with Frederick Hihn's new mill scheduled to open shortly afterwards.[145]

Monte Vista mill burns to the ground

Only two days after opening for the year, in the early hours of May 13, 1885, the Loma Prieta Lumber Company's primary lumber mill at Monte Vista burned to the ground. The *Sentinel* reported on May 14:

> *Wednesday morning at 4 o'clock flames were seen issuing from the planing mill of the Loma Prieta Lumber Company. The flames quickly spread, and soon the mill was in a sheet of flames, resisting all efforts to subdue it. The fire spread to the cook-house, lumber on the ground, and two carloads of lumber standing on the track. All in a short time were in ashes. The loss is about $40,000.*
>
> *J. W. Linscott, who was formerly superintendent of the mill, says that about one hundred thousand feet of lumber was burned, and it will take three months to rebuild the mill. The machinery was of the best kind, one edger alone costing $2,000. The boilers were not destroyed, as they were protected by a wall of sandstone three feet in thickness. The steam pumps and tank were burned, and the men were unable to make use of the water, of which there was an ample supply. The origin of the fire is unknown. The flames were discovered by the watchman, who was firing up the engine.*
>
> *Nearly 150 men will be thrown out of employment in consequence of the fire. The mill had a capacity of forty thousand feet per day. Eighteen men were employed in the mill and the others in the redwoods. There was no insurance on the property. Following are the members of the lumber company and upon whom will fall the loss: A. C. Bassett, J. T. Porter,*

> T. Hopkins, T. Bishop and the heirs of the late A. Sanborn.
>
> John Copp, proprietor of the boarding-house, estimates his loss at $1,600. He had recently laid in a large supply of provisions for the summer, to feed the eighty boarders staying at his place.
>
> The Loma Prieta mill was one of the finest in the State, and was built a year ago, at a cost of $20,000, and was started up just one year ago to-day (May 14th). As soon as the ashes cool the work of rebuilding will begin.
>
> The fire is supposed to be the work of an incendiary, and is now believed to have originated near the edger, which was in the center of the planing mill.

The fire at the Monte Vista mill had far-reaching consequences for the Watsonville Mill & Lumber Company and its subsidiary Loma Prieta Lumber Company. The day after the fire, Bassett and William Dougherty visited the ruins of the mill—what they saw was almost total devastation. With no insurance payout, the cost of rebuilding the facility was left entirely to the companies' investors and financiers, and resources were tight. Even with funding, rebuilding was expected to take a year to complete, which meant that the companies could not expect substantial revenue from their operations on Aptos Creek. Other than revenue streams from splitstuff, tanbark, and shakes cut in the hills above the burned-out mill, the main source of funds was from the Eureka Canyon mill, which was limited in the amount of timber it could process annually. And with the agreement with Frederick Hihn ended, the Loma Prieta Lumber Company was responsible for substantial amounts of contracted lumber that it could no longer deliver.

The solutions the companies decided upon came rapidly and changed just as quickly. Crews immediately were sent into to clear out the wreckage from the fire and begin rebuilding the mill. The hope was that the mill could resume producing rough-cut lumber within three months using logs from the millpond that had survived the fire. The initial focus was on reconstructing the primary lumber mill, so all other support facilities such as the planing mill and shingle mill would wait. As construction began, company directors realized that they needed to look at the destruction of the mill as a blessing in disguise and plan for a different future than they had envisioned four years earlier.

Though desperate, the Watsonville Mill & Lumber Company was not a reckless corporation. Back in 1881 when it purchased the stumpage rights to Tract 9, it sent out cruisers to determine the expected timber yield of the massive property. Following a second survey, the cruisers established a line from the 1,000-foot point of Aptos Creek, just north of Five Finger Falls, to a similar point along Hinckley Creek to the west. This line marked the point where an equal amount of harvestable timber was located to the north as to the south. In reality, it was about sixty percent below the line and forty percent above it, but the number to the north was still considerable.

The Southern Pacific Railroad had intended to extend its Loma Prieta Branch an additional 0.68 miles to the top of what was then called Aptos Falls, now Five Finger Falls, but the cruisers reported extremely difficult terrain in the vicinity. They concluded that if the railroad was extended, as agreed to by the Pacific Improvement Company, and a mill was built at the new end of track, the cost in building and maintaining skid roads alone would far exceed any profits gained through selling lumber derived from the area. That being said, skid roads from Monte Vista to the 1,000-foot elevation point would already average a seven percent grade, while beyond that point, they could reach up to twelve percent. These types of inclines were simply not feasible for the modes of transportation available. Although the potential timber yields in the upper reaches of Tract 9 were promising, it would take all of the talent and ingenuity of Partridge and Knox to harvest that timber at a profit.

The Loma Prieta Lumber Company management found ready allies in Charles Crocker, Collis Huntington, and Leland Stanford, who were already heavily invested in the logging and resort activity within Tract 8 just to the south of the Loma Prieta operations. Having already built the Loma Prieta Branch to its current terminus, the men agreed that reaching the 1,000-foot elevation point was vital to ensuring a return on their investment. If they could extend track even further, all the better for everyone. However, the issue of rebuilding the mill at its original site also came up for debate. While the Monte Vista mill had worked adequately at its location, the narrowness of the canyon and limited space in the clearing where the mill was built restricted its expandability. The millpond itself also provided an obstacle to further rail expansion up the canyon. In the future, the company likely would want to increase its capacity, add a pole-making facility,

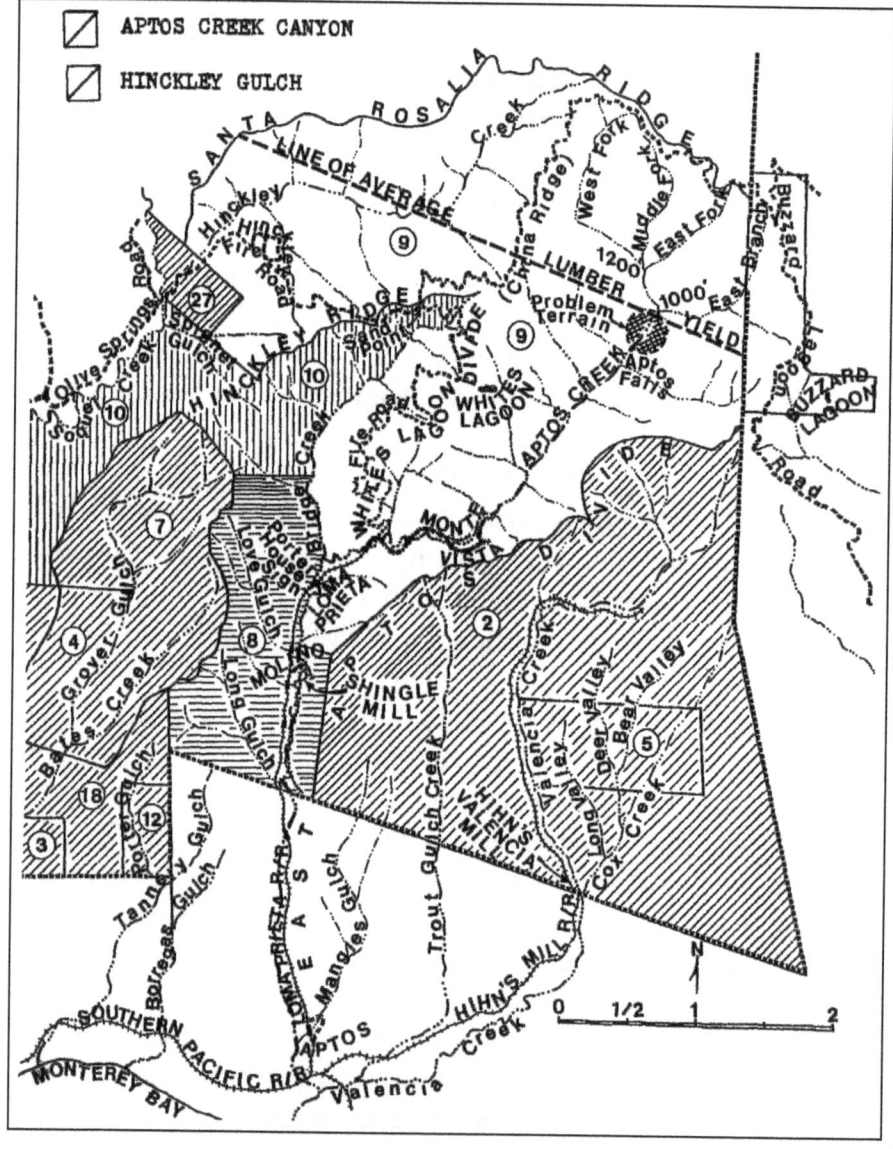

Figure 4.12 Line of average lumber yield in the Augmentation

and possibly expand its planing and shingle mills, all of which would also require more workers and housing for them. And with the mill six miles north of Aptos and only accessible via rail, the predicament of the Monte Vista mill site became clear.

After much discussion, a new vision for the Aptos Creek operations was agreed upon by all concerned parties. Three mills would be built. First, a small rough-cut lumber mill would be erected at Monte Vista. Second, lumber from the mill would be used to build a new, larger mill on a property near the Southern Pacific Railroad depot at Pajaro. Logs from the millpond at Monte Vista would be shipped via railroad to the new mill, where they would be cut and, after drying, loaded onto waiting freight cars. And third, a still larger mill would be erected off the Molino spur on the boundary of Tracts 8 and 9 in the Augmentation, where a wide flat area provided ample room for expansion. Construction on the mill at Pajaro began in early June as the board of directors began seeking new investors.

At some point later in the year, Mary Hopkins purchased 1,380 shares valued at $100 each in the Loma Prieta Lumber Company. She likely purchased these shares on behalf of the Pacific Improvement Company, although she retained ownership of them for the rest of her life. Hypothetically, these could have given Hopkins a powerful position within the lumber company, but she never chose to use her position, possibly because she lived on the East Coast. This influx of capital infused the company with enough revenue to finish the mill at Pajaro, begin the new mill near Molino, and start the extension of the railroad beyond Monte Vista. When precisely she purchased the shares is unknown since they only came to light after her death when the property passed to her adopted son, Timothy Hopkins. Regardless, the company wasted no time putting the funds to use.[146]

Valencia Creek mill opens

After several delays, Frederick Hihn formally opened his new mill at the confluence of Valencia and Cox Creeks in June 1885. The new mill had a respectable capacity of 30,000 board feet of lumber per day.

The opening of the mill prompted the subsequent development of the area around it into the village of Valencia, akin in many ways to the nearby village of Loma Prieta on Aptos Creek. The Valencia School District actually predated the establishment of the settlement, having been formed on May 14, 1881 as a breakaway from the Aptos School District. The number of pupils at the end of the first semester was listed as 23.

The hamlet itself emerged shortly after the mill relocated to the site. Hihn himself was responsible for its continuing development, even advertising parcels for sale and a township layout in A. J. Hatch's famed map of the county in 1889. Around 1886, Hihn funded the construction of Valencia Hall, which was to be used as a community center, church, and meeting house for local residents. The schoolhouse was located near the hall on today's Valencia School Road.[147]

Monte Vista mill reopens

Less than two months after the mill burned down, a smaller, temporary mill opened at Monte Vista by the Loma Prieta Lumber Company at some point in early July 1885. The mill's primary purpose was to process rough-cut lumber to be used to build a larger mill at Pajaro, although it also was used to fulfill outstanding contracts and process logs from the millpond that survived the fire.[148]

Lucius Sanborn resigns

Following the death of his brother Alvin and a lingering illness, Lucius Sanborn resigned from his positions as secretary and general manager of the Loma Prieta Lumber Company on July 11, 1885.[149]

Charles Ford resigns

Barely two weeks after the resignation of Lucius Sanborn, Charles Ford also resigned from his position as president of the Loma Prieta Lumber Company on July 31, 1885. In his stead, John Porter was appointed interim president pending an election. Ford retained ownership of his shares in the Watsonville Mill and Lumber Company for another two years, selling them to the Loma Prieta Lumber Company around May 1887.[150]

The Luck of Roaring Camp   1885 – 1886

Thomas Fallon dies

On October 25, 1885, Thomas Fallon, Californian revolutionary, one-time mayor of San José, and ex-husband of Carmel, daughter of Martina Castro, died of kidney failure at Russ House in San Francisco.[151]

Hotel Bohemia, the Mountain Home, and the Willows

In the mid-1880s, Z. A. Cotton and his wife purchased a small parcel of land from Birney Burrell located a short distance up Loma Prieta Avenue north of Summit Road. After his home was completed, Cotton constructed a hotel that would soon become known across the United States as Hotel Bohemia. Over its short life, the hotel catered to some of the best-known celebrities on the West Coast, including Jack London, George Sterling, Ambrose Bierce, Herman Scheffauer, and Samuel Clemens (Mark Twain). The primary attraction was not the hotel itself, but rather the nearby cottage of Josephine McCrackin, Monte Paraiso, which was colloquially nicknamed the Bohemian Bungalow.

Across Loma Prieta Avenue, the Jeffery family built around 1886 a small hotel known as Mountain Home. An article in the *Surf* published July 16, 1889, reported:

> *Having an hour to spare, our driver turns into "Jeffery's" and lands us at the "Mountain Home Hotel." It is difficult to realize that the spacious, comfortable house, with the surrounding cottages, set in the midst of flower beds, clumps of shade trees and bosky shrubs, have been built within the last three years. The cool verandahs were filled with summer visitors. Beneath the shade trees others swung in hammocks; at the base of a clump of noble redwoods others were hid under sun umbrellas, and there was in the air a flavor of yellow shoes, a gleam of straw hats, a flutter of light drapery and the sound of laughter and pleasant badinage.*
>
> *From the "lookout" on the top of the house (to which our host conducted us) there was a view of valleys, glens and mountain slopes and a glimpse of the bay. The garret through*

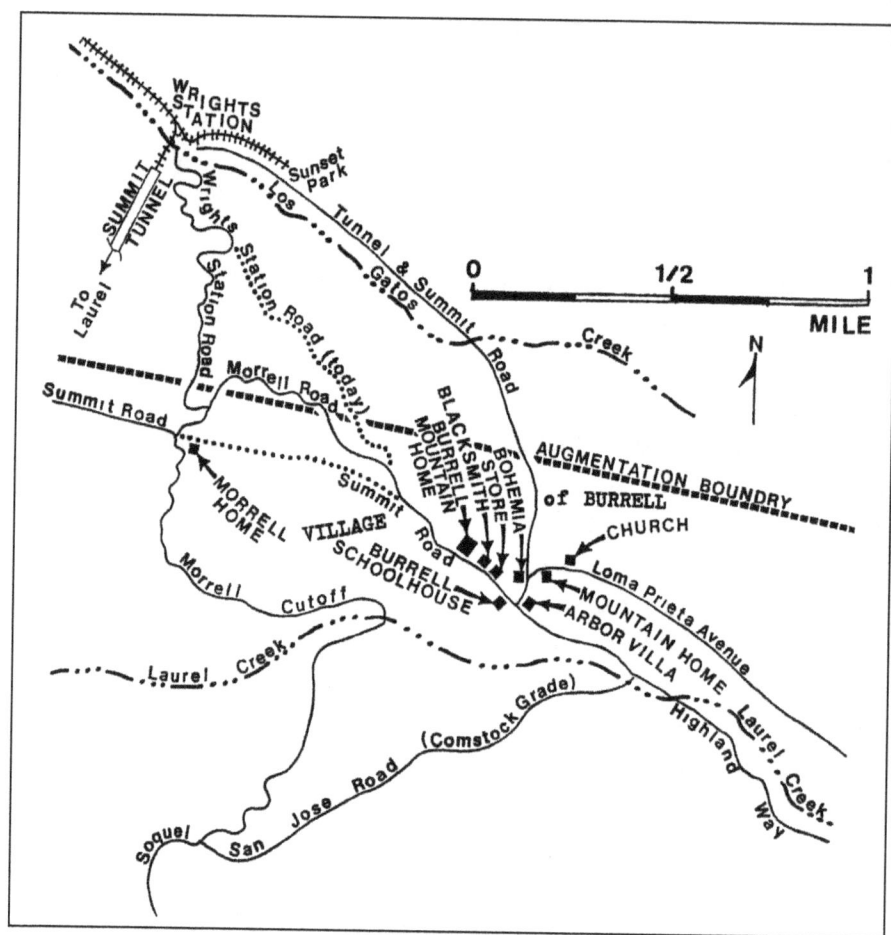

Figure 4.13 Hotels and resorts in the Summit area

which we passed on our way to the roof was hung with bunches of grapes rapidly changing to raisins. We imagined spoony couples going up there to enjoy themselves under a canopy of dried grapes and cobwebs!

By the 1890s, the area around Hotel Bohemia, Mountain Home, Arbor Villa, and the Burrell School had become known as Burrell, a town without a post office centered around the intersection of Loma Prieta Avenue and Highland Way. The town was not without amenities, however. In addition to the local resorts, a Presbyterian church had been built by Reverend

James Wright, a small community store was run by H. D. Ingram, and a blacksmith shop was operated by Earl T. Smith and his son, Jack. The *Surf* reporter continued:

> ...we come out near the head of Burrell Creek [Laurel Creek], having passed on our way the junction of roads leading right and left. At this road crossing there stands a neat building, used as a schoolhouse through the week and as a meeting-house on Sundays. Opposite is the entrance to 'Arbor Villa'—a beautiful estate, brought to its present state of high cultivation by Mr. Wright and his sons within a decade of years. As we go on past the neat vineyards of this homestead we are told that a single acre of grapes from here returned $3,000 to those who gathered, packed and sent the fruit to San Francisco last Christmas season.

About four miles away down Skyland Road at its intersection with Stetson Road, Donald Beadel purchased a section of land from Charles Herman Allen within Tract 20 in the Augmentation. Beadel owned and operated a large shipping company that operated between the Central Coast of California and East Asia. After he purchased the land, he built a large home along with several cottages that he planned to rent to vacationers. He surrounded his home and cottages with an impressive garden and hired a Mrs. Hannon to manage the resort, which he named The Willows. In 1904, Beadel sold the property to a Mrs. Holt, whose daughter married Beadel's son, Alec.

Alec and his wife quickly took over operation of the resort and turned it into one of the showplaces in the entire Santa Cruz Mountains. They added new cottages, which surrounded their beautiful rambling central home, and upgraded their home to the style of an English farmhouse. They added a swimming pool, enclosing it within glass walls and a ceiling, thereby creating the largest privately-owned indoor swimming pool in the United States. Under its huge canopy of glass, the great double pool of concrete and tile brought the curious from miles around while Eastern newspapers extolled its virtues.

The Beadels also planted terraces full of exotic garden plants from all corners of the globe and built fountains and rock gardens that transformed the surrounding forest and resort into a fertile paradise. In 1933, a Fresno rancher, J. V. Enloe, purchased the estate and began renovating it. After running it for six years, he then sold it to Rolland T. R. Hastings of Chicago, who made further improvements.

On a personal note, in the mid-1960s, my wife, four children, and I spent a pleasant week at The Willows. The cottages were still there, one of which we occupied. The pool was also still in use, although it was no longer enclosed but open to the elements. I cannot remember if any of the described attractions still existed, but I do remember that we enjoyed our stay there. The resort has since become a rural trailer park and the pool sits empty and unused.[152]

Construction begins on new mill and village near Molino

As soon as weather permitted, construction of a second bridge at Molino began in the early spring of 1886. Once completed, this bridge was the longest along the first five miles of the Loma Prieta Branch at 320 feet. However, construction took time, so crews prepared the area for the new mill by leveling the site of the mill and clearcutting the half mile upstream along both sides of Aptos Creek to allow for its eventual inundation into a millpond. Many of the larger trees cut from along the banks of the creek were cut into sections to be used in the millpond's dam. The dam took several months to construct, and the valley was not inundated until the winter rains arrived. The completed structure measured 300 feet across and a towering 26 feet high at its center.

The construction of the mill itself was overseen by Jake Scheers, who situated the structure just south of the millpond dam. The foundations of the mill were made of raised log beams connected to the redwood floor with large bolts. The partial walls and the roof were connected using dowels rather than nails, although it is unknown why Sheers chose this method.

The relocation of the mill to just north of Molino also required a substantial rearrangement of railroad tracks in the area to cater to the mill, the millpond, and the other facilities in the vicinity. The Southern Pacific Railroad installed a 1,600-foot-long bridge and viaduct across Aptos Creek from Molino to access the new mill site. It was the single longest bridge along the entire Loma Prieta Branch. The first track built to the mill took a circuitous route that kept the spur's tracks out of the lumber yard. Once the mill was completed, two additional spurs were extended into the lumber yard, alternating with tramway tracks used by lumberjacks to transfer lumber from the mill to the lumber stacks. In later years, the tramway tracks were elevated in order to simplify the transfer of lumber from the mill to the lumber stacks. This greatly improved the efficiency of lumberjacks and, as a result, made shipping lumber from the mill easier and quicker.

On the west bank of Aptos Creek above the millpond, several short tracks were installed. The two sidings furthest to the east were used for dumping logs into the millpond. Two other tracks allowed northbound and southbound trains to pass, when necessary. At least three other spurs of varying lengths on the west side of the mainline could be used by trains waiting to unload their logs or as simple holding tracks for unneeded rolling stock.

To the north on the east bank of Aptos Creek, another spur broke off and then forked, with one branch heading south and the other branch making a 180-degree turn to the northeast. The southern millpond spur—referred to as the "log-way"—was used to relieve traffic congestion on the west side and allow the offloading of long logs that would be turned into telegraph poles. After about 750 feet, the spur crossed a shallow gulch over a long bridge, beyond which it is unclear how far the spur continued. It is possible that it continued all the way to the mill. As of the late 1990s, the remains of the bridge were still lying along the north side of the gulch while several rails were visible on the south side. The northeastern spur, meanwhile, curved to the northeast to follow today's Aptos Fire Road, then a wagon road to Trout Gulch and Aptos. The spur continued gradually up the side of the East Aptos Divide until the grade became too steep for trains. This track was used to collect logs brought down from the divide and slightly beyond.

While the mill site was under construction, crews also moved into the the village of Loma Prieta and prepared it for a much-needed upgrade. Prior to this time, the location, which had begun life as the railroad's construction camp, hosted a modest settlement composed of low-quality

1886 — The Reign of the Lumber Barons

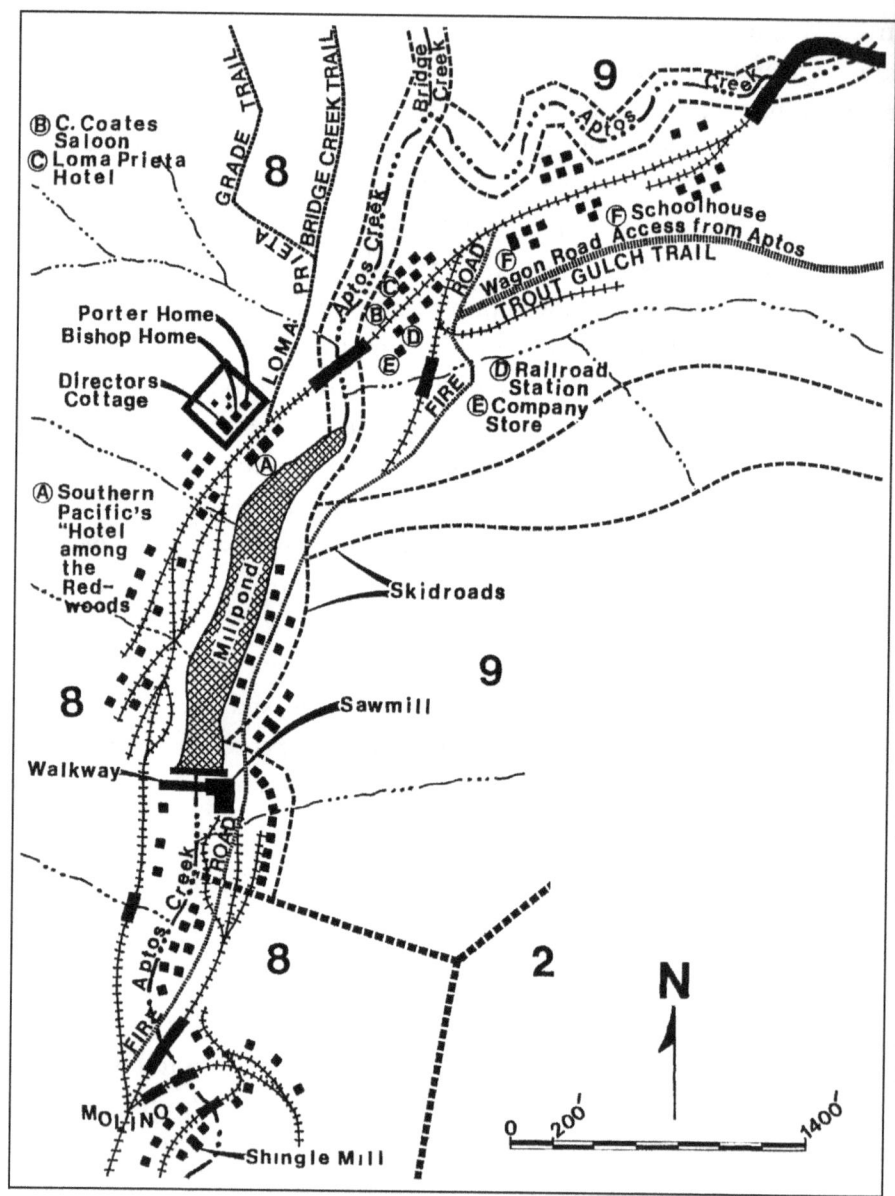

FIGURE 4.14 VILLAGE, MILL, AND COMPOUND AT LOMA PRIETA

worker homes and a railroad spur for a spring-fed water tank. However, after the Monte Vista fire and the decision to relocate the primary mill downstream, the settlement became the heart of the local community.

Within a few short months, the lumber company built at or moved to the site the company store with its accompanying post office, a new hotel for tourists and visitors, a field office for the Loma Prieta Lumber Company, C. Coates' Saloon, and several improved cottages and homes. The company also built a dance hall for both workers and visitors and several storage warehouses of various sizes. The Southern Pacific Railroad also erected a depot, which included a Wells Fargo express parcel service office.

The town's population, almost entirely composed of mill workers and their families, primarily lived in cottages built on the east bank of Aptos Creek upstream of the mill and beside the millpond. When the mill opened, at least thirty-six cottages were built in this section. Because the Pacific Improvement Company hoped to turn the Loma Prieta area into a resort, all of these cottages were built of superior quality so as not to detract from the visual splendor of the locale. They were painted on the outside and wallpapered on the inside and featured running water. Most had landscaped gardens, and the descendants of flowers planted around these homes can still sometimes be found on the east bank of Aptos Creek today. Some of the homes also had multiple rooms and were large enough to support families.

Although the entire area between the Molino and Loma Prieta railroad station points is often considered to be "Loma Prieta," there were three distinct areas that the lumber company and railroad recognized. In addition to the village and the mill, there was the compound along the railroad tracks on the west bank of Aptos Creek southwest of the village. The compound consisted primarily of three buildings: individual homes for the Loma Prieta Lumber Company's president and secretary, and a multi-room meeting hall and guest lodge for visiting company directors. The purpose of these buildings was to make the company's management more directly involved in the operations of the mill by giving them a place to stay when they visited. The president's house was only used periodically by Thomas Bishop, who was elected to replace Charles Ford on April 10.

The secretary's house became a primary residence for Warren Porter, who replaced Lucius Sanborn in the same election. As secretary, Porter was also general manager of the company and took his role seriously. As soon as the home was completed, Porter moved to Loma Prieta and lived there throughout the summer months, returning to live in Watsonville during the winter. When his father, John, visited the mill, he stayed at his son's house rather than in the director's cottage. His home was described over the years as elegant and of a similar aesthetic quality as the nicer homes in Aptos.

The director's cottage had rooms for all of the remaining directors, who each had their own dining room, kitchen, and cook's quarters. While directors came and went as they pleased, they tried to meet at the cottage once a month. Warren Porter, as the only permanent director living on the site, arranged for the delivery of local supplies for the cooks to use. Each director was responsible for furnishing their rooms.

The community—village, mill, and compound—grew quickly in the first two years after it was built, with several new facilities and features added to cater to workers. The community was linked together via a telephone system that also connected to the Pacific Improvement Company's mill at Molino, the small mill at the end-of-track three miles to the north, and Aptos Station to the south. The hotel quickly proved unfeasible and became a boarding house for specialist workers and visitors to the camp. Meanwhile, a rapidly expanding population of children led to the creation of the Loma Prieta School District in September 1885, the schoolhouse for which was built north of the village around 1887. The building doubled as a meeting hall at night and as a nondenominational church one Sunday every month. Around the school and along the Loma Prieta Branch north of town, a number of homes were built for the more important employees of the mills. The town dump was also located near this area, as were the public outhouses for the town.

The primary drinking water supply for the town came from a gulch a half-mile to the north of the village and just beyond the long compound railroad bridge across Aptos Creek. Two large wooden catch boxes were installed along two arms of the gulch, each box measuring about seven feet square. Because of its status as a water supply, the stream that flowed down the gulch was named Spring Creek. The catchments were both maintained at roughly 800 feet above sea level, which was 440 feet above the village. This difference meant that it had substantial pressure, so did not require pumps to operate. Over time, Spring Creek proved inadequate as a water supply in the summer months, so several wells were dug near the schoolhouse north of the village. The water for the compound—the only part of settlement on the west bank of Aptos Creek—came from a smaller spring to the west that was piped into a large, elevated water tank tucked above the buildings.[153]

Loma Prieta Lumber Company sacks all Chinese workers

After two years of employing Chinese workers to construct railroad spurs, grade skid roads, and work in a limited capacity within its mills, the Loma Prieta Lumber Company announced on April 6, 1886 that it was sacking all of its Chinese workers, effective immediately, pledging to never employ Chinese workers again. This reflected a wider anti-Chinese movement that was gaining ground across California and the United States.[154]

Mills throughout county prepare to fire up their boilers

At the end of April 1886, the mills at Molino, Monte Vista, and Valencia fired up for the season. At Monte Vista, both boilers with their headrigs had been repaired, although the building around the machinery was still under construction and no finishing works were planned. Molino resumed its production of shingles, shakes, and various splitstuff. The *Sentinel* reported on the Monte Vista mill on May 2:

> *This mill, after having been shut down during the winter, commenced running on the 27th ultimo, under the supervision of C. Cummings, who has taken the work by contract. Mr. Cummings has engaged Edward Davenport as shipping clerk, who is well qualified for the position, having served former employers faithfully during years past. Over 125 men are at present employed at this extensive and well-appointed mill, and 40,000 feet of lumber per day are turned out, besides thousands of cords of slabs and stove-wood. S. Jefter, who has charge of the wood-cutters, employs sixteen men, and Wm. Hudner, also a wood contractor, employs as many more. The*

pack-mule is used in bringing the wood to the station from the spot where it is cut, along a steep and almost impassable trail. Fourteen mules and four horses are engaged in this work. As soon as the pack-saddle (with two iron bows projecting from each side of the animal), is loaded with four-foot wood, the mule starts down the hill without the assistance of a driver and goes direct to the place of unloading, now and then stopping to rest. Eight men are busy daily in cutting tan-bark, which is a very remunerative business, the bark selling at $8 per cord on the ground. The great bulk of wood from this portion of the county is shipped to Peterson's brick-kiln at San Jose, while considerable is sent to Pleasanton and San Francisco.

It is safe to say that there is more shipping down over the Loma Prieta railroad than at any line on the S. P. R. R. From May 4th to Dec. 1st last year conductor Gayton tells us he handled 5,000 freight-cars, and the outlook is that a greater number will be handled during the coming season.

Since last year extensive improvements have been made in the logging system at the mill. Formerly five ox teams were engaged in hauling the huge logs to the saw, but now a track has been laid up the canyon beyond, a distance of nearly a mile, where the logs are loaded on cars and started on a down-grade to the mill. By this improvement nearly $8 per day are saved in grease, formerly used in making the work easier for the ox teams. Before next winter the Loma Prieta Lumber Company...will, it is said, have the mill moved further down the canyon, near Molina station, and steps will be taken to make a dam for the purpose of floating logs to the mill. This will be done in order that the mill may be enabled to run all winter. An extra force of men will be employed to cut logs for the winter use, and these will be rolled into the dam, and there lay until floated to the mill and sawed.

The first two car-loads of lumber from the mill this season were shipped Friday [April 30], together with eight car-loads of four-foot wood, and the train bearing the same sped down the grade and around the sharp curves at a careful speed, the hind cars at times being lost sight of on this somewhat zigzag road.

The Luck of Roaring Camp 1886

At five o'clock Aptos was reached, and a successful trip made.

Meanwhile, Frederick Hihn's newly-relocated mill on Valencia Creek opened in March only to shut down in April due to heavy rains. It reopened in May. On May 31, the *Surf* gave its own assessment of the mill following a visit:

> One of the pleasantest of our many delightful mountain drives is the Valencia Creek road. Leaving Aptos and following this road for three miles, with the mountains and the trees growing taller as we advance, we arrive at a point on Valencia Creek where is located probably the finest and best appointed lumber mills in the county, owned by F. A. Hihn and known as the "Aptos Mill." The steam power is generated by two powerful engines, and is sufficient in quantity for the operation of several different but connected industries.
>
> The Lumber Mill
> Itself cuts an average of 25,000 feet per day, and in order that there may be no waste of material, a box and shingle mill has been erected upon a natural plateau one hundred feet above the lumber mill. The material for this upper establishment is raised to the plateau from the mill below by a tramway, by steam, and the power for this purpose as well as for the running the box and shingle mill, is obtained from the engines before mentioned. Everything about this latter structure is of the latest and most improved patents, and Engineer French, who presides over these monster steam generators, takes the utmost pride in the fine appearance and perfect order of this domain. He is an acknowledged master in his profession.
>
> Upon the natural plateau before spoken of are located, besides the box and shingle mill, a lumber yard and the
>
> Houses of the Employes,
> Arranged in orderly rows, and each one whitewashed and surrounded by its own plot of ground. The care of the proprietor for the comfort of those in his employ has also provided clear mountain water which is brought in pipes from Valencia creek and supplied at the door of each family in

quantities sufficient for domestic use and for irrigation. To do this, *Valencia Creek has been tapped at a point some 8,000 feet above where it passes the little settlement, and thus has been provided an immense and never failing supply. The land about the mills is divided, as fast as it is denuded of the virgin forest, into small farms which are sold, with right of water, to settlers and soon turned into smiling homes surrounded by vineyards and orchards.*

The Timber,

Which supplies the mills with material is situated at a distance of one and a half miles. The logs are transported this distance by two flat cars drawn by two powerful mules over an iron tramway. Each car brings from five to ten logs which are unloaded into the log-way by steam. U. S. Nichols, the experienced millwright of the establishment, has in hand two new cars which will soon be finished. Mr. Nichols constructed both the mills at this place.

Lumbermen estimate that there still remain uncut upon this property some 40,000,000 feet of lumber, which, at the present rate of consumption, will keep these mills busy for

Ten Years or More.

By that time, if the present wise plan of turning the uncovered country into small ranches is pursued, these hills will be covered with fruit and vine and sustaining a large and busy population. There are now on the pay roll eighty-five men, many of whom are married and have their homes in the little settlement on the plateau already described. All the buildings and bridges are whitewashed, showing picturesquely against the dark green background of the hills.

It is a remarkable fact that each man employed here in any responsible or special position, is an acknowledged master of his business, and that all the employees are selected for their known competence and fidelity.

Mr. Fred. W. Cook

Is the General Superintendent, and an hour's observation would convince anyone that his position, so faithfully filled, is no sinecure.

The Luck of Roaring Camp 1886

William Baird, Superintendent at the mill, is a man of large experience and judgment, and has for his head sawyer, Alex. Bedell, whose skill is well known throughout the mountains. Thomas Leonard, Clerk, although a young man, has already established a reputation as a measurer. We have before spoken of Engineer French and the fine condition in which his department is kept. The boarding house is under the efficient charge of John Copp, who caters for some sixty-nine boarders. Mr. Copp also keeps

The Settlement Store,

So well supplied as to make it a great convenience to the families located there. It may well be imagined that the roads for hauling timber and shipping lumber, together with all the bridges thereon, must be kept in "apple-pie order" to secure the best results, and this work is in the hands of "Boss" Sargent. There are three roads which give an outlet to the retail trade in this region; one to Aptos; one, considered the finest in the county, to San Andreas, and another to Quatros Legus.

The wholesale shipping is done at Aptos, three miles distant from the mill, where there is an ample lumber yard. At present the lumber is hauled by team over the regular road but Tom Wright, C. E., has recent surveyed and located

A Narrow-Gauge Railroad

Which, when built, will lessen both distance and time materially. This road will follow the general direction of the wagon road but will dispense with many curves and turns. The railway will be 14,600 feet in length. For the first 9,300 feet it will be level; for the succeeding 3,400 feet there will be a grade of three feet in each 100 feet, and the remainder of the distance will be level. The sharpest curve will be 25° on a level and less on the grade.

Our mountains and forests conceal many a scene of busy activity in this county with their outward aspects of grand repose, but it is doubtful if any more busy or more profitable camp than this one can be found among them all.

Hihn had hoped to increase productivity by bringing his mill closer to the timber. The problem was transporting the finished goods to Aptos Station, which was now three miles to the south. Technically, it was relatively straightforward to transport the products to the station, since all it required were roads and wagons. But it proved far from efficient since the wagons had to cross over into Trout Gulch before continuing on to Aptos, and the roads became mud with only a light sprinkling of rain. Furthermore, once the area around the mill was cleared, which was completed early in 1886 before the mill opened, the task of bringing logs to the mill became difficult, with an increasing number of steep skid roads required to navigate the narrow valley and its many gulches and feeder streams.

Hihn's decision to construct a mule-drawn railroad between the mill and Aptos was, therefore, a logical solution to all of his problems. Most importantly, it could be extended beyond the mill to reduce the mill's reliance on skid roads. Once built, mules found the route relatively easy to navigate since only empty cars were ever sent up the grade. Laden cars were sent down to Aptos by gravity with a brakeman controlling the descent. Indeed, the railroad increased the productivity of the mill by an additional 10,000 board feet per day, making it the most efficient mill in the county at the time.[155]

Land transfer from the Watsonville Mill & Lumber Company to Mary Hopkins concerning land in Eureka Canyon

On May 26, 1886 in San Francisco, the Watsonville Mill & Lumber Company sold 138 acres of land in Eureka Canyon just east of the Augmentation and north of Buzzard Lagoon to Mary Hopkins.[156]

Loma Prieta Lumber Company opens new sawmill in Pajaro

Sometime around late June 1886, the Loma Prieta Lumber Company's mill in Pajaro began processing logs from the millpond at Monte Vista. With this operation supplementing the rough-cut lumber mill at Monte Vista and the two Watsonville Mill & Lumber Company mills along Eureka Canyon, the two firms were able to anticipate a successful season.

Valencia Creek mill exceeds expectations

Near the end of its first season at its new site, Frederick Hihn's mill exceeded its original output projections. The *Surf* reported on October 20, 1886:

> *F. W. Cook, Esq., Superintendent of the Aptos Mill informs us that the mill is averaging 30,000 feet per day; that the demand is such that the output would be doubled if transportation could be had for the lumber.*
>
> *The grading for the narrow-gauge railroad has been completed a distance of seven miles, three to the mill and four beyond into the timber. A substantial bridge is in course of erection over the creek and it is expected that within thirty days the track will be laid and the road in operation. The cost of improvements now so near completion will be not far from $45,000.*

Meanwhile, the *Surf* also revealed the progress that had been made on the new Loma Prieta Lumber Company mill at Molino:

> *Mr. Cook will superintend the construction of the new mill of the Loma Prieta Company at Molino. The mill will have a capacity of 50,000 feet per day. The lumber yard of the company at Aptos will be discontinued and Molino will be made the distributing point. The expenditure in and about Aptos in improvements by the mill companies the coming fall and winter will not be far from $70,000.*[157]

Grover & Company's new mill opens

With the autumn rains beginning, many of the lumber mills in the Augmentation began to shut down in mid-October 1886. The Loma Prieta Lumber Company used this opportunity to finalize its relocation of the Monte Vista mill from its original site to just south of the village, a process that would take several months to complete. The Valencia Creek mill planned to stay open as long as possible, pending weather.

Meanwhile, Grover & Company was just wrapping up construction of its new mill on Bates Creek and planned to keep it running as long as possible through the end of the year. In an article published on November 2, the *Surf* reported:

> Three miles from Soquel, on Bates' Creek, Grover & Co., the enterprising lumber men of Santa Cruz have built and have now in operation their new mill. This firm has been to a large expense in grading roads and excavating for the site of the mill. The mill has been running about two weeks, and cutting an average of about 30,000 feet per day and will shortly be run to its full capacity of 35,000 feet per day. Among the orders now being filled is one from Davisville for 1100 telegraph poles; also for sawed timbers for the railroad bridge over the Salinas river on the Soledad extension of the S. O. Co.; forty sticks 12x18 and forty-one feet in length having a part of the contract. Among the improvements going on is the new cook-house and dining hall 24x70 feet; also grading for a tramway. This tramway will be one and three-quarters miles in length, reaching from the main mill to the shingle mill and will greatly facilitate the shipment of lumber. The company have six hundred acres of the finest timber in the county sufficient for a ten years' run. Fifty men are now employed in and about the mill, and the lumber, as fast as cut, is shipped away to fill orders—delayed through the loss of the Centennial mill, lately destroyed by fire. The proprietors feel perfectly satisfied with their prospects for a profitable business, and will keep everything in and about the mill on full time as late as possible this season.

The Centennial Mill was an independent lumber concern located on the west branch of Bean Creek in Centennial Gulch. The mill was built by C. W. Pyatt in 1876 and acquired by Grover & Company in 1881. The mill burned down in September 1886.

Two days after the above article was published, the *Surf* clarified that the mill's capacity was 35,000 in shingles rather than lumber. It added that it also produces 500 apple boxes per day. The new mill was placed under the management of John Keough, a contractor.[158]

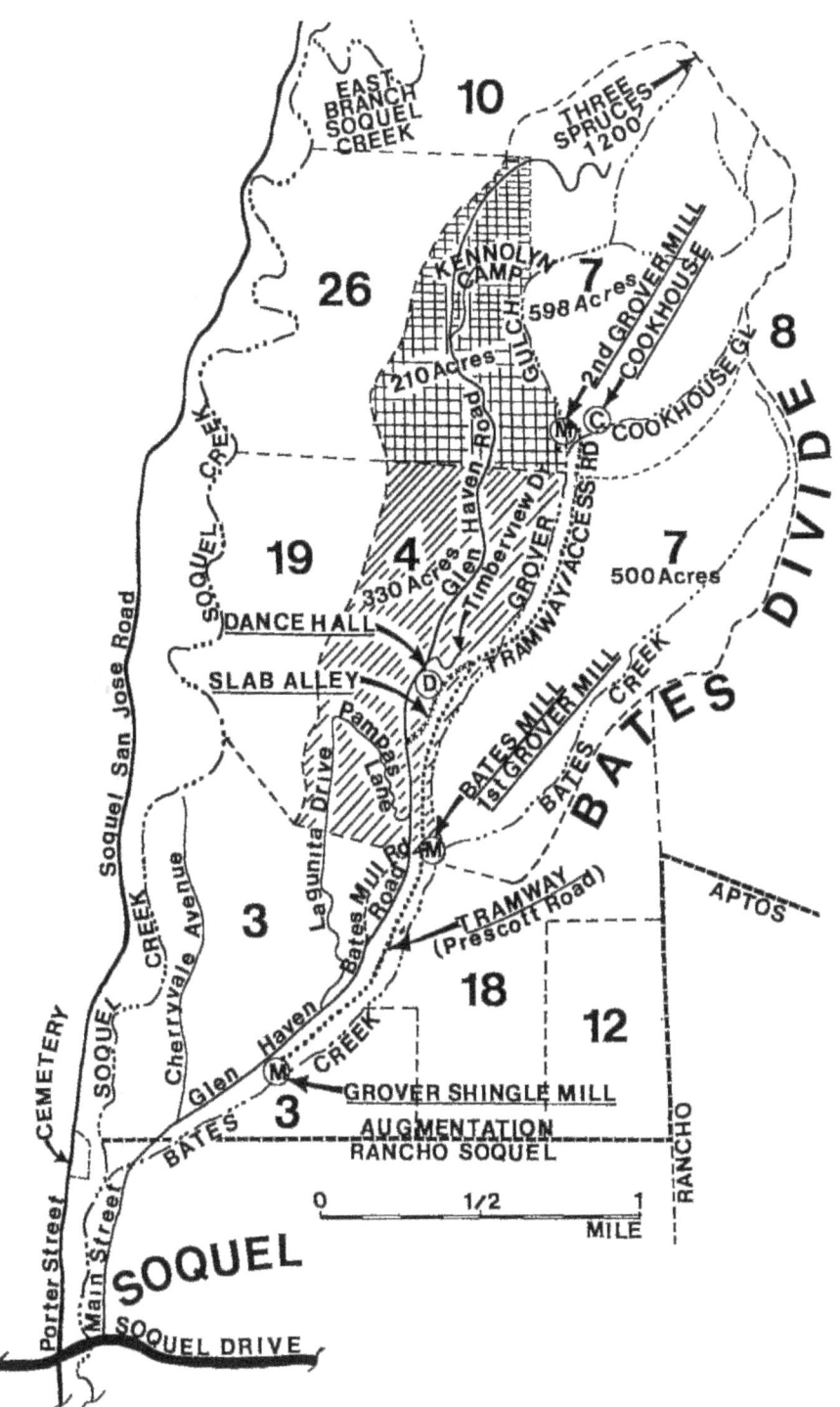

Figure 4.15 Grover lands in Tracts 4 and 7 in the Augmentation

Valencia Creek mill burns down

In a year that had already seen the destruction of the Monte Vista mill and the Centennial Mill in unexpected fires, it came as no surprise when Frederick Hihn's new Valencia Creek mill burned to the ground on the morning of November 29, 1886. The *Surf* reported:

> *In June last the Surf gave quite an extended account of F. A. Hihn's Aptos Mill, one of the finest and best appointed mills in the county, where some 30,000 feet of lumber were daily sawed, besides pickets, shingles and box material. To day this fine building lies in ashes, having been destroyed by fire on Sunday morning, between 2 and 3 o'clock. On Saturday, the regular watchman, Thomas Flynn, came in to Santa Cruz and failed to catch the return train in the afternoon. He at once telephoned the fact to Mr. Wm. Baird, the general foreman, who detailed Thomas Kirby as watchman for the night, giving him careful instructions and many cautions to use the utmost vigilance.*
>
> *At one o'clock, Kirby felt somewhat ill, and first looking about to see that all was quiet, went to his house to take some medicine, leaving his post entirely deserted. About two o'clock J. S. Stanley discovered fire at the mill and gave the alarm. In a short time a number of the employees had gathered to the rescue, but the water supply proved inadequate and it was soon seen that the saving of the mill was an impossibility.*
>
> *Every energy was then directed to keeping the fire hedged in so that it should extend no further than the mill, and in this the impromptu firemen were successful. The mill building, the dimensions of which are 100x60 feet, was entirely destroyed, and much of the machinery with it. An engine and boiler were saved, and one planer besides the box mill, which was situated in an L. A few thousand feet of lumber which were in the mill were lost, but the flames were fortunately kept from the lumber yard, and many thousand feet of logs in the logway above the mill were also saved.*
>
> *Mr. Hihn was apprised of his loss at 8 o'clock yesterday*

morning and spent the day at the scene of the fire. He estimates his loss at about $10,000, though this estimate may be modified upon further investigation. There was no insurance upon the property, Mr. Hihn's plan being that of self-insurance. No time will be lost in rebuilding. Already the debris is being cleared away and Mr. Hihn has telegraphed to J. A. Rabb, the expert, of San Francisco, to come down and consult with him upon plans, etc. for the new structure. This will probably be completed some time in March next and will be ready for the opening of the season.

The mill just destroyed was moved to the present location of the lumber camp, some three miles above Aptos, on Valencia Creek, two years ago, the machinery was new four years ago and included the newest and most approved patents for the work it was designed to do. The engine was of great size and power and generated steam for the operation of the saw, box and picket mills, besides two planers and hoisting works for the loading and unloading of material. The origin of the fire is not positively known. A blow-pipe started from the interior of the mill and led to the saw dust pit where the saw dust is kept burning. The draught for this pit-fire was supplied through this blow-pipe, the blower for which was operated by the engine. It is supposed that during the inaction of the blower at night, gases had generated in the pipe which forced themselves out at the blower, drawing after them the fire from the pit. Had the watchman been on the alert to discover this at its inception, the mill might have been saved, and Mr. Hihn expresses the opinion that to this carelessness is due the entire loss.

Some sixty men have been employed about the camp. These will be, as far as possible, kept at work still in getting out shakes and pickets, clearing away debris and helping to rebuild the mill, which would not have shut down for the winter so long as favorable weather continued. The railroad from the mill to Aptos will be completed in about a fortnight, and this together with the railway leading into the timber above the mill, will be of the greatest service in transporting material, &c., for the work of reconstruction.

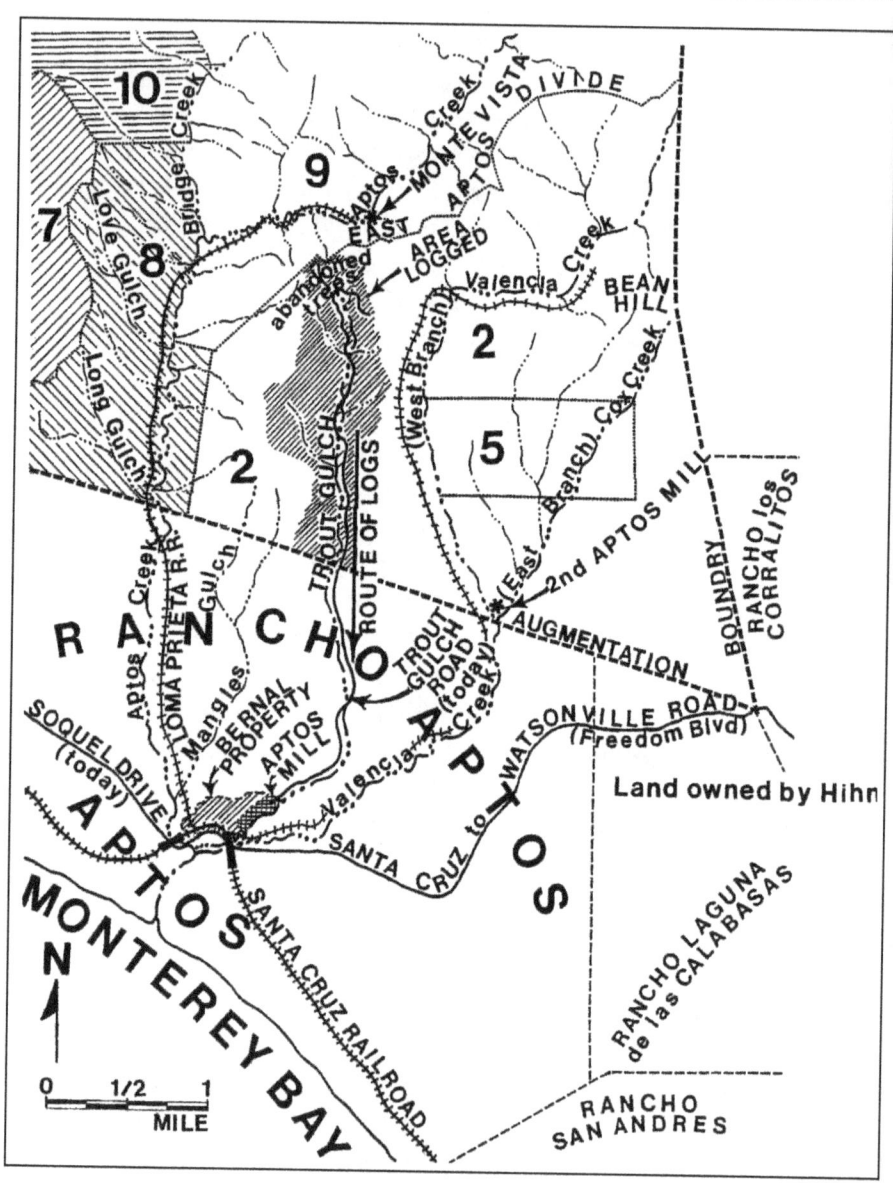

FIGURE 4.16 LOCATION OF HIHN'S MILL ON VALENCIA CREEK

After Hihn assessed the damage, because times were good and the lumber market was booming, he opted to rebuild. But instead of simply restoring production to the mill's pre-fire capacity, he decided to increase its output to match his competitor, the Loma Prieta Lumber Company.

Thus, the new milling complex would have the capability of producing up to 70,000 board feet of lumber daily. He also decided to improve his box factory, increase his shake and shingle output, and add a planing mill. In order to meet the increased freight requirements brought on by such a large facility, Hihn decided to upgrade his small mule tramway into a full steam railroad. After considering several makes of locomotives, he settled on a Porter type 0-4-2 saddle tank engine. The locomotive was again named 'Betsy Jane,' just as Hihn had named the first locomotive used on the Santa Cruz Railroad, but this was a new model. It would continue to work in the Valencia Creek canyon until the mill shut down in 1892.[159]

Spring Creek spur installed

Around the end of 1886, as the Loma Prieta Lumber Company was wrapping up operations for the year, construction began on the first substantial Southern Pacific-built spur off the Loma Prieta Branch at Spring Creek. Spring Creek was the only exclusive logging spur to appear as a formal railroad station in Southern Pacific records and that was likely because it was an expensive undertaking. The spur broke away from the mainline just beyond the long compound bridge that crossed over Aptos Creek twice on its way to Monte Vista. This location is still visible today. Hikers on the Aptos Creek Trail, after crossing Aptos Creek and climbing to the old railroad grade, can find it breaking off to the north through a long cut.

The primary reason that the spur was built is quite clear. Following the fire that destroyed the Monte Vista mill, the Loma Prieta Lumber Company needed to harvest more timber. However, the extension of the Loma Prieta Branch beyond Monte Vista was still at least a year away from completion. Thus, the company needed a short-term solution and turned to the untapped timber along the bottom of China Ridge and up Spring Creek Gulch. Therefore, the purpose of the Spring Creek spur was threefold: first, it received logs that came down from the upper reaches of Spring Creek Gulch; second, it provided railroad access along the southern end of China Ridge to the west above Bridge Creek; and third, it provided that same access to the east. Because water from the creek was used to supply the nearby town with drinking water via two cisterns near the 800-feet elevation point,

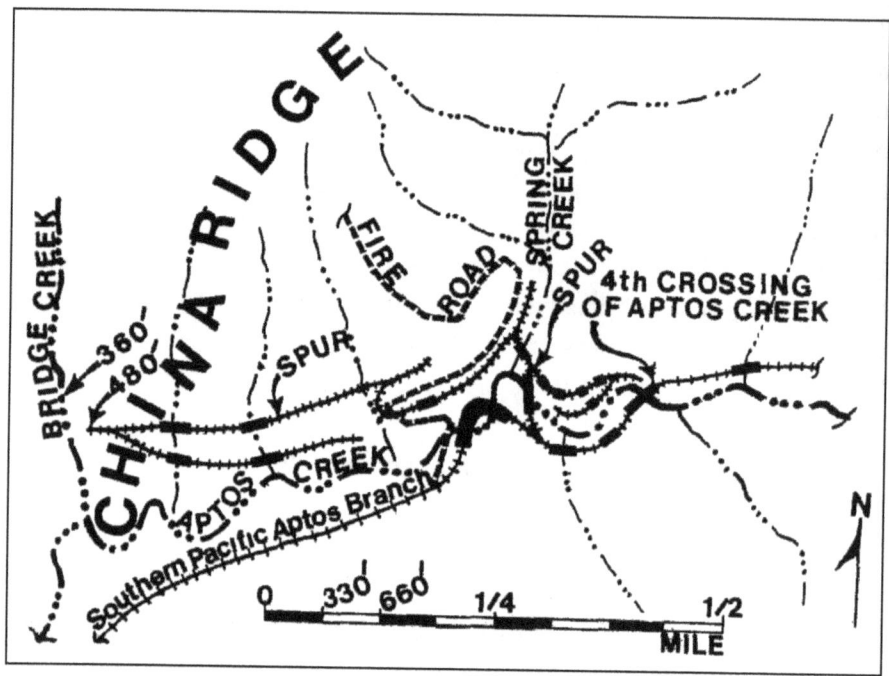

FIGURE 4.17 THE SPRING CREEK AND SOUTH CHINA RIDGE SPUR

none of the timber above that line was harvested until after 1900.

The first 500 feet of the Spring Creek spur was graded bed but at Aptos Creek, a 100-foot-long bridge was required to reach the west bank of the creek and then an additional shorter bridge was needed to cross Spring Creek just below today's Aptos Creek Fire Road. About 500 feet to the north of the second bridge, at the top of the railroad grade within the gulch, a loading area was set up where logs cut from either side of Spring Creek could be hauled and loaded onto waiting flatcars.

The loading area doubled as the end of a switchback for a track to the west along the bottom of China Ridge. After crossing a short bridge over a gully, the track made a tight 180-degree turn to the east near a substantial turn on the modern Aptos Creek Fire Road. At the end of this curve, the line double-backed to the west again, crossing over two more shallow gulches via short bridges before stopping about 120 feet above Bridge Creek. At this point, the line switch-backed toward Aptos Creek, crossing the two gulches again before paralleling the mainline from the west bank of the creek.

Meanwhile, just north of the main spur's bridge across Aptos Creek, a different track broke off via a switchback and went about 1,000 feet to the east above the creek before ending near the point where the mainline crossed Aptos Creek to the west bank. A switchback sent the track to nearly creek level, stopping just below the spur's bridge. The Spring Creek spur was likely only used for two seasons, but it remained on Southern Pacific Railroad records until 1890 and the first 500 feet may have remained in place for several years to park rolling stock.[160]

Mills reopen for the season

Even as rebuilding efforts continued on the Valencia Creek mill, the other mills within the Augmentation began to open again in March 1887. The Loma Prieta Lumber Company's new mill south of the village was not yet completed but enough work had been done to fire up its boiler and headrig. One of each had been transferred south from the Monte Vista mill, while the other boiler and headrig remained at Monte Vista to continue processing lumber until construction was completed on the new mill. Meanwhile, Southern Pacific Railroad surveyors were searching for a route from Monte Vista to the new logging camp and shingle mill site near the bottom of Aptos Falls, two miles to the north.[161]

Loma Prieta Lumber Company opens offices at Loma Prieta

Around April 19, 1887, the corporate offices of the Loma Prieta Lumber Company were moved to the village of Loma Prieta. Most of the company's planners, bookkeepers, secretaries, and support staff would work and live here while the mill was operating. Prior to this time, all of this staff shared space in the Watsonville Mill & Lumber Company's offices in Watsonville.[162]

Game Cock mill opens on Corralitos Creek

In May 1887, the Watsonville Mill & Lumber Company began erecting a new mill in Game Cock Gulch along a tributary of Corralitos Creek. On June 5, it was announced in the *Surf* that D. A. Rider & Sons was awarded the contract for operating the mill. An advertisement for lumbermen appeared in the newspaper the same day. Charles Ford estimated that the harvesting of Game Cock Canyon would take from three to four years.[163]

Monte Vista mill shuts down permanently

Sometime in late May or early June 1887, the second boiler and headrig at Monte Vista joined the first at the new mill south of the village of Loma Prieta. With this relocation, the mill at Monte Vista shut down for the last time. Most of the remaining logs in the millpond were taken to the new pond down Aptos Creek, but some were shipped to the Pajaro mill in order to keep it operating for the rest of the year.

Valencia mill reopens

The first week of July 1887, Frederick Hihn's Valencia Creek mill finally reopened with an increased capacity and a new narrow-gauge railroad to deliver wood products to Aptos. The *Sentinel* announced that "At Hihn's Aptos mill 50,000 feet of lumber per day are being cut. A new engine and boiler will be put in the mill this week. This addition will give the mill 350-horse power."[164]

South Pacific Coast Railway is leased to the Southern Pacific Railroad

After months of speculation and suspicious backroom bargaining between officials of the South Pacific Coast Railroad and the Southern Pacific Railroad, the truth finally began to emerge: the rivalry between the two companies was over. Despite the financial success of the South Pacific Coast Railroad and its several subsidiary companies, James Fair had lost interest in the company and sold his shares to the Southern Pacific in April 1887 via a complex lease agreement valid for fifty years, during which time he would receive around $220,000 annually. For whatever reason, he soon afterwards sold his bonds to Farmers Loan & Trust Company, permanently abandoning the South Pacific Coast Railroad.

Prior to the finalization of the transfer and to better manage the South Pacific Coast portfolio of companies, the various subsidiaries of the railroad were consolidated to form the South Pacific Coast Railway Company on May 23. The new firm would be run as an autonomous unit, first as a subsidiary of the Southern Pacific and later as the Narrow-Gauge Subdivision of the Coast Division. The official transfer of the company to the Southern Pacific was completed on July 1. The southern end of the route would remain narrow-gauge until the April 18, 1906 San Francisco Earthquake, at which point Southern Pacific standard-gauged all of the tracks and fully integrated the system into the Coast Division. The South Pacific Coast Railway retained a semblance of corporate independence until the expiration of the fifty-year lease in 1937, at which point Southern Pacific consolidated the railway into its parent company.[165]

Timber cutting record set at Loma Prieta mill

An article in the *Surf* published on July 30, 1887 revealed that a new state record had been set for the amount of board feet of lumber cut in a single day. Over a period of 11 hours, 45 minutes, a total of 92,325 board feet was cut by the Loma Prieta mill's crew. Crews began bragging to the Valencia mill workers in Aptos, sparking a rivalry that would continue into the following year.

It should be noted that, to accomplish this feat, it required days or even weeks of preparation by the mill's crew. The entire mill and its supporting functions had to be ready. There had to be enough logs of proper size and length waiting in the millpond and only the simplest lumber could be made in such a high volume. In other words, the settings on the saws for the headrigs, edgers, and trimmers could not be altered to any great extent to maintain such a high output level.[166]

Land transfer from John Hacker to George Olive concerning Tract 27 in the Augmentation

On August 31, 1887, George Olive purchased the 126-acre Tract 27 in the Augmentation from John Hacker. Olive had taken over the Olive & Company lumber firm from his father and added this new tract to his timber holdings in the area.[167]

The *Surf* reports a lumber boom in the Santa Cruz Mountains

An article was published in the *Surf* on October 5, 1887 revealing the full extent of the lumber industry at the time. The reporter revealed that:

> James Dougherty, of the Loma Prieta mills was in town last evening and reports business is booming. For the last three months the mills have been cutting an average of 55,000 feet of lumber daily, and have orders ahead for all that can be manufactured this year.
>
> When it is realized that one day's cut from one mill like this would furnish material for six or eight ordinary dwellings, some idea of the rapid development of California can be gained.[168]

Game Cock mill burns down

On October 21, 1887, the lumber mill in Game Cock Canyon owned by D. A. Rider & Son burned down. The *Los Angeles Herald* reported that 155,000 board feet of lumber was lost at a cost of $12,000. The Riders had not taken out any insurance on the mill.[169]

Frederick Hihn opens new mill on Spignet Gulch

Because the shake and shingle mill at the Valencia Mill could not keep up with customer demand, Frederick Hihn decided to increase output by establishing a new purpose-built mill on Spignet Gulch within Tract 10 of the Augmentation. The tract was divided between the Soquel Creek watershed to the west and the Aptos Creek watershed to the east, with Hinckley Ridge dividing them. The 453 acres to the west, along the East Branch of Soquel Creek, had high quality standing timber and was easily accessed from the Soquel Turnpike.

The mill was built near the 900-foot elevation mark along the south fork of Spignet Gulch. In order to reach the site, a road was extended from the vicinity of today's Olive Springs Road along the gulch's south side for about a mile. While this road was steep in places, wagons loaded with shakes and shingles could easily maneuver its twists and turns. An old surveyor map of the road and gulch clearly shows the road to the mill. From there, some path—either a road, trail, or skid road—continued up to the top of Hinckley Ridge and down toward Bridge Creek. About a half mile below the ridge, the road made a sudden turn south. Part of this route today is the Big Stump Gap Trail within the Forest of Nisene Marks.

In truth, the shake and shingle operation did not last long. An article

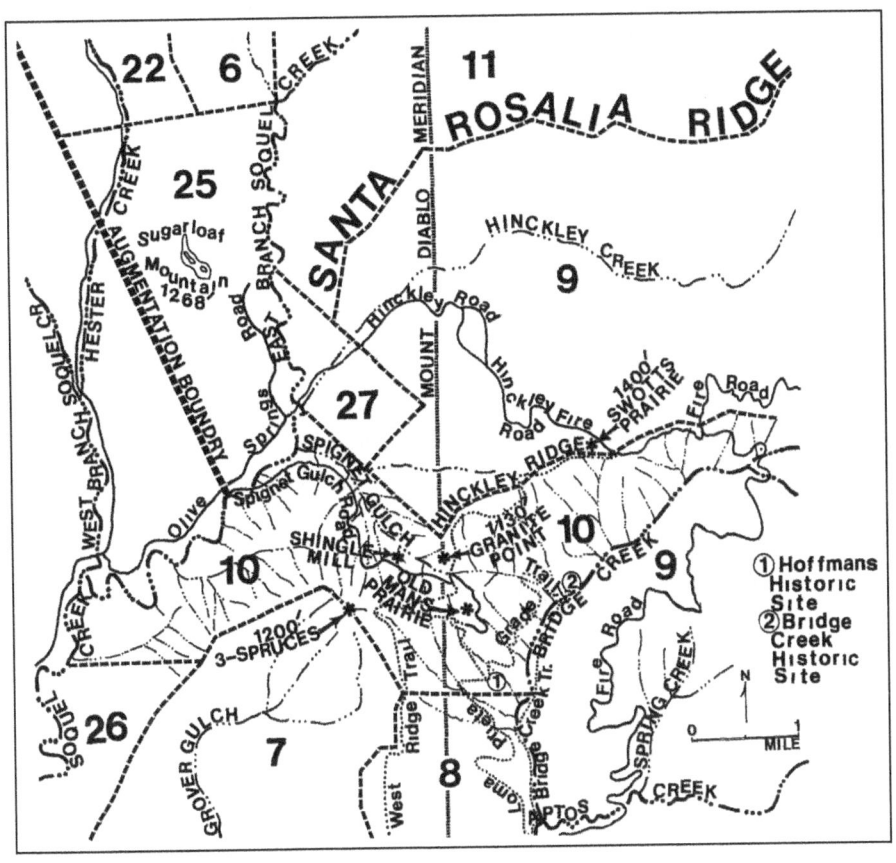

FIGURE 4.18 SITE OF HIHN'S SHINGLE MILL ON SPIGNET GULCH

in the *Surf* published September 28, 1903 stated that "The timber in the Spignet Gulch did not prove as valuable as expected and instead of a five year run at the shingle mill it has been abandoned after a year and a half's cutting." In 1917, the Loma Prieta Lumber Company purchased the eastern 610 acres of Tract 10 and discovered what they called "spot rot" in many of the redwood trees. This meant that an extra amount of trimming was required, often resulting in overly short lumber. What they likely encountered was actually root rot, which is decay in a tree's root system caused by a fungus. The fungus enters a tree through a wound and then passes into the heartwood and down into the root system.

The etymology of several places along Hinckley Ridge deserve mention at this point. First, there are two locations identified as prairies along the ridge, labeled as such by Thomas Wright, who was county surveyor in the 1860s. The term seems to have been used almost exclusively for locations within the Augmentation, suggesting that Wright either had a penchant for the term or conducted a more careful study of this area. By definition, a prairie is an extensive tract of land, mostly level, destitute of trees and covered with grass. Both prairies were located near the top of the ridge, where the redwood trees had thinned out.

The name Old Man's Prairie has an unknown origin complicated by the fact that its physical characteristics at the time it was named are also unknown. It easily qualifies as one of the most mysterious and mystifying places within the Forest of Nisene Marks. Its approximate location is within Tract 10 near the top of Hinckley Ridge on the Bridge Creek side. Considering the amount of maps that note the location, it clearly served as an important location well into the twentieth century, but its exact purpose or value remains uncertain. Today, the remnants of the prairie are surrounded by the West Ridge Trail and the Big Stump Gap Trail. The area is largely populated by poison oak interspersed with short hardwood trees.

Hinckley Ridge's other prairie—Swett's Prairie—lies along the north side of the West Ridge Trail near where the trail meets the Hinckley Fire Road. Historically, another road also met here to provide Henry Clay White access to the Soquel Turnpike. The origin of the name for this prairie remains a mystery and only appeared on Wright's 1864 map of the county between Tracts 9 and 10.

Wright and his team of surveyors gave more generic names to other locations they found on Hinckley Ridge. Granite Point, for example, lies east of Spignet Gulch's headwaters between Hinckley and Bridge Creeks just north of today's West Ridge Trail. The location is marked by a granite boulder that resembles the bow end of an upside-down rowboat. The site is along the top of Hinckley Ridge, while the trail followed by the surveyors and other travelers passes along its west side. Today the area is overgrown with small bushes and trees.

To the west near the headwaters of Grover Gulch and on the boundary line of Tracts 7 and 10 was the Three Spruces. It is a strange name for an area that, at least today, has no spruce trees of any variety. In all likelihood, the term actually referred to three Douglas fir trees, which resemble spruce trees in certain conditions. The location marked the junction of Hinckley Ridge with the Bates Divide and the unnamed ridge separating Grover Creek from Soquel Creek.[170]

Loma Prieta Branch extension completed

On March 14, 1888, the extension of the Loma Prieta Branch from mile-marker 5.0 to mile-marker 7.08 was completed. It proved to be one of the most difficult and expensive stretches of track constructed or maintained in Santa Cruz County.

A half-mile north of the former Monte Vista mill site, the extension line crossed the Zayante Rift Zone, which shifted minutely but regularly and caused endless landslides and sinks. Making matters worse was the predictable but costly damage caused to the right-of-way every winter that the branch operated. In a bid to avoid some of these potential problems, the railroad's engineers decided against building fills along these two miles since they would just wash away. However, even the bridges and half-trestles were not immune from the movements of the earth. To save on costs, Southern Pacific went with a cheaper option than the prefabricated bridges that linked Aptos to Monte Vista. Instead, all the pilings, bents, and beams were cut at the Loma Prieta mill and constructed on site, giving a rustic and transitory nature to the extension.

The most significant obstacle along the new track was a perilous loca-

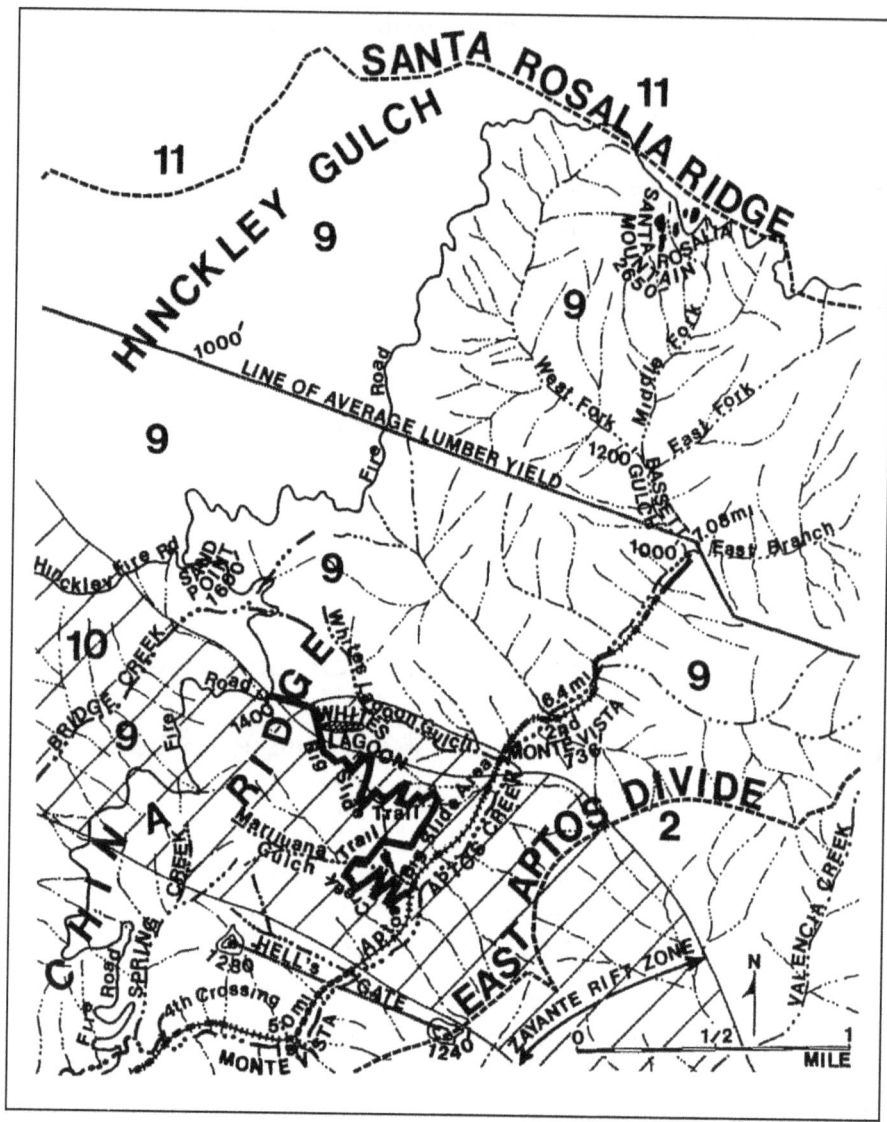

Figure 4.19 Route of the Loma Prieta Branch to mile marker 7.08

tion named Hell's Gate, named for a narrow passage between a 1,280-foot peak along China Ridge and the 1,240-foot summit of the East Aptos Divide. This location a quarter-mile north of Monte Vista was considered nearly impossible to surmount and it was said by crews afterwards that "to build a railroad beyond this line could only have been concocted in Hell itself." The location today can be found along the Aptos Creek Trail and is identified by the fine white sand along both sides of the trail. Just north of the 'gate' is the aptly named Hell's Gate Gulch.

From Hell's Gate to about a half-mile north through the Big Slide area is the Zayante Rift Zone. In total, this zone covers nearly twenty percent of the entire Forest of Nisene Marks, leaving a one-mile by three-mile gash through the mountains, although it is not easily visible due to foliage and the varying elevations of the landscape. The Loma Prieta Branch experienced its most extensive and continuous problems in this area, with frequent misalignments at its margins and constant slide activity in between.

The route from the original Monte Vista and the 1,000-feet elevation point 2.08 miles to the north was a sometimes-perilous journey that stuck closely to Aptos Creek. It began just above Monte Vista near the 4.78-mile mark, where the mainline began its descent toward the original mill that sat on a narrow shelf on the west side of Aptos Creek. Thus, the distance from the start of the new track to Hell's Gate was approximately a half-mile.

Despite the short distance, ten small trestle bridges and half-trestles of varying lengths as well as two long cuts were required to reach the squeeze of Hell's Gate. Throughout this section, Aptos Creek ran about 60 feet below the right-of-way. Most of the bridges were no more than 50 feet, but at least three reached closer to twice that length. An eleventh and final bridge of about 150 feet was required to cross Hell's Gate Gulch. For the 0.4 miles north of this point, no bridge nor cut was needed.

Nearly a mile beyond the start of the extension track, crews reached Marijuana Gulch. Despite the Spanish origin of the name, the name is recent and refers to cannabis. In the late 1960s or early 1970s, several ambitious individuals forged a path to Aptos Creek from the east, crossed the creek, and worked their way up Marijuana Gulch for a quarter mile. Where the steepness of the hillside proved too great, the people set up an illegal pot garden. They terraced the hillside using large boards and hand tools, and installed hoses and pumps to irrigate and cultivate the marijuana plants. The remote operation remained undetected until mid-1978 when several park rangers led by Gerry Waggoner were surveying a continuation of the Aptos Creek Trail to Five Finger Falls. The rangers discovered the well-worn path across the creek and followed it to its end, where they found forty-three healthy cannabis plants ready for harvest. They quickly pulled all of the plants and turned them into the Santa Cruz County Sheriff's office.

For many years, State Parks staff tried to suppress the nickname for the gulch. Waggoner was ordered not to use the term by his superiors

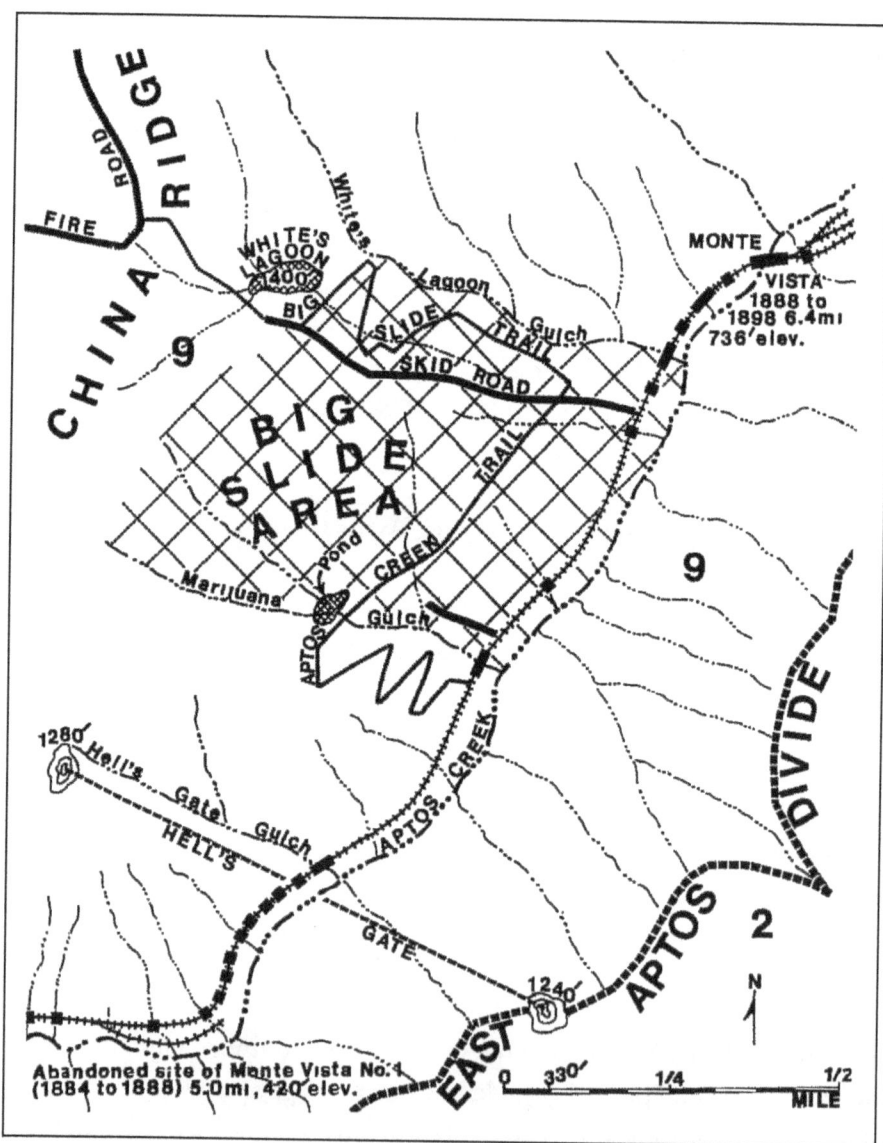

FIGURE 4.20 ROUTE FROM HELL'S GATE GULCH TO WHITE'S LAGOON GULCH

and the instructions were passed on to staff as well as myself. I began to ponder other names to identify the gulch, finally settling on Emerald Pond Gulch, a name arrived at because of a small artificial pond that sat in the gulch high above Aptos Creek. Over the years, an abundance of duckweed has collected in the pond, which tends to turn it into an emerald-green color at times during the year. But, because the pond was so isolated at the time (Aptos Creek Trail now passes directly beside it), the name never caught on. Today, despite resistance from State Parks officials, the name Marijuana Gulch has stuck.

It was shortly after the discovery of the marijuana operation that I began my exploratory journeys in The Forest of Nisene Marks. In late 1978, I accompanied Waggoner and his assistant ranger to help dismantle the terracing and bring out the equipment left by the growers. It was felt that the area had to be destroyed in order to discourage further planting. But the effort was not necessary because Mother Nature had plans for the gulch as well as for the entire canyon. On the night of January 4, 1982, the entire lower quarter mile of the gulch was wiped almost entirely clean of vegetation and remnants of human occupation, with portions cut through to bedrock.

Marijuana Gulch today marks the southern boundary of today's Big Slide Area, a section roughly 0.6 miles wide that stretches the same distance to near the top of China Ridge. This roughly square section of steep hillside originally held nearly ten million board feet of lumber and required such a unique and unprecedented solution to harvest it that many today refuse to accept it. Because of the damage from the massive landslide of January 1982, it is difficult today to imagine what the scene looked like for grading crews working in the canyon nearly a century earlier.

According to the best estimates, the 0.6-mile section of track between Marijuana Gulch and White's Lagoon Gulch was not an overly problematic stretch of right-of-way. Its main issue was that the ground was soft and gave way easily, so grading crews made the right-of-way extra wide to compensate. At Marijuana Gulch, a trestle bridge of not less than 150 feet was required, but no other substantial bridge was needed in this section. Just north of the bridge, a wide section of track allowed for a 500-foot-long spur where logs could be loaded from a 50-foot-long skid road that ran along the north side of Marijuana Gulch above the railroad grade.

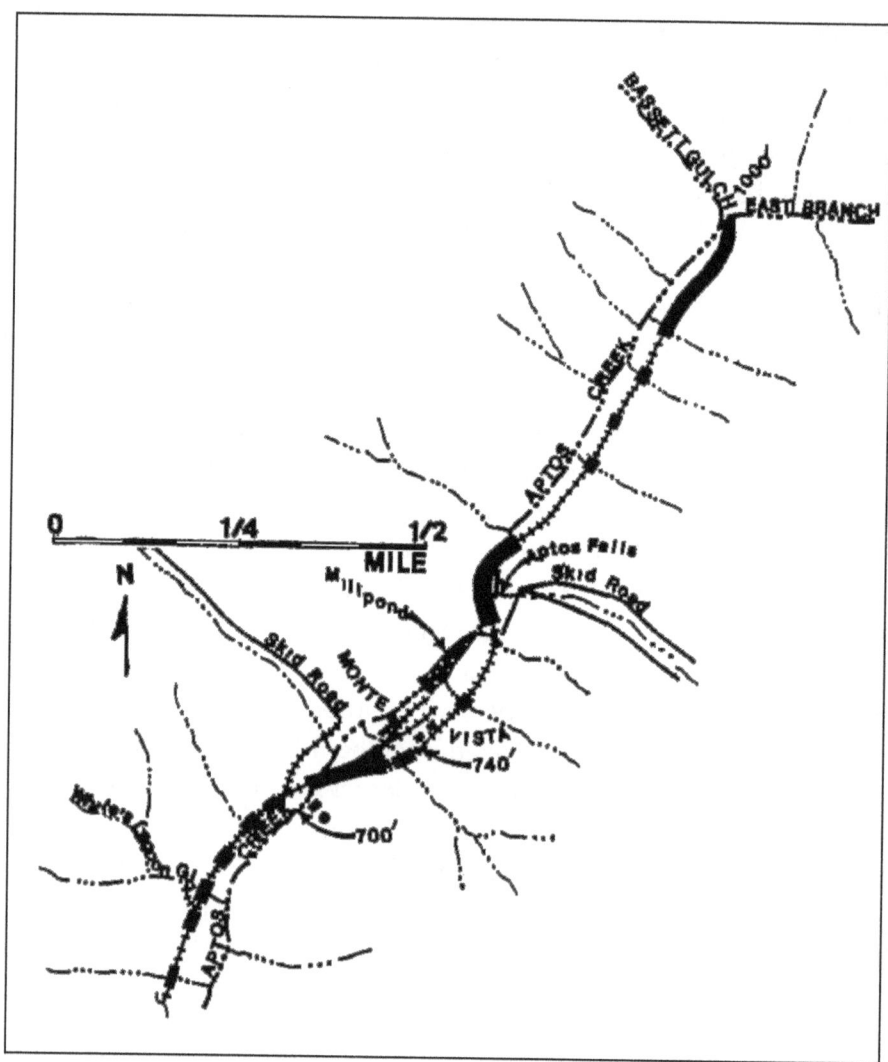

FIGURE 4.21 ROUTE FROM WHITE'S LAGOON GULCH TO BASSETT GULCH

About 250 feet beyond the northern side of this loading station, a short bridge crossed an unnamed gulch. From here for about 2,000 feet, the line ran along a half-trestle in order to avoid the difficulties caused by the moist soil. Another trestle bridge crossed an unnamed gulch before the tracks reached a skid road that ran up the north side of the gulch for a distance of nearly 500 feet to White's Lagoon near the top of China Ridge. A short spur line branched off here to receive logs that were brought down by oxen from along the gulch. From here, the tracks crossed another short 100-foot trestle bridge and then reached White's Lagoon Gulch, named for the fact that the lagoon would overflow into the gulch during periods of intense rain. An approximately 150-foot-long trestle bridge crossed the gulch, moving the right-of-way out of the later-named Big Slide Area.

North of White's Lagoon Gulch, the extended railroad entered the area that would borrow the name Monte Vista from the mill that once sat a mile and a half to the south. Despite the similar names, the scope of the operations at these two locations was vastly different. The earlier Monte Vista was a full-scale lumber mill while the later Monte Vista was more of a transloading center with some small-scale milling facilities. The 500 feet of right-of-way between the gulch and Aptos Creek south of the second Monte Vista was a narrow shelf that required three short trestle bridges to cross a gulch and two shallow depressions. At the north end of this stretch, a spur continued along the west side of the creek to the bottom of a gulch to access a skid road that ran along the gulch's north side. The main track continued across a low, curving trestle bridge that brought the railroad line to the east side of Aptos Creek for the first time along the extension. At the end of the bridge, the track split, with two spurs terminating at the mill site at the 6.4-mile marker and the main track continuing to the east of Monte Vista in order to reach the desired end-of-track 0.68 miles further upstream.

As soon as the extension track reached the site for the second Monte Vista, construction began, and it would continue to be expanded in some capacity for the next decade. The original purpose of the site was to house logging crews working far up Aptos Creek and to provide a transloading site for local skid roads. As such, there were cottages for workers, corrals for oxen and mules, and some rudimentary facilities for buckers and fallers to store and maintain their equipment. Southern Pacific also kept a small crew of workers at the camp to maintain the rolling stock, and the Loma Prieta Lumber Company maintained an office, including living quarters, for a company officer. To support the workers in their daily life, the camp included a small store with phone and telegraph facilities, as well as Wells Fargo Express and postal services, which functioned as satellites of the offices at Loma Prieta.

Monte Vista was also a tourist destination, however. With Aptos Falls just north of the camp and miles of yet-uncut timber upstream, adventurous campers came from across the world to explore the headwaters of Aptos Creek. To support these activities, the camp included a campground, picnic area, barbecues, a small saloon and hotel, a dance pavilion, and guest rooms for visiting bands that came up to Monte Vista to entertain vacationers in the summer. All of this activity, both freight and tourist, naturally required a Southern Pacific depot to support it and one was built just north of the bridge over Aptos Creek.

A report by the *Surf* in May 1890 describes in detail a visit to Monte Vista by students at Chesnutwood's Business College in Santa Cruz:

> *Quite a large crowd, about 150 in all, of College students and their friends left on the broad-gauge train at 10 o'clock Saturday morning for Loma Prieta to attend Prof. Chesnutwood's annual picnic.*
>
> *The only incident of importance that happened on the way was near the Loma Prieta Lumber Company's mill, a log protruding from a shute* [sic] *tore the steps from the platform of the foremost car, which caused the car to lurch to one side, somewhat frightening several of the picnicers* [sic].
>
> *When "Monte Vista," the little station, was reached the passengers, with baskets and other paraphernalia, were bundled off the cars and directed up the mountain to the picnic ground, and by the time the grounds were reached it was lunch time by everybody's watch. Table cloths were spread under every shady tree and the contents of the lunch baskets were displayed.*
>
> *From the picnic grounds a majority of the merry picnicers adjourned to the dance hall, where Hastings' band of seven pieces furnished dance music for the rest of the afternoon. Those who were not votaries of Terpsichore wandered about the woods and gathered flowers and ferns or watched the loggers sending huge logs down a hundred-foot bank into the water above the mill dam.*
>
> *The train pulled out from the station with all aboard at 6 P.M., making the run to Aptos in twenty minutes, where there was a wait of forty-five minutes for the regular train,*

> which arrived in Santa Cruz at 7:27 P.M.
> Mr. and Mrs. Chesnutwood were, as usual, admirable host and hostess and made the entire party an enjoyable one for all.

Two years later, in his *History of Santa Cruz County, California*, Edward Harrison recounted that:

> [W]hile the [Loma Prieta] mill possesses all the advantages of modern machinery, having a daily capacity equal to any mill in the county, the main and conspicuous point of advantage possessed by this company over its competitors is the branch railway to the mill and beyond it into the timber land, connecting with the main line of the Southern Pacific Company at Aptos, and furnishing the very best facilities for shipping their manufactured products. They have eight and a half miles [sic] of railroad, built with the co-operation of the Southern Pacific Company, over whose line all their building materials, etc., are necessarily shipped.
> This road is one of the most picturesque in the State, winding through a tortuous cañon from Aptos to Monte Vista, a station three and a half miles above the present site of Loma Prieta Lumber Mill. The company this year is extending this line about one-half mile further up the cañon, in order to tap the timber which is necessary to obtain from that locality. I have said that this is a wonderfully pretty route, and I will add that its completion is the consummation of a very difficult feat of engineering. One who had seen these forests in their virgin condition, unacquainted with the possibilities of railroading, would never have dreamed that the whistle of the locomotive would some day break the deep stillness of these wild and rugged mountains.

When precisely the millpond and small lumber mill mentioned by the *Surf* was built at Monte Vista is unclear. It seems most likely that the mill was an original construction, built shortly after the line reached Monte Vista, possibly to cut crossties, bents, and posts for the railroad and support construction projects elsewhere along the line, including at the larger Loma Prieta mill. Bert Stoodley made a passing reference to a mill at Monte Vista in his memoir but did not elaborate on it. Meanwhile, the *Surf* article clearly mentions a millpond but gives no further information either.

Monte Vista was the terminus for passenger service but not the end of the line. The right-of-way wrapped around Monte Vista to the east of the camp, slowly climbing the hillside to gain elevation along what reached a seven percent grade at its steepest point. After crossing the main bridge over Aptos Creek, the main line immediately crossed a short gulch over a trestle bridge and then proceeded along a narrow, sloping shelf for about 1,000 feet. Near the middle of this shelf, a second short bridge was required to cross another small gulch. At the end of this stretch, the tracks encountered another steep gulch blockaded to the north by a sheer rock wall that could not easily be passed. A loading station was set up here to access a skid road that climbed up the gulch to the east.

A natural cul-de-sac was formed at this site due to the dual presence of a solid rock wall and a phenomenon unique to Aptos Creek: the 25-foot-high Aptos Falls, often called Monte Vista Falls and now known as Five Finger Falls. The creek has no other waterfall along its main route and it caused a major engineering problem for Southern Pacific. The railroad could either dynamite the rock wall to cut a passage through to the other side, potentially damaging or destroying Aptos Falls in the process, or it could cross Aptos Creek again and wrap around the falls from the other side. The railroad chose the latter option.

Thus, the extension track turned sharply away from the east bank of Aptos Creek and to the west bank across a trestle bridge still elevated 40 to 50 feet above the ground in order to keep the grade manageable. After curving around Aptos Falls, the tracks finally found purchase on the steep hillside of the west bank of Aptos Creek, but the shelf was so narrow that at least three bridges or half-trestles, as well as several culverts, were needed to maintain a level right-of-way for the next 800 feet. At this point, even the occasional shelf disappeared entirely with almost sheer hillsides flanking either side of Aptos Creek nearly fifty feet below the grade.

Because of the canyon's narrowness, there was no room for a railroad line on either side of the creek. Therefore, from the end of the last shelf to

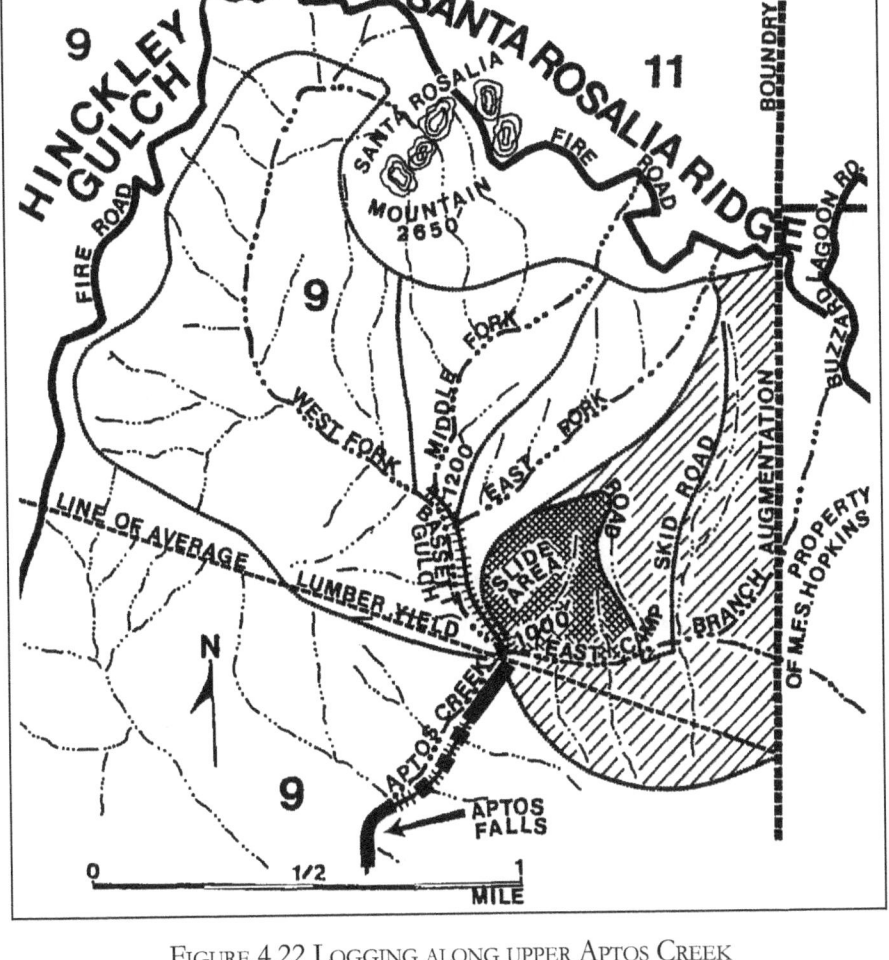

FIGURE 4.22 LOGGING ALONG UPPER APTOS CREEK

the 1,000-foot elevation point, the line was entirely elevated along a trestle viaduct. The grade of the railroad was less than that of the slope of the creek, so as the tracks continued north, they slowly approached the level of the creek. During my exploratory hikes, I came across several 100-foot-long one- to two-inch diameter cables hanging from the west bank that nearly reached the creek below. My guess is that the cables were used to support this viaduct. The right-of-way finally found solid ground again atop a narrow shelf just above the creek level at the confluence of the east branch of Aptos Creek and Bassett Gulch, named after the railroad's superintendent, A. C. Bassett. At the site, lumber crews established a small, rugged logging camp where they could receive logs from the surrounding area.

Plans were in place to extend the track another 0.36 miles up Bassett Gulch to the 1,200-foot elevation point, but that project would take another three years to complete. In the meantime, one of the goals of the Loma Prieta Lumber Company was to harvest the timber along the east branch of Aptos Creek. It was not possible to extend a track up the branch since the way was blocked by a wall of boulders, some 25 to 30 feet high, followed by a steep climb up the southern leg of Santa Rosalia Ridge. Therefore, logging crews found other means of transporting the logs along the east branch to waiting flatcars at the logging camp.

The biggest obstacle along the way was not, in fact, the wall of boulders or the steep grade, although both caused considerable difficulties. Instead, it was an area just beyond the boulders, where a large slide encompassed nearly 40 acres of rocks and boulders separated by crevices, narrow ravines, and seasonal streambeds, all interspersed with low growing vegetation and fallen trees. During my exploratory hikes into this area, I found no hint of a skid road. Therefore, it seems unlikely that logs were pulled through this area and there were no other telltale signs that logging occurred here.

The solution logging crews decided upon was to establish a staging area on a narrow shelf just east of the slide area. Logs to the south were dragged or hauled to the area using donkey engines, while a skid road ran up to the north alongside a seasonal feeder creek. Oxen in tandem with donkey engines were used to haul logs down from this section. From the staging area to the northwest, a 100- to 150-foot-wide road was built that skirted all the way around the slide area, first up the hillside on the east and then around the back of the slide area to the west, with the road ending just above the 1,000-foot elevation logging camp at the end of the Loma Prieta Branch. Logs at the staging area were tethered via a chain to a donkey engine that was installed at the top of the slide area. At the top of the grade, logs were attached to the chain of another donkey engine that then hauled them due west across the top of the slide area. Finally, a third donkey engine lowered the logs to the 1,000-foot elevation logging camp below the end of the road, where they could be loaded onto a flatcar. Because of the narrowness of the canyon and the difficulty of loading the logs, an elaborate loading device was built to ensure logs were properly secured on flatcars. Filled flatcars were probably rolled under brake power to Monte Vista where they were either processed or taken by train to the main mill at Loma Prieta.[171]

James Grover dies in Santa Cruz

James Grover died from a prolonged illness at his home in San Francisco on May 13, 1888. His passing left a hole in Grover & Company management that would not be filled for several months.[172]

Pajaro & Santa Cruz Railroad consolidated into Southern Pacific Railroad Company

On May 14, 1888, sixteen subsidiary railroads including the Pajaro & Santa Cruz Railroad were consolidated into the Southern Pacific Railroad Company. The renamed Santa Cruz Line and the Loma Prieta Line became part of the new Coast Division, with A. C. Bassett appointed general superintendent.[173]

CHAPTER 5

~

The Gilded Age

Hihn's Mill News

On May 18, 1888, the *Surf* ran its first entry in a long-running series of columns about news in the Santa Cruz Mountain logging towns. These columns were contributed by residents in the communities and supplemented the *Surf*'s regular "Personal Splashes" and "Shifting Sands" columns that focused on local happenings. From 1888 to 1894, they ran irregularly and alternated between the communities adjacent to Frederick Hihn's mill at Valencia Creek and the Loma Prieta Lumber Company mill on Aptos Creek. The columns eventually were given comedic titles and were usually signed with often farcical pen names. For the sake of completeness and to give an idea of life in local logging communities, all of these happenings columns are interspersed throughout the following two chapters, beginning with this column submitted to the *Surf* on May 14:

Hihn's Mill News

The Valencia School will give an exhibition in the evening at the closing of the term.

Mr. Hanahan has been engaged to work at De Harte and White's saw mill for the season.

All who attended Mr. and Mrs. Horstman's party last week are still talking of the delightful evening they spent.

Miss Rose Barbree, of Salinas, who has been visiting Mrs. M. Hanahan at her "Shady Nook Farm," near Hihn's Mill, has returned home.

Some folks say the boom is dead, but they wouldn't say so if they were at "Hihn's Mill," which has been undergoing many improvements in the past month. New machinery has been placed in the mill; a store, office, and many unique cottages built. Likewise everything and everybody are in a flourishing and lively condition. VERNON.[174]

Aptos and Loma Prieta Items

The *Surf*'s Hihn's Mill News expanded to include the Loma Prieta mill in its second column, published on May 26, 1888:

Aptos and Loma Prieta Items

Miss Jessie Nichols is visiting friends in Santa Cruz.
Fern Fall is beautiful, but how about the barbed wire fence?
Walking is said to be good between Aptos and Loma Prieta.
The Loma Prieta Mill is now cutting 75,000 feet of lumber daily.

J. H. Nichols, of Illinois, is visiting his brother, Judge Nichols.

Hamlin's colored minstrels played at Loma Prieta Thursday evening.

A handsome cottage is in course of erection at Loma Prieta for the management.

A new store is to be opened at Hihn's Mill, which will be

under the management of Mr. Bert Hihn.

Mr. Manges has commenced the erection of his new dwelling and expects to have it completed Sept. 1st.

A gentleman sitting in the front seat at the minstrels the other evening arose to get more light on the subject, but created a total eclipse of the stage to the rest of the audience.

ORLEANS.[175]

Grover & Company selects new management

On July 2, 1888, the officers of Grover & Company met with its investors to read the will of James Grover and determine his stake in the company. After some discussion, it was agreed that he owned $225,000 in shares, which he had passed on to his son, Dwight. In addition, it was revealed that James had owned extensive timber tracts in Santa Cruz County, including several with company mills operating on them; a ranch in San Joaquin County; timberland in Humboldt County; Unity Church property; shares in the Farmers' Union; and an elegant home in Santa Cruz on Walnut Avenue.

Following the meeting, new articles of incorporation were filed to reflect the change in leadership. Stephen Grover was elected president and Dwight vice president.[176]

Charles Crocker dies

Charles Crocker passed away on August 14, 1888 at the Hotel del Monte in Monterey from complications caused by diabetes. At the time of his death, he was secretary of the Central Pacific Railroad Company and the Southern Pacific Railroad Company. Crocker was the second member of the Big Four to die following Mark Hopkins. In the 1860s, he had overseen the construction of the western half of the first transcontinental railroad.[177]

Valencia mill breaks Loma Prieta lumber cutting record

A year after the Loma Prieta Lumber Company set a daily record in the state for cutting the most lumber and a month after Aptos Creek lumbermen openly bragged about their achievement during Fourth of July festivities, the lumber team at Frederick Hihn's mill on Valencia Creek finally fought back. Weeks of preparation at the mill had been required to attempt to beat the Loma Prieta mill's record on August 14, 1888. The *Surf* reported:

> *The Aptos Mill, owned by F. A. Hihn, and situated on the Valencia creek, is a thoroughly equipped and efficiently manned saw-mill of great capacity. The average daily run is a large one, but for some time the men under the effective foremanship of Alex. Bedell, have believed that the powers of the mill and men were only half drawn upon, and one and all determined to show the "stuff that was in them." So preparations were made, and everything placed was ship-shape for a steady pull that should tell what the mill could do, and yesterday morning at six o'clock began the race for record.*
>
> *The giant logs were lifted from the dam and swung upon the carriage, which rolled them swiftly under the whizzing circular saws. No one of them measured less than 1,000 feet of lumber, and many tallied as high as 1,600, 1,700 and 1,800 feet. They were cut into boards, slabs and railway ties, edged, and taken care of as rapidly as possible, but the lumber yard looked something as if a cyclone had struck it; for so rapidly did the manufactured product accumulate that it had to be pitched wherever it would go. The scene was one of intense excitement. Every man was determined to break all past records, and the spectators were hardly less enthusiastic. The watches began to come out, and as the ponderous engines drove the circular saws faster and faster, the excitement rose as high as if a pair of trotters were trying neck and neck for the home stake. First, three of the logs were ground up into ties, boards, slabs and pieces, in ten minutes, then one that measured considerably over 1,000 feet went under the saw and came out mince-meat in a trifle less than two minutes; and so it went on, "without haste, without rest," till a halt was called, and the unprecedented record of 143,000 feet—sawed and stored from 125 logs in six hours—was declared amid*

The Gilded Age   1888

rousing cheers.

The regular day's run over the railway took down to Aptos several thousand feet of the morning's product, which was duly shipped to Pajaro, en route *to Coyote, whence it was ordered, and this morning, in less than twenty-four hours from the time the lumber was in the shape of clumsy logs floating in the Valencia creek, they will be on the ground, nearly a hundred miles away, where they are to be used.*

Aptos Mills challenges the State to beat that record—and well it may.

Following are the names of the men who, under the foremanship of Alex. Bedell, accomplished this great run, by means of a mill as perfectly appointed as any in the State.

George Bowes, Charlie Horstmann, James Marham, George Mackrell, Wm. Tracy , A. N. Hedgpeth, T. Nolan, Wm. Amaya, Charles Edmond, W. C. Heddrick, W. A. Wing (gang edger), J. T. Finnamore, J. R. Finnamore, L. T. Shriedes, John Hanahan, H. Lassen, H. Tichenor, James Lower, Joe Daniels, Joe Prother, Wm. Samuels, H. Castor, J. M. Taylor, C. C. Hoffman (Engineer), Wm. Bryan (Fireman).[178]

Chips From Hihn's Mill

Following a gap of several months, the irregular *Surf* column on logging community happenings resumed on August 23, 1888 under a new name: "Chips From Hihn's Mill." It reported:

CHIPS FROM HIHN'S MILL

Mr. Al. Buswell, of Oakland, spent Sunday here with his family.

Mrs. O. Blodgett, of Ben Lomond, is visiting her parents Mr. and Mrs. T. J. Hubbell of this place.

Harry, infant child of Mr. and Mrs. McGovern, died here last Thursday, after a few days illness.

The pupils of the Valencia school, (Hihn's Mill), gave their teacher, Miss Esther V. Malcolm, a surprise last Thursday, of a delicious birthday lunch.

"*What's that you say? Loma Prieta mill can cut twice the number of feet of lumber in a day that Hihn's can? I'm thinking, Mr. H, Loma Prieta will have to get up rather early in the morning to even cut 143,000 feet in a day, let alone six hours.*"

Mr. E. Hundley gave his sisters, Mrs. Dr. Dawson of Oroville, and Mrs. Al. Buswell, of Oakland, who have been visiting him for the past three weeks, and his friend, Mr. W. Samuels, a very pleasant surprise party at his "Brier Farm," last Saturday evening. Dancing, with a bounteous supper sandwiched in, was the feature of the evening. At a very late hour the merry party departed, after spending a most enjoyable evening, wishing the "Fair ladies" pleasant dreams, and Mr. S. many more such happy birthdays.

"Vernon."[179]

September 12, 1888: Hihn's Mill Happenings

The next entry in the recurring *Surf* column focused on local logging matters occurred on September 12, 1888, accompanied by yet another name change:

Hihn's Mill Happenings

Miss Dolly Hubbell, spent last Sunday in Santa Cruz.

Mrs. Julia Winchell of San Lucas, is visiting her sons, Messrs. Matt and Newton Hedgepath of this place.

Mrs. H. Hanahan from the "Pajaro Valley mill" is visiting her parents, Mr. and Mrs. Morehouse of this place.

Mr. Hundley departed for his home in Oroville, the following Wednesday and his many true and warm friends regret the loss of one who has been such a "Star" among them.

Mr. John Fenimore, while piling lumber at Aptos, Sunday week, accidentally let a heavy board fall on his hand, bruising it so severely that he has been unable to work since.

Mrs. A. Buswell of Oakland and Mrs. Dawson of Oroville, sister of Mr. Hundley of this place with whom they have been spending their summer vacation, returned to their homes last week.

All who attended the dance given by Miss Mary Lee Saturday week, spent a very pleasant evening, but those who attended the farewell surprise party given to Mr. Eugene Hundley at his Sweet Brier Farm, on the same evening, had, as the boys say, a "bang up" time. It was a late hour when the "merry dancers" departed for their respective homes, bidding farewell to Mr. Hundley wishing him success in his new undertaking and trusting they will soon again see him in their midst. VERNON.[180]

Loma Prieta mill reclaims state lumber cutting record

It took the Loma Prieta Lumber Company less than two months to attempt to reclaim its lost lumber cutting record from the crew of Hihn's mill on Valencia Creek on October 6, 1888. The *Surf* reported:

> One of the most pleasing features of the Independence Day parade in this city last July, was the fine array of lumber men in line from the various saw-mills of the county. Their appearance and behavior was very justly praised by the spectators and visitors, but the employees of the Loma Prieta Company carried a little ensign which had more significance than they dreamed of at that time. It bore the legend "our biggest day 93,000 feet." Now, the employees of Hihn's Aptos mill believe that is the finest mill in the State, yet they had never cut 93,000 feet of lumber in a day. They therefore sought, and gained permission of the proprietor to try their speed, and accordingly one fine day last month astonished the world with the announcement that they had cut in six and one-fourth hours 143,000 feet of lumber. This astonishing feat was duly chronicled in this paper at the time, and the sequel was last Saturday, when the Loma Prieta mill turned out 181,000 feet.
>
> Interest in the undertaking, combined with curiosity to witness the fastest lumber sawing ever performed in the county, attracted quite a company of persons to the mill on Saturday.

Among them was a large sprinkling of local candidates for office, including the Democratic nominee for Senator, Jesse Cope, for Assemblyman, J. A. Hall, for Sheriff, E. Dakan, for County Clerk, Wm. Ellery, for District Attorney, W. T. Jeter, and the Republican nominee for Treasurer, W. H. Bias. Among the plain citizens were noted S. Drennan, F. G. Menefee, S. S. Sears, F. O. Hihn, D. W. Grover, C. H. Lincoln and several others from Santa Cruz, Capt. A. J. Trask, W. B. Drew and I. N. Hayes from Felton, Jas. Dougherty and O. R. Harmon of Boulder Creek, J. T. Porter of Pajaro, and several representatives from Aptos and the surrounding section.

The Loma Prieta mill is located about five miles from Aptos station on the S. P. R. R. and is reached by a railroad that winds up the canyon of the Aptos creek three miles beyond the mill into the very heart of the redwoods. The scenery is that charming combination of the sublime and the beautiful which we term the picturesque, every road a revelation of new beauties, and every mile leading farther and farther into the secret recesses of Nature, where only a few years ago the purling of the brook or the scream of the eagle were the only sounds to be heard. Now, the warning whistle of the locomotive reverberates through the canyon, and the distant hum of the saw breaks the stillness that then echoed to the call of the coyote.

The train that traverses this canyon, either of empty "flats" going up, or of lumber and wood coming down follows so meandering a course that seldom can engine and caboose be both seen at the same time, so sharp are the curves and so continuous the succession of S's that served the surveyors for models when laying out the line. But the way though sinuous is not long and a few minutes found the tourists swinging their hats to the gallant crew of mill men who were working so valiantly against time.

At the mill the scene was an exhilarating one. Two score men were working "might and main." Every muscle, every nerve on tension, and every man's will exerted to "do his best," while the massive machinery, steady as a watch, but mighty as a ship, was moving with a precision and a velocity that astonished every beholder.

The huge logs from three to five feet in diameter, straight as an arrow and smooth as a candle, lying by the hundreds in the storage pond or reservoir illustrated forcibly the majesty of Nature, while the ease and rapidity with which man and machinery reduced these mighty monarchs into merchantable material, was a striking demonstration of the majestic power of Man over Nature.

The arrangements for handling logs and lumber were practically perfect, and the transit of the log past the saws, from storage pond to railroad car proved a wonderful and pleasing panorama.

W. R. Porter, the resident representative of the Lumber Company, informed the visitors on arrival that the "cut" of the first hour's run was 30,553 feet, so that each was aware that they were witnessing some of the best work that had ever been performed in that line. For an hour or more (until the break) the spectators formed a cordon along the line of work and watched with admiration the leviathan logs drawn up by huge chains on an iron "skid" track, rolled on to the carriage, and in three minutes transformed from logs to lumber, passed along, and in another three minutes loaded on the cars ready for shipment. The perfection of the machinery and the celerity and enthusiasm of the workmen alike challenged compliment.

It was a proud morning for W. J. Hudner, the master of ceremonies, and his good spirits seemed to be shared by every man in the mill.

Then came the moment when a broken cog upset all chance of making a competitive record.

The "carriage" could not be moved, and the monster saws, that with three hundred revolutions a minute had been pushing their sharp teeth through the timber, stood still.

But these Mill men were not daunted. Frank S. Bartlett, our local machinist, who was present assisted in making repairs, and in an hour the wheels were in motion.

From this point the "cut" proceeded without hindrance, and when "time" was called the Loma Prieta Lumber

Company's stock had been increased by 181,000 feet of lumber that existed only in the log at 6 o'clock in the morning. The lumber was tallied by W. J. Hudner, Superintendent of the mill, and by T. J. Leonard, of Hihn's mill, and J. V. Follett, of Chace & Co's. mill.

The score, as announced every hour, was as follows:

Time.	No. feet.
From 6:45 to 7:45	30,553
" 7:45 to 8:45	25,741
" 8:45 to 9:20	15,724
" 10:08 to 11:08	29,392
" 11:08 to 12:08	29,900
" 12:08 to 1:08	29,601
" 1:08 to 2:00	20,089
Total No. feet lumber sawed	181,000

This lumber was all cut from 88 logs, each 16 feet in length, and averaging about 4 feet in diameter.

Those familiar with the lumber business will appreciate the figure of 181 M. feet, but the magnitude of the job may be better understood by others by some explanatory figures. The sawed lumber when loaded on broad-gauge cars filled 23 cars; the slabs which were cut into 4 foot lengths for wood, and also loaded, filled 4 cars, making 27 car loads of manufactured material. To haul this to market requires two locomotives making two train loads as the result of a day's work at the mill. If loaded on wagons and hauled away by teams it would have made a procession over a mile in length of teamsters.

Of the 23 cars of sawed lumber 17 were loaded with railroad ties and 6 with plank, posts and square timbers of various sizes. The number of ties cut averaged over 70 per minute for the entire time, and were sufficient in number to lay one and three fourth miles of railroad track. They were all cut for the S. P. Co. and will be used in the new extension beyond Templeton.

The same measurement of lumber sawed into fencing material would be sufficient to build over ten miles of four-board fence, or if converted into ordinary building material would

The Gilded Age — 1888

be ample for the construction of nineteen 5 room cottages.

The little water power saw mills that "cut up" the forests of New England and the Middle States at the rate of three or four thousand feet a day, are left as far in the shades of oblivion by the modern mill as has been the stage coach or the scyle [sic].

Jas. C. Haughy, one of the proprietors of the California Saw Works, on Mission street, San Francisco, the establishment which furnished the saws to the Loma Prieta Company, was present and personally superintended the working of the saws, which prove to have the "cut" and "go" in them to meet all demands.

The "crew" which did "the job" was composed of the following men:

O. A. Lanthier, Sawyer; J. Richardson, Engineer; P. Kearny, Edgerman; L. Lanthier, Screw Turner; Jos. Cox, Trimmer; W. Irwin, Trimmer; J. Love, T. Morrison, George Lachemnaier, C. Mucier, C. Pierce, D. Ross, J. Harveston, W. Scott, M. Cantwell, J. Buckhart, J. Dent, J. Perry, J. Dougherty, C. Craighill, J. Hall, H. Kyle, F. Valencia, T. Cremer, T. Clancy, P. Molasky, J. Brown, C. Speed, A. Barnard, D. Chisholm, W. Poole, M. Rogers, W. Lockhart, J. W. Wright, L. D. Heath, W. White, W. Stacey, Jos. Williams, J. O. Walker, Jas. McGurty, G. A. Dennis, C. Dresti, E. Roza, F. Carroll.[181]

Hihn's Mill Happenings

The next entry in the *Surf*'s ongoing Hihn's Mill Happenings column was published on October 17, 1888, based on information provided to the newspaper on October 10:

Hihn's Mill Happenings

———

Mrs. H. Antrim of Santa Cruz, is visiting her parents, Mr. and Mrs. T. J. Hubbell of this place.

Mr. J. Snyder, daughter of Mamie, and son Roy, have gone to Michigan on a visit to Mr. S.'s old home in Grand Rapids.

> *Mr. Ed Cockens, who has been employed at Hihn's Mill for the past year, left for his home in Iowa last week. His many friends wish him a successful and happy trip.*
>
> *On last Saturday even, Mr. and Mrs. W. Samuels entertained their friends in their "right royal style." It is needless to say that a most enjoyable time was hand [sic] by all, for Mr. and Mrs. S. are renowned for their hospitality.*
>
> *Mr. Joseph Prothers and Miss Lizzie Eaton, both of this place, were united in marriage at Santa Cruz, Sept. 23d. On the night of their return home, the "Mill Band Boys," gave them an "old fashioned country serenade," which will long be remembered by Mr. and Mrs. Prothers. Last Saturday week Mr. and Mrs. P. gave a supper and dance at their new home on "Valencia Hill," in honor of their "wed-lock," and the "Band Boys' serenade."*
>
> *Mrs. Castor on Wednesday last, Oct. 3d, gave her daughter, Carrie, one of the most pleasant surprise parties ever witnessed at Hihn's Mill. The occasion being Miss Carrie's 13th birthday, she was the recipient of many useful and beautiful presents. A very merry time with games and dancing was indulged in until 11 o'clock, when each and every one did ample justice to the "luscious feast" prepared by Mrs. Castor. Another hour of merriment and the happy throng dispersed, wishing Miss Carrie many such "gay and festive" times.*[182]

Loma Prieta Lumber Company moves Pajaro mill to Watsonville

Sometime in November 1888, the Loma Prieta Lumber Company shut down its small mill at the Southern Pacific Railroad yard in Pajaro and relocated the machinery to the lumber yard of the Watsonville Mill & Lumber Company at Beach Road and Pine Street in Watsonville. In place of a lumber mill, a planing mill was built on the site since the mill on Aptos Creek was now capable of handling all lumber orders by itself. The planing mill at Watsonville employed between forty and fifty men and would remain in use for the next twenty-four years, only shutting down in 1912.

Loma Prieta Lumber Company repays debt to the Bank of Watsonville

When the Loma Prieta Lumber Company purchased Tract 9 in the Augmentation from Carmel Fallon in 1883, it did so by taking out a loan of $53,000 at seven percent interest from the Bank of Watsonville. In the intervening years, the bank had acted as treasurer for the lumber company. On January 2, 1889, that loan was finally repaid. The company released its bank-appointed treasurer from its board of directors on March 18. At the next meeting of the board of directors, N. T. Smith was elected treasurer of the Loma Prieta Lumber Company. Smith would remain in the position for the rest of his life.[183]

Loma Prieta Loglets

The first column dedicated exclusively to the community beside the Loma Prieta Lumber Company's mill appeared in the *Surf* on February 5, 1889:

> **LOMA PRIETA LOGLETS**
>
> **LATEST NEWS FROM OUR LOFTIEST MOUNTAIN TOP**
>
> *Dan Ross is soon to take up his residence in Loma Prieta.*
> *Mr. and Mrs. A. C. Bassett are still rusticating at Loma Prieta.*
> *The morning frosts here on the mountain continue quite heavy.*
> *Mr. John D. Wright, our local wrestler, is recovering from his illness.*
> *Mrs. Brouse, a recent arrival from Missouri, says there is no place like Santa Cruz.*
> *Mr. Morrow has been very sick but has recovered sufficiently to take a trip to Watsonville.*
> *Mr. and Mrs. Cox have taken up their residence here and have settled down to domestic happiness.*
> *Mr. William Erwin, who operates the slab saw, sustained*

a slight fracture of the leg on Thursday.

Mr. Brown, who was lately attacked and beaten by "Pyburne," a pioneer, is still under the weather.

Nathan Roberts, while rolling logs, met with a painful, though not serious accident, on Wednesday last.

Robert Davit, after a long vacation, has resumed work and many of our cottages show signs of his artistic taste.

Mrs. Cantwell, our jolly hostess, is doing a thriving business, the company's cool house not being running.

One of our most promising young men is about to solve the problem: "Is Marriage a Failure?" at no far distant date.

Mr. George Hudner, of Hollister, is visiting his cousin, W. J. Hudner, the Superintendent of the Loma Prieta Mill.

The Loma Prieta school has commenced and we are glad to have our much esteemed teacher, Miss Barny, again in our midst.

Mr. Smith and a detachment of employees of the Western Telegraph Company, are examining and shipping telegraph poles to San Jose.

The Loma Prieta Lumber Company are now cutting a large quantity of lumber for the new bridges to be constructed on the Northern Division of the S. P. R. R.

Yours truly, "Skaggs."[184]

Dickamon Rider moves to Mendocino

In mid-February 1889, Dickamon Rider of D. A. Rider & Son purchased a mill and logging rights from John S. Kimball and moved to Westport in Mendocino County. Rider's son Homer remained to manage the Game Cock mill on Corralitos Creek for the 1889 season before joining his father in the north. Another son, Frank L. Rider, managed the Game Cock mill through the 1891 season. That same year, D. A. Rider & Son opened a mill near San Francisco using logs rafted down the coast from Westport.

Two years later, in May 1891, Dickamon, as well as John Kimball and his son-in-law Fred W. Pease, W. P. Plummer, and C. E. Wilson, incorporated the Western Lumber Company in San Francisco. This short-lived firm was likely set up as a commercial distribution company to ship lumber products across California from the Rider mill in Westport.[185]

Loma Prieta Loglets

A new column of "Loma Prieta Loglets" was published in the *Surf* on February 18, 1889:

LOMA PRIETA LOGLETS

ITEMS OF INTEREST FROM THE MILLS IN THE WOODS

Mrs. John T. Porter of Pajaro is visiting her son, W. R. Porter.

Mike Walsh, a former resident of Santa Cruz, is living in Monte Vista.

Mr. Wakelee and family of Aptos paid a visit to Monte Vista on Friday.

Mr. Kemm has taken a trip to San Francisco which combines business and pleasure.

John Dougherty is again in Loma Prieta and is trying to organize a brass band.

Mr. Philip Molasky met with a very painful and almost fatal accident last Monday.

Miss Josie Valencia of Santa Cruz has been visiting her brother, Frank Valencia. She returned to Santa Cruz last week.

Mrs. Nathan Roberts has been very ill and is now at the residents of her parents, Mr. and Mrs. John Daubenbis, of Soquel.

Mr. James Saxton is at present conductor on the Loma Prieta train. Mr. Gaton the regular conductor taking a vacation.

Loma Prieta Mill will shut down for the season on or about March 10th. It is now cutting about 40,000 feet of lumber per day.

Loma Prieta is now enjoying a religious boom; weekly services are held in the hall by the Episcopal clergyman of Watsonville.

The many friends of Miss May Nagle will be very sorry to hear of her illness. Dr. Bixby of Watsonville was called on Wednesday evening.

William Talbot, better known as "Wild Bill," who visited Carmel Mission, Monterey Co., to recuperate, mentally, is again in our midst.

Mr. Michael Prindevill of Loma Prieta and Miss Mary A. Kelly, of Watsonville, were united in marriage at Watsonville by Father Marron on Tuesday the 12th inst. They will soon take up their residence here and will be a great addition to Loma Prieta society.

Prof. Owens, the noted phrenologist, visited Loma Prieta last Monday and Tuesday; the citizens of this place and Monte Vista gave him a rousing welcome and believe that he understands his business. During the evening a knight of the anvil strolled in and the Professor was heard to mutter something about "Darwin" and the "missing link."

Yours truly, SKAGGS.[186]

Frederick Hihn plans a railroad from Soquel into the Augmentation

On March 20, 1889, the *Surf* published an article that gives insight into Frederick Hihn's plans regarding harvesting the upper tracts of the Augmentation along Soquel Creek. It reported:

> There is considerable life and interest in the local railroad circles concerning the developments of the year 1889. The Southern Pacific has been improving their line between this city and Pajaro for months, and much additional work is in contemplation, exclusive of changes in this city which are yet in abeyance.
>
> A projected road from Corralitos to Moss Landing has attracted some interest in the southern part of the county, but of all the projected branches the one most likely of construction at the present time is one planned by F. A. Hihn to extend

> *from the bay shore to Highland.*
>
> *The proposed line will start from a point on the bay shore about a half mile below Capitola and by a circuitous route extend up the easterly side of the Soquel canyon, into and through the immense timber belt on the upper Soquel owned by Mr. Hihn, and have its ultimate terminus far up in the Highland region. The line passes through lands of* [Augustus] *Noble, thence on the easterly bluff above the Soquel church, through lands of* [Joshua] *Parrish, and so on up the canyon.*
>
> *Surveys have been made, right-of-way procured and the line located for the greater part of the distance, altho' still subject to some modifications.*
>
> *The road will be broad-gauge, and operated in connection with the Southern Pacific, but whether the road will be constructed by that company or not, is not yet definitely determined.*
>
> *At the junction of the new road with the S. P. line at the coast, a capacious saw mill will be erected, and to this the entire timber resources of the Soquel canyon will be tributary. The extent and value of this timber can only be approximately estimated, but it is calculated that with all the modern appliances for slaying the forest, that it would require twenty-five years to exhaust the supply and the revenue will run into the millions.*
>
> *The first and main use of the proposed line, of course, will be as a lumber road, the same as the Loma Prieta branch, but there are many other resources in the section through which it will pass, and it will undoubtedly lead to the development of some choice mountain resorts on the upper Soquel.*

The railroad was Hihn's first attempt to build a lumber road of some type from Soquel to Tracts 1, 6, 10, 11, and 25 in the Augmentation. Although portions of the route have appeared on maps since 1889, no map showed the exact route except for that created by the A. M. Elam Company of San Francisco, dated to about 1915. Whether the map is entirely accurate is unknown, but it was created shortly after Hihn's death and depicted the status of his lands in Rancho Soquel and the Augmentation at that time.

The route of the planned railroad, not including any spurs, was to total a little more than 20 miles. It would not have been a simple or cheap line to build and maintain, which is likely why Hihn solicited Southern Pacific support for its construction. However, the owners of Southern Pacific were not interested. The company had already invested heavily in local Santa Cruz area railroads and was actively in the process of extending the Loma Prieta Branch and streamlining the South Pacific Coast Railway. In addition, the company had several costly projects elsewhere in the state. But more importantly, the company was already directly involved in the Loma Prieta Lumber Company, so helping Hihn build his line would lead to a conflict of interest and potentially reduce its overall profit.

Details on the Elam map show that the railroad would break off from the Pajaro & Santa Cruz Branch just east of Capitola Station near Washburn Avenue. Just north of Monterey Avenue, it would cross Noble Gulch, where a mill would be built to cut the lumber brought down from the Augmentation. The right-of-way would then continue north along today's Rosedale Avenue, crossing the County Road (Soquel Drive), and then swinging in a wide westerly arch before turning north again at the end of today's Hannan Lane.

From this point, the Hihn Railroad Grade actually exists as a geographic entity for some distance, running through the backcountry behind homes, Main Street Elementary School, and local businesses. At Bates Creek, the right-of-way curves gently across where a bridge would have been built before crossing Glen Haven Road and then paralleling Cherryvale Avenue to its end. During this journey, it crosses over High Gulch Road three times but always remains to the east of Soquel Creek. Only one bridge across a stream near the end of Cherryvale Avenue would have been required in this section. At 2.7 miles from Hannan Lane, the remnant portion of the Hihn Railroad Grade abruptly ends at the boundary of Tract 26. This may mark a place where Hihn had not yet secured a right-of-way when he abandoned the railroad project. Nonetheless, the proposed route continued on for many more miles.

Through Tract 26, the line would have continued in a mostly straight line until reaching Hihn's Tract 10, where the narrowness of the canyon

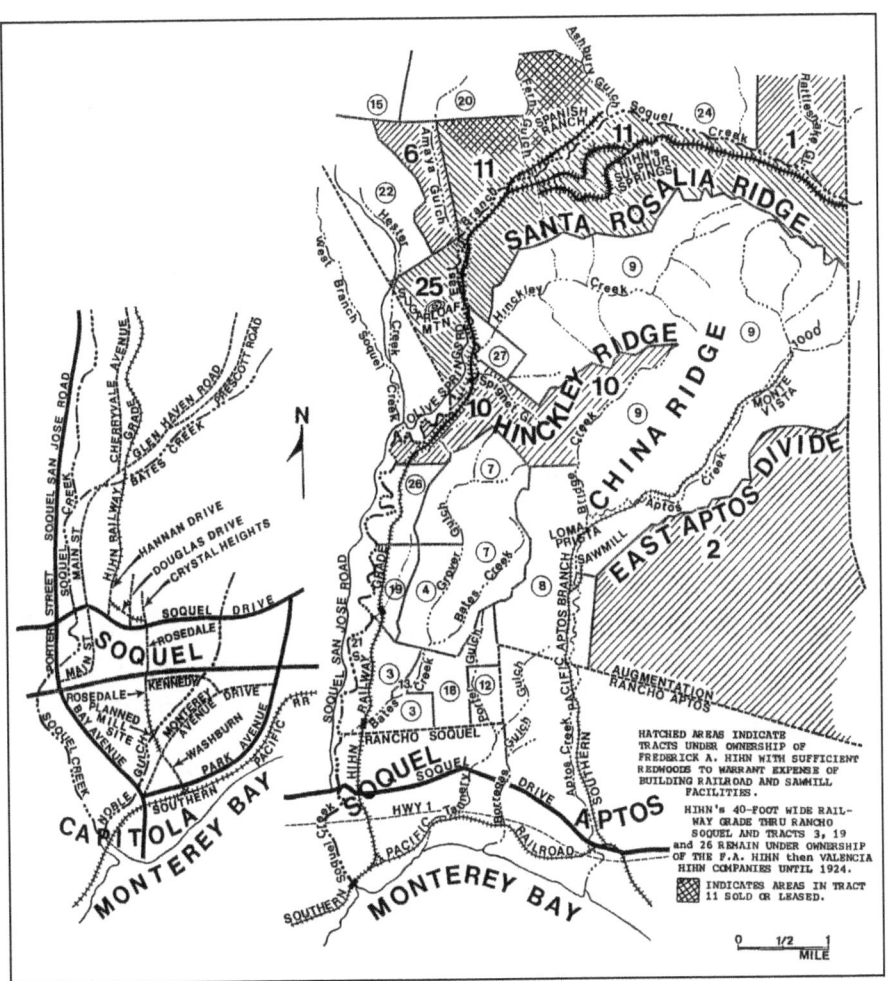

FIGURE 5.1 ROUTE OF HIHN'S PROPOSED RAILROAD ALONG SOQUEL CREEK

would force the right-of-way closer to Soquel Creek to maintain an even grade. The first crossing over Soquel Creek would occur just before the grade reached Spignet Gulch, at which point the line ran parallel to Olive Spring Road and within Tract 25. It is unclear how many times the railroad would have needed to cross Soquel Creek for the next two miles, but it likely would have been several times as the confines of the canyon would have required the grade to run almost in the creek. After two miles, at Amaya Gulch, the tracks would cross to the east side of Soquel Creek for the last time before the line turned to the east into Tract 11, where much of Hihn's timber stock was located.

Within Tract 11 and Tract 1 beyond, the ultimate route of the railroad is purely speculative and, in reality, would have changed according to needs. The ill-defined Hihn Mill Road, which appears on some maps today, may match some of the proposed route. A spur would have likely broken off near Fern Gulch to reach Ashbury Gulch to the north, while another spur would have gone south, probably breaking off near Hihn's Sulphur Springs and turning back west to reach Badger Springs. The main track would have likely continued to the east up the East Branch of Soquel Creek beyond Rattlesnake Gulch until reaching the eastern boundary of the Augmentation, north of the headwaters of Aptos Creek.

Talk of this proposed railroad reappeared in the *Sentinel* in May 1891. The newspaper reported that:

> *The mill will be located in Tannery Gulch, near Capitola. The railroad will begin at the broad-gauge track at Capitola and continue up Soquel Creek. One branch will extend in an easterly direction to Laurel, connecting with the narrow-gauge road, while the other branch will continue westerly and tap the redwood forests, which will furnish material for the mill. There will be twenty miles of track. Much new country will be opened up for homes, and the road will be arranged for the carrying of passengers and freight. It is estimated that the project will necessitate the expenditure of about $200,000.*

The only remnant of this proposed railroad is the partial forty-foot-wide right-of-way that runs behind the east of downtown Soquel for nearly three miles. Besides appearing periodically in maps, it also is entered into property deeds and arises in court cases dealing with adjacent property. In reality, though, Hihn never graded any of the line and the name is purely wishful thinking.[187]

Loma Prieta Loglets

A tongue-in-cheek edition of the "Loma Prieta Loglets" was published in

The Gilded Age 1889

the *Surf* on March 21, 1889, recording information submitted to the newspaper on March 20:

LOMA PRIETA LOGLETS

Henry K. Goodwin of Watsonville is about to open a butcher shop at this place, as there has been too much delay in getting meat up from Aptos.

Frank Valencia has opened a tonsorial establishment here and all the place needs is a shoemaker's shop and, perhaps, another establishment or so, and Loma Prieta will be big enough to incorporate as the liveliest young town in the county.

Skaggs is dead. BAZOO.[188]

Happening's at Hihn's Mill

On April 3, 1889, the next column focused on Hihn's Mill was published in the *Surf*, recording information provided to the newspaper on March 29:

HAPPENINGS AT HIHN'S MILL

PERSONALS, SOCIAL DOINGS AND THE PRETTY FERN GATHERERS

Mr. J. Bowes, of Maine, is here visiting his brother, George.

Miss Clara Hubbell of Santa Cruz, is paying her parents, of this place, a visit.

Hihn's Mill is undergoing repairs in order that it may commence work soon.

Miss Julia McDonough, of Santa Cruz, is spending the week with Mrs. Geo. Bowes.

Mr. M. Hanahan is also making wonderful improvements on his "Shady Nook" farm.

Mr. C. Horstman is making great improvements with his home situated on "Forest Hill."

Miss Jennie Shirley, who is attending the State Normal School at San Jose, is expected here the last of this week to visit her cousin, Sophie Shirley.

Miss Minnie Otto and Miss Lizzie Merrill, both of Santa Cruz, have returned home, after spending a few jolly weeks with Miss Merrill's sister, Mrs. Wilder.

The new hall on "Knob Hill" is completed and ready for service, so not many more Saturday nights will pass before the lovers of the "light fantastic toe" will be skipping o'er its beautiful laid floor.

Mrs. T. J. Hubbell, living on "Fern Hill," gave her daughter, Della, a birthday party last Friday evening. When we add that the chief sport of the evening was a "candy pull," you may know that a sweet and happy time was had by all. Dancing was added to their sweetness and a bounteous supper was sandwiched in, so it was a late hour when the merry party dispersed for their homes, each wishing the fair Miss Della many more such pleasant times.

If we do live in the mountains and are known as the "back-woods" people, we've "caught on" to the boom, and believe in prosperity and improvements. Come up and just take a "birds eye view" of us and our beautiful green hills, and you'll surely buy and remain with us. We have all that is requisite to make you "healthy, wealthy, and wise."

"Ferning Hunt." Two of our charming damsels started fern searching a few evenings past. Knowing that they'd be compelled to travel through mud and damp ravines, they appropriately, costumed themselves. One of the fairer sex looked so charming, she couldn't help remarking to her friend, "I'd bewitch a meek old cow, if we should meet one." After walking a few miles, they came to the long searched-for spot, "Nature's Fernery." When their baskets were filled and they had refreshed themselves from the cool babbling brook, their steps were turned homeward, as night was overtaking them. In order to get to the main road again, they were compelled to climb a very steep mountain and just as they had reached the top, face to face they came with a "cow with crumpled horn." The three stood still staring at each other for a moment, when the braver of two frightened girls, took a long stick, and poking *it at "boss," asked her to pass on. But instead of passing on, she gave her head a toss and with a "ba-ba" made for them. She didn't even give them time to say "so-boss, so," but sent them, ferns and all, whirling down the mountain. Believing in the motto, "try, try again" they gathered up the hard worked-for ferns and started up the mountain again, "boss" was still at her post and the poor girls' hearts sank with them. Just as they were planning a stratagem for their escape, one of the "Lords of creation" appeared on the brow of a mountain. Need I say more than he came at their signal and they were saved, saved from being mutilated and a muddy grave.*

Last heard from they were planting the few treasured ferns that were saved and blessing the "Lords of creation."

VERNON.[189]

Hihn's Mill Items

An unprecedented edition of the usual Hihn's mill column appeared in the May 9, 1889 issue of the *Sentinel* rather than the *Surf*. The columnist's signature implies that it was written by a new author, as well:

HIHN'S MILL ITEMS

Wm. Wing is being visited by his brother from Maine.
Mr. Hedrick is the happy father of a eleven pound girl.
Henry Rastar anticipates a trip East some time this fall.
The rain of Saturday night and Sunday did considerable damage to hay.
John Finmore, one of our society young men, has gone to Loma Prieta to work.
We have one of the nicest halls of any country place for miles around, donated to our use by F. A. Hihn.
Mrs. Newton Hedgpeth is lying very sick at her home. Mrs. Winchel, her mother-in-law from San Lucas, is taking care of her.
Our Lyceum is progressing finely, and some of the grandest talent was displayed last Tuesday night you ever heard of.

But the most amusing part is a jumping-jack that is there every night. Our Marshal keeps fine order, and when his "tootsy wootsie" comes down it can be heard plainly.

May Day passed off very quietly here, only a few going on picnics.

Misses Merrill and Otto came up from Santa Cruz on a visit to Mrs. Wilder, and a company composed of Mrs. Wilder, Mrs. Wing, Misses Merrill and Ott, and Messrs. Leonard, Hihn, Jones and Wing went for a picnic up the grove.

SAW MILL DUDE.[190]

Happenings at Hihn's Mill

Another entry in the *Surf*'s news reports on Frederick Hihn's mill at Valencia was published on May 15, 1889:

HAPPENINGS AT HIHN'S MILL

"VERNON'S" VALENCIA TOWN NOTES—
NEWS AND PERSONALS

At the Valencia School, taught by Miss Esther V. Malcolm of Watsonville, the following pupils were neither absent nor tardy: Cay Marham, Lila Taylor, Alanson Burgess, Milton Castor, Ross Hedrick, Iva Hedrick, Lucy Day, Birnice Haines, Alford Teichner, Mary Burgess, Delphine Meynier, Clarance Marham and Newtie Marham. Cay Marham, Lila Taylor and Alanson Burgess also receiving 100 in deportment were awarded prizes.

Miss Dollie Hubbell is spending the week at Loma Prieta.

Mr. W. Sanders, of Boulder Creek, is visiting his cousin, Mr. Marham.

Misses Josie and Clorinda Valencia are here visiting their mother.

The 16th of last month, a Lyceum and Literary Society was organized at this place, with a membership of thirty three. Following are the officers: President, Ed. Hihn; Vice

> *President, Thos. Leonard; Secretary, Esther V. Malcolm; Treasurer, Sophia Shirley; Marshal, Geo. Shreves; Editress, Mrs. Walker. The Lyceum meets every Tuesday evening, and so far has been a great benefit as well as a pleasure.*
>   *The following resolution has been adopted:*
>   *Resolved, That the community of Valencia Town (Hihn's Mill), represented by the "Lyceum" and the "Sunday School," do most heartily thank Hon. F. A. Hihn for his great benevolence and kindness in erecting the Valencia Hall for their pleasure and benefits.*
> ESTHER V. MALCOLM, *Sec.*
> VERNON.[191]

Frederick Hihn establishes the F. A. Hihn Company

Frederick Hihn became a megalithic force in Santa Cruz County over the four decades after his arrival in the county in 1851. Once he entered the real estate industry, his fortune grew exponentially, and he repeatedly founded new companies to manage his many different enterprises. But on June 4, 1889, he decided that the time had come to consolidate many of his gains. He founded the F. A. Hihn Company as a family business and appointed his son August Charles Hihn to serve as president. Other children and sons-in-law were also appointed officers of the company, with Frederick Otto Hihn appointed treasurer, William Thomas Cope (husband of Katherine Charlotte Hihn) appointed secretary, and Louis William Hihn, Frederick August Jr., and the latter's wife, Therese Hihn, appointed directors.

When the company was established, its main assets were its logging operations on Valencia Creek and its vast land holdings in the Augmentation and elsewhere in the county. However, over time, F. A. Hihn Company expanded its property interests to housing subdivisions at Fairview Park in Capitola and Valencia north of Aptos, vacation homes in Camp Capitola, and various types of land within the former Rancho Zayante in Felton. The company also bought the Shasta and Commodore Hotels in San Francisco. Hihn retained personal control over the Soquel-

Capitola water system and several properties throughout the county, which were spun off after his death into the Hihn Investment & Building Company, the Hihn Water Company, the Capitola-Hihn Company, the Santa Cruz Water Company, and the Soquel Water System Company.[192]

Happenings at Hihn's Mill

A further report on events at Valencia was published by the *Surf* on July 19, 1889:

HAPPENINGS AT HIHN'S MILL

Miss Cora Bowes is visiting her uncle Geo. Bowes.
Miss Sophia Shirley is spending a week with her parents.
Frank Snyder had his hand badly cut Wednesday by a saw.
  The Valencia school will reopen Monday, July 22d, with Miss Pearl Alford of Santa Cruz, formerly of Tulare, as teacher, the trustees being unable to obtain Miss Esther V. Malcolm, whose loss is deeply regretted.
  A barbecue and picnic will be held at Valencia Grove Sunday, July 21st, given by the citizens of Valencia. A grand time is anticipated.
  The installation of officers of the Valencia Lyceum for the ensuing term was held Tuesday evening. The officers were installed as follows: A. J. Hihn, President; S. L. Gibson, Vice-President; Mrs. C. Walker, Secretary; Thos. Leonard, Treasurer; C. A. Kent, Marshal; Neil Forden, Marshal. The exercises closed with a minstrel performance by Prof. Hoffmann's renowned troupe, which was highly appreciated
                                      MADRONE.[193]

Chips from Hihn's Mill

Yet another *Surf* summary of happenings in Valencia appeared in the August 24, 1889 issue:

Chips from Hihn's Mill

Literary and Musical Enjoyments—Neighborly Visits With Loma Prieta

Mr. James Taylor and family left this week for their new home in Texas. All wish them a bon voyage.

Miss M. Hoffmann has returned to her home in San Jose after spending several weeks visiting her brother, C. C. Hoffmann, and Mrs. O. Wilder.

The usual debate took place Tuesday evening, August 20th. The question debated on was, "Resolved, that the modern inventions are detrimental to the laboring classes." The debate was warm and interesting, and the decision was given in favor of the negative.

We have a fine poet and composer in our midst in the person of Mr. Ed. Haines, and if his songs were set to music and sang in open air concert in Santa Cruz, they would undoubtedly draw as large an attendance of listeners as ever the Vigor of Life and Wizard Oil troops have.

The regular entertainment given at Valencia Hall took place a week ago last Tuesday evening when the following program was given: Original song, dedicated to the Hihn's mill barbecue, Ed. Haines; recitation, "The Storm," Miss Pearl Alford, of Santa Cruz, our local school teacher. The style in which the young lady delivered the recitation proved her to be an elocutionist of rare ability. Recitation, Miss. Addie Hedrick, which was well delivered and merited a round of applause; song, "Shaking of the Hand," Miss Lina Hedrick, which was rendered in her own dulcet voice; recitation, "Advertising for a Wife," Mr. Hedrick, which was well given and delighted the audience with its humor. The entertainment closed with a couple of plays by our local minstrel company, which well pleased the boys and were pronounced by all as very good.

Some few weeks ago Hihn's mill gave a barbecue under the auspices of Mr. C. C. Hoffmann, to which, among *several others, our neighboring mill, the Loma Prieta residents were invited, and on last Sunday, in response to an invitation from the Loma Prietas, several of our towns-folk attended their barbecue. Both one and all agree that it was among one of the finest events of the season. The delightful odor that was transmitted from the broiling meat made each one hunger for the dinner hour, and when noon arrived all sat themselves down to tables that were fairly groaning under the weight of good things, including luscious fruits and all the delicacies of the season. Suffice it to say all did justice to the tempting viands in satisfying the inner man, and when the hour for homeward bound arrived, all departed, wishing many more returns of Loma Prieta barbecue, and also thinking that it was a day long to be remembered in the social annals of saw mill history. More anon.*

RURAL.[194]

Happenings at Hihn's Mill

Still more news from Valencia was published in the *Surf* on August 30, 1889:

HAPPENINGS AT HIHN'S MILL

A LIVELY LITTLE SETTLEMENT AND PLENTY OF BRIGHT PEOPLE THERE

Mr. Wm. Shirley is visiting his brother, Theo. Shirley.

Mrs. W. J. Hudner, after a short visit to her sister, Mrs. Geo. Bowers, returned to her home at Loma Prieta, Wednesday.

Mr. L. I. Shrieves, one of our popular young men, has left us to seek a better position.

Miss Esther V. Malcolm made a flying visit Tuesday evening, returning home Wednesday morning.

Mr. J. N. Marham and family will shortly leave for their former home in Texas.

An ice cream social will be given at the hall in the near

future for the benefit of the organ fund for the Lyceum.

The Valencia school is in a flourishing condition under the tutorship of Miss J. Pearl Alford. The scholars are all advancing and are delighted with their new teacher, as are also the people of this community.

The Valencia Lyceum met in regular session at the hall Tuesday evening, and after transacting their usual business, the president announced a short literary program for the balance of the evening. Mr. Ed. Hames opened the program with a song entitled, "Loma Prieta Barbecue," proving himself to be a composer of no small ability. Miss Esther Malcolm, by request, recited the "Johnstown Flood" in a pathetic manner and which was highly appreciated by all those present. Misses Birucie and Blanche Haines and Lucy Day sang "Christine Leroy" in a pleasing manner. Little Ivy Hedrick delighted the audience with a short recitation. This being Miss Sina Hedrick's last appearance before us, on account of going away, she sang, by request, "The Beautiful Voices" in a manner that was loudly applauded. Last, but not least, was a recitation by Miss Pearl Alford, who again showed her ability as an elocutionist to be far above the average. By request, Mr. William Curran closed the meeting with a song in his usual heart-rending manner. WOOD BEE.[195]

Chips from Hihn's Mill

September 27, 1889 saw another entry in the ongoing *Surf* column about happenings at Valencia:

CHIPS FROM HIHN'S MILL

PERSONAL, SOCIAL AND RELIGIOUS SAW-DUST

Miss Carrie Kastor went to Monterey last Friday to visit her aunt, Mrs. Frank Clark, wife of the well-known architect and contractor of that place.

Misses L. Merrill and M. Otto returned to Santa Cruz

Monday after spending a few days visiting Mrs. O. Wilder.

Mr. P. McGovern and family and Mrs. John Klough were in Santa Cruz Sunday of last week to witness the dedication of the new Catholic church.

Religious services were held in the hall on last Sunday evening by the ministers of the Latter Day Saints denomination.

The Sunday-school reorganized on last Sunday, when Mrs. E. Kastor was unanimously appointed Superintendent and Mr. N. Hedgepath Assistant Superintendent.

The weather for the past few days has been unusually warm, owing to mountain fires.

The members of the Valencia Lyceum have taken an indefinite vacation, but upon the event of its reopening we may anticipate a rare treat in the oratorical and elocutionary line.

Mr. A. Baird is happy, the cause being an additional son and heir in the family on Sept. 22d.

Mrs. R. Blodgett is visiting her mother, Mrs. T. J. Hubbell, on Fern Flat.

Who is the young gentleman that Dame Rumor has it is seriously contemplating joining the benedicts?

RURAL.[196]

Chips from Hihn's Mill

Even in the depths of autumn, Valencia was hopping. The *Surf* reported on November 8, 1889, based on information provided on November 4:

CHIPS FROM HIHN'S MILL

DOINGS OF THE PAST FORTNIGHT—
SOCIAL, PERSONAL, ENTERTAINING, ETC.

Mr. P. McGovern visited Loma Prieta last week.

H. Kastor visited friends in Watsonville two weeks ago.

Miss Carrie Kastor has returned from her visit to Monterey.

Mr. and Mrs. Jos. Cox of Loma Prieta have taken a res-

idence here.

The Valencia Lyceum will reopen Tuesday evening, the 12th instant.

Messrs. Gibson and Roso have returned from their visit to the metropolis.

Mr. P. Kearney and family of Loma Prieta, will reside among us during the present week.

G. C. Bowes was the guest of Mr. and Mrs. W. J. Hudner, of Loma Prieta, Thursday of last week.

Miss Pearl Alford intends having closing exercises, by her pupils, previous to the Christmas vacation.

We were pleased to learn by last week's papers that the debt on the Y. M. C. A. building had been liquidated.

Mr. W. A. Wing, formerly of this place, has gone to Loma Prieta, and will move his household goods there this week.

The damage done the logging roads by the recent rains has been repaired, and the mill resumed operations Monday.

The weather is lovely and one would imagine it was spring time, as the hills are clothed with Nature's carpet of green.

The mother of Mr. A. Carrier, who came here recently from Bradley, Monterey county, is confined to her home by illness.

Prof. Byuped, wife and sister, will give an exhibition in ventriloquism, fire eating and snake charming this evening at the hall.

Mr. and Mrs. Keough, who had been spending a week in Santa Cruz with Mrs. Keough's sister, Mrs. S. Lockhart, have returned.

James Finnemore, brother of Mrs. Chas. Horstman, has gone to Texas to engage in farming. May success attend you, James, in your new enterprise.

The families of N. Marnham and P. Emmons, who left here some time ago for Texas, are occasionally heard from. The former is interested in cotton raising.

Mrs. Chas. Walker makes frequent trips to Santa Cruz to visit her little daughter, Byrel, who is receiving tuition at the boarding school of the Holy Cross.

Mrs. D. O. Wilder and family, who had been spending the week in Santa Cruz with Mrs. Wilder's mother, Mrs. Merrill, returned Thursday, accompanied by Mrs. Chas. Lovett.

A social dance was given here on Friday evening, which was well attended. Among those present were noticed the following from Loma Prieta: Mr. and Mrs. Jos. Cox, W. M. Wing and J. Finnemore.

A surprise party was tendered Miss Clara Hubbell, at the residence of her mother, Mrs. T. J. Hubbell, on last Saturday night. The evening was pleasantly passed in singing, games, refreshments, etc.

Mr. Robert Moss and family who were formerly residents of this place, but lately of Tulare, have returned and upon the completion of the boarding house, situated at the Bear Spring logging camp, will assume charge of the same.

Our little town of Valencia has a bright and cheerful aspect. Not one of the eighteen houses in the immediate vicinity of the mill has been vacant, not including the logging camp or the several surrounding little farms occupied by employees of the mill. With the buzzy hum of the saws and the merry laughter of children, a fine store, comprising groceries, dry goods and provisions with Bert Hihn as smiling salesman; telephone communication with Aptos and Santa Cruz in charge of the courteous and affable Thomas Leonard, resident clerk of the county; daily mail, railroad communication to Aptos, a meat delivery wagon twice weekly, from the Aptos market of J. D. Chace; a flourishing school under the official management of Miss J. Pearl Alford of Santa Cruz; and a fine hall donated by Mr. F. A. Hihn, for religious, entertaining and educational purposes, one can easily see we have anything but a monotous dwelling place, and should the town continue to progress in the future year as it has in the one now drawing to a close, we will in all probability get ahead of (though we would not like to) our sister towns, Aptos and East Santa Cruz, and become annexed to the city of Santa Cruz. RURAL.[197]

Loma Prieta Loglets

After an extraordinarily long gap between updates, a new entry in the *Surf*'s column on happenings at the Loma Prieta mill appeared on November 20, 1889:

LOMA PRIETA LOGLETS

NEWS NOTES AND PERSONALS FROM THE MILLS IN THE MOUNTAINS

Mr. Chas. Long, who has been quite ill is slowly recovering.

Mr. and Mrs. W. A. Wing have taken up their residence here.

Mrs. M. Prindeville will reside in Watsonville during the winter.

Mrs. J. Love celebrated her 19th birthday by giving a social dance.

Mr. T. B. Bishop and family are now occupying their cottage here.

Miss Mary McCartey, of Watsonville, is the guest of Miss May Nagle.

Mrs. A. Lanthier and son spent Saturday and Sunday in Santa Cruz.

Mr. Jas. Morrow made a flying business trip to Watsonville Saturday.

Mr. John Morrison is now in the employ of contractor Cummings at Monte Vista.

Mr. Wm. Lockhart, our local mill wright, visited friends in Santa Cruz Sunday.

Mr. R. Devitt has again resumed work and it is to be hoped that his health will enable him to continue.

Our local blacksmith continues to make his usual trips to Watsonville. What's the attraction Newt?

Divine services continue to be held here once a month conducted by the Rev. Mr. Lewis of Watsonville.

Mr. Joseph Harveston, a former employee of the

mill, is now traveling salesman for the Richmond, Va., Publishing Company.

The mill will continue to manufacture lumber all winter, as the supply of logs in the pond is sufficient to keep it in operation.

Although so many feet above the level of the sea, we are refreshed every morning at 7:15 by the ever welcome Santa Cruz Surf. More anon.

On Thanksgiving night a sheet and a pillow-case party is to take place at the hall, under the able management of Mrs. Wm. Scott.

The family of Mr. S. Jeter will reside in Los Gatos during the winter. Mr. Jeter will remain here looking after his business interests.

Mr. W. R. Porter left Monday morning for Ogden, where he is to meet his mother, on her return homeward from a visit to the Eastern States.

Messr. A. Jeter, S. Jeter, C. Cummings and C. Craighill intend going to Stockton next Sunday. It is to be hoped they will be allowed to return.

A prominent young couple of this place are soon to be united in marriage. On Sunday last they were looking up a site for the erection of their future residence.

Mr. and Mrs. W. J. Hudner and Mr. and Mrs. C. Craighill were up the coast Sunday last gathering mussels, and, judging from the quantity brought home mussels must be very plentiful.

Last Saturday a very pleasant and enjoyable evening was spent at the residence of Mrs. Cantwell. The participants all went by invitation extended by mine hostess. The leading feature was a candy pull.

After the services held last Wednesday evening a Sunday School was established and the following officers were elected for the ensuing term: Mr. Cox, formerly of Fresno, superintendent; Mrs. C. Craighill, organist, and Mr. J. Richardson, leader of the choir. CHIPS.[198]

Loma Prieta Loglets

On December 14, 1889, another enthusiastic entry in the "Loma Prieta Loglets" series was published in the *Surf*:

Loglets from Loma Prieta

Plenty of Weather Up That Way— But no Dearth of News

Rain! Rain!! Rain!!!

Mrs. John Love returned home yesterday.

Mr. Morrow, in charge of a gang of men, visited Aptos yesterday for provisions. We still live.

The telephone wire was down for a short time Tuesday, owing to a big tree falling across the line.

Mr. McCloud, civil engineer for the S. P. R. R. Co., is in town to-night, looking to the condition of the road.

Bert still counts ties. How many are there between the office and?—well we won't give it away, but you know.

Miss Grace Barney left Loma Prieta Tuesday on a hand car for Aptos, where she takes the regular train for Watsonville, her home.

Newt and Bert are seen nightly together. Wonder where they go? Coal oil has reduced greatly in price these bright moonlight nights.

Mr. Wakelee, of Aptos, accompanied by Assistant Superintendent Haydock, visited our little burg yesterday, inspecting the road.

Mr. John Hubbars, of this place, has left for a few days, it is whispered to be married. We all wait anxiously his return, so as to welcome his fair bride home. Good luck, John.

Mr. Wm. Hudner, our Superintendent, is continually seen standing on the "dam at midnight" watching the terrible volley of water pouring through the gate. Who wouldn't with these snappers on his great rubber boat.

Large improvements have been made in the Loma Prieta

Music Hall in anticipation of the great crowd who will hold their first grand masquerade ball there New Years' evening, given by our local carpenters, Wm. Scott and Wm. Higgins. A grand time is expected.

The train has been unable to run for the last ten days, owing to the many slides and washouts on the road. Mr. Cautrell, assisted by a large force of men, is working early and late repairing the damages. If no more slides occur the track will be clear by Wednesday next. Our mail, however, is not delayed, as it is carried daily by Mr. Mitchell.

Owing to the heavy rains of the last two weeks the steep hillside back of Mr. Lanthier's dwelling took a slide last Friday morning. The house had a cellar about twelve feet high. As the earth struck the building it slid gently to the ground. Besides scaring the occupants nothing was damaged. Men have already been put to work on the new dwelling for our popular head sawyer.

At a meeting of the Loma Prieta Athletic Club Wednesday evening it was decided to offer Sullivan and Jackson the handsome purse of $75,000 to fight to a finish at their club rooms, members of the club only being admitted. The decision was immediately telegraphed to the gladiators and we wait breathlessly their reply. The winner will be challenged on the spot to a bare knuckle fight by one of our heavy weights, Mr. B. Fowler. He has been in training since the storm, punching sand in the pond. Two to one on Fowler.

The gate of the dam was filled with driftwood last Sunday, causing the water to rise very high in the pond. Our much beloved secretary was on hand, however, early and late, assisted by a large force of men clearing out the debris. Owing to the number of saw logs in the pond, work was slow but after many a bath the boom was fixed so as to wash out considerable sand, etc. About 3:30 P. M. a terrible cry was heard, and on looking in that direction our gallant "commander" was seen falling into the water, as he was in the act of laughing at our local blacksmith, who was just dragging himself out of the pond. At present everything is O. K. with little or no damage to the company. STICKS.[199]

December 27, 1889: Hihn's Mill

The regular columnist for the *Surf* covering the Valencia area provided one last entry for 1889 on December 27:

HIHN'S MILL

HAPPENINGS OF THE PAST FORTNIGHT IN VALENCIA TOWNSHIP

Mr. C. C. Hoffman, our local engineer, has gone to San Jose to spend the holidays with his parents.

Mr. D. Ross started yesterday for his home in Mendocino county to remain during the holidays.

Mr. and Mrs. John Keough left Tuesday for a week's visit to San Jose.

Mr. and Mrs. Jos. Cox leave to-day to spend the holidays in Santa Cruz with Mrs. Cox's father, Mr. William Lockhart.

We have had an immense amount of rain, yet considering the severity of the storm the damage done is slight, being mostly confined to the logging roads, and a few washouts on the railroad. Although it is mid-winter and the rain has been much in excess of other winters one would imagine to see the perennial look of Spring that Mrs. E. Castor's garden presents, that no such thing as winter was known, as genial is our mountain climate. Some improvements in real estate are noticeable during the past fortnight, Mr. Hall having fenced in the lot surrounding his residence, besides adding other improvements. The foundation for a new house in the lower town is already laid and Dame Rumor has it that when the same is completed it will be occupied by a bridal party.

The Aptos Market has changed hands, Mr. J. D. Chace having sold to Mr. Carter, who will send the delivery wagon here.

On Tuesday eve of last week Mr. and Mrs. H. Castor tendered a party to their daughter Carrie and Mrs. S. Omnes. The evening's pleasure consisted of a candy pull, euchre playing and dancing. A novel feature of the evening's enjoyment was an antique German dance, which was participated in by the hostess, Mrs. E. Castor, Mrs. Keough, Messrs. Samuels and Keough. At mid-night all departed well pleased with the evening's entertainment and the jolly hospitality of the host and hostess. Those present were the following: Mesdames Castor, Stuart, Haines, Keough, Cox, Bowes, Omnes, Samuels, Hall, Misses Castor, Clark and Stuart; Messrs. Castor, Hall, Samuels, Bowes, Keough, Cox, Haines, Jones, Hihn and Ross.

On Sunday last a report was spread in camp that a California lion had been seen in the vicinity of Long Valley, so early Monday morning a half dozen or more hunters thoroughly equipped with rifles, ammunition and hounds repaired to the located spot. Soon the hounds scented and gave chase and a lively battle between the dogs and lion (for surely it must be the lion) ensued. The anxious hunters dared not enter the brush lest the lion might spring and thereby wound the daring hunter. Finally one of the party, braver than the others, peeped in and fell, elated over the success. Some of the party went to his assistance and the animal was brought out, the dogs having killed it. Meanwhile the dogs had "treed" a wild-cat and a shot from one of the rifles brought him to the ground. Both animals were then tied and placed on a stick and born on the hunters' shoulders into camp as trophies of the adventure. Upon inspection the supposed lion proved to be an immense wild-cat. His majesty has since been seen. Don't give up boys; the game is yours next time.

Messrs. F. A. Hihn, A. Hihn and Wm. Cope were here Monday on a visit of inspection.

The usual entertainment took place at the Hall on last Tuesday evening. The program consisted of vocal music by Mr. Parker, an original song by our poet Mr. Ed. Haines; Mr. Ross also sang, Mr. W. Wing of Loma Prieta accompanying on the organ. Recitations by Miss Carrie Castor, Vernice Haines, Clara and Louisa Shirley and Master Allie Bowes. The gem of the evening was the song by two little tots, Jennie Blodgett and Maud Haines, also the song "There's a

Baby in the House," sung and acted by little Jennie Blodgett, only six years old.

Owing to the inclemency of the weather the debate which was to be discussed last week did not take place, so the question was debated on last Tuesday evening. Resolved, "The nicotine of cigarettes is more injurious to the lungs than whisky." From the arguments adduced the committee could not arrive at a decision.

One of the leading parts of Tuesday evening's programme was acted by Johnnie Jones, who, under the sobriquet of Miss Clark, sang and danced. Johnnie had donned some of the finest ladies' wearing apparel he could find, and undoubtedly Johnnie's fine feminine features are well adapted to impersonate a lady, and many a fine daughter of Eve would be pleased to possess them.

Miss Sophie and Master Herman Shirley, who have been attending the Watsonville schools, are home spending their vacation.

Little Miss Beryl Walker, who has been at the boarding School of the Holy Cross, is spending her vacation with her parents, Mr. and Mrs. Chas. Walker.

Through all the storm we were refreshed with the news of the Daily Surf. RURAL.[200]

Happenings at Hihn's Mill

The inaugural entry for 1890 of the *Surf*'s Valencia column appeared in the newspaper on January 13:

HAPPENINGS AT HIHN'S MILL

NOTES, PERSONALS AND EVENTS OF THE PAST FEW WEEKS

Carrie Castor spent a few days last week in Santa Cruz.
J. E. Wise has returned from a trip to Seattle and vicinity and reports no place like California.

>   *Fred Hubbell has left for Mendocino county to enter into the employ of D. A. Rider & Son, of Westport.*
>
>   *T. D. Sargent and his crew of Celestials are at work repairing the railroads, so that the trains will be running between the mill and Aptos within a week.*
>
>   *Probably the happiest man hereabouts is M. Hanahan, who received a bright bouncing baby girl as a New Year's present. Both child and mother are doing well.*
>
>   *New Year's Day passed very pleasantly, every one seeming happy except the party who ate cotton in their biscuit. They can't see the joke and promise to seek revenge.*
>
>   *The Valencia school will re-open about February 1st. Miss Pearl Alford having secured a position in the Santa Cruz schools, Miss Teresa Leonard, daughter of James Leonard, of Aptos, will officiate as teacher.*
>
>   *Mr. and Mrs. Forden have returned from their honeymoon and are about to occupy their new residence on the hill. May their voyage on the matrimonial sea be long and prosperous are the wishes of their numerous friends.*
>
>   *An enjoyable social dance was given at the hall New Year's eve and was kept up until 12 o'clock, when "Happy New Year" was shouted. The participants then danced one more quadrille and dispersed, much pleased with the evening's pleasure.*
>
>   *Owing to the continued absence of President Day, the Valencia Lyceum declared the office vacant and elected Theo. Shirley in his stead. Mr. Shirley is the real originator of the Lyceum and to him much is due for the success of it. Notwithstanding the stormy weather, the Lyceum is still in a prosperous condition, thereby causing our friends in Hungry Hollow to follow our example, as they organized last Tuesday evening and intend to challenge Valencia to a debate.*
>
>   WASHED OUT.[201]

January 21, 1890: Happenings at Hihn's Mill

On January 21, 1890, the *Surf* published another entry in its social column on the Valencia mill. Curiously, two separate entries were included in the column, the first dated January 19 while the second was presumably submitted on January 21:

Happenings at Hihn's Mill

Notes, Personals and Events of the Past Few Weeks

P. McGovern and family have left for Boulder.

Miss Sadie Neagle, of Loma Prieta, and Miss McCarty of Watsonville, spent Sunday with Mrs. P. Kearney.

Owing to the continual rains, making it an impossibility to attend, the Valencia Lyceum adjourned last Tuesday evening for one month.

Cars are now running over the Aptos railroad, the track having been repaired the past week.

Mr. and Mrs. N. Forden are now occupying their new residence on the hill.

It is expected a masquerade ball will take place at the hall on February 21st.

Work will be commenced to-day driving piles at the washouts about the mill.

Wm. Hudner and wife, of Loma Prieta, made Mr. and Mrs. Geo. Bowes a short visit last week. Mr. Hudner expects to have the Loma Prieta mill in running order shortly.

The continued stormy weather has caused a lull in our social well as business events, but, as is said, there is an end to everything, we hope to see our little burg keep up its name as one of the most prosperous little places in the county.

Washed Out.

Miss Carrie Kastor has returned from her visit to Santa Cruz.

Mrs. S. Ommenes went to Santa Cruz Wednesday.

Westley Wing of Loma Prieta is rusticating in this vicinity.

Misses S. Nagle and M. McCarthy came over from Loma Prieta Sunday to visit Mr. and Mrs. Jos. Cox.

Mr. and Mrs. P. J. McGovern, who resided here for the past eighteen months, have moved to Boulder Creek, Mr. McGovern having entered the employ of Cunningham & Co.

A social dance was given here New Years eve which was well attended. Music was discoursed by Wilder's string band and the light fantastic was tripped until the old year was out and the new year had dawned.

There is some talk of having a masquerade ball here some time next month and there are many who favor the question.

School will, in all probability, the weather permitting, reopen on or about February 1st with Miss Teresa Leonard of Aptos as teacher. Miss J. Pearl Alford, who taught last term, has obtained a position in the Santa Cruz schools. Though parents and pupils much regret to lose such an affectionate and competent teacher we are pleased to have Miss Alford obtain a superior position and heartily wish her success. Miss Leonard comes well recommended, and no doubt will merit the same approbation as former teachers.

The pile driver has arrived preparatory to doing work in its line in the yard, and in a few days the shrill whistle of the engine will sound familiar.

On New Years Day Mr. Neil Fordham and Miss Ida Day, daughter of Mr. and Mrs. D. Day, were united in marriage by Rev. Mr. Osborn at Watsonville. After spending a few days of the honeymoon the young couple returned, and are domiciled at the residence of the bride's parents, awaiting the completion of their new home when they will go to house-keeping. The groom is an industrious young man of sterling qualities, and is well thought of by his employers and his associates. The bride is a most estimable young lady, a loving daughter and affectionate sister, and though her residence will be almost in the vicinity of home, she will be missed by the family circle. That their joys may be many and their sorrows few, is the earnest wish of all who know them.

Chinese New Year is next week, and already the celestials are purchasing poultry, and good things for the coming feast.

VERDANT.[202]

The Gilded Age 1890

Hihn's Mill Items

On February 18, 1890, the *Surf* published another column on Valencia:

HIHN'S MILL ITEMS

DOINGS OF THE PAST FORTNIGHT AT THE MOUNTAIN MILL

Raining again.

Miss Eva Leonard, of Santa Cruz, is visiting her aunt, Mrs. E. Haines.

Mrs. Morehouse has a slight attack of la grippe.

Miss Lizzie Merrill is spending a week with her sister, Mrs. O. H. Wilder, who is down with la grippe.

A candy pull was given at the residents [sic] of Ed. Haines, Saturday evening. The evening was pleasantly spent in games, etc.

Messrs. Geo. Stewart, T. D. Sargent, Theodore Shirley and Blodgett are all suffering more or less with the prevailing epidemic, la grippe.

The Valencia Lyceum, at their meeting last Tuesday evening, decided to give a social dance next Saturday (Washington's birthday) Eve. Supper will be served by Mrs. Day. Admission, including supper, $1.50. The lyceum at their next meeting will elect officers for the ensuing term.

The attendance at the Valencia school has so increased (now numbering thirty-six scholars, occupying every seat in the building) that the trustees have decided to build an addition to the school house, as there are several more pupils who wish to enter.

The Valencia Galoot Club held its nightly meeting at the mill office Tuesday night. The members enjoyed an eloquent debate on the Chinese question indulged in by T. Shirley and T. Sargent. The meeting then adjourned. The clerk of the mill has requested the club to procure new quarters for their meetings. The request seems to have no effect.

SUNBEAMS.[203]

Loma Prieta Loglets

1890's first "Loma Prieta Loglets" column appeared in the *Surf* on February 19, with the information submitted to the newspaper on February 16:

LOMA PRIETA LOGLETS

A FINE LOT OF NEWS FROM THE MOUNTAIN MILL TOWN

Milk has gone down since the last rain.
A heavy shower of rain fell here yesterday and last night.
Mrs. S. Jeter and family is again a resident of our happy burg.
We are glad to see the smiling face of James Gayton on his train again.
New clothes and black eyes will be scarce in the gulch next summer. The producer is gone.
The proposed road from Monte Vista up the Bassett gulch is being surveyed by Mr. McCloud.
Miss Minnie Nagle has been sick at her home, but with the careful nursing she is convalescent.
It is not yet decided when to start the mill, but probably with fair weather it will run in two weeks.
Loma Prieta is a very lively place again as the carpenters and section men all stop at our little town.
Ten car loads of lumber was shipped last week by the Loma Prieta Lumber Co., and many more are loading.
Mr. Cantwell is pushing work between Loma Prieta and Monte Vista very fast. He has sixty men on the section.
Mr. John Wright is daily seen smoking some of Nagle's fine Mexican cigars. They come high, but we must have them.
Mr. Richard Nagle has gone to San Francisco for a few days to go through the Hammam bath treatment for sickness.
Valentine's day passed very quietly. Only a few valentines were received, but what were, deserve praise, as they only suggested the truth in many cases.
Pop corn is selling fast at our store, owing to the low price

asked by Mr. Kent. In fact, one family just lives on it. Great Scott! but how they love it.

A meeting of the directors of Loma Prieta Lumber Company was held here Saturday and Sunday. Messrs. T. B. Bishop, A. C. Bassett, Wm. Dougherty, John T. Porter, T. Hopkins and Capt. Smith were all present.

We are sorry to write that Charles Cummings has sold out his contract to Mr. James Dougherty. Charles was one of the boys and a good one too. We all hope luck and prosperity will follow him in any undertaking he attempts in the future.

The mentioning of a fine piece of cabinet work will not be out of place in this column. It was executed by Charles Craghill. It is a cupboard, the front finished with bird's-eye and curly redwood, highly polished, and a fit piece of furniture for the best house in the land.

A new and novel raffle was held here the other night for a box of No. 1 cigars, for the benefit of a poor widow woman in the city. The proceeds will surely gladden her poor soul and fill her larder with provisions for the spring. Who says Loma Prietans are not generous? STICKS.

It is interesting to note that the writer of the article states that the railroad line through Bassett Gulch is being surveyed, while work between Loma Prieta and Monte Vista is being pushed. This latter effort probably involved one of the spur lines between the two locations.[204]

Bill Baird takes over as logging manager at Loma Prieta

On February 19, 1890 in the "Loglets" column, the *Surf* revealed that Charles Cummings had sold his half interest in the logging contract with the Loma Prieta Lumber Company to his business partner, James Dougherty. The next day, Dougherty turned around and sold that interest to William "Bill" Baird, who had served as the logging manager at the Valencia mill since 1886. The *Surf* noted of Baird that he "is one of the most skillful managers in the logging line in this county, and probably understands more about the business than any other person in Santa Cruz."[205]

Loma Prieta Loglets

A new column of "Loma Prieta Loglets," dated February 22, 1890, was published in the *Surf* on February 27 detailing a boxing match between two men from the mill:

Loma Prieta Loglets

Last evening was one of much enjoyment at our little town. The Music Hall was lit up at 7:30, when a large crowd gathered to see the event of the season, Cantwell vs. Bossano's fight to a finish. At 8 o'clock time was called by W. R. Porter, who acted as referee and timekeeper; Will Scott second for Cantwell; Joe Perrie, second for Bassano. Owing to a former bare fist fight a few weeks previous, in which young Cantwell came out victorious, this promised to be a good battle. Six-ounce gloves were used, gate receipts going to winner.

The first round they shook hands, but there was fire in the eyes of both. Some severe blows were exchanged, both sparred carefully.

Second round—Cantwell led with his left, bringing claret from Bossano's nose.

Third round—Careful sparring during which time was called.

Fourth to tenth rounds—There was a hot exchange of body blows, Bossano getting a terrible smasher on the eye.

Eleventh round—First clear knock down for Bossano. Cantwell recovering, came back with a terrible right hander on Bossano's eye, which partially closed it.

Twelfth round—Cantwell came up smiling, but pale. Bossano a little the worse for wear. Cantwell aimed a blow at Bossano's nose, which fell short. Cantwell followed with a dandy on Bossano's abdomen, when cries of foul were heard from all sides of the audience.

Mr. Referee decided there was no foul. During this, the hottest round of the fight, time was called. Both went to corners hot and mad.

Thirteenth round—Both rushed this round, determined

to do each other up. Hot and hard fell the blows, Bossanno getting in some terrible jaw smashers; Cantwell planting them thick and fast on Bossano's ribs, nearly knocking the latter out, but one in the snoot brought him to life, and also his round, for he went in and pushed the fight until time was called.

It was then agreed to divide the purse of $125 and to call the fight a draw.

Sheriff John Wright then addressed the crowd, complimented the referee, spoke in the highest praise of both fighters and seconds, and dispersed the crowd in a very orderly manner.

Among the crowd who witnessed this great battle for blood were E. Kemin, W. R. Porter, John Wright, Mr. Cantwell, Chas. Cummings, J. T. Porter, T. B. Bishop, A. C. Bassett, Mr. Wakelee, Pat Walsh, Edw. Barnard and many others of note. JOHN L.[206]

Happenings at Hihn's Mill

Another entry in the "Happenings at Hihn's Mill" column appeared in the *Surf* on May 26, 1890:

HAPPENINGS AT HIHN'S MILL

DOINGS OF THE PAST FORTNIGHT IN THE HIGH REDWOODS

Geo. Bowes and family have moved to Loma Prieta.
Miss Tillie McKay is visiting her cousin, Neil Forden.
Mrs. T. Shirley will soon leave for Nevada on a visit to relatives.
H. Castor intends making a trip East this fall.
Mr. and Mrs. J. Keough have gone to Bartlett Springs. Mr. Keough's health being rather poor of late, necessitated the change. He is reported as improving rapidly.
Martin Leek, now residing in Santa Cruz, will soon move back to his ranch on Bean Hill.
Mr. L. Lanthier and Miss Dollie Hubbell were united in

marriage at the residence of P. Welsh, Aptos, Saturday, May 10th. The happy couple immediately left for Visalia, where Mr. Lanthier has secured a position as sawyer in one of the saw-mills near there. May their voyage on the matrimonial sea be long and prosperous is the wish of many friends.

An entertainment and dance for the benefit of Mrs. Hall, whose husband left her in rather destitute circumstances, was given Saturday evening, May 10th. The program consisted of songs, dialogues and recitations, participated in by the amateur talent of Valencia. Dancing was indulged in until midnight, concluding one of the most pleasant parties yet held at the hall. The entertainment was given under the auspices of the Valencia Lyceum, and the success was largely due to the untiring efforts of Misses Carrie Castor, Della and Clara Hubbell, Messrs. C. C. Hoffmann and James and William Buckhart. About $20 was realized.

It is rumoured a wedding will take place some time this fall between an elderly gentleman, a widower, and one of Valencia's fairest daughters.

Mr. T. J. Hubbell having secured charge of a box mill at Los Angeles, will move his family there. Clara, Fred and Mrs. Blodgett will leave next Tuesday, while Mr. Hubbell and Della will start later on.

A fire occurred in the roof of A. Stewart's residence the other day, causing a bit of excitement for a short while. The Valencia Fire Department responded nobly, for in two minutes fifty men were at the scene. The blaze was soon extinguished. The damages were nominal.

A subscription has been started for the purpose of raising funds towards paying for a flag for the Valencia school house. About $20 has already been realized. Appropriate exercises will be rendered on the hoisting day, which in all probability will be Memorial Day.

The closing exhibition of the Valencia school will take place next month. The scholars are now learning their parts under the direction of Miss Leonard, the teacher. An excellent program is being prepared. WILDWOOD.[207]

The Gilded Age 1890

Happenings at Hihn's Mill

The *Surf* published another entry on its ongoing column about Valencia on June 11, 1890:

HAPPENINGS AT HIHN'S MILL

NOTES, PERSONALS, ETC., AT THAT LIVELY LITTLE BURG

J. D. Chace spent a day last week with us.

D. Stewart is again employed at the mill.

Mrs. T. Shirley leaves next week for Nevada.

Miss Lizzie Merrill, of Santa Cruz, spent Sunday with her sister, Mrs. O. H. Wilder.

J. Keough has returned from Bartlett Springs much improved in health.

Mrs. C. W. Horstman, after quite a visit to Boulder Creek, has returned home.

J. Fenimore had the middle finger of his right hand badly cut by being caught by a hook.

Miss Tillie McKay, after spending a few weeks with her cousin, Neil Forden, has returned to Stockton.

P. Kearney's infant child was suddenly seized with spasms last week, caused by eating cherry stones. Dr. Morgan attended the sufferer and she has now recovered.

At the school election last Tuesday twenty-one votes were cast. Theodore Shirley, O. H. Wilder and H. Castor were elected to serve three, two and one years respectively.

A pleasant farewell party was given Miss Tillie McKay, Saturday evening, May 31, at Valencia hall. Dancing was indulged in until midnight when a bountiful repast was served the hungry guests. Music was furnished by Flores' band of Soquel. Among those present were Mr. and Mrs. T. J. Gullic, S. Ourmes, N. Fordin, J. Keough, J. Cox, J. Burkhart, Misses Carrie Castor, Addie Fisher, Della Hubbell, Eva Stewart, Nellie Craig, Mary Lee, Lottie Day, Tillie McKay, Mary

Smith, Messrs. T. Gresham, J. Buckhart, Wm. Buckhart, W. Day, Chas. Buckhart, Ed. Hihn, Bert Hihn, H. Galligan, H. Shirley, J. R. Jones, L. Smith, P. Richards, T. Leonard, W. Curran, J. Fenimore.

The hoisting of the flag at Valencia school house will take place Friday, June 13th, at 2 P. M. The program will be rendered as follows:

Presentation address...Miss Lottie Day
Reply...Theo. Shirley
Raising of Flag...Misses Lucy Day and Clara Shirley
Song, "Star Spangled Banner"...Miss Addie Hedrick
Oration...J. M. Kenyou
Song, "Columbia"...by the Pupils
Original Poem...Miss Teresa Leonard
Song, "America"...by the Pupils
Recitation, (Drakes address to American Flag)...Theo. Shirley

In the evening the closing exercises of the school will be held at Valencia Hall. The pupils are rehearsing every night this week and an excellent program is expected.

MADRONE.[208]

Land transfer from George Olive to Harriet Blackburn concerning Tract 27 in the Augmentation

George Olive had been in the lumber business for many years by 1890 but had grown tired of the industry and local politics. He listed for sale his Santa Cruz and San Lorenzo Valley lumber yards and mills, retaining only his mill and yard near Watsonville. His exit from the lumber industry placed an unanticipated burden on Santa Cruz residents since his was the only local company to not fix prices with its competition. Olive also sold Tract 27 in the Augmentation to Harriet B. Blackburn on June 23, 1890 as a part of his divestment.[209]

Loma Prieta Branch extended to 1,200-foot elevation

In late April 1890, it was revealed in the *Surf* that the Southern Pacific Railroad

The Gilded Age   1890

was surveying for another extension to the Loma Prieta Branch. While this last section was short—only 1,900 feet or 0.36 miles long—what made it difficult to complete was its increase in elevation, which averaged 10.5 percent. A grade this steep could not be overcome by the types of locomotives used by Southern Pacific thus far, and it has been doubted by some historians that the railroad even went beyond the bottom of Bassett Gulch.

The route appears to have been opened around June 28, 1890. For proof, we once more turn to Woods Mattingley's letter from Southern Pacific, which made it clear that the railroad did continue up the gulch to the 7.44-mile mark, where three forks of the west branch of Aptos Creek converge. I found the proof myself in the mid-1980s when, in the company of two hikers, I climbed from the junction of the Aptos Fire Road and Buzzard Lagoon Road down to the 1,200-foot elevation in Bassett Gulch. While working our way downstream to the bottom of the gulch, we found railroad parts: the joint bars used to bolt the ends of rails together. The parts were partially buried beside the creek. We left them there for doubters to find.

The way that this extension operated with the steep grade was not clear until I came across an interview given many years ago by Vincent Leonard, the former president of the Mid-County Historical Association. In the interview, Leonard discussed how timber was harvested in areas that were too steep for trains to reach without assistance. He stated specifically that the cars were pulled up the steep sections by long cables "just like Southern Pacific did above Aptos." He did not state where this steep section was located, but based on the known route of the mainline and its major spur lines and their percentage grades, Bassett Gulch is the only reasonable location. Thus, cars were pulled up and lowered down the steep section of track using the cables of a donkey engine in the manner of a cableway.

However, the steep grade in Bassett Gulch was not the only problem the terrain presented to grading crews. The gulch was also crooked and narrow across its entire length, with some turns curving over 25 degrees, making it difficult to pull or lower cars. The south side of the gulch is an almost sheer wall rising several hundred feet vertically, while the north side has a gentler grade and rises only 25 to 35 feet before opening onto a shelf near the summit of Santa Rosalia Mountain. While it is possible that parts of the gulch were graded for the railroad, it seems more likely that the en-

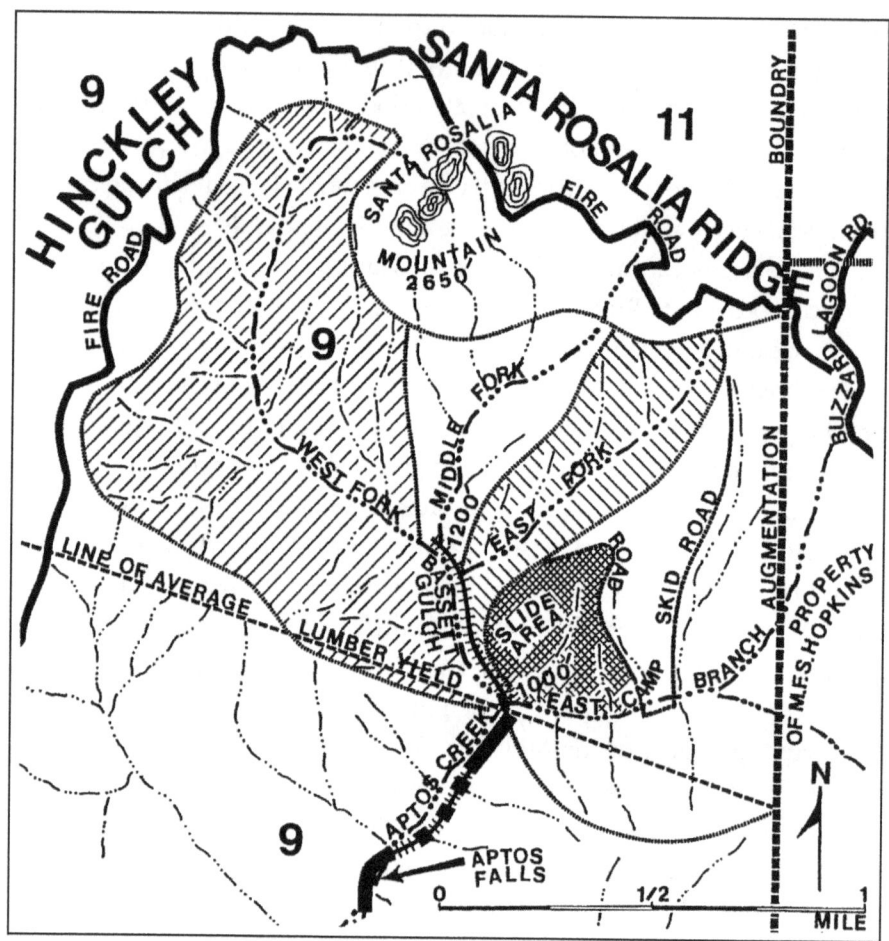

FIGURE 5.2 ROUTE OF THE LOMA PRIETA BRANCH TO 1,200-FOOT ELEVATION

tire section ran atop a level viaduct. No matter how the track was built, it was a Herculean task to complete and operate.

The manner in which the timber along the upper gullies of Bassett Gulch was harvested is still largely a mystery and will probably never be known with certainty, but some basic conclusions can be made based on my extensive exploratory trips into the gulch. It seems clear that the area was harvested in an almost identical fashion as the east branch of Aptos Creek except that no oxen were used along Bassett Gulch. I never found any evidence for even one skid road, not even one hidden along obvious paths heading into one of the three forks or in their side ravines. This was probably because of the steepness of the gulch. Instead, the Loma Prieta Lumber Company had to rely almost exclusively on donkey engines and gravity to get logs to the right-of-way below. If any oxen were used on this section, their activity was restricted to the immediate vicinity of the creek and railroad line. This also makes the logging above Bassett Gulch the first operation in the county to run without the use of animals.[210]

Logging update at Loma Prieta

On September 2, 1890, the *Surf* reported that Baird & Dougherty, who were responsible for cutting the timber for the Loma Prieta Lumber Company, were employing more than ninety-five men and producing 75,000 feet of logs per day. This provided the mill with 2.5 million feet of logs in their millpond. According to William Baird's calculations, this was enough logs to run the mill for up to eight weeks.[211]

Loma Prieta Saw Dust

Another local social column, retitled "Loma Prieta Saw Dust" from "Loglets," was published in the *Surf* on September 8, 1890 based on material provided to the newspaper two days earlier:

LOMA PRIETA SAW DUST

NOTES, PERSONALS, ENTERTAINMENTS AND NEWS FROM THEREABOUTS

Mr. J. Richardson, our local engineer, spent Sunday with friends in Santa Cruz and was present at the dedicatory services of the Garfield Tabernacle.
Mrs. W. A. Wing has returned from a visit to San Jose.
Mr. and Mrs. Charles Craighill were in Santa Cruz Sunday.
Jos. Parker of the Mechanics' Store, was here on Wednesday.
Chas. Winterhalder was here last week delivering the

premium dictionary to subscribers of the Surf. *Judging from the amount of books he brought with him the* Surf *is undoubtedly well represented in this burg.*

A Party of Surveyors is Here.

Our genial knight of the anvil, Newt. White, departed for San Jose on Tuesday. How the ladies will miss you, Newt.

Chas. Fitch of Santa Cruz has opened a butcher shop here.

Weekly raffles are fashionable.

John Richardson offers $10 reward for the arrest of the man who took his can of kerosene.

Prof. Gibson lectured on phrenology Wednesday and Thursday evenings. On Thursday evening prizes were awarded to the handsomest lady and homeliest man. Miss Grace Jeter was awarded the ladies prize, and W. R. Porter the gents.

The mill presents a busy appearance as everything in and around it looks brisk. It is running to its fullest capacity, the company having put on a full crew two weeks ago. To see the amount of lumber and ties that is sent out daily, and how busily the boys are occupied, Loma Prieta seems to be as busy, if not the busiest mill in the county.

The latest improvement in camp is that the private residences are all numbered in neat figures on nickle plates. There is some talk of a free delivery system in the near future.

The boys are already commencing to be politically inclined. All desirous of becoming registered in this precinct can be attended to upon application to Mr. J. Morrow.

Miss Barney, our school teacher, and Mrs. Bert Ray left Friday for San Francisco to attend the celebration of the Native Sons on Admission Day.

More anon. BILL NYE.[212]

Loma Prieta Sawdust

Another entry of the "Loma Prieta Sawdust" appeared in the *Surf* on October 20, 1890, based on a submission to the paper made on October 17:

Loma Prieta Sawdust

Bill Nye on Democracy, Dancing, and Mountain Doings Generally

Mrs. W. J. Hudner and Mrs. G. C. Bows and her little son Allie, have returned from a week's visit to friends in Coyote and San Jose.

Mrs. M. Cantwell and family have gone to San Francisco where they will make their home in future. The Loma Prieta Hotel formerly kept by Mrs. Cantwell has been leased by Mr. and Mrs. O'Brien lately of Gilroy. A very pleasant dance was held at the hall, a week ago last Saturday night. Music was discoursed by Cox's string band, and a fine supper at the hotel, in which mine host of the house, Mr. O'Brien, showed that he understood all the good things necessary to please his guests.

John Brouse and family left last week for Missouri.

Mr. and Mrs. Ray spent Sunday in Watsonville.

Mr. and Mrs. Murdock left Tuesday for Stockton.

Miss Clara Hamilton is visiting her parents in Monterey.

Miss Grace Barney is attending the Teacher's Institute in Watsonville.

A. C. Bassett and a number of gentlemen were here yesterday.

Mrs. Chas. Craghill spent a couple of days this week with friends in Santa Cruz.

W. J. Hudner was in Aptos on last Sunday.

Miss Leland of Watsonville is visiting Mrs. Ray.

Felei Deere started yesterday for Missouri, but upon reaching Aptos was surprised to meet his brother and a friend who was coming to visit him. Felei returned, and will defer his trip to Missouri until later on in the season.

Rumor has it that the heart of one of our mill boys has been pierced by cupid's arrow, and that a wedding in the near future with a young lady of an adjoining county will be the result.

Things have a lively appearance here. The pond is full of logs, and the bank all along the pond is piled with logs. Twenty six carloads of logs arrive daily from Monte Vista under the supervision of contractor Baird, who, it may be candidly said, is not only the most competent woodsman in the State, but by his energy and far sightedness will undoubtedly by the end of the logging season beat the record for all previous logging in the county. About seventy thousand feet of lumber is being sawed daily at the mills.

The Democratic meeting was held here on last Tuesday evening. The hall was tastefully decorated with evergreens, the stage overhead being a canopy of green foliage. Around the wall in the immediate vicinity of the stage, stars were formed of the evergreens, showing the artistic taste of Jos. Nagle. W. J. Huder presided as chairman, and after making a few remarks appropriate for the occasion, introduced the first speaker of the evening, C. B. Byrne, nominee for Assemblyman. After Mr. Byrne had concluded his remarks, Enrico de Tomaso was introduced amid applause, and favored the audience with "Rocked in the Cradle of the Deep." Several ladies were present, undoubtedly attracted there to hear Tomaso sing, and were well repaid for attending. The several speakers of the evening were introduced and made brief addresses to the point at issue, in which the Australian ballot system recommended. Mr. Steinmetz paid a glorious tribute of praise to woman in his remarks, and from what the ladies were overheard saying, Mr. Steinmetz may rely that if ever the ladies are permitted to vote in this county he will certainly receive their vote, not only for Treasurer, but will try and nominate him for Governor. Dr. Vaux made a brief speech, interspersed with his usual humorous anecdotes. Harry Garrett sang "Old Black Joe," in his usual fine tenor tones, but the gem of the evening in the vocal line was the duet "Larboard Watch" by Messrs. Thompson and Garrett, and upon being encored, repeated the song. The original songs dedicated to the aspiring candidates, sung by Mr. Wilson, with banjo accompaniment pleased the audience well, the encore being an original composition dedicated to the opposite party, "Marching Out of Office." The meeting *on the whole was a pleasant one, and be it said to the credit of all candidates for office that the absence of raillery and detraction of the opposite party, usually indulged in on such occasions, was praiseworthy.*

BILL NYE.[213]

Peak lumber year for the Augmentation ends

When the mills shut down in mid-November 1890, it marked the turning point for the lumber mills within the Augmentation. A. C. Bassett stated in an interview with the *Surf* in 1897 "that in 1890 no less than 70,000,000 feet of lumber were cut in Santa Cruz County. The employees formed a regiment or more in themselves, their pay was good and nearly all of it spent here. The annual 'cut' has gradually diminished, until 17,000,000 would be a generous estimate for last year's [1896], and the current year's, unless improvement comes, will be scarcely more than 7,000,000 feet."[214]

Chapter 6

~

Life in the Woods

Charles Ford dies

Charles Ford was never a healthy, robust man and he suffered many illnesses during his lifetime including the last, which was a long illness. Ford died on November 14, 1890. While he was not one of the Loma Prieta Lumber Company's directors, he did co-found its predecessor and sister company, the Watsonville Mill & Lumber Company, of which he was its first president. He also formed the Bank of Watsonville with John Porter, which was responsible for loaning the funds required to buy Tract 9 in the Augmentation from Carmel Fallon. In the end, his input was instrumental in the successful logging of Tract 9 and the success of the Loma Prieta Lumber Company. The Ford Company remained in business in Watsonville for another hundred years, only shutting down after the company's main building was damaged beyond repair in the 1989 Loma Prieta Earthquake.[215]

Loma Prieta Loglets

On November 26, 1890, the *Surf* published another column in its "Loma Prieta Loglets" series:

Loma Prieta Loglets

A grand masquerade ball will be given at Loma Prieta next Saturday evening. Good music will be provided and a fine time is assured to all who attend. The ladies, together with the committee in charge, will surely make it a pleasant affair.

It is expected that the Loma Prieta mill will shut down about the 10th of next month until after the holidays, when work will be resumed for the winter, as they have a large supply of logs already on hand.

Wm. J. Hudner, superintendent of the Loma Prieta Lumber Co., reports the demand for lumber the present season as very good and has several large orders on hand.

Jack Valencia, who had his hand severely jammed some time ago, is again at work in the mill.

Messrs. James Dougherty and Wm. Baird, who have had the contract to furnish logs for the mill, have laid off all the teams except one, which they will use for a few days to finish the work for the season.[216]

Loma Prieta Loglets

Another column of the "Loma Prieta Loglets" was published in the December 6, 1890 issue of the *Surf*:

Loma Prieta Loglets

The Feasting and Festivities of Thanksgiving Time and Thereabouts

Mr. James Morrow has returned from the metropolis,

where he participated in the festivities of the great Scottish festival, St. Andrews.

A fine dinner was given to the men on Thanksgiving Day by the Loma Prieta Company. Chickens, pound cake and the proverbial mince and squash pies were served in abundance. Suffice it to say that justice was done the viands and many good wishes for the benefactors were expressed.

Bert Hihn, of Hihn's mill, came over to attend the bal masque *on Saturday evening, and was the guest of Mr. and Mrs. W. J. Hudner on Sunday. Bert appeared to enjoy his first visit to Loma Prieta.*

The logging camp has about closed for this season, but Messrs. Dougherty and Baird will soon commence work for the coming season.

It seems our mountain burg has been the first to open the carnival season, a grand masquerade ball having taken place on last Saturday evening. The attendance was the largest that has ever been seen here, and many were en masque. *The supper was served at the hotel by the host and hostess, Mr. and Mrs. J. O'Brien, and was one that would be hard to excel by the most noted caterers of our times. After supper all joined with the merry masquers in having a general good time, and the terpsichorean art as indulged in until the wee sma' hours of morn. A list of those in costume would take too much of your valuable space, but mention of a few of the characters would not be amiss. Several of the young men from Hihn's mill and a few ladies and gents from Aptos were present. Jos. Nagle, as a Chinaman, made a capital John. Will Scott, as Harlequin, did well. Miss Nichols, of Aptos, was becomingly attired as Night. Chas. Craighill, as the "Fat Man," was well made up. Miss Grace Barney, Domino; Mrs. Ray, Domino. Bert Ray, as a lady, looked and acted well. Johnnie Birmingham was handsomely attired. Mesdames Scott and Valencia, and Miss Jeter and several others were* en masque.

Chas. Craighill has completed a cupboard in "burl" redwood for W. J. Hudner. It is a beauty, and the work shows Charlie to be a workman of no inferior merit.

> *W. J. Wing will soon leave for Templeton, where he and Mr. J. Farren will engage in the hotel business.*
>
> *The sad intelligence of the death of Miss Alice Leibrandt reached here by telephone yesterday forenoon. The family, up to a month ago, resided here, when they moved to Aptos. Alice was a pupil at the school here, and by her affectionate disposition and gentle qualities won the affection of her teacher and schoolmates. The young lady attended the ball here on Saturday evening and was in good health, and seemed to enjoy herself en masque. She was taken ill on Sunday and removed to her home in Aptos. Medical assistance was summoned, and all that was possible to alleviate her suffering was done, but all proved futile, as the angel of death had marked her for his own. Her parents and friends have the sincere sympathy of all their Loma Prieta neighbors and the community to whom they are known in their sorrow. A floral piece will be presented for the casket from her teacher and schoolmates.*
>
> BILL NYE.[217]

Internal strife surfaces within Loma Prieta Lumber Company management

Following many years of success, the Loma Prieta Lumber Company finally began facing serious management problems around the beginning of 1891. Since incorporation, the company's officers had slowly drifted into two opposing camps: the old timers closely associated with the Watsonville Mill & Lumber Company and the newer generation connected to the Southern Pacific Railroad. With the death of Charles Sanborn, the strength of the old guard weakened considerably and there were fears that A. C. Bassett, N. T. Smith, and Thomas Bishop—all linked to the railroad—would take a more dominant role in the daily management of the company. Woods Mattingley reported in the 1960s that rumors began circulating that the railroad men were going to freeze out some of the opposition by leveling assessments against their stocks. This led several shareholders to surrender their stocks in order to avoid assessment.[218]

Life in the Woods — 1891

Hihn's Mill Shavings

The first *Surf* column on Valencia of 1891 released on March 26 under the name "Hihn's Mill Shavings," a title that apparently did not stick:

> **HIHN'S MILL SHAVINGS**
> ---
>
> *Mr. Higgens is the happy father of an eight-pound son. More anon.*
>
> *Mr. C. Hoffman, of San Jose, paid a flying visit to our town last Sunday.*
>
> *Arthur Carrier and bride returned home Tuesday after an absence of eight months.*
>
> *Mr. T. Leonard, of this place, who has been on a visit to 'Frisco returned home Sunday.*
>
> *Miss Lizzie Merill, of Santa Cruz, is spending a few days with her sister, Mrs. Orville Wilder.*
>
> *If reports are true, two of Valencia's fair daughters are soon to be led to the hymeneal altar.*
>
> *A very pleasant party was given in honor of Miss Louisa Hihn, of Santa Cruz, who has been spending a week with Miss Lotta Day. The evening was pleasantly spent in dancing and games until a late hour, when the company dispersed well pleased with the evening's enjoyment. Those present were: Mesdames Buckhart, Baucom, Shirley, Wilder and Walker. Misses Louisa Hihn, Lotta Day, Eva Stuart, Lizzie Merill and Lucy Day. Messers Will Baucom, S. Gibson, H. Galligan, Ed Hihn, Bert Hihn, T. Shirley, J. Perry, O. Wilder, C. Buckhart, H. Hoig, R. Buckhart, C. Combs, Rob Day, Chape Day, Z. Nunemaker, George Lee and C. Walker.*
>
> "TWINS."[219]

A. C. Bassett resigns from the Southern Pacific Railroad

A. C. Bassett had been a stalwart of the Southern Pacific Railroad since its early days, but on May 8, 1891, he resigned from the company after his position as Coast Division superintendent was reorganized. Earlier in the year, railroad president Collis Huntington led an internal restructure of the management of the railroad. In effect, he took several existing divisions and organized them into a system, with the Pacific System in charge of the West Coast. A. N. Towne was made general manager of the new system, effectively demoting Bassett without revoking his title or reducing his pay. Bassett only discovered the reality of the new system when he travelled to New York to meet Huntington in person. When told he would now be forced to report to Towne, a former colleague, he felt it was a slap in the face. Bassett resigned at that meeting, although he did not submit a signed resignation until he returned to San Francisco on June 2. He made the resignation effective June 10.

The June 4 issue of the *Surf* discussed Bassett's resignation in detail:

A. C. BASSETT.

HE DECLINES TO BEND THE KNEE.

WILL RETIRE FROM THE RAILROAD.

TO THE REGRET OF COL. CROCKER AND THE PEOPLE ON THE COAST DIVISION.

The following from the San Francisco Chronicle is not unexpected news to those informed concerning railroad matters, but the loss of Mr. Bassett from the Coast Division will be keenly felt by all concerned with railroad matters and the general public. Mr. Bassett's private business lies largely in this county, and it is to be hoped that he will become a resident of this city. The Chronicle says:

The merging of the coast division into the Pacific system on the same footing as the Western division, Sacramento division and any of the other divisions of the Southern Pacific road took place some weeks ago. Considerable speculation was indulged in at the time as to the position to be occupied by Superintendent A. C. Bassett. Prior to the change he was in as independent a position as General Manager A. N. Towne, while the change brought the entire division and its officers directly under the latter gentleman.

Vice-President [Charles Frederick] Crocker was seen yesterday about the matter and his statement was substantially as follows. He said: Mr. Bassett has resigned his position as superintendent and manager of the Coast division after twenty years service with the company. As the reasons for his resignation had nothing whatever to do with the efficiency and ability of his management, Mr. Crocker said he was glad to have the opportunity to make an explanation, which is Mr. Bassett's due and which should convince his friends and the public of the high esteem in which he is held.

Yesterday Mr. Crocker received a letter of resignation from Mr. Bassett, explaining that he had taken the step because he had received a letter from C. P. Huntington to report to A. N. Towne and turn over the business of his division to the general manager.

"We regret," said Mr. Crocker, "Mr. Bassett's retirement very much, as the directors of the company have looked with pride and admiration of the management and condition of that portion of the company's property. Mr. Huntington did not consult with Mr. Stanford or me before directing Mr. Bassett to make the change. If he had done so we should have opposed the change and it would not have been made. The resignation was directed to me and has been sent on to Mr. Huntington. It will go into effect on June 10th."

In further comment the first vice-president said that no other course was open to Mr. Bassett. He had held the position for many years, and Mr. Towne had always felt hurt that this portion of the system should not, like all the other divisions, be under his jurisdiction. Any railroad manager who could show operating expenses as low as 46 per cent of the gross earnings must be a capable man, as 50 percent is considered an excellent showing for any road, while 70 percent is common. As to President Huntington's idea in making the change Mr. Crocker said he supposed it was a move in the direction of economy, but for himself he could not see that anything would be saved by the change.

It is understood that Mr. Bassett will devote himself to the affairs of the Loma Prieta Lumber Company, in which he is largely interested.[220]

Loma Prieta Saw Dust

The last social column focused on Loma Prieta in the *Surf* was published on May 18, 1891, based on information provided on May 15:

LOMA PRIETA SAW DUST

SECURED FROM ONE OF THE LIVELIEST LUMBER TOWNS IN THE COUNTY

A. C. Bassett was here Wednesday on a business tour.

Harry Street and wife, of Santa Cruz, were among the visitors here on Tuesday.

M. Lemmons is visiting his daughter Mrs. Wm. Scott.

Chas. Craighill spent a couple of days this week in Santa Cruz on a business trip.

Mr. J. Richardson, the former engineer has resigned, having obtained a more lucrative position in San Francisco. His successor is Mr. Chas. Christine, of San Francisco, who comes highly recommended.

Captain Smith, one of the stock-holders of the L. P. L. Co., accompanied by Mrs. Smith and a lady friend, spent Saturday and Sunday at the cottage.

The mill started Monday for the season with a full crew and will turn out daily about sixty thousand feet of lumber. For the past two weeks Geo Bowes, the sawyer, and a gang of assistants have been busily engaged repairing the mill preparatory to starting, while the engineer has been busy with his department. Chas. Craighill has been superintending the building of the logway for dumping logs from the cars into the pond, and several men have been busy as bees in the yard shipping lumber and putting the yard into order. Though the mill has not been operating for the past few months, yet we have not been idle, as the shipment of lumber from here has been extensive. The shipping of one order for two million feet is almost completed.

Do not think because Loma Prieta is situated on the Santa Cruz mountains that it is an isolated place; far from it, for here we have all the modern improvements to be found in a good sized village. Loma Prieta communicates by rail with Aptos. By taking cars at Aptos one has about three and a half miles of a ride, which is sure to be a safe one while under the management of our experienced and courteous conductor, James Gayton. You soon reach the yard and the next object of interest is the mill. Here one will find fifty men employed turning out lumber and shingles. Passing on you come to Loma Prieta proper. Here is the hotel, store and main office, where the genial Secretary of the company, W. R. Porter, and the two book-keepers, Messrs. Keeum and Rea, will be found at their respective desks. Adjoining is the store managed by J. B. Kent, who also has been busy replenishing stock for the season, even to the millinery line, But why is it, Blair, that while you have provided for the gentlemen against being sunburned, you have slighted the ladies? There is a Wells, Fargo express and a postoffice and a telephone communication with the offices of Baird and Dougherty, contractors, situated at Monte Vista, three miles distant from the mill, and Wm. J. Hudner's, situated opposite the mill. Thirty-six houses, all occupied, are situated adjacent to the mill, good houses, papered, painted and water inside and outside. Little garden spots of vegetation are everywhere noticeable, while fair Flora has adorned the hills with her rarest gifts until they are converted into a regular flower bed and present a pleasing sight and a balmy fragrance. Adjacent to the hotel are the private cottages of J. L. Porter and W. Bishop, members of the company, while the commodious cottage of the directors adjoin. The grounds in and around the last named cottages are handsome but special notice must be given to the garden of J. T. Porter, as some very choice flowers are in bloom. Mrs. Porter personally superintends the fixing of her garden in the growth and beauty of the same, and she is well repaid for her pains taking.

James Morrow, who went to San Rafael a week ago, has returned and is in charge of the picket department.

W. A. Wing has returned from Templeton and is again filling his former position as edgerman.

Wm. Wallbridge, our experienced raftsman, is again seen on the pond.

A pleasant party was held at the hall on Saturday evening, the occasion being a farewell tendered Jos. Nagle, as the young gentleman left on Tuesday for the metropolis to permanently reside. A goodly number attended. Supper was served by mine host and hostess of the hotel, Mr. and Mrs. W. O'Brien. Music was discoursed by Love's string band and the terpsichorean art was indulged in until all hied themselves home.

It reminds one of old times when perusing the Surf *under its present management. Long may it wave.*

BILL NYE.

It is interesting that Nye places the Loma Prieta Hotel in two different places. He situates it first beside the company store and office on the northeast side of Aptos Creek. Later, it is adjacent to the Porter and Bishop cottages in the Compound. Could there have been two hotels operating for a period? According to several previous articles, large affairs were held in the hotel, which from their descriptions were too large and elaborate to be held in the small building next to the C. Coates' saloon.[221]

Valencia Saw Dust

After a long pause, the *Surf* resumed its irregular series focused on Frederick Hihn's mill, with the column now going by the name "Valencia Saw Dust," copying the name recently applied to the "Loma Prieta Saw Dust." The first new column appeared in the May 21, 1891 issue:

Valencia Saw Dust

Doings of the Past Few Weeks at Hihn's Mill

Mrs. A. C. Carrier left for Monterey last week with the intention of soon going to her old home in Michigan.

Miss Sarah Lockhart, of Santa Cruz, spent a few days last week with her sister, Mrs. J. Keough.

Miss Pearl Alford, the popular ex-teacher of Valencia school, made a short visit to Mrs. M. Hanahan Sunday.

The happiest person in the vicinity at the present time is J. Keough, who is the proud possessor of an eleven pound son, born last Thursday.

Wm. Buckhart, attending Chestnutwood's Business College, made his parents his usual semi-monthly visit, Sunday.

Misses Bernice and Blanche Haine returned Sunday from a pleasant visit to relatives at Glenwood.

M. Hedgepeth and Wm. Day, students of Chestnutwood's Business College, will work in the mill this summer, with the intention of resuming their studies in the college next winter.

The dance given by the Farmers' Alliance Saturday night was the best attended and most enjoyable ever held at the hall. Fully one hundred persons sat down to supper, excellently prepared by Mrs. D. W. Day. To the committee of arrangements, H. Galligan and S. L. Gibson, is largely due the success of this pleasant affair.

The mill will resume operations sometime during the present week. The pond is being rapidly filled up with logs which are hauled a distance of five miles from the woods by a locomotive purchased last season, but which has undergone considerable repairs since last winter. WOOD BEE.[222]

Valencia Saw Dust

On May 26, 1891, the *Surf* published another entry in its "Valencia Saw Dust" series:

Valencia Saw Dust

Doings of the Past Few Weeks at Hihn's Mill

Mrs. S. Morehouse is suffering from the effect of an attack of la grippe, contracted last winter, but from which she has not been able to recover.

H. Leibrandt, C. B. Cox, Jno. Barrcom, J. M. Hoit, and families have lately taken up their residence with us.

While working in the mill last week, J. Keough met with a painful if not serious accident. A piece of steel entered the pupil of his eye. He was compelled to go to Santa Cruz to have it extracted after which cold set in, causing him considerable trouble.

There is some talk of having Valencia make a showing at the baby show to be held in Santa Cruz this week. Valencia contains six of the largest and brightest infants to be found anywhere in a community of its size. They are all boys excepting one and range from one to five months old.

The social dance held on the 16th ult., proving such a grand success, probably another one will be given on June 20th.

The mill started up for the season last Thursday with same crew as employed last season, excepting the engineer; J. Dunham filling that position, as C. C. Hoffmann has engaged in other business. It is generally admitted we have the finest mill site in the county. Situated upon the Valencia Creek between two gently sloping hills; on the hill west of the mill are situated the single employes' [sic] cabins, some twelve in number, and it is commonly known as "Bologna Height." On the east side are the dwellings occupied by employes and their families while just south of this is the town of Valencia proper. Water is brought to the mill from the head of the Valencia Creek, some two miles north, by a flume which empties into a reservoir east of the mill. This supplies the mill and families occupying dwellings close by. The overflow or excess water passes through a flume south to a smaller reservoir. This supplies the inhabitants of Valencia town. We have a fine large hall in which church services are held every Thursday evening, conducted by I. N. Archibald of Santa Cruz. Sunday School is also held here regularly every Sunday.

The hall contains one of the best spring floors in the county, this is admitted by all those who have danced upon it. The mill office, store and cook house are all situated just south of the mill. A trip through the surrounding country would inspire almost any who enjoys the beauties of nature. The hills are covered with beautiful and rare varieties of wild flowers. Delicious wild blackberries are also in abundance and are being gathered daily. Valencia is easily reached by four or five different roads, the best of which is to drive along the county road past Spreckels ranch, then turn off at the Corylos Park (Dr. A. Lilliencrantz), which brings you direct to the mill.

WOOD BEE.[223]

Valencia Saw Dust

Only a week after the previous "Valencia Saw Dust" column, the *Surf* released an entry in the series on June 3, 1891. For the first time, the column went unsigned, and all the subsequent columns for the year also lacked a named author:

VALENCIA SAW DUST

DOINGS OF THE PAST WEEK AT HIHN'S MILL AND VICINITY

Mrs. R. Devett is visiting Mrs. O. H. Wilder.

Mrs. F. E. Hallock is on an extensive visit to her mother, Mrs. D. W. Day.

Mrs. S. Morehouse is seriously ill, and shows no signs of improvement.

Mrs. O. H. Wilder entertained a few invited friends at a euchre party Friday evening. At the conclusion of this interesting game a delicious repast was served.

The social census of Valencia District has been taken the

past week by Miss Carrie Castor.

Rehearsals are being held weekly by those taking part in the school exhibition which takes place the latter part of June.

Miss Carrie Castor intends leaving for other parts this week.

Mrs. Wm. Baucom made a visit to her mother, Mrs. Fisher, who lies dangerously ill in Santa Cruz.

Among other things worthy of mention are the well-kept and arranged gardens of the inhabitants of this village, the beds adorned with large and beautiful varieties of flowers, the size and fragrance of the roses being most notable. The ladies are deserving of a compliment for the care and attention paid to their gardens.

The annual election of school trustees of Valencia District will take place Tuesday, June 2d, to fill the expired terms of F. Leonard and H. Castor.

The engagement is announced of one of our well known young men to a Watsonville lady. The wedding will take place sometime during the present week.

For some time past there has been a difference of opinion as to which place, the logging camp or the mill, contained the best man with the boxing gloves among the younger class. To settle the dispute it was arranged to have a set-to last Sunday at the mill, the principals being M. McGurty of the mill and F. Trevethan of the logging camp. The boys fought ten rounds, McGurty proving himself to be by far the better man. A large crowd witnessed the combat.[224]

Valencia Saw Dust

Continuing its almost regular column on Valencia happenings, the *Surf* published another article on June 17, 1891:

VALENCIA SAW DUST

HAPPENINGS OF THE PAST WEEK AT HIHN'S MILL

Miss T. Gannon spent Sunday with Mrs. J. Cox.

Miss Carrie Castor left for San Jose last week where she has secured employment in a fruit cannery. Miss Luta Waters of Corralitos accompanied her.

A party of ladies and gentlemen from Watsonville chaperoned by Miss Esther V. Malcolm, spent Sunday in the vicinity gathering ferns.

Mrs. O. H. Wilder is spending a few days in Santa Cruz.

At the annual election of school trustees of Valencia District, R. T. Holmes and Chas. Horstman were elected to succeed Thos. Leonard and H. Castor.

Owing to other attractions the dance which was to take place on the 20th, has been indefinitely postponed.

A fire completely destroyed the dwelling occupied by A. Carrier a week ago Friday. The furniture and other household goods were saved. Had the wind been in another direction other buildings would have suffered. The mill hands worked nobly to save the building, but the fire had gained such headway before discovered, it was impossible to save anything but the household effects.

Percy Richards met with a bad accident Friday. While removing some box shooks in the box mill he accidentally struck his hand against a circular saw. His fore finger was cut at the joint necessitating its amputation, while his thumb and other fingers met with less serious injuries.[225]

Valencia Saw Dust

June 25, 1891 marked the last substantial column focused on events happening at Valencia. After this date, only periodic articles appeared in the *Surf,* with four articles in 1892, one in 1893, and two in 1894. The final column of 1891 appears here:

Valencia Saw Dust

Doings of The Past Week at Hihn's Mill and Vicinity

Miss Tillie Staub spent Sunday with her sister, Mrs. A. C. Baird.

Miss Cora Otto is visiting Mrs. O. H. Wilder.

Chapin Day had his hand severely cut by a box saw last week.

Mr. and Mrs. R. H. Pringle, accompanied by Mrs. C. Hoffman and daughter, spent Sunday with Mrs. S. M. Hoit.

Miss Sarah Lockhart is suffering from a severe attack of the measles and pleurisy, at the residence of her sister, Mrs. J. Keough.

There is some talk of organizing a minstrel troupe, to be composed of local talent. If the project materializes, some fine entertainments will be the result as there is some excellent talent to be found in this neighborhood.

At the semi annual election of officers of the Valencia alliance held last Wednesday evening, the following were elected: A. N. Hedgpeth, President; H. Gallegan, Vice-President; S. L. Gibson, Secretary; Mrs. S. Buckhart, Treasurer. The alliance is in a flourishing condition having rented the hall, put up curtains and otherwise improved the appearance of the hall. Thirty-eight names are now on the roll.

A very successful entertainment was given by the Aptos Sunday School at the Aptos Hall last Saturday evening. Strawberries and cake, coffee and lemonade were served by the fair young ladies of Aptos.

The closing exercises of the Valencia School will take place next Friday evening, June 26th. Numerous applications for the position of teacher have been received by the trustees, but no one has been chosen as yet.

While laboring in the box mill Monday, J. Keough cut his right thumb to the bone.

Miss Stella Walker of Watsonville has been spending a few days with her aunt, Mrs. J. Buckhart.[226]

Mary Hopkins dies

On July 25, 1891, Mary Hopkins, owner of one-fourth of the Southern

Pacific Railroad and its related companies, died. According to the *San Francisco Chronicle*, she "died after a long and painful illness at the residence of her husband, Edward F. Searles, in Methuen, Mass., early this morning." She had first fallen ill in 1890 during a trip to Europe and quickly went to California in the hope that she could recover there; however, she returned to Massachusetts after a brief period of slightly improved health. Hopkins "was nearly 70 years of age at her death. She is reported to be worth over $70,000,000, making her the richest woman in the United States.... From the moment of her death the house has been under guard. All the servants and workmen were sworn to secrecy on penalty of immediate discharge."

The *Chronicle* continued:

> *Mrs. Searles died without issue by either of her husbands. Her adopted son, Timothy Hopkins of this city, treasurer of the Southern Pacific Company, is now in Japan with his family. Mrs. Timothy Hopkins is a niece of the deceased, and another niece is the wife of Mark S. Severance.*
>
> *Mrs. Searles' property was managed until recently by Timothy Hopkins, and latterly by Moses Hopkins, M. S. Severance and J. S. Sproule. Her interest in the Southern Pacific directory was represented by Hubbard & Stillman of New York....*

Timothy Hopkins, upon hearing of the death of his adopted mother, returned to Massachusetts to hear the contents of her will, which was read on July 30. He discovered before he returned that he had been intentionally left out of the will with the entire estate passing to Searles. Indeed, the will stated outright: "The omission to provide in this will for my adopted son, Timothy Hopkins, is intentional, and not occasioned by accident or mistake." Immediately upon his return, Timothy filed suit against his step-father. His position was that his mother's decision had been made under undue influence by Searles. Meanwhile, newspapers speculated that it was due to Timothy's criticism of Mary's second husband. The trial between Hopkins and Searles lasted months and dominated the newspapers coast to coast. The trial packed the Salem courthouse with curious spectators waiting to hear the details of Searles's romance and dealings with Mark Hopkins's widow. However, when Searles saw the crowd, he retreated and approached his step-son's attorney to settle out of court.

The eventual amount agreed between the two men is unknown, but the *Boston Globe* stated on March 5, 1892 that it was about $3 million. Searles retained the majority of the fortune, including most of the railroad stock, but he retired from the public and never interfered with the affairs of the companies from which he derived so much wealth. Timothy kept his position with Southern Pacific but never divulged the details of his arrangement with Searles. He did, however, admit that Mary had given him a substantial cash payment as part of the estate settlement following Mark Hopkins's death in 1878.[227]

Board of Equalization evaluates the F. A. Hihn Company's timber tracts in the Augmentation

On July 27, 1891, the *Surf* revealed that the timber lands of the F. A. Hihn Company in the Augmentation had been evaluated by an assessor hired by the Santa Cruz County Board of Equalization, or rather the Santa Cruz County Board of Supervisors. The article states:

> *As patiently and attentively as jurors, the members of the Board of Equalization sat all day Saturday and listened to testimony concerning the value of the timber lands of the F.A. Hihn company, and rarely is the examination of witnesses in a Court conducted as energetically and as ably as by Messrs. Hihn and Mattison before the Board. Neither gentlemen missed a point from start to finish. The examination of the main witnesses for the Hihn company, Messrs. Kent, Brown and Armstrong, was continued and the Assessor introduced J. T. Freshour, L. J. Mason and Nathan Hart, Sr., of Soquel, and Wm. E. Emory, and E. B. Morrill of Highland.*
>
> *Evidence was taken upon the character and amount of the timber and general value of the land in each lot of the immense tract known as the Soquel Augmentation Rancho,*

> *and every witness was called upon for his estimate of what the land would bring if offered for sale at auction. Nearly all the witnesses agreed that good redwood timber land would sell for $50 per acre at auction. Mr. Morrill valued a considerable part of the timber in Hihn's Highland tract [Tract 16] at $100 per acre, and offered to back his judgment by purchasing it then and there at that price, but no sale took place. Mr. Emory estimated good fruit land in Highland at from $50 to $75 per acre and offered to procure a purchaser for Mr. Hihn's fruit land at Highland at that price.*
>
> *From evidence it appears there is about 1,400 acres of redwood timber in the Soquel canyon. Mr. Brown, a witness for Mr. Hihn, estimated the lumber at about 75,000,000 board feet, others made it higher. From 1,000 to 2,000 cords of tan bark oak could also be procured on the tract.*
>
> *The main contention of Mr. Hihn concerning this upper Soquel tract [Tracts 1, 6, 10, 11 and 25] appeared to be its inaccessibility. Because it would require the construction of seven miles of railroad to reach it, he claimed that it should not be rated as high as lands of otherwise equal value.*

Hihn argued that his properties and those of the F. A. Hihn Company had been assessed at a higher rate than adjacent properties and that he was being singled out. As a result, he demanded a reduction from the assessor. Arthur Taylor, the *Surf*'s editor, however, challenged Hihn directly in his editorial, pointing out the advantage the wealthier landowners in the county had over people with substantially smaller properties, such as those owned by Hihn's neighbors.

The next day, the *Surf* continued reporting the assessment:

> *[Hihn] said that it was practically inaccessible, that the available shake timber and the tan bark had already been taken off, and the construction of a road to it would be very costly, it would not pay at present prices and probably would not for many years. Regarding the Highland tract he read a copy of a letter which he stated had been sent to E. B. Morrell, offering*

to sell him the timber land at the price he had offered for it on Saturday, in his testimony before the Board, and also on to Mr. Emory offering to sell the fruit land at the prices he said could be obtained for it. He said that the timber was in small tracts and that no mill site was available. He compared the assessment of his land on the upper Soquel with that of F. Averon, which he said was worth ten times as much as his land.

On cross examination he admitted that he had testified in the case of Wilding vs. Hihn, that it was his intention to build a railroad into this timber tract at once.

Robt. Stanley was called by the Assessor to testify as to the value of the Aptos Mill. J. B. Brown had sworn that the Aptos mill was not worth as much as the Loma Prieta mill. Stanley testified that he considered the Aptos mill the better of the two. In cross examination, he stated that the cost of the Aptos mill was $16,000 (assessed for $8,000)."[228]

A. C. Bassett's business conflicts evaluated by Collis P. Huntington

A. C. Bassett left the Southern Pacific Railroad on bad terms and Collis Huntington felt it necessary to assess his former employee's business dealings to ensure that Bassett had not been excessively exploiting his position. Following the investigation, the *Surf* reported on August 8, 1891:

> *The Examiner yesterday made public a letter from C. P. Huntington, President of the Southern Pacific Railroad, written to Col. Crocker relative to the resignation of A. C. Bassett, the former Superintendent of the Coast Division. Mr. Huntington says:*
>
> *Perhaps it is just as well, as Mr. Bassett has "extensive interests of his own, to which he will devote his attention," referring particularly to the San Jose Improvement Company in which Mr. Bassett is a "heavy stockholder." I understand also that he has a large interest with the Loma Prieta Lumber Company, and also in the Southern Pacific Milling*

> *Company, so that with these large interests to attend to, very likely it would be better for him and as well for the railroad company that he should have resigned, and very likely it will be more satisfactory to him, as it is no doubt somewhat difficult for a man to occupy the relations that he has to, as manager of a railroad owned by others, transporting large tonnage that he would necessarily have to transport for the said railroad, which tonnage belongs to himself. But certainly with the wonderful thrift that has followed him since he came to the railroad company, he cannot complain that he has not had opportunities for acquiring wealth sufficient to allow him to retire from this position without fear of coming to want.*

Following his departure from Southern Pacific, Bassett remained vice president of the Loma Prieta Lumber Company alongside other railroad officers.[229]

F. A. Hihn Company requests survey of East Aptos Divide between Tracts 2 and 9 in the Augmentation

As the harvesting of timber climbed up the East Aptos Divide between the east branch of Aptos Creek and Valencia Creek, conflicts arose between the Loma Prieta Lumber Company and the F. A. Hihn Company over property lines. Thus, Frederick Hihn decided in September 1891 to hire A. T. Hermann and R. R. McLeod, both of San José, to survey the boundary between Tracts 2 and 9 within the Augmentation.

Final timber cutting operation in Eureka Canyon begins

In an article published in *The Pajaronian* on January 14, 1892, the Loma Prieta Lumber Company announced that it was accepting bids for the milling of the remaining timber in Eureka Canyon along Ramsey Gulch north of Corralitos. The company "proposed to move the Game Cock mill into the gulch and cut timber with it." The article further explained that "the timber in the Ramsey Gulch is the last of the large bodies of timber in the Pajaro hills. There is considerable uncut timber in the Taylor Gulch, and on the Hughes, Laning and Casserly tracts, but they are not such large tracts as that of the Ramsey Gulch. The rise and decadence of the lumbering interests of the Pajaro hills has not covered many years." In the end, William Baird of Loma Prieta was given the job of harvesting the timber in Ramsey Gulch.

By this point, it seems clear that the Watsonville Mill & Lumber Company, which owned the land and the mill, had been reduced to a junior partner to the Loma Prieta Lumber Company. This decline had been happening for years but was probably accelerated by the death of Charles Ford.[230]

Land transfer from Edward Searles to Timothy Hopkins

On March 2, 1892, Edward Searles began the transfer of 8,529 acres of property in Santa Cruz County to his step-son, Timothy Hopkins, as part of an out-of-court settlement relating to Mary Hopkins' estate. The *Surf* reported extensively on the transfer in an article published on March 25:

> *In common with all Californians, and the world in general, Santa Cruzans have taken a lively interest in the disposition of the Hopkins-Searles estate, but this interest has also been considerably heightened by the fact that the estate had large land holdings, the final disposition of which would not be without influence upon the development of Santa Cruz county.*
>
> *It is therefore a matter for congratulation not only to Mr. Timothy Hopkins, but to the people of the county, that this property, by the terms of the settlement, is to be transferred to Mr. Hopkins, for he is a liberal-minded and progressive young man who may be depended upon to manage his estate in a manner which will promote the general welfare as well as advance his private interests.*
>
> *The property of the estate in this county consists mostly of redwood timber lands, selected some years ago. A portion of it is tributary to the Loma Prieta mills, and a portion is accessible to the mill now located in the Ramsey Gulch near Corralitos.*

Life in the Woods 1892

> There are several fine tracts on the Zayante, Newell and Boulder creeks, but the largest body lies up the coast, and is tributary to Scott's creek and the Waddell. The assessed valuation of these lands aggregates about $150,000, but it would undoubtedly require at least half a million to purchase them.
>
> The distribution is such that the Hopkins property is found in thirteen different school districts, in acreage as follows:

District.	Acres.
Castle Rock School District	200
Dougherty " " " "	570
Browns " " " "	840
Zayante " " " "	80
Boulder " " " "	640
Newell Creek " " " "	440
Sequoia " " " "	480
Sunnyside " " " "	320
Seaside " " " "	1,944
Agua Puerca " " " "	346
Eureka " " " "	957
Loma Prieta " " " "	1,117
Hazel Dell " " " "	595

> As long as the title was vested in Mrs. Searles this timber was practically under the control of the Southern Pacific, but Timothy Hopkins will be an independent citizen and may prove an important factor in future enterprises in this county.

Shortly after Searles signed over the property to Hopkins, a letter from Stillman, Hubbard & Company of New York informed Hopkins that the firm held 1,380 shares of stock in the Loma Prieta Lumber Company under his mother's name. He immediately made arrangements to have the stock certificates reissued in his name. These shares gave Hopkins a forty-two percent stake in the lumber company. He also separately obtained full ownership of Tract 8 in the Augmentation, including its long-running shingle mill operation, which he took over in earnest.[231]

Lines From Loma Prieta

On March 26, 1892, the *Surf* published its latest column on happenings at Loma Prieta:

LINES FROM LOMA PRIETA

Last Tuesday evening the L. P. L. Society gave a very enjoyable entertainment at their hall, the most interesting feature of which was a tableau entitled "Bluebeard's Closet." Among those who took part were Mrs. Mercier, Mrs. Craghill, Misses Sadie Nagle, Lillie Nagle and Grace Barney. Just as the "young ladies" had assumed the most excruciating countenances the curtains were drawn, the red lights thrown on, when lo! and hold, a most serious accident befell them. The rigging, which had been previously prepared by one of the "young ladies" and Mr. Fuller, unfortunately gave way, and the wives of poor old "Bluebeard" were left hanging by the hair in full view of the audience.

A grand masquerade is to be given at the S. P. Hall on April 2d. A good time is guaranteed all who come.

Miss Louise Kidder of Watsonville, is the guest of Miss Grace Barney, and Saturday evening a euchre party was given at the house of Mr. and Mrs. C. B. Rea in honor of Miss Kidder. Those present were Mr. and Mrs. C. B. Rea, Mrs. Cowling; Misses Sadie Nagle, Lillie Nagle and Louise Kidder of Watsonville, and Grace Barney; Messrs Porter, Kemm, Hedgpeth and James Bishop of San Francisco. Miss Sadie Nagle carried off the first prize and Miss Louise Kidder the booby prize. After the game the guests were treated to a sumptuous repast, after which all retired to their homes well pleased with the evening's entertainment.

"MOLINO."[232]

Life in the Woods 1892

Happenings at Hihn's Mill

After an absence of nearly a year, new entries in the *Surf*'s column on Valencia began to appear again, starting on April 9, 1892:

HAPPENINGS AT HIHN'S MILL

DOINGS OF THE PAST FEW WEEKS AT VALENCIA

The mill will commence operations about May 1st, with Geo. McCrell, formerly head-sawyer, as foreman.

J. Keough will operate a shingle mill at San Jose this season.

A farewell party will be given Wm. Buckhart Saturday evening at the residence of Ed Hames. Mr. Buckhart will enter the employ of J. Keough as a bookkeeper at San Jose.

A match game of baseball will be played between the Valencia and Loma Prieta nines Sunday. The game will be hotly contested, and a large crowd is expected to attend.

Miss Annie Snyder of Kansas is visiting her cousin, Mrs. C. W. Horstman.

James Buckhart, after an absence of two years has returned and will be with us this season.

W. T. Douglass, formerly of the U. S. A. and who as a soldier, spent a month in 1887 in Santa Cruz has temporarily located at the mill.

Geo. W. Nichols of New York is visiting O. H. Wilder. Messrs. Nichols and Wilder were brought up in the same city.

The opening dance of the season will be given at the hall Saturday evening, April 23d. Wheaton's full string band of five pieces will furnish music. A grand time is promised.

The Valencia Lyceum so long demised for lack of interest, will be revived this summer, with much better prospects of success than ever before.

Taken all together, the prospects for a lively season are good. VAL.[233]

Happenings at Hihn's Mill

A week after the last column, another Valencia article appeared in the *Surf* on April 16, 1892:

HAPPENINGS AT HIHN'S MILL

DOINGS OF THE PAST WEEK AT VALENCIA— TIMES GETTING LIVELY THERE

Mr. and Mrs. Chas. Craighill of Loma Prieta have taken a house in Valencia and are moving thereto. Charlie will manage the box mill and file the mill saws this season.

Great preparations are being made for the opening dance on the 23rd inst, no doubt it will be a grand success.

The residents of Valencia intend holding a picnic on the Aptos beach, Mayday.

Mrs. P. Correll is lying dangerously ill at her home.

Alex. Bedell long in the employ of the Aptos Mill, has formed a partnership with Wm. Baird and they will operate the Game Cock mill in Ramsey gulch. Success to them both.

The game of baseball between the Loma Prieta and Valencia nines was won by the latter by a score of 8 to 5. The brilliant fielding and excellent batting work of both nines were features of the game. A contest between the Aptos and Valencia nines is on the tapis for next Sunday.

A farewell party given to Wm. Buckhart at Mrs. Ed Haines' was well represented by the society element of Valencia. The evening was pleasantly spent in games, songs, music and dancing until midnight, when an excellent repast was served. Those present were: Mr. and Mrs. J. Buckhart, C. W. Horstman, Ed Haines, O. H. Wilder, Misses Carrie Castor, Annie Snyder, Tillie Dunham, Schilling, Haines; Messrs. W. Day, R. Day, H. Galligan, J. Buckhart, W. Buckhart, Chas. Buckhart, Bert Hihn, W. T. Douglass, G. W. Nichols, H. Stuart, H. Johnson and others. VAL.[234]

Happenings at Hihn's Mill

Two weeks passed after the second Valencia news update in the *Surf* before a third column was published in the April 30, 1892 edition:

HAPPENINGS AT HIHN'S MILL

DOINGS OF THE PAST WEEK AT VALENCIA—TIMES GETTING LIVELY THERE

The mill will start shortly.

Miss Julia Daubenbiss of Soquel is spending the week as the guest of Mrs. C. W. Horstman.

Wm. Buckhart came over from San Jose to attend the opening ball.

Hugh Forden is stopping with his brother Neil.

Mr. and Mrs. Frank Rider spent Sunday with Mrs. J. Buckhart.

The opening dance given on the 23rd was one of the most enjoyable held at the hall, fully forty-five couples were on the floor at one time. The dancers came from all directions, Santa Cruz, Soquel, Aptos, Loma Prieta, Corralitos and Watsonville being well represented. The music furnished by Wheaton's Band was exceptionally fine. Another party will be given some time in June.

A grand picnic will be held at Aptos on Friday the 29th by the schools of Corralitos, who have joined together to celebrate this day as their May day. The May Pole dance and other features will be executed by the school children. The Corralitos brass band of fourteen pieces will furnish music. The band is said to equal any amateur band in the State in its playing. A good time is anticipated at the picnic and a large crowd will attend.

There will be a match game of base ball between the Aptos and Valencia nines at the Valencia grounds. The grand stand is in good condition and no doubt will be illuminated by the pretty faces of the fair sex with merry voices shouting for their favorite team. The Valencia nine have procured elegant suits and will wear them Sunday for the first time. Success to the boys. GILHOOLY.[235]

Loma Prieta mill shuts down and Valencia mill starts up

Following a wildly successful winter season that saw the mill at Loma Prieta shut down for only two days, the mill closed indefinitely beginning on May 1, 1892. *The Pajaronian* elaborated: "This will be the first time the mill has been closed down for any length of time since its erection. Their mill at Ramsay [*sic*] Gulch, above Corralitos, will supply their lumber market this season. There is 10,000,000 feet of lumber in Ramsay Gulch and it will take two years to mill the same."

At the same time, the Southern Pacific likely used the shut down as justification to abandon the part of the Loma Prieta Branch beyond the 1,000-foot elevation point. This section along Bassett Gulch was exceedingly costly to maintain and most of the nearby timber had been sufficiently harvested by the beginning of 1892.

Meanwhile, Frederick Hihn opened his mill on Valencia Creek on May 16 "with a large force of men."[236]

Happenings at Hihn's Mill

The last *Surf* column on Valencia for 1892 appeared on June 9, over a month after the previous column:

HAPPENINGS AT HIHN'S MILL

DOINGS AT THAT LIVELY SAW-MILL VILLAGE FOR THE PAST MONTH

The mill has commenced running and is sending out a large amount of lumber.

Misses Sadie and Lillie Nagle of Loma Prieta are spending a few days visiting Mrs. Chas. Craighill.

A social dance will be given at the hall Saturday evening, June 11th. Everything is being done to make this dance one of the usual successes for which Hihn's Mill is noted.

At the school election held Tuesday T. Leonard and Neil Forden were elected trustees for the ensuing term.

Quite a number of citizens being in favor of celebrating the glorious 4th in this vicinity, a meeting has been called to consider the advisability of the same. It is expected to give a picnic and dance.

The Valencia nine were defeated in a game of baseball by the High School nine of Santa Cruz last week by a score of 14 to 6. MADRONE.[237]

Southern Pacific's Coast Division reorganized

On July 1, 1892, the Southern Pacific Railroad Company announced a substantial reorganization of its local lines. The Santa Cruz Line was renamed the Pajaro & Santa Cruz Branch and the Loma Prieta Line became the Loma Prieta Branch. Meanwhile, the South Pacific Coast Railway Division, previously operated autonomously, became the Santa Cruz Division. The latter name did not last long, however. Beginning September 3, 1896, the Santa Cruz Division began appearing in the same employee timetable book as the Coast Division. A year later, on September 27, 1897, the Santa Cruz Division was reduced to the Narrow Gauge Subdivision, at which point all the Southern Pacific Railroad's infrastructure in Santa Cruz County became a part of the Coast Division.[238]

Loma Prieta Mill remains closed

After shutting down most of its operations on Aptos Creek in 1892, the Loma Prieta Lumber Company decided to keep the mills closed for the following year as well. This was done so its machinery could be upgraded. It will be remembered that when the mill first opened in 1887 following the Monte Vista fire, one of its headrigs and two boilers were brought over from the destroyed mill. After heavy repairs, the second headrig was also salvaged and brought to the new mill at Loma Prieta. Thus, for six years, the Loma Prieta Lumber Company's primary mill used substandard, salvaged equipment. By the beginning of 1892, it became clear to management that this long-neglected machinery needed replacement in order to keep up with the number of logs that continued to be dumped in the millpond. The initial solution the company chose to pursue was adding a new headrig and boiler to the mill, but since the older machinery was in such a state of disrepair, the directors decided to buy three new headrigs and boilers instead.

With its primary mill shut down for another season, the company depended upon the output of the mill operating in Ramsey Gulch on Corralitos Creek to maintain its lumber stocks. Fortunately, the company had several lumber yards located throughout the area including in Watsonville at Beach and Pine Streets, in Santa Cruz at 110 Pacific Avenue, and in Hollister, Moss Landing, Salinas, Monterey, Pacific Grove, and San Juan Bautista.

The lapse in production for 1893 may have also been the result of internal disputes within the Loma Prieta Lumber Company management. With Timothy Hopkins now in possession of forty-two percent of the firm's stock and A. C. Bassett owning another eighteen percent, the two former Southern Pacific men effectively owned sixty percent of the lumber company—a controlling interest. Hopkins soon began pushing his advantage at the expense of the other shareholders. After some behind-the-scenes struggle, the company's president, Thomas Bishop, resigned at some point late in 1893, selling his stock and moving back to San Francisco permanently.[239]

Happenings at Hihn's Mill

The only *Surf* article on happenings at Valencia that was published in 1893 appeared on February 28:

HAPPENINGS AT HIHN'S MILL

NOTES FROM THE LIVELY BERG OF VALENCIA IN THE REDWOODS

The weather is delightful.

Grant Dotson is visiting his cousins.

Mrs. G. Wenban of Santa Cruz made a flying visit to Mrs. T. Leonard Thursday.

Miss Lillie Waltrup has returned home after a pleasant visit to friends and relatives.

Mr. Jno. Buckhart and three sons are working on their ranch near Corralitos clearing land and otherwise improving their ranch.

Dan Madeira once of Santa Cruz, who married Clara Ryder has bought the Martin Leske ranch and will make this his future home.

One of the most pleasant parties of the season was held at the residence of Mrs. J. Buckhart last Saturday evening. The evening was enjoyably spent in games and dancing until midnight when a most bountiful supper was served the hungry guests. The jolly crowd then dispersed wishing the hostess many thanks for the pleasant evening spent. Those present were:

Mr. and Mrs. Haines, Craghill, Wilder, McCrell, Gibson, Hoig, Castor, Mrs. A. C. Stuart, Misses Birdie, Minnie, and Mattie Maxwell, Dora Lewis, Blanch and Boyce Haines, Emma Stuart, Kate Harris, Bertha Stuart, Carrie Castor, Messrs. Waler Maxwell, J. Spencer, Ed Hihn, Geo. Roberts, Bert Hihn, Dave Haines, R. Hastings, Grant Dotson, Percy Richards, Herb Stuart, Chas. Wm. and Jas. Buckhart, Eli Stuart.

Mrs. Geo. Roberts is rapidly recovering from the effects of the injury to her wrist received by being precipitated from a cart some time ago.

Mrs. H. Kerns, who received dangerous injuries to her right ankle three months ago is able to be about on crutches.

Several of our Four Hundred attended the drama Confederate Spy at Aptos and state it was the best amateur play ever given in the vicinity.

Dame Rumor has it about that one of our fairest belles is about to be carried on the sea of matrimony by one of our rising young men. MADRONE.[240]

Valencia post office opens

Thomas Leonard petitioned for a post office for the village of Valencia on February 11, 1893. He estimated that the total population of the immediate vicinity was 250 residents, with another 150 in the wider area who could also access the location. The post office was approved on April 22 and opened shortly afterwards.[241]

Hihn's Mill Notes

The previous reporter for the Hihn's mill society column disappeared following their February 28, 1893 column and was replaced with a new author only named "P. C." This mysterious new reporter, however, chose to publish their column in the *Sentinel* rather than the *Surf*, the first article of which appeared on April 26:

HIHN'S MILL NOTES

Ed. Sentinel:—Niel Fordan and Harry Hoig returned from a trip to Hollister Saturday, where they had been to purchase some horses.

Wm. Baucom has purchased a horse and buggy.

Mrs. L. Schilling has been suffering from a severe attack of rheumatism for the past two weeks.

Miss Delia Hubbell, of Santa Cruz, is the guest of Mrs. Buckhart.

A. J. Hihn, our genial clerk, is filling Mr. Johnson's place in the lumber office at Aptos during the illness of that gentleman.

Miss Emma Stuart returned from Watsonville Saturday where she has been spending a few days with her friend, Miss Stella Walker.

George Mackrell has bought a new horse and buggy, which fact has gladdened the hearts of some of our young men, as they will not now have to go to Aptos for a stylish turnout.

Thomas Leonard and wife visited Santa Cruz last Saturday, returning Sunday.

Among our week's visitors to Watsonville were: H. Hoig and wife, Mrs. G. Mackrell, Mrs. Ed. Haines, Misses Minnie and Mattie Maxwell, W. Baucom and wife, Mrs. T. Leonard and Mrs. O. H. Wilder.

Mrs. Corey, of Santa Cruz, visited her daughter, Mrs. C. Craghill, of this place, last week.

Mrs. Richardson, of San Francisco, is the guest of Mrs. T. Leonard.

One of the most pleasant affairs of the season was a party given by G. M. Roberts on Saturday evening last. The house was beautifully and tastefully decorated with evergreens, and lights were hung so as to give a most artistic coloring to the whole scene. Mr. and Mrs. Roberts exerted themselves to such a degree that the guests were continually interested and amused, and not a moment was allowed to lag. A repast that would very readily tempt the appetite of an epicure was placed before the guests, to which they did ample justice, and at the late hour of twelve the merry crowd, after bidding good-nights with many best wishes to the happy host and hostess, broke up, and separated to their different homes.

The people of Hihn's Mill will celebrate May-day on the Aptos beach, where they have arranged to have a grand time.

P.C.[242]

Hihn's Mill Notes

The mysterious *Sentinel* columnist known only as "P. C." contributed a second update on happenings at Hihn's mill on May 4, 1893:

Hihn's Mill Notes

The first of May dawned bright and clear, and everybody and everything seemed to have on their gala-day attire. The sun seemed to shine several degrees brighter, while the air never before seemed so fresh and balmy as it did to a merry car-load of our pleasure-loving people, who left the mill on Monday morning en route for the Aptos beach, where the day was spent as only a jolly crowd of picnicers can spend a lovely day.

The day was all that could be asked for, in the shape of weather, and the forenoon passed rapidly amid games and merry-making. At noon the lunch baskets were opened and a delicious repast was placed before the hungry crowd, who did it complete justice. J. T. McKean, of McKean & Ort, took some views of the different groups. To Messrs. Ed Haines, G. M. Roberts and H. Hoig many thanks are due for their care in providing a car and team. At six o'clock the party once more arrived at the mill, tired but happy. So closed a day that few regret, and many, yes all, look forward to a return of the same a year hence.

The dance given by the young people of this place last Saturday evening was a very successful affair and well attended, many being present from Santa Cruz, Soquel, Aptos and Glen Haven.

Harry Hoig and wife have changed their residence and are now living in the upper part of the city, while Mrs. Day has once more assumed charge of the cook-house.

The familiar face of Joe Perry was seen on our streets Sunday.

M. L. Markley, of Indiana, is the guest of ol O. H. Wilder.

Henry Gobbs has moved his family from Soquel to the mill, where he will reside in the future, as he has secured employment here.

G. M. Roberts sports a new top buggy.

Mr. and Mrs. O. H. Wilder visited Santa Cruz Wednesday.

An unusual number of visitors have been attracted to our little burg by its clear, bracing air and lovely scenery, for which it is noted.

P. C.[243]

A world financial panic and economic depression begin

Since the financial recovery of 1879, the United States' national economy had faired relatively well. But by 1893, foreign investors were becoming concerned with a lack of industrial progress in America, with many projects held up, delayed, or simply abandoned. Thus, they began to divest. A series of slumps in the New York Stock Exchange in May and June led to the devaluation of the silver dollar on June 26. However, President Grover Cleveland avoided a crash by borrowing $6,000,000 from clearinghouse banks. He also instructed the Treasury to sell bonds for gold, which ultimately totaled $293,000,000.

Despite these preventative measures, 500 banks and 15,000 companies, including 194 railroads, went bankrupt, with a high percentage of them in the Midwest and on the West Coast. National unemployment skyrocketed with around 2,500,000 persons out of work by the end of 1893. Most mills in Santa Cruz County and the Bay Area shut down or operated at a reduced capacity for several years, with low demand for building materials due to a widespread lack of capital. Democrats blamed Republicans for imposing high tariffs and spending excessively during President Benjamin Harrison's term. Republicans blamed the recently-elected Cleveland for financial mismanagement, especially after Cleveland borrowed $65,000,000 in gold from J. P. Morgan and the Rothschild family. Gold standard advocates blamed the recession on agitation for more and cheaper money. The Populists blamed the gold standard and a shortage of currency. The economy improved slowly, with a second panic in 1896. By this point, the mills in Santa Cruz County had resumed full operations and business returned to normal the next year.[244]

Hihn's Mill Notes

Less than a week after the previous Hihn's Mill Notes, the *Sentinel* published another entry in the ongoing series on May 9, 1893:

Hihn's Mill Notes

In a baseball game between the Aptos and Hihn's Mill clubs Sunday, the Mill club was worsted by a difference of nine runs. But never mind boys, try 'em again.

Ed Haines is working a crew of Japanese on his trails and wagon roads at the logging camp preparatory to getting out the four thousand cords of wood for which he has taken a contract from the F. A. Hihn Co.

As the Christian Endeavor Society of this place was unable to send a delegate to the Convention at Oakland, Miss Snedecor, president of the Santa Cruz County Union, came up and entertained our society with an interesting report of the doings of the convention, on Sunday afternoon.

Mr. and Mrs. T. Leonard visited Santa Cruz Sunday.

R. Hastings, Dave Haines and Misses Blanche and Bernice Haines made a trip to Highland Saturday afternoon, returning home Sunday.

Misses Birdie Maxwell and Lucy Day visited Soquel Sunday.

J. Mortimer gave an interesting talk at the hall on Sunday afternoon. Mr. Mortimer resides at Corralitos.

A. J. Hihn visited Santa Cruz Monday.   P. C.[245]

Hihn's Mill Notes

Ten days after the last column, "P. C." contributed another update on the happenings at Hihn's mill to the *Sentinel* on May 19, 1893:

HIHN'S MILL NOTES

The shower of rain Wednesday morning was just the thing we've been looking for; it laid the dust in fine shape.

Ben and Eli Stuart visited Watsonville Sunday.

The saw-mill started up in full blast Saturday. It looks quite natural to see so many of the boys who have been away all winter at their old places in the mill again.

Rob Day is suffering from a severe cold.

Elder Baucom, of Corralitos, preached an interesting sermon at the hall last Sunday afternoon.

The farmers say there is a poor prospect for hay this year, as the grain is very short and thin, but as there is so much old hay on hand the price will not be materially affected.

The entertainment for the benefit of T. Crilley, given by

the *A. L. and A. of Aptos, was a pronounced success, the programme being well rendered. Of the parts taken by Hihn's Mill talent we can but speak with pardonable pride. The entertainment was opened by an instrumental solo by Mrs. Stout, followed by a reading, "Mona's Water's," by Miss T. Leonard; recitation, "Bessie and I," by Miss Carrie Castor; an original solo by Ed Haines, followed by some feats in gymnastics by Messrs. Amoore and Datson; vocal duet by Messrs. Ord and Amoore; instrumental and vocal solo by Miss Blanche Haines, followed by a very laughable farce by James Tracy, Wayne Rice, and Red Brady that ended the programme, after which the seats were moved back and the rest of the evening was spent in tripping the light fantastic.* P. C.[246]

Frederick Hihn executes his will

On May 23, 1893, Frederick Hihn executed his will. In it, he declared that all of his property was community property held in tandem with his wife, to whom he also bequeathed all of his household items. In addition, he bequeathed monthly and one-time payments to various siblings and employees. Hihn's children acted as his executors, namely: Theresa, August Charles, Frederick Otto, Katherine Charlotte, Louis William, and Agnes.

Hihn's Mill Notes

"P. C." submitted a short update to the *Sentinel* regarding happenings at Hihn's mill on June 1, 1893:

HIHN'S MILL NOTES
———

Mrs. Lizzie Leonard visited Santa Cruz Saturday.
Mr. and Mrs. D. Adams, of Soquel, were the guests of H. Kerns and family Sunday.
Miss Dora Lewis had one of her fingers fractured last Friday.
Mr. and Mrs. Willis, of Nebraska, spent several days of

last week with the family of O. H. Wilder.

D. W. Day died at his home near Valencia on May 26th. He was aged 65 years. His death was sudden and unexpected, as he was taken ill at 7 o'clock in the evening and at 10:30 passed quietly away. The deceased was an old and respected resident of this place and was of an honest and upright character. The bereaved family have the sympathy of the entire community. P. C.[247]

Leland Stanford dies

At midnight on the morning of June 21, 1893, United States Senator, former California state governor, and president of the Southern Pacific Railroad Leland Stanford was found dead at his home in Palo Alto, California. He was the third member of the Big Four to die, leaving control over the company in the hands of the survivor, Collis Huntington. Throughout his life, Stanford had worked to connect Santa Cruz County in some way to the main Southern Pacific Railroad network, spearheading the effort to purchase the bankrupt Santa Cruz Railroad in 1881 and, later, lease the South Pacific Coast Railway in 1887.[248]

Valencia mill temporarily shuts down

Opening in early May, the lumber mill of the F. A. Hihn Company on Valencia Creek shut down unexpectedly on August 8, 1893 due to an oversupply of lumber in the market. This put the majority of the company's 200 employees out of work and delayed plans to shut down the mill at the end of the 1893 season. Planing and shingle mill operations were not impacted by this shutdown.[249]

Warren Porter marries Mary Easton

Warren Porter had lived seasonally in the compound at Loma Prieta since April 1887, but throughout that time, he lived alone. That changed on August 23, 1893 when he married Mary Easton, the daughter of

Reverend G. A. Easton, rector of St. Mark's Episcopal Church in Berkeley. Following their honeymoon, the couple moved into Porter's mountain home and started a family.[250]

Valencia mill reopens

Following a gap of about two months of inaction, the F. A. Hihn Company mill on Valencia Creek restarted its small lumber mill in early October 1893 and continued to run it until November 30.[251]

Timothy Hopkins elected president of the Loma Prieta Lumber Company

The resignation of Thomas Bishop as president of the Loma Prieta Lumber Company in late 1893 left vacant an important position that needed to be filled. As the person who possessed the largest percentage of shares in the company, Timothy Hopkins put his name forward as Bishop's replacement and was duly elected president. With the support of fellow directors A. C. Bassett and N. T. Smith, Hopkins was in a position to advance his interests without regard for potential rivals.

Hihn's Mill Notes

A flurry of weekly updates on Hihn's mill happenings began publication in the *Sentinel* on December 6, 1893 following six months of no news from the community. The first was submitted to the newspaper on December 2:

Hihn's Mill Notes

After a long period of silence, during which spring has melted into summer, and summer into autumn, P. C. issues forth from his corner of rustication, and brushing the cobwebs from his mind, bring forth his ink and quill, and will once more attempt to keep pace with the world by carefully scrutinizing its current literature, and by offering up unto the hungry mortals, whose souls are thirsting for knowledge, such brilliant and interesting thoughts as may occur to him as he hashes up the "newest" and latest items and happenings of Valencia. While we are pursuing this line of thought, and before dropping into the act of itemizing, we will remark that our new Post office is doing a large business, with Thos. Leonard as Postmaster, and our genial friend, A. J. Hihn, as an efficient assistant.

The saw-mill, which has been running at full blast the last two months, closed down for the winter on Thursday last.

Ed West and wife have moved into the house formerly occupied by Geo. Maxwell. Mr. and Mrs. West are very desirable additions to the social circle of this place.

Miss Eva Leonard returned to her home in Santa Cruz on Tuesday last, after spending a pleasant week with friends and relatives at this place.

Miss Birnice Haines visited Santa Cruz Tuesday.

Miss Clara Hubbell, Santa Cruz, is visiting among friends at Valencia.

Miss Louise Hihn, who for the past four months has been keeping books in the mill office at this place, on Wednesday last returned to her home in Santa Cruz, where she expects to take up the study of shorthand and typewriting. During her brief stay here Miss H. has made hosts of friends, all of whom regret the necessity that takes her from them, but all join in best wishes for her success in the future.

The dance given at the hall last Saturday evening was, despite the mud and rain, a pronounced success, as all seemed to enjoy themselves thoroughly.

A number of our young folks attended the dance given by the "Wheelmen's Club" of Pajaro valley at Watsonville Thursday evening.

Last Thursday evening about thirty-five friends and neighbors gathered at the home of Mr. and Mrs. D. Moncrief, taking completely by surprise their son Frank, in whose honor the party was held. After numerous games were participated in by nearly all present refreshments were served, and shortly *afterwards the guests departed, all uniting in sounding the praises of the host and hostess and expressing themselves as having spent a most enjoyable evening.*

O. H. Wilder and family are spending a couple of weeks visiting friends and relatives in Santa Cruz.

Percy M. Newhall closed a very successful term of school at the Valencia school-house on Wednesday last. Mr. Newhall has discarded his duties as a teacher in a manner deserving of much credit. The interior of the school-room was tastefully decorated with ferns and evergreens artistically placed about the pictures, windows and doors of the room. After an excellent programme of songs, recitations and dialogues, which were rendered in a very credible manner by both teacher and pupils, Mr. Newhall closed the exercises with a few appropriate and well-chosen remarks, in which he bid adieu to the pupils and friends who were present.

P. C.[252]

Hihn's Mill Notes

The next column from "P. C." regarding happenings at Hihn's mill appeared in the *Sentinel* on December 12, 1893:

HIHN'S MILL NOTES

Lovely weather and good roads, such as we are enjoying at present, are productive of plenty of travel and lots of trade.

G. M. R. and wife spent Sunday with Mr. R.'s father, H. H. Roberts, of Corralitos.

Miss Clara Hubbell returned to her home in Santa Cruz Thursday after a pleasant visit among friends at that place.

Geo. Lee visited his sister, Mrs. Thos. Greesham, of Loma Prieta, Thursday. Mrs. G. has been quite ill, but is reported as improving at present.

Mrs. Thos. Leonard visited her mother in Santa Cruz Wednesday.

Mrs. Ed Haines was called to Redwood City Friday on ac-

count of the severe illness of her brother, R. Taylor, of that place.

The C. E. Society of this place held a social at the hall Saturday evening. After a programme of reading, recitations and music, refreshments, consisting of cake, pie and coffee, were served.

P. C.[253]

Hihn's Mill Notes

Yet another report from Hihn's mill appeared in the *Sentinel* on December 17, 1893:

HIHN'S MILL NOTES

A. J. Hihn visited his mother in Santa Cruz Sunday.

Ed Haines and wife were in Watsonville Wednesday.

Ed West and wife, and D. Moncrief and wife, attended the New England Supper given by the Ladies' Aid Society of Soquel Tuesday.

Mrs. C. W. Craghill was a Santa Cruz visitor from Thursday to Sunday.

Mrs. Ed Haines returned from Redwood City Tuesday, where she had been called to attend the funeral of her brother, R. Taylor, of that place.

Little Eddie Stuart is suffering from a severe attack of pneumonia, but is receiving good care and medical treatment.

Rev. Hartley of Watsonville will preach at the hall this Sunday. Mr. H. is a very earnest speaker, and is always accorded a hearty welcome by all who have heard him.

S. L. Gibson will take charge of the F. A. Hihn Co.'s work at this place, as T. Leonard, who has been foreman, takes charge of the company's interests at Aptos.

Times are very dull at the Mill, as there is no work going on except ranch work, the cook-house being closed up for the first time since the establishment of the mill.

W. A. M.[254]

Life in the Woods 1893

Hihn's Mill Notes

Still another column on Valencia appeared in the *Sentinel* on December 31, 1893:

Hihn's Mill Notes

Farmers again resume their plowing and sowing.

Christmas was a dull day at Valencia, as a number of our people spent the day elsewhere.

Ed West and wife spent Christmas with Mrs. W.'s mother at Tres Pinos.

Robert Day and Frank Moncrief attended the Christmas tree at Aptos Monday evening.

Charlie Buckhart spent several days of last week in Watsonville, returning home Sunday.

James Buckhart, Geo. Lee and Dick Buckhart were among the visitors of Santa Cruz Tuesday.

A. J. Hihn visited Santa Cruz Saturday, remaining there over Christmas.

Thos. Leonard and wife spent Christmas with Mrs. Merrill, Mrs. L.'s mother, Mrs. Leonard remaining in town until Thursday.

Mrs. Day and Lucy spent several days of last week, including Christmas, in Monterey county, with Asa Day.

Percy F. Richards and wife spent Christmas with Mr. R.'s mother in Santa Cruz.

James Buckhart and Thos. Clancey are collecting an exhibit of curly redwood panels, cases, etc., which they intend placing on exhibition at the Midwinter Fair.

Geo. Lee and Dick Buckhart are keeping bachelor's hall over in Bear Valley, where they are engaged in slaughtering quail, rabbits and other game in immense numbers.

A. J. Hihn is often laughingly accused, by his friends, of complimenting himself through the "Mill Notes," as it is generally believed that he is the author of them, but we must clear him of such charges by saying that Bert has nothing whatever to do with the "Notes."

As Chas. Stewart was returning from Santa Cruz Saturday evening he had a narrow escape from being injured by a runaway horse which, attached to a light cart, came up behind him, barely giving him time to turn out of the road as it dashed past.

W. A. M.[255]

Land transfer from Timothy Hopkins to the Loma Prieta Lumber Company and the Porters

On January 2, 1894, Timothy Hopkins signed two deeds transferring his land to the Loma Prieta Lumber Company and John and Fannie Porter. In the first deed, he transferred 1,170 square feet of land, which encompassed the entirety of Thomas Bishop's home in the Compound, to the lumber company under the condition that the property return to Hopkins when there was no further need for the land or the home. The land eventually reverted to Hopkins on June 12, 1916, when Bishop's widow, Josephine Hall Bishop, gave up the property. Although its purpose is unclear, the home was likely used as a summer retreat by the Bishop family.

Similarly, Hopkins sold approximately 18,295 square feet of land to the Porters for their home and adjacent properties in the Compound. The sale included the same clause that the property would revert to Hopkins if the home was no longer used. However, unlike the Bishops, the Porters refused to release their land. After John and Fannie died, their descendants used the home as a summer retreat until it began to deteriorate to the point that it was no longer safe to enter. When the Parks and Recreation Department acquired the adjacent land on June 25, 1965, they opened negotiations with the family to force the reversion. The Porters finally released it under the condition that a picnic area would be established at the site under the name Mary Easton. Mary Easton was Warren Porter's wife. Shortly afterwards, the dilapidated home was demolished leaving behind only a few bricks to mark the site. A sign was later installed by California State Park officials to explain the history of the Compound.

Life in the Woods 1894

Hihn's Mill Notes

After a week break over the new year, the Hihn's Mill Notes column resumed in the *Sentinel* on January 10, 1894 under a new author:

HIHN'S MILL NOTES

Considerable ice is now formed in pools and water troughs o'nights.

Miss Annie Schilling returned from San Francisco Monday, where she has been the past two months.

David Moncrief and son Frank visited Boulder Creek last Thursday, returning home Saturday.

Ed West and wife attended the installation services of the Rebekahs at Soquel last Wednesday evening.

Henry Gaub and family are now living in the house formerly occupied by O. H. Wilder.

Miss Sina Hedrick spent several days of last week visiting her sister, Mrs. Ed Goldsmith, at Loma Prieta.

Rob Day was a Watsonville visitor Saturday. Rob reports everything as flourishing in that part of the country.

George Lee was called to the deathbed of his sister, Mrs. Thos. Gresham, of Loma Prieta last Sunday evening. Mrs. Gresham was quite well known by many of this place.

As Mr. James, a music teacher, whose residents [sic] *is about a mile and a half from this place, was returning to his home Saturday evening, he was taken sick, and was found in a fainting condition by G. Remy, who took him to his home and cared for him until Monday, when he was removed to his own home. His wife, who is in Oakland, was sent for.*

The remains of J. J. Ely, who was found dead at his home in Santa Cruz last Saturday morning, were interred in the cemetery at this place on Sunday afternoon last. The deceased was a former resident of this place, and now sleeps beside his first wife, in the quiet little cemetery in the valley. M.[256]

Hihn's Mill Notes

The second of the Valencia news columns for 1894 appeared in the *Sentinel* on January 18:

HIHN'S MILL NOTES

Miss Blanche Haines spent several days of last week in Santa Cruz.

Mrs. A. C. Stuart is suffering from a severe attack of pleuro-pneumonia.

Birdie and Mattie Maxwell were Watsonville visitors Saturday.

George Mackrell and wife spent Saturday visiting friends at this place. Mr. M. now resides near Whisky Hill, where he is engaged in farming on quite a large scale.

We were slightly misinformed in regard to the death of Mrs. Thos. Gresham, as stated in our items of last week, her death having occurred in San Francisco instead of Loma Prieta.

The home of Mr. and Mrs. H. Gaub was the scene of a delightful surprise party last Friday evening. The party consisting of a large number of our fun-loving people who, after meeting at the home of G. M. Roberts, marched to that of Mr. and Mrs. Gaub, who, after recovering from the effects of the real surprise, did the honors of host and hostess in a highly creditable manner. The evening was spent in games and amusements until a late hour, when refreshments were served, after which the merry crowd separated for their different homes.[257]

Hihn's Mill Items

After appearing exclusively in the *Sentinel* for the previous year, the Hihn's Mill Items column returned to the *Surf* on February 1, 1894, although it continued to be published in the *Sentinel* as well. The column was also written by a new author, Valencia:

Hihn's Mill Items

Happenings at the Mill for the Past Few Weeks or So

Colonel A. J. Hihn will soon re-open his store.

G. M. Roberts returned from San Francisco, after a day's rest, Thursday.

Mrs. L. Moncrief and two youngest sons are in Boulder for a visit.

Mrs. Ed Haines has been spending a few days in Santa Cruz.

Mrs. Buckhart has been visiting Mrs. D. W. Day.

The birthday party given to Henry Roberts was a pleasant affair and was well attended. The evening was pleasantly spent in dancing, games and singing, after which a sumptuous repast was partaken of by the hungry guests. Those present were: Mr. and Mrs. Richard, Mr. and Mrs. Hoig, Mr. and Mrs. Loomis, Mr. and Mrs. Roberts and Mrs. Gaubb. Misses Eva Leonard, Blanche and Bernice Haines, Dora Lewis, Grace Osborne, and Carrie Roberts. Messrs. Charles Stuart, Robert Hastings, Dave Haines, Ed Haines, Mr. Osborne, Frank Moncrief, Charles and Dick Buckhart, A. J. Hihn, Harry Haines, and Henry Roberts.

The very latest sensation that has been created in Valencia is that Messrs. H. A. Hoig and P. F. Richards have become boys again. They have shaved off their bountiful mustaches and they each look very much like a "Vizier."

Frank Moncrief is batching at home while his mother is in Boulder. He says "it is pretty hard, as he never gets his breakfast dishes washed till it is time to wash the dinner ones." We hope bachelor Moncrief will get along nicely with his batching till his mother gets back.

Mr. and Mrs. Thomas Leonard have moved to Aptos.

Valencia has lost one of its most worthy and esteemed families. Every one regrets the absence of Mr. and the Misses Maxwell in all their social gatherings. They have taken up

their abode in a beautiful and elegant mansion in Aptos.
Valencia is a "way up" now, and Aptos is "not in it," we will close by saying there is no place like
                                              VALENCIA.[258]

Hihn's Mill Notes

The final social column focused on happenings at Valencia appeared in the *Surf* and *Sentinel* on February 10, 1894. Following this, all Valencia and Loma Prieta community news updates were published in the general society sections of the newspapers:

HIHN'S MILL NOTES

HAPPENINGS AND PERSONALS AT THE MILL FOR THE PAST WEEK

Mrs. D. Moncrief has returned from Boulder.
Mrs. Buckhart and her son Will returned from Loma Prieta Monday.
A. C. Stuart and family have moved in to the house lately occupied by Mr. Kern.
Mr. Charles Remy has a collection of snakes which he will send to San Francisco.
Farmers have finished plowing for the Hihn Company.
Mrs. D. W. Day and her daughter Lucy, visited Mrs. Galligan in San Andreas last week.
Robert L. Day has returned from a visit to Watsonville.
A few families from Valencia visited Loma Prieta last Saturday evening to hear the play entitled "Poor Pillicody."
Quite an enjoyable time was had at the party at Mrs. Kartor's last Thursday evening. The evening was pleasantly spent in games and singing, after which a bounteous supper was served, and not until the evening wound up with a stuffed sock fight, between Messrs Ed West and Charlie Craghill, did the guests bid adieu to their host and hostess and wend their

way homeward.

Miss Dora Lewis made a flying trip to Watsonville Sunday.

Mrs. Harold West has returned to her home after visiting Mrs. Ed West.

Messrs Charles Stewart and Everett Loomis have captured a couple of ferocious wildcats at the Promontory vineyard. AUNT DIANA.[259]

The Loma Prieta Lumber Company and the F. A. Hihn Company form the Santa Cruz Lumber Company

The idea of a Santa Cruz Lumber Company was not new in the spring of 1894. Two iterations of such a concept had already been formed, with the most recent collapsing in court only months before Frederick Hihn and the Loma Prieta Lumber Company agreed upon a third such company. But the economic conditions of the mid-1890s meant that demand had dropped far below supply and the market was oversaturated with lumber. Thus, the best solution was to join forces to control the cost and supply of lumber in Santa Cruz County.

The compact between the F. A. Hihn Company and the Loma Prieta Lumber Company was heavily weighted toward the latter, which was by far the larger company. Following negotiations, it was decided that Hihn's firm would own one-third of the Santa Cruz Lumber Company, while the Loma Prieta company would own the remaining two-thirds. The focus of operations would, unsurprisingly, be the existing mills on Aptos Creek, Corralitos Creek, and Gold Gulch. However, because Hihn and the Loma Prieta directors failed to convince Grover & Company and Cunningham & Company to join the combined firm, their price-fixing scheme was undermined, negating much of the initial intent of the alliance.

A later retrospective on the combined company published in the *Surf* in November 1897 explained some of the difficulties the firm faced:

> *prices have been cut so low and the competition of Santa Cruz county's greatest rival—the northern forests of the Humboldt*

country, has been so keen, that it has been cheaper for the lumber companies here to fill their orders by purchasing in San Francisco than by manufacturing from their own forests. As a consequence, and as the citizens of the county know to their cost, mills have lain idle, the logger's axe has been almost silent and the industry in all its branches has languished.

It took several years for the market to stabilize such that it was worthwhile for the Santa Cruz Lumber Company to buy advertisements in local newspapers. Staff of the Hihn company took a leading role in running the lumber yards for the business while the directors of both the F. A. Hihn Company and Loma Prieta Lumber Company bickered over finances and responsibilities throughout the duration of the corporate alliance.[260]

Logging ends on upper Aptos Creek

While the precise date that the upper reaches of Aptos Creek were logged out is unknown, operations elsewhere along the creek began in earnest in 1895. This suggests that there was little profitable timber left to harvest outside of Bridge Creek after 1894. Thus, in the early months of 1894, the final two standard-gauge spurs of the Loma Prieta Branch were built within the upper reaches of Aptos Creek.

The first spur was installed beside the fourth crossing of the main line across Aptos Creek about 700 feet east of the former Spring Creek spur. The composition of the bridge required for this spur to cross Aptos Creek twice is unknown. Two bridges may have been used, but if it was composed of one long curving bridge, it would have been between 400 and 500 feet long. At the southern end of the bridge, the spur climbed a short distance up a gulch until the grade became too steep for a train to continue forward. This track functioned as a switchback, with another track breaking off just beside the creek and then continuing west an indeterminate distance above the mainline track, crossing two shallow gullies along the way. Like the other spurs that ran along the steep hillsides of Aptos Creek, this was used to collect logs that had been felled from along the ridgeline to the south and southeast.

This location left an impression on me during my fourteen plus years

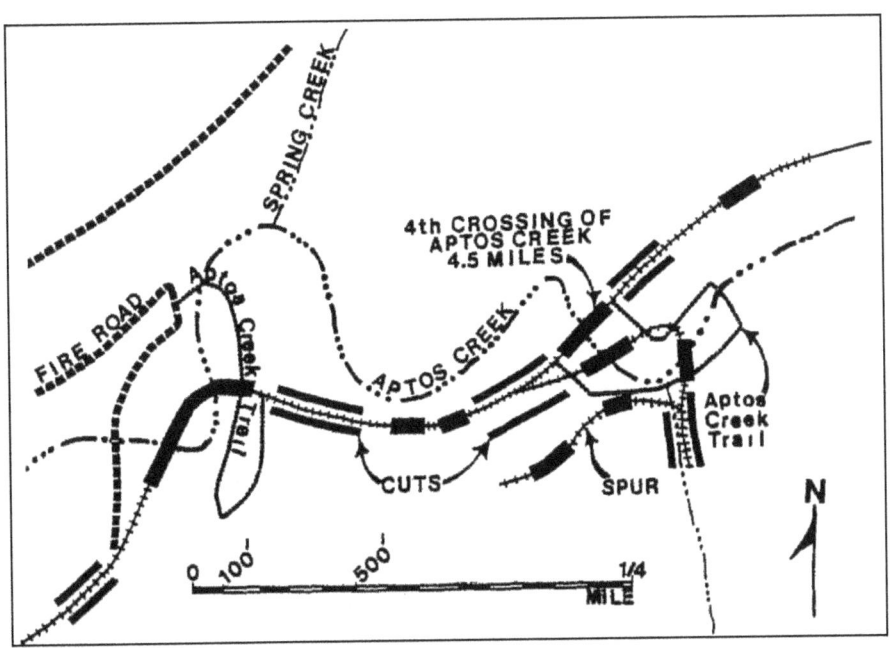

FIGURE 6.1 LOGGING SPUR NEAR THE FOURTH CROSSING OF APTOS CREEK

of exploring the Augmentation, which included many trips in The Forest of Nisene Marks State Park. Each time I hiked the Aptos Creek Trail and reached the area where the railroad crossed Aptos Creek for the fourth time, I noted with curiosity that the long cut between the third and fourth crossings was twice as wide as the upstream cut. The question of why entered my mind every time. It was not until I began exploring the east side of the creek that the explanation to this mystery was finally revealed.

Where the Aptos Creek Trail makes a wide half-circle bend, I came across a road, the remains of a graded railroad bed. I followed this bed for a short distance upstream, discovering that it entered a small gulch that had been modified by pick and shovel. Not only was the gulch widened, but it had been extended further back into the side of the canyon, far enough to accommodate a locomotive pulling four flatcars. With this discovery, it was obvious why the cut was twice as wide as the other nearby cuts: it was widened to accommodate a switch, which required crossties of at least sixteen feet in width.

The second spur was more complex since it dealt with the timber situated within the Big Slide Area between Marijuana and Whites Lagoon Gulches just south of Monte Vista. The timber around Whites Lagoon was very difficult to extract due to the steepness of China Ridge, especially to the southeast. Timber on its north and west sides was cut after 1894 and hauled down to Bridge Creek, where it was taken by train to the mill near Loma Prieta. Logs on the east side of the lagoon were hauled down a skid road that paralleled the gulch until reaching a loading area beside the railroad grade below. Remnants of this skid road can be viewed today along the Big Slide Trail. However, around three-quarters of the area's timber was located to the south of the lagoon and the area was too steep and the ground too unstable to support a skid road. The solution, therefore, was the most audacious railroad spur built along the Loma Prieta Branch.

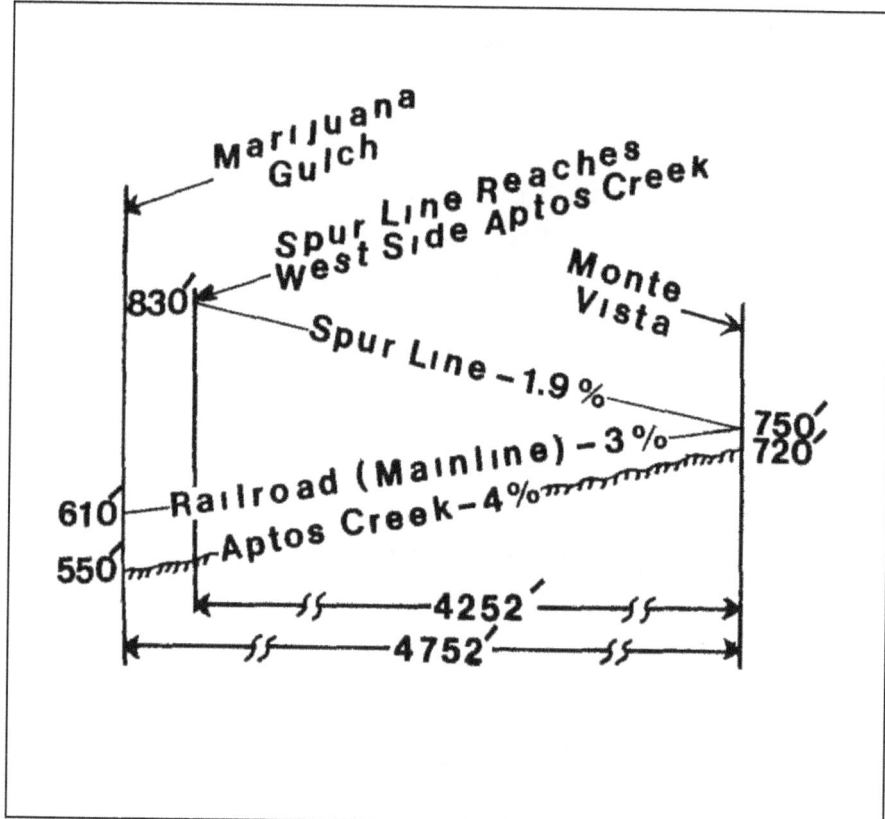

FIGURE 6.2 TRACK ELEVATIONS AND GRADES IN THE BIG SLIDE AREA

Life in the Woods 1894

Southern Pacific surveyors working with lumber company engineers determined that approaching the southern side of Whites Lagoon from the west bank of Aptos Creek was impossible. The lowest stable shelf where a spur could sit was 220 feet above the mainline track and no switchback could climb such a steep grade without a firm footing and a lot of space. So, surveyors decided to find more space.

Beginning from Monte Vista, they inspected the east bank of Aptos Creek, across from the Big Slide Area. By building a spur along the more stable hillside, graders could slowly increase the elevation of the track until they were 220 feet above the Loma Prieta Branch mainline. At this point, they would cross the creek via a bridge and enter the area they wanted to harvest. This spur would only need to maintain a 1.9 percent grade to achieve this goal, although the total length of the spur would need to be around 4,250 feet. Ultimately, an indeterminate number of short bridges were required to cross at least seven gullies and gulches along the eastern wall of the canyon. About 500 feet north of Marijuana Gulch, a long curving truss bridge was installed over the mainline track, carrying the spur line to a high shelf in the Big Slide Area.

Once back on the west bank of Aptos Creek, the spur split. The northern branch turned upstream and continued for a short distance, curving up a gulch near the 900-foot elevation point before ending. A switch was installed below here for the other spur to continue downstream to Marijuana Gulch. The southernly spur crossed a narrow gully over a bridge before reaching the gulch, at which point the evidence for how the spur continued is lost. What is certain is that the track continued in a wide arc away from the gulch and passed through a marshy area before returning to the gulch near Emerald Pond.

Today, there is almost no evidence of this long spur line. Prior to the storm of January 4, 1982, there were three trestle pilings remaining high above the Aptos Creek Trail along the canyon's east side between White's Lagoon and Marijuana Gulches. At this time, the Aptos Creek Trail ran directly alongside the creek between the two gulches. The first piling heading downstream was located just below White's Lagoon Gulch sitting high above the trail, while below it was a junk pile of fallen railroad and trestle parts. A little further down the trail, a second piling remained, while 500

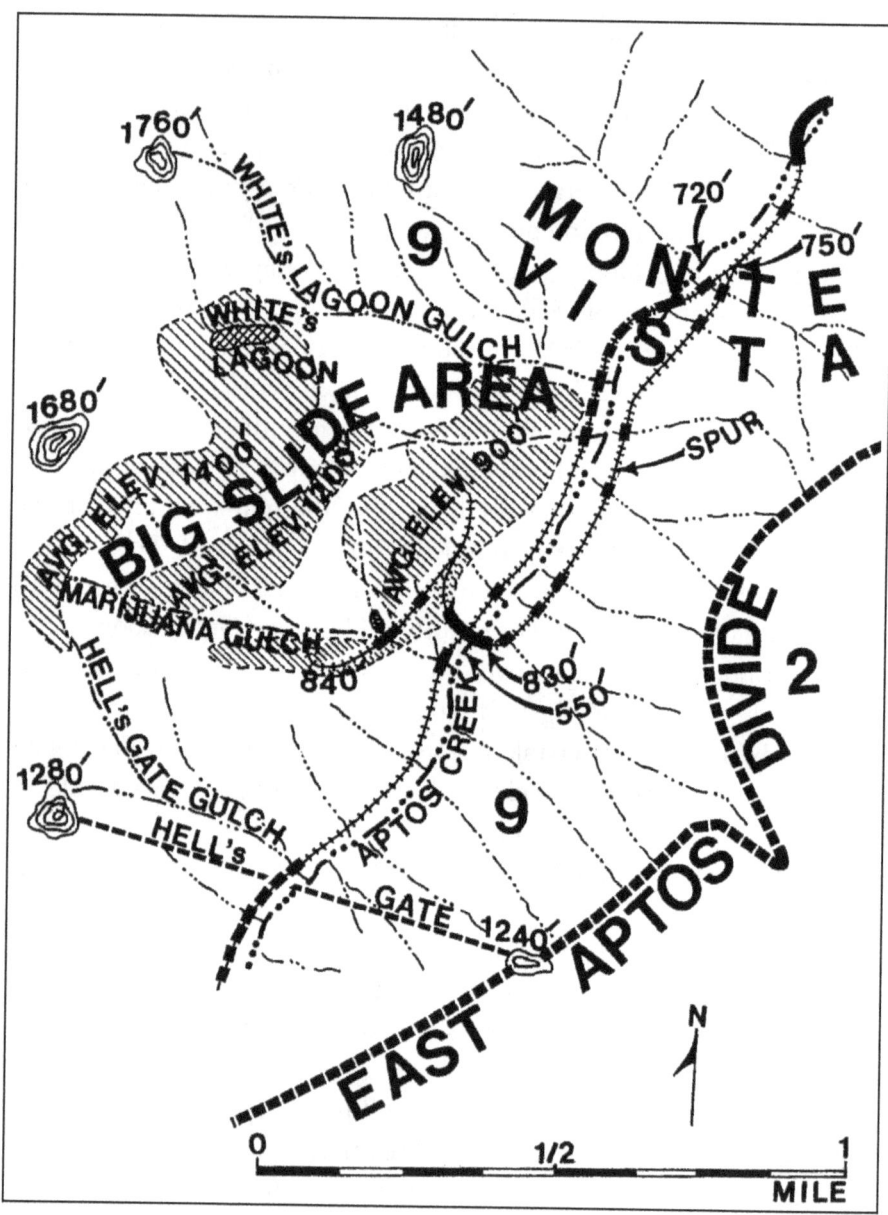

FIGURE 6.3 LOGGING SPUR IN THE BIG SLIDE AREA

feet short of reaching Marijuana Gulch, high overhead until 1990, sat precariously the third remaining piling sitting at least 15 feet higher than the mainline across the creek. It was clear that this was only the lower section of the piling and that it had once been much, much taller.

Several persons have put forth their opinion that the three remaining pilings held the mainline and were built to bypass the original line due to difficulties encountered and the expense of maintaining the line through the Big Slide Area. But if the east bank track was a replacement mainline, how did a track get up so high on the west bank?

Further proof that the line existed can be found on the west bank's shelf. Sections of graded railroad bed can be followed including the cut used today for the Aptos Creek Trail. Meanwhile, metal detectors reveal nails and other metal parts near where the two ends of a bridge would have been located across Marijuana Gulch. Furthermore, the graded bed that ended just a short distance from Emerald Pond can still be seen in places.

Loma Prieta Lumber Company mills open for the season

The Loma Prieta Lumber Company's mills in the Santa Cruz Mountains resumed operations in mid-March 1894 despite a difficult economic environment. The newly-renovated mill at Loma Prieta started up for the first time in two years, while the Monte Vista and Ramsey Gulch mills also heated their boilers for the season. The latter mill was expected to finish cutting its remaining 5,000,000 board feet of lumber this year, after which it would shut down permanently, ending the last harvesting operations along Corralitos Creek. Meanwhile, the new mill at Loma Prieta had a substantially increased capacity, with new planers, a new refuse conveyor, and three large stationary boilers. Nearby, the shingle and shake mills were also upgraded in order to mass produce 60-foot-long telegraph poles and railroad crossties.

William Dougherty dies

On March 20, 1894, local lumber magnate William Dougherty died of heart failure at his home in San José, California. At the time of his death, Dougherty served as president of the Santa Clara Valley Mill & Lumber Company and also was a director on the board of the Loma Prieta Lumber Company. His younger brother, James, took over as president and director.[261]

Grover, Cunningham & Company incorporates

On April 25, 1894, articles of incorporation were filed effecting the merger of Grover & Company with Cunningham & Company, creating as a result Grover, Cunningham & Company. The board of directors was divided between the firms, with Dwight and Stephen Grover of Grover & Company on one side and James and Jeremiah Cunningham of Cunningham & Company on the other. Theodore Vinton Matthews, a local politician and businessman, acted as the final director, having no prior relationship to either family or firm. The new Grover–Cunningham combine was still nowhere near the size of the new Santa Cruz Lumber Company, but its presence signaled to the larger firm that its dominance over the local lumber industry would not go unchallenged.[262]

Valencia Creek mill opens for final season

The F. A. Hihn Company waited until the first week of September 1894 to open its mill for its final season. A. J. Hihn earlier in the year had estimated that the final season would only last two months before all of the available timber was cut. Based on this estimate, the mill shut down permanently some time in November.[263]

Logging begins along Bridge Creek

Following two slow years of lumber cutting and the end of substantial logging efforts in the vicinity of Monte Vista, the Loma Prieta Lumber Company shifted its focus closer to its primary mill at Loma Prieta in late 1894. This began the three-stage process of harvesting the timber along Bridge Creek. The reason this task took so many years is because the creek separated three tracts within the Augmentation, with Tract 8 on the west bank owned by Timothy Hopkins, Tract 9 on the east bank owned by the Loma Prieta Lumber Company, and Tract 10 further north on the west bank owned by the F. A. Hihn Company. The first section chosen for harvesting was the section along the east bank between China

Life in the Woods

Ridge (the Fire Road) and the creek bed, encompassing around 810 acres of timberland in Tract 10.

In his book on Santa Cruz County place names, Donald Clark writes that Bridge Creek's name dates to before 1863. Thomas Wright's first map of the area shows a Bridge Creek Ravine, over which a trail crossed far north of the creek's confluence with Aptos Creek. This trail was probably built by Henry White to provide him with a route to Soquel from his home beside White's Lagoon. At this time and for many years after, Bridge Creek was also known as the West Branch of Aptos Creek until that name was borrowed to describe the creek running through Bassett Gulch.

The Loma Prieta Lumber Company logged the east bank of Bridge Creek using axe and saw. The logs were moved with oxen teams whenever possible and with donkey engines or gravity otherwise. The entirety of this area—the 1.5 miles between Aptos Creek and Maple Falls, and the 2,000 feet north of the falls through Bridge Ravine—was extremely steep. The main skid road to Aptos Creek ran parallel to the creek throughout its whole route, crossing the creek on suspended platforms on several occasions. Many of these redwood skids can still be found embedded in the ground along either side of the creek, while more skids can be found up several of the gulches on the east side of the ravine.

The logs that were cut higher up along the steep side of the ravine were either allowed to make the descent to Bridge Creek by gravity or, when necessary, had their descent controlled by a donkey engine's cable. Once a log was next to Bridge Creek, it was put on the skids according to its weight and size before heading off behind a team of oxen or a donkey engine to the millpond. Logs that were felled above Maple Falls were not lowered down the face of the waterfall, as many believe. The cables that still hang over the falls today are actually remnants of a later operation that is described in the next book, *The Shadow of Loma Prieta*. Instead, the skid road continued around the top of the falls to the east until reaching a small gulch. Here, gravity brought each log down on skids until it reached Bridge Creek below. Once the logs were all down the gulch, they were arranged and then pulled the remaining 1.6 miles to the millpond.

The upper 2,000 feet of Bridge Creek north of Maple Falls is a broader basin that climbs gradually to the top of China Ridge. Today's Fire Road

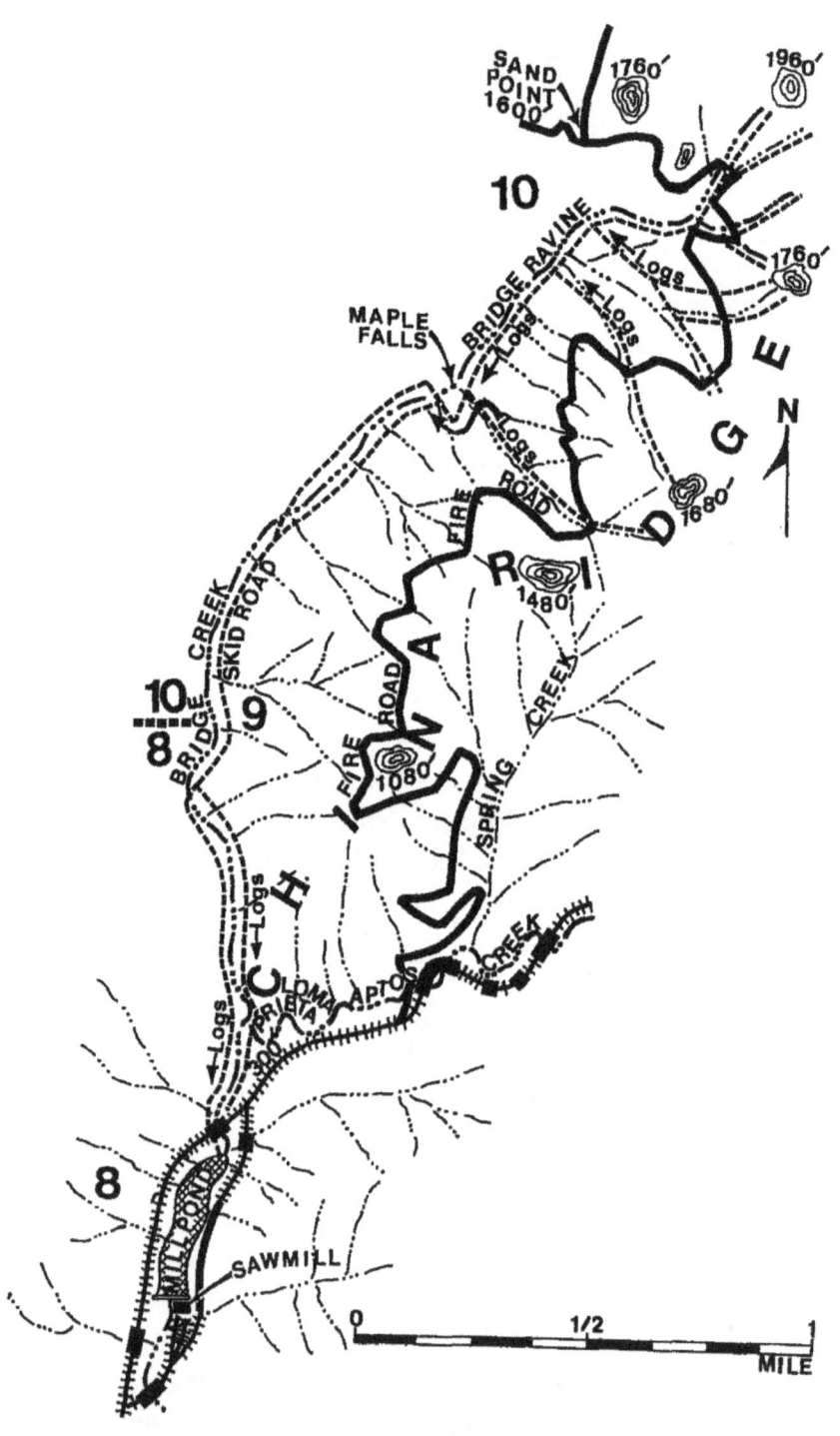

FIGURE 6.4 ROUTE OF THE BRIDGE CREEK SKID ROAD

Life in the Woods   1894 – 1895

wraps around the basin on its way to Sand Point and Whites Lagoon. Because of this more level area, oxen were able to operate in many different areas resulting in a confusing crossroad of skid roads that all led to the 1,000-foot elevation point. Here, the lumber company established an assembly point for all timber harvested in the area. Once assembled, the logs were removed using a combination of oxen and donkey engines the main skid road to the Loma Prieta millpond to the south.[264]

Hihn's Mill moves to Gold Gulch and Valencia declines

At the beginning of the 1893 lumber season, the F. A. Hihn Company decided that the timber along the upper reaches of Valencia Creek was becoming too difficult to cut and drag to the railroad grade and the mill. Meanwhile, Frederick Hihn's timber tract along Gold Gulch south of Felton in the San Lorenzo Valley was readily available for harvesting. To entice the company further, Hihn personally was part owner of two gold mining companies that operated in the gulch, but neither had proven profitable enough on their own. The obvious solution was to kill two birds with one stone. If he extended a railroad spur from the narrow-gauge Old Felton Branch of the Southern Pacific Railroad up Gold Gulch to his proposed mill, he could also use this spur to ship out unrefined gold ore. Indeed, this was the only way that mining in the gulch would be profitable.

Due to the economic crisis, however, the F. A. Hihn Company delayed relocating the mill until April 1895, when its boilers were shipped to Aptos and the tracks were carefully removed to build the new Fahihn spur on the Old Felton Branch. The *Surf* reported on April 20 that "Work on the mill is being pushed rapidly forward, and it is expected that by the first of June it will be completed and 20,000 feet of lumber turned out daily." In May, the new workers' village up Gold Gulch was christened "Hihnport" by its residents, a name that never caught on.

By this point, the village of Valencia was already in decline, albeit a slow one. When the mill closed, many of the local millworkers chose to remain behind to plant apple trees, farm, and ranch. As such, the disappearance of the mill did not immediately lead to the abandonment of the town, as would be the case with the village of Loma Prieta. The F. A. Hihn

359

Company supported its former employees by selling them land cheaply and helping them grow apples. By November 1905, the Valencia brand of apples became a commercial product shipped out of a warehouse at Aptos to the United Kingdom, India, and elsewhere.

The post office was the first to close on August 14, 1909. This was followed in the early 1930s by Valencia School. Valencia Hall still stands, however. In 1933, Theresa Hihn Moore donated the building to the Valencia Farm Center which continued to use it for local events until 1975, when the hall was sold to Santa Cruz County. The county still owns the hall and it continues to be used for events, with the old schoolhouse now sitting directly across from it.[265]

Chapter 7

~

The Turn of the Screw

Mills open for the season

As the depression of the 1890s continued, local lumber companies struggled on, firing up their boilers for another lackluster season in the spring of 1895. The mills at Monte Vista and Loma Prieta both resumed operations at a decreased output, while Grover–Cunningham's main mill in Grover Gulch and its shingle mill at the junction of Cherryvale and Main Streets along Bates Creek also started up again.

Fortunately for the rival firms, the season was injected with new life when the Southern Pacific Railroad placed an order for half a million railroad crossties in January 1895. The railroad needed the crossties to complete its extension of the Coast Division from San Luis Obispo to Elwood. Shortly afterwards, another order was placed by a telephone company in Ventura County that needed 5,000 telegraph poles by the end of 1896. While neither of these orders required lumber, they would keep the splitstuff and pole-making facilities busy all year long.

The end of logging in Ramsey Gulch in 1894 also meant that Timothy

Hopkins could relocate the Game Cock mill to its new home beside Buzzard Lagoon, just to the east of the Augmentation's eastern boundary. Hopkins owned 571 acres of land within the vicinity of the lagoon, as well as some uncut timber along the upper reaches of Aptos Creek and another 386 acres elsewhere in Eureka Canyon. In total, this land could produce up to 34 million board feet of lumber, which would take at least seven years to completely harvest and process through the small mill.

While it may have seemed reasonable for Hopkins to just transport logs down to Aptos Creek, where a railroad car could take them to the Loma Prieta mill, there were several reasons this would not work. First, about half of the land in question was on the Corralitos Creek side of the ridge, meaning logs would first have to be pulled to the top of the ridge before they could be lowered down the other side. Second, there was no railroad directly below Buzzard Lagoon—it sat above the eastern-most branch of Aptos Creek, which was too steep and precarious for a railroad line. Therefore, all logs would have to transit around the slide area to the landing at the 1,000-foot-elevation end-of-track. Third, Hopkins was running this mill separately from the Loma Prieta Lumber Company, so he would have to pay for permission to use the mill at Loma Prieta and he would need to keep his lumber separate from that produced at the mill from its own properties. And fourth, with the track north of Bridge Creek mostly idle except for occasional shipments of splitstuff from Monte Vista, the Loma Prieta Lumber Company and Southern Pacific Railroad had hoped to repurpose the line for a new project, to be discussed below. Any increase in activity along this track could negatively impact that plan. Thus, Hopkins chose to use the old Game Cock mill rather than attempt to negotiate all of the above.

D. A. Rider & Son mill reopens on Soquel Creek

After shutting down several years earlier while Dickamon Rider was running a mill in Westport, the former Corralitos Creek mill was reopened by D. A. Rider & Son in August 1895. Its new location appears to have been at the top of Santa Rosalia Ridge between the headwaters of Aptos, Soquel, and Corralitos Creeks. Buzzard Lagoon Road was extended at this time to reach this new mill.[266]

The Turn of the Screw   1895

George Olive opens Olive Springs resort in Hinckley Gulch

On October 25, 1895, Harriet Blackburn transferred title to the 140 acres in Tract 27 in the Augmentation that she had purchased in 1890 from George Olive to her real estate broker, Edward L. Williams. That same day, Williams sold 126 acres of the land back to Olive. He retained 14 acres for himself to be used as a summer home within a resort that Olive planned to build.

The Olive Springs resort was a callback to plans Olive had abandoned in 1890 when he sold the land to Blackburn. After five years, however, it appears Olive changed his mind and got most of his land back. The area had been known for its mineral springs for many decades. Scant newspaper evidence reveals that Olive began redeveloping the resort in mid-1894, which suggests he had already negotiated the purchase of the land a year prior to its realization. Throughout the summer of 1895, he brought people up to the property to picnic and camp. Soon after he completed the reacquisition, he set to work expanding his resort. He subdivided 5 acres to sell for homes or summer cabins. Meanwhile, he sold another 26 acres along the north side of the Santa Rosalia Ridge above the East Branch of Soquel Creek to E. L. Smith. This was the land once harvested by Roger Hinckley and John Shelby and later sold to Richard Savage. The remaining 95 acres would remain in the Olive family for the next twenty-five years, after which it was bought by Elizabeth J. Corcoran.

An article in the *Surf* published on April 29, 1897 explains the merits of Olive Springs:

> *When Mr. George Olive a few years ago retired from the lumber business in this city and located on a tract of woodland at the junction of the Soquel and Hinckley creeks, about four miles above the village of Soquel, he did not dream that he was taking a step destined to make his name widely known and to attach it to a health and pleasure resort, of, as yet, unknown possibilities.*
>
> *Mr. Olive was only looking then at the wood and timber as resources for a livelihood. In developing these Mr. Olive discovered indications of mineral waters flowing into the creek,*

365

and a little exploration developed several strongly impregnated springs. In two of these sulphur predominates, in one soda and in another iron.

All these are yet in a primitive state, but the waters, in connection with a most beautiful and romantic canyon, have proved a sufficiently strong attraction to develop a camping resort, where several families find summer homes, and which, on Sundays and holidays, is thronged with visitors from this city and sojourners from abroad.

Nowhere in the Santa Cruz mountains can one get nearer to Nature's heart than in this sequestered canyon, and hundreds are already willing to testify to the medicinal value of the waters.

Mr. Olive this year is preparing facilities for sulphur baths, and expects to be able to add a restaurant to the camp accommodations.

If with greater development the supply of the mineral waters prove copious, these springs are destined to become famous.

Olive operated his resort facilities for six seasons with little interference from the Loma Prieta Lumber Company until 1900, when the lumber firm built its Hinckley Creek mill just upstream from Olive Springs. At this time, Olive took the lumber company to court, claiming it infringed on his rights by passing through his property, but the court sided with the lumber company according to the decisions made in the Shoquel Augmentation partitioning case.[267]

Southern Pacific Railroad surveys for a tunnel to Hinckley Creek

For the two years before January 1896, the last three miles of the Loma Prieta Branch had sat mostly dormant with the majority of the logs up Aptos Creek harvested and Monte Vista running at minimum capacity, simply cutting splitstuff and processing what little remained. Yet the Loma Prieta Lumber Company still had plans for the track. The company's next area to harvest after Bridge Creek was the upper part of Hinckley Creek,

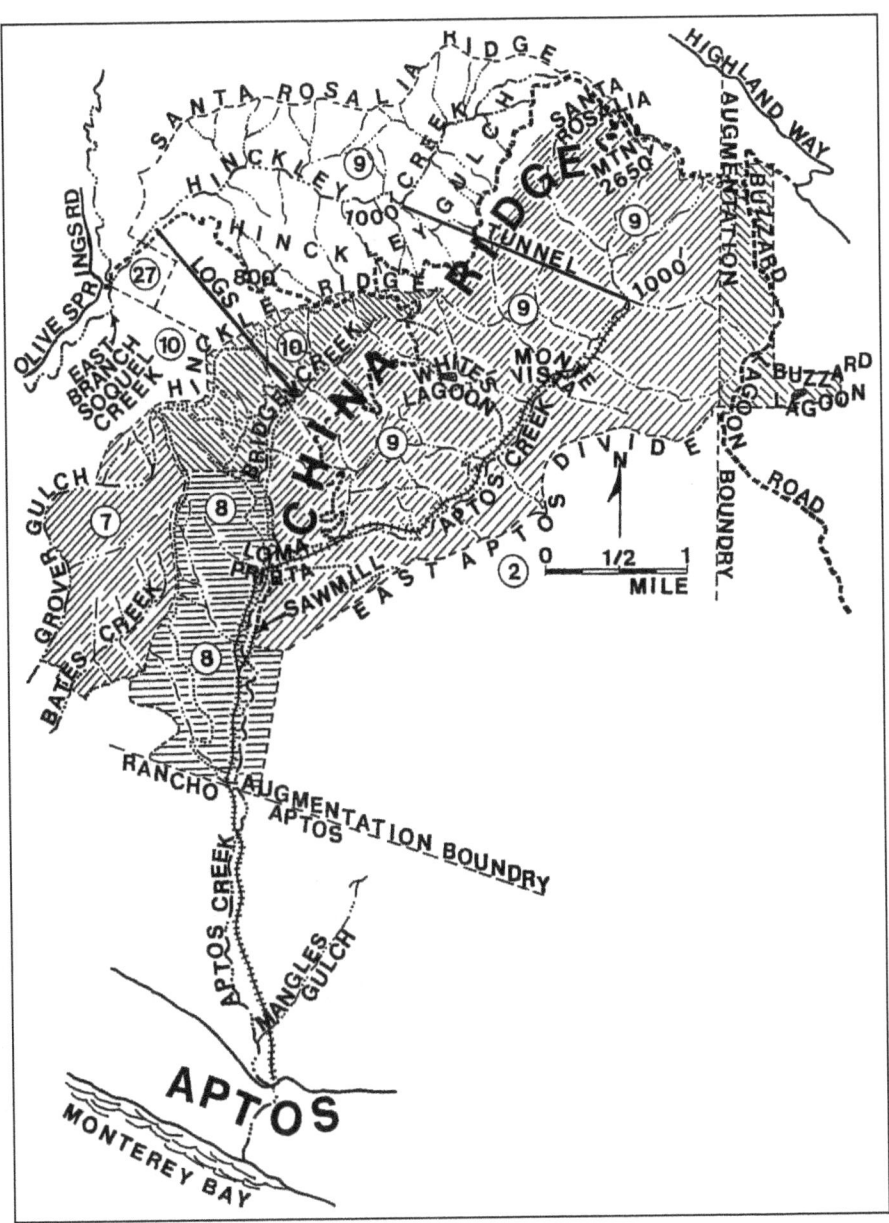

FIGURE 7.1 PROPOSED ROUTE FOR A TUNNEL TO HINCKLEY CREEK

which was in the Soquel Creek basin on the west side of Hinckley Ridge. With large, old-growth redwood trees dominating the area, it only made sense to continue processing the trees at the large mill at Loma Prieta.

Therefore, Timothy Hopkins approached Southern Pacific Railroad management with a proposal to construct a 1.75-mile-long tunnel and 4-mile extension of the Loma Prieta Branch between Bassett Gulch and the top of Hinckley Gulch. The tunnel would ensure that the branch line remained viable for at least another decade, and it would also reduce the cost of building a new mill in Hinckley Gulch and transporting lumber from that mill by wagon to the railroad station at Capitola. The railroad promptly dispatched surveyors to investigate such a route.[268]

Mills reopen for the season

Another lackluster lumber season began in the spring of 1896. Most lumberyards in the county were oversaturated with lumber, both their own and imported. As a result, the Loma Prieta Lumber Company decided not to operate its primary mill at Loma Prieta. Officially, it claimed that little timber remained along Aptos Creek and the company hoped to build the branch line to Hinckley Gulch, but it also still had 11,000,000 board feet of lumber of various types and grades sitting beside the mill. Nevertheless, it continued to process telegraph poles for its Ventura County contract and may have cut shingles, stakes, and splitstuff at Monte Vista and elsewhere. Other mills likely remained closed for the year as well. A. C. Bassett later noted that less than 17,000,000 board feet of lumber was cut across the county in 1896, suggesting most mills were running far below capacity, if at all.[269]

Grover & Company buys out Cunningham & Company

The good relationship between the Grover family and the Cunningham family collapsed in the summer of 1896 when the board of directors of Grover, Cunningham & Company shifted strongly to favor the latter family. After Cunningham officials attempted to break into the company's safe in July 1896, a war of letters, lawsuits, and countersuits resulted in a petition by the Grover family to dissolve the joint stock company. The Superior Court of Santa Cruz County declined the petition in August, forcing the two families to come to terms. The result of these negotiations was announced in the *Sentinel* on September 27, 1896:

Compromised.

The Troubles of Grover, Cunningham Co. to be Amicably Adjusted.

Grover & Co. Will Purchase the Cunningham Interest—Arbitrators to Determine Amount.

For months the troubles of the Grover, Cunningham Mill and Lumber Co. have been more than an open secret. Suits, counter-suits, arrests and threats of insolvency have played prominent parts. At one time matters became so serious that no one could predict how they would end.

The troubles of the corporation have now been amicably adjusted, all the papers looking towards a compromise having been signed Saturday. According to the terms of the compromise Grover & Co. will purchase the interests of Cunningham & Co. The amount to be paid will be decided by arbitration. Cunningham & Co. have selected H. L. Middleton to represent them, and Grover & Co. have chosen W. C. Hoffmann. The two referees will select a third. For a period of nearly four years the two firms have been doing business together, so the amount due Cunningham & Co. by Grover & Co, will be ascertained by the arbitrators. Grover & Co. will be allowed to pay the debt at the rate of 2 1/2 per cent per month until paid. The present officers of the corporation are to resign.

It has been agreed that each company shall abide by the decision of the arbitrators.[270]

Frederick Hihn adds a codicil to his will

On October 15, 1896, Frederick Hihn added a codicil to the will he executed on May 23, 1893. Contrary to popular belief, the codicil did not change who controlled his estate following his death. It only appended monetary tokens of gratitude to former employees and increased the amount given to the Hihn Charity Fund.

Grover, Cunningham & Company files for insolvency

On January 18, 1897, Grover, Cunningham & Company filed a voluntary petition for insolvency with the Santa Cruz Superior Court. The relationship between the Grover and Cunningham families during the tenure of their business partnership had been tenuous at best and nearly came to blows on several occasions. Indeed, in addition to the attempted safe theft earlier in the year, Cunningham agents tried to trick debtors into paying their debts directly to Cunningham representatives rather than the company's collectors. In both cases, the Grovers responded with litigation against their erstwhile business partners.

To make matters worse, by mid-January 1897, $29,767.75 of claims were held against the company, primarily by the company's attorneys and officers. According to the *Surf*, among the liabilities for the company were $438.10 owed to Dwight Grover as manager, $69.19 owed to Stephen Grover as president, $302.44 owed to Alfred Williams as secretary, and $16,529.11 owed to Cunningham & Company. The bills payable were $6,000 to Cunningham & Company and $3,110.12 to Grover & Company. The personal property of the company consisted of horses, wagons, harnesses, office furniture etc., which amounted to a value of only $1,156.27, of which 27¢ was liquid cash held by the county bank. The former Cunningham & Company planing mill and lumber yard on River Street adjacent to Quintana Street in Santa Cruz was assessed at no value since it had been in disuse since 1892.[271]

Mills open for season

The depression of 1893 continued for a final year through 1897. Most of the county's lumber mills ran at a low capacity if they ran at all and A. C. Bassett predicted only 7,000,000 board feet of lumber were cut this year. Timothy Hopkins and Frederick Hihn took advantage of the poor economic conditions to send cruisers out to their remaining timber tracts, respectively Tracts 8 and 10 in the Augmentation. Hopkins decided that the time had arrived to finish cutting the last standing timber from Tract 8's northern boundary with Tract 10 to just south of Love Gulch. This decision was motivated by the realization that the mill at Loma Prieta would likely shut down in 1901 if the Southern Pacific Railroad decided not to build the tunnel to Hinckley Gulch, which seemed likely due to high construction costs and low potential returns.

Hihn, meanwhile, became aware in 1897 that his timber tracts in Gold Gulch were already reaching their end. Furthermore, he worried that the isolated section of Tract 10, which was located on the eastern side of the Bates Divide far above the west bank of Bridge Creek, might get trapped if the Loma Prieta Branch were to be abandoned by Southern Pacific. Thus, Hihn sent out cruisers and approached Hopkins to discuss easement rights through Tracts 8 and 9 in order to reach the timber and use Bridge Creek to haul it out of the ravine.[272]

A visit to Rider's Saw Mill

On June 19, 1897, a group of reporters for the *Sentinel* visited the lumber mill of D. A. Rider & Son on Corralitos Creek. One of them described their trip in detail:

Very often the question is asked, Where is Rider's Saw Mill? Many people have heard of the mill, but its location in the county is entirely unknown to them. It is situated about three miles southeast of Loma Prieta, and is at or near the heads of the Soquel, Aptos and Corralitos Creeks. D. A. Rider is the owner of the mill, and is one of the oldest settlers in the Corralitos district. As the timber has been slowly cut out, the mill has been slowly moved up far into the mountains, until it has reached its present location.

The "Sentinel" representatives turned off the Corralitos road near McKean brothers' place and drove up through Pleasant valley, or Hungry Hollow as it is commonly called. After traveling a steep, sand road they arrived at noon at Frank Rider's farm, where, through Mr. Rider's hospitality, they secured hay for their horses, and were allowed to "fill up" on cherries. The mill was reached after a long, hard pull, and when the visitors approached the settlement they really caused quite a sensation. Guests are uncommon and are looked upon with awe. There are many hands at the mill, and they do a lot of work every season.

The trip down the hill along the Corralitos Creek was an eventful one. Although this is the road over which all the teaming to Watsonville is done, there are portions of the road which are very steep. It was found necessary to lock the wheels in order to hold back the load. But upon entering the valley below, the road was well watered, the orchards were neat and prosperous, and green verdure appeared in all its loveliness.[273]

Grover family no longer involved in Grover & Company

The economic crisis of the 1890s ultimately destroyed Grover, Cunningham & Company, although Grover & Company had been hemorrhaging money even before the merger. Newspapers at the time were only able to glean what they could from court records, meaning that the full story of the company's rise and fall came later, after much of the dust had settled. A statement by the directors of Grover & Company was published in the *Surf* on December 8, 1900 and summarizes, through the eyes of the company's directors, events that occurred in the summer of 1897:

In 1897, when Logan, Makinney and Schwartz came into the directory of Grover & Company, that corporation owed over $75,000, and was bankrupt. It had been losing money for seven or eight years before, estimated at about $1,000 per month during all of that time. Among the largest creditors of Grover & Co. were The Bank of Santa Cruz County and Santa Cruz Bank of Savings and Loan, which were secured by mortgage. Grover & Co. was several years behind in its interest. The banks, deeming themselves secure, allowed the interest to run, and Grover & Co., being very hard pressed for money could not and did not pay any interest. From time to time Grover & Co. sold lands mortgaged to the banks, and the proceeds were credited on that indebtedness. The affairs of Grover & Co. were in a hopeless tangle. All of their property, *except some old machinery that had been taken from the lands mortgaged to the bank, was either mortgaged to the bank or was in litigation in the suit of Grover & Co. vs. Besse, and Burke vs. Cunningham, or pledged to Stone and Hoffman for $1,300, the balance of Stone's fee of $3,000, claimed from Grover & Co., and about $500 due W. C. Hoffmann. The company owed laborers' bills amounting to about $5,000, and other unsecured notes and debts, amounting to a large sum. These laboring men had to be stood off until Stone and Hoffmann were paid. The corporation could not borrow a dollar. After Stone and Hoffmann were paid, Grover & Co. made arrangements with The Bank of Santa Cruz County to make an assignment of the lumber and perhaps the old machinery to get money to pay these debts. The bank advanced money from time to time—waiving any claim of its own to be paid its back interest from these sources. The amount at one time reached the sum of about $4,000. The directors, realizing that Grover & Co. were bankrupt, and that it would require the best of management to pay all of its just debts, went to work to accomplish that end. They determined to close out the business that had been run so disastrously for the past seven years, and was then being run at a large loss. Right here came the first kick from the Grovers. They, father and son, were drawing from the company a monthly sum of $200 as salaries. Naturally they were anxious to continue in business so profitable to them, yet so disastrous to others. Like Artemus Ward, who was willing to sacrifice all of his wife's relations in the Civil War, they were willing to sacrifice all the money of any sucker who could be induced to put up the coin, so long as they could draw their monthly $200. But who was going to put up the money for this purpose? Nobody could be found, and the bank prudently refused to put up any more to carry on the lumber business. There was no other recourse but to close up the business of this insolvent corporation. The most of the lumber of Grover & Co. was involved in litigation with the Cunningham Co. and Robert Dollar, and the suit of Burke vs Grover-Cunningham Mill* *and Lumber Co. The latter suit was decided by Judge Smith in favor of Burke, giving him a lien on the property for about $18,000, with Robert Dollar in charge of it for Burke. We made overtures to Mr. Dollar, and found him willing to settle, giving Grover & Co. a full proportion of the property put into the Grover-Cunningham Mill and Lumber Co., or about sixty-three per cent, Dollar retaining thirty-seven per cent, that being the proportion each received on dividing the property, the amount coming to Grover & Co. being about $14,000. If this settlement had not been made the property, which afterwards sold for less than $23,000, would have been sacrificed on execution sale for the $16,000 due on Burke's judgment, and Grover & Co.'s unsecured creditors would have got nothing.*

As to the Bank of Santa Cruz County and Santa Cruz Bank of Savings and Loan, who were the principal creditors, Grover & Co. were treated with the greatest forbearance. They were not only not called on for any money, either as principal or interest, but the Bank of Santa Cruz County aided them and advanced all the money it could consistently with prudent business, when they could get money nowhere else; yet these banks were in a position at that time to have closed out Grover & Co., and if they had done so, would have made a clean sweep of all of its realty, leaving all of the unsecured creditors with a pittance of their claims. These debts were all due, and could have been demanded in full payment of their debts, all of which were secured. The question may well be asked here if the banks had wanted to get all the property of Grover & Co. for the debts due it, why did they not do so at this time, when Grover & Co. were helpless and insolvent, instead of waiting two years later to accomplish by fraud, as alleged, something that could have been done years before in a way everywhere recognized as legitimate? When a debt is due, the right of a creditor to press his claim is undisputed. These being the facts, the directors of Grover & Co. made the best terms they could with the banks for all the creditors of Grover & Co., and the banks extended all the leniency possibly to such creditors. That anything was left to the holders of thousands of dollars of claims against Grover & Co. was due solely to the forbearance of the banks in waiting for their money until the lands could be sold to the best advantage. The validity and justice of the debts due by Grover & Co. to these banks have never been and can not be questioned, and we have no apology to make for assisting in their payment. We pay our own debts, and we would not, as directors of a corporation, lend ourselves to repudiating its just debts, even to a bank.

Lieutenant-Governor Jeter in all his dealings with Grover & Co., acted most fairly. He wanted to close up the matter, and frequently offered to S. F. Grover to take the money due the banks and release the property. This Grover did not do. He could neither raise the money for the banks on mortgages, nor even sell the property for the amount of the bank's mortgage.

As to the fraud charged by plaintiff Grover against the undersigned as directors of Grover & Co., we characterize it as unqualifiedly false in every particular. Every director of Grover & Co. is a bona fide stockholder of Grover & Co., and has been ever since his connection therewith. Even admitting that the directors were "dummies",—which we deny—we do not recall any statute of this State that makes it a crime to be a dummy director, nor do we know of any principle of law or justice that would permit L. F. Grover to recover any sum of money whatever from The Bank of Santa Cruz County for that reason.

Grover & Co. had money deposited in the bank belonging to the Savings Bank, and received from sales of property mortgaged to it, and which the bank by memorandum checks transferred to the Savings Bank in payment of just debts, and for which the Savings Bank released its security. The money belonged to the Savings Bank, and it was no fraud to so transfer it. The same can be said of the payments into The Bank of Santa Cruz County of money belonging to Robert Dollar. The propriety of depositing this money in The Bank of Santa

Cruz County at all might be questioned as an irregularity, but that it should be paid to the parties who owned it is certainly unquestionable. At any rate, what right has Grover to recover anything from the banks by reason of those acts? Further, the charges of Grover that the directors were tools of Lieutenant-Governor Jeter are absolutely untrue. That such directors often conferred with Mr. Jeter is not denied. The banks had liens on most of the property of Grover & Co. all of the time, and on all of its property some of the time. That we should confer with him as to the disposition of that property was most proper. We could not sell a dollar's worth of it until it was arranged with the banks as to its release and the disposition of the proceeds. That Lieutenant-Governor Jeter dominated the directors in anything is not true; that he ever attempted to control them in any matter pertaining to the general business of Grover & Co. is equally false.

As to the institution of these suits, we claim that they were not instituted in good faith, or for the money that could be made out of them to a holder of 250 shares of stock in a bankrupt corporation. Lieutenant-Governor Jeter says that either Grover or his attorney came to him before the suits were brought, and proposed that if the mills and property on Pacific Av. were conveyed to him for the sum of $7,000, he would satisfy all of his claims. As this property was worth $12,000 it would be a very good speculation on 250 shares of stock in a bankrupt corporation, held by him a few days, and for which he had paid nothing. The whole tenor of the complaint, and the acts of plaintiff since, show that these suits were instituted to injure the banks, and for what purpose and with what end in view, we leave to the citizens of Santa Cruz for their own conclusions.

The other director of Grover & Co., who seems to be the only straight director of the corporation, S. F. Grover, what of him? We charge that from the 4th of June, 1897, he has been trying to get into his possession all of the property of this bankrupt corporation that he could, and now is posing as the injured stockholder of Grover & Co. In the spring of 1897

Grover & Company borrowed of S. F. Grover's son-in-law, C. L. Gibbins, $400, and gave him a mortgage on about thirty acres of land, near Soquel. When the mortgage came due a few months later, he tried to get Grover & Co. to convey the land for the balance due on the mortgage, being about $370. This was refused. Grover & Co. were offered $800, and S. F. Grover afterwards took it for $900, soon after selling it for about $1.50. About the same time he got a deed from Grover & Co. for three houses on Chestnut Av., in Santa Cruz, for $1,500, and shortly after sold them for over $2,000. About the same time he bought a half interest in the 450 acres of land at Clear Creek for $1,000, and it is worth today $7,000 or $8,000. We do not state these things to show that S. F. Grover was guilty of any fraud in these transactions, but to show that S. F. Grover, in the winding up of Grover & Co.'s affairs, has not allowed any golden opportunities to pass by, and can not very well pose as the injured stockholder of Grover & Co.

We further charge S. F. Grover with buying property of Grover & Co. at very much less than its value, a fact known to him, and unknown to any of the other directors. He bought falling wedges, as good as new, of the company for fifty cents, which cost $6, the other directors supposing them to be cheap wedges costing less than a dollar. He bought about thirty tons of railroad iron in good condition for $150, worth $30 per ton, or $900, representing that it was worn out and fit only for junk.

We respectfully ask citizens of Santa Cruz to consider these matters.

J. H. LOGAN,
J. G. TANNER,
H. E. MAKINNEY,
J. W. FORGEUS.

The situation at Grover & Company was such that the Grover family divested itself and left. The first to leave the company was Dwight Grover, the leading figure among the second generation of the family in Santa Cruz County. The *Surf* reported on June 9, 1897:

Dwight W. Grover

Retires From Business as a Capitalist and Lumber Merchant

The Collapse of the Fortune Left by His Father—He Will Have a Homestead Left

For more than twenty years the firm of Grover & Co. have been engaged in the lumber business in Santa Cruz county. The firm at the time consisted of J. Lyman Grover, S. Freeland Grover, brothers, and Dwight W. Grover, a son of J. L. Grover. Their business was extensive and profitable and the Grovers were counted among the "solid men" of the county and State.

About eight years ago Mr. J. L. Grover died, leaving an estate that was appraised at between seventy and eighty thousand dollars. His property would easily have realized from $125,000 to $150,000 in the market at that time.

It included his share in the extensive timber tracts, and lumber mills owned by the firm in this county, a valuable ranch in San Joaquin county, timber lands in Humboldt county, the handsome residence property on Walnut avenue hill in this city, the Unity church property, shares in the Farmers' union and various other assets.

The control and management of this estate, together with that of his own personal share in the business has since devolved upon Dwight W. Grover.

The success which has attended his financiering is attested by the fact that today his property consists of a house and lot on Walnut Avenue. The J. L. Grover estate has left the residence property adjoining, (which has been deeded to the two daughters of the late J. L. Grover) some timber land in Humboldt county and some minor assets. The ranch in San Joaquin county is considered worth more than its encumbrances, but how much is uncertain.

The affairs of Grover & Co., have been subject to

notoriety for some time, owing to complications with the corporation of Grover, Cunningham & Co. but the corporation of Grover & Co. has now been reorganized, by the elimination of Dwight W. Grover and the estate of J. L. Grover. The indebtedness of Grover & Co., Estate of Grover and Dwight W. Grover to the Bank of Savings and Loan, the Bank of Santa Cruz County, and the estate of L. Schwartz, has all been readjusted, by the transfer of real estate and stock.

The board of directors of the company as organized consists of J. H. Logan, J. L. Schwartz and H. Makinney, representing the bank, and S. F. Grover and L. F. Grover, his son.

Few young men in this community—few anywhere have had such opportunities in life spread before them as Dwight W. Grover had. His cactus hedge enterprise and his scheme for building a city at Pismo beach are examples of his financial astuteness, familiar to the business public.

It is understood that Frank M. Stone received a fee of $3,000 for extricating D. W. Grover from his connection with the Grover Company, leaving him free to engage in other independent enterprises.

As an aside, one day in about 1988, I got a telephone call from the mayor of Grover City. He wanted a picture of Dwight Grover, the founder of the city. He stated that in the 1890s, Grover had entered a general meeting of town representatives, presented them with plans for their city, and then promptly disappeared.[274]

Santa Cruz Lumber Company purchases Grover & Company

After a year of financial disaster for Grover & Company, including lawsuits, bankruptcies, and police investigations, the company finally threw in the towel and sold out to its competitors, the F. A. Hihn Company and the Loma Prieta Lumber Company, thereby merging the three largest companies selling lumber in the county. The *Surf* reported on November 10, 1897:

A Lumber Deal

Grover Interests in This City Purchased

By the Combined Loma Prieta and F. A. Hihn Companies—Resumption and Extension of the Manufacture Promised for the Future

It is now some four years probably a little more, since a "combine" was made by two of the great lumber companies of this county—the Loma Prieta Company and the F. A. Hihn Company. They formed the "Santa Cruz Lumber Company," the former owning two-thirds of the stock and the latter one-third.

At that time an effort was made to get the Grover-Cunningham Company—which had been formed a short time before by the union of the interests of the Grovers and J. F. Cunningham—to join the combine, but it failed, so that the lumber interests of the county remained divided and the business of manufacture continued to languish....

The result is that, while the big companies have weathered the storm so far, the smaller ones have fared less well. The Grover-Cunningham Company became the Grover Company, the Cunningham interest being absorbed, and yesterday afternoon the purchase of the Grover interests in this city by the Santa Cruz Lumber Company was consummated. The deal has been in consideration for a month or more but now that it is accomplished work will at once proceed—the long-silent Grover mill has, in fact, started up and the lumber camps throughout the county will resume activity, and many unemployed men will be given remunerative labor, as it is not intended to "cinch" wages.

The mill, lumber and machinery were purchased and the ground leased for five years.

The Loma Prieta has as its president Timothy Hopkins, whose personal timber holdings are vast, and include a goodly portion of the Big Basin; A. C. Bassett is vice-president and general manager; W. F. Smith, treasurer; Warren R. Porter,

The Turn of the Screw 1897 – 1898

secretary: the other directors are John T. Porter, Thomas Bishop, Joseph Dougherty, J. M. Thorp and J. J. Sevrons. The F. A. Hihn Company's personnel and officers are F. A. Hihn, his sons and daughters.

It is understood that the debts of the Grover Company are assumed by the purchasers and that the Grovers will complete all contracts now on hand before turning over the mill and yard in Santa Cruz.

While this deal gives the Santa Cruz Company virtual control of that industry in this county, the Grovers still own timber property uncut, and Middleton, of the Boulder, should also be taken into account, as he is manufacturing the product from his own property and on an independent scale.[275]

Shingle and shake mills at Molino shut down permanently

It will be remembered that Timothy Hopkins owned a shingle and shake operation at Molino within Tract 8 of the Augmentation. He had purchased this property in 1884 and transferred it to his adopted mother, Mary Hopkins, who had the Pacific Improvement Company build the railroad tracks and mills. Timothy reacquired the property in March 1892 and it continued to process the timber of the eastern half of Tract 8 for several more years. A photograph from 1897 shows that the mill was still operating in that year, but it is not mentioned in sources afterwards suggesting it shut down shortly after the photograph was dated.

Mills open for season

The future was bright for Santa Cruz County lumber companies in the spring of 1898 as the depression of the past several years was finally at an end and operations in the Santa Cruz Mountains could resume. In the Augmentation, the Loma Prieta Lumber Company warmed up its mill at Loma Prieta for the first time in over a year, while the Monte Vista mill likely continued to process the remaining logs cut over the previous two years from the upper tracts of Aptos Creek.

Timothy Hopkins also realized that he was running out of time to complete the harvesting of timber in the northern half of Tract 8. Loma Prieta management was already looking toward Hinckley Gulch as its next area to harvest, and such an operation would require the relocation of the mill at Loma Prieta. Although there was still a small chance that the Southern Pacific Railroad would agree to build a tunnel to Hinckley Gulch, the odds of such a massive undertaking were decreasing annually. Thus, Hopkins once more employed the Southern Pacific to help him remove his cut timber. The railroad obliged by building two short spurs, one that continued beyond the buildings of the Compound to the confluence of Bridge and Aptos Creeks and another that climbed a short distance up the east bank of Love Creek.

The first logs to be cut were located in the northern end of Tract 8, just south of the boundary with the F. A. Hihn Company's Tract 10. William Baird was contracted to build a skid road from the west branch of Bridge Creek to the new spur, a length of approximately 3,000 feet. At the transloading site, a log-built ramp was installed where a donkey engine pulled logs one at a time onto waiting flatcars. The spur itself was about 1,700 feet long and required at least three short bridges and one longer bridge across a gulch located just north of the Porter family's home. The northernmost 500 feet of the spur was also built in a shallow cut to allow logs to be rolled directly onto flatcars. The cut can be observed from the Bridge Creek Trail to the right near the confluence of the creek with Aptos Creek. The log ramp was still visible until January 4, 1982, when a storm destroyed the last traces of it.

The logging operation adjacent to Bridge Creek likely lasted only one season, at the end of which the spur was removed and the track repurposed for a new track along the east bank of Love Creek south of the Compound. This spur was slightly shorter than the Bridge Creek spur, being around 1,300 feet long. It created a sharp curve separating from the mainline across from the millpond and turning to the west until it paralleled the creek. Today, several sections of the spur are easily identified, allowing its entire length to be followed with little effort. Hikers will notice the right-of-way along the Loma Prieta Grade Trail to the left just after crossing the bridge over Love Creek. Remains of the mainline's bridge over the creek are still visible in the creek while the indentation from the spur continues alongside

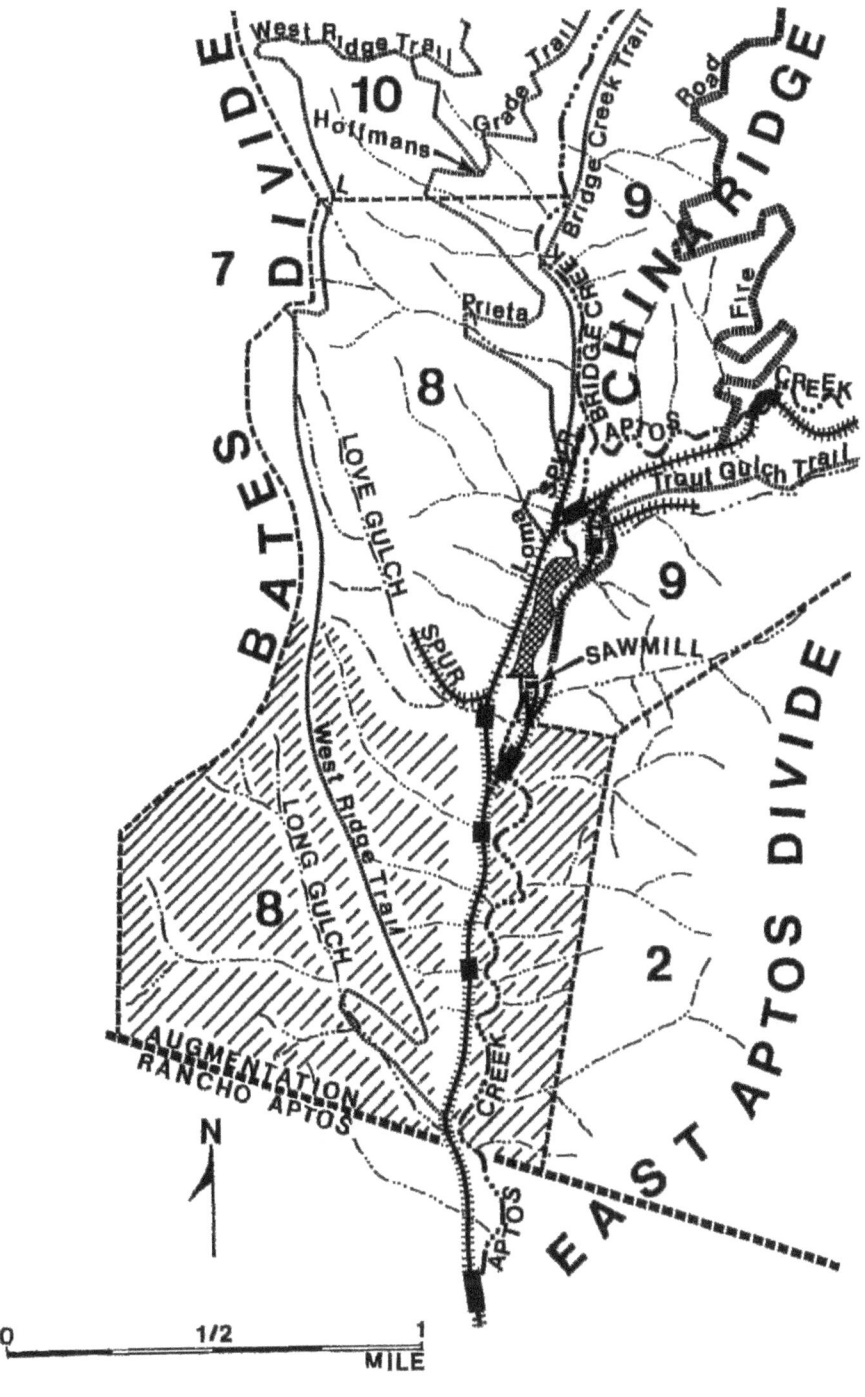

FIGURE 7.2 PART OF TRACT 8 USED TO HARVEST TIMBER FOR SHAKE BOLTS

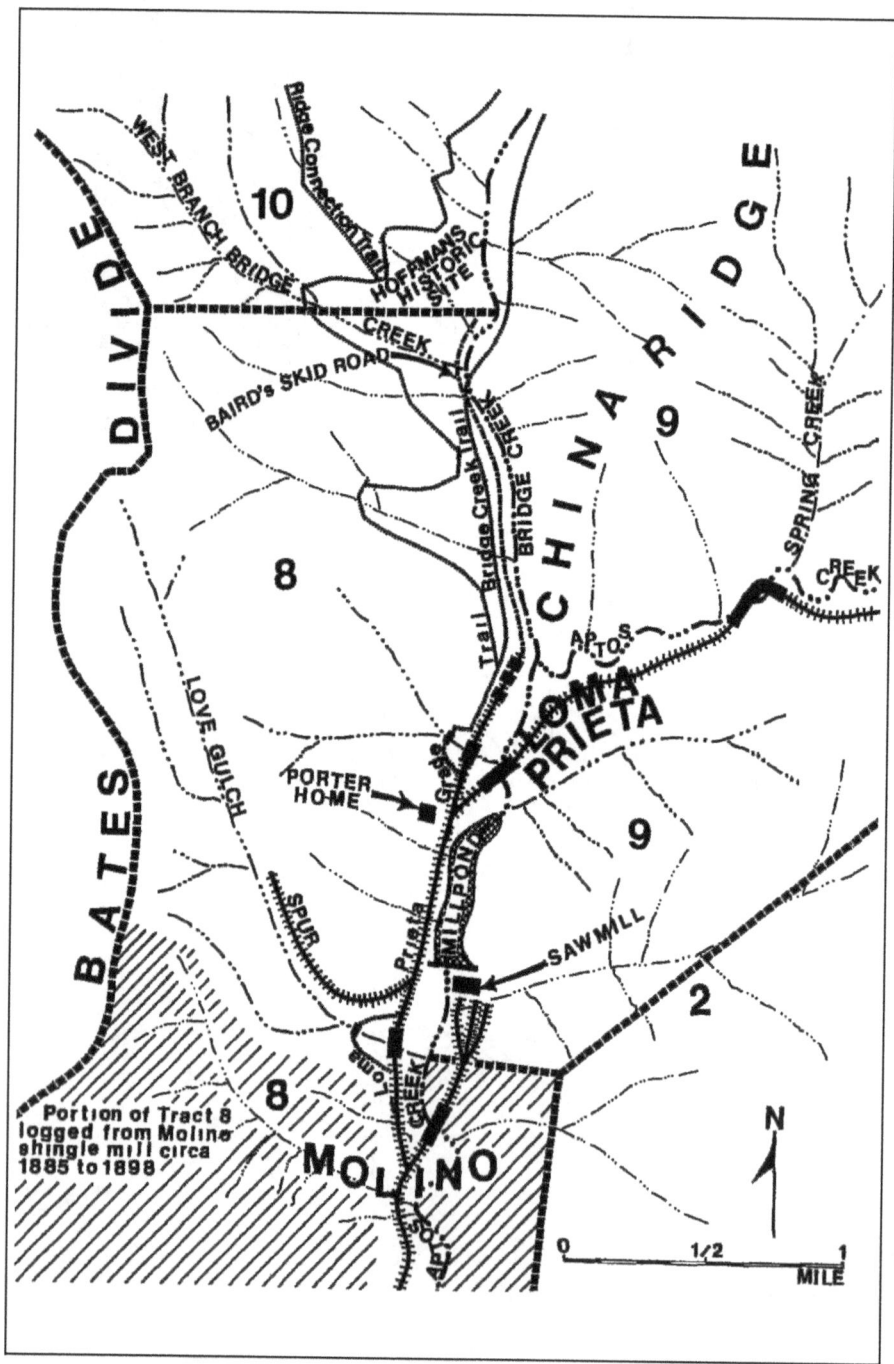

FIGURE 7.3 THE UPPER PART OF TRACT 8 AND THE FIRST BRIDGE CREEK SPUR

the creek for a short distance up the gulch.

During the two years that it took to harvest the remainder of Tract 8, a little over 14,000,000 board feet of lumber was cut. Together with the 24,000,000 board feet that was processed at the former Molino mill, Tract 8's total output between 1884 to 1900 amounted to approximately 38,000,000 board feet of lumber, shingles and shakes, and other splitstuff.

There remains some uncertainty regarding where Hopkins cut the timber derived from the upper part of Tract 8. Bert Stoodley, who became an employee of the Loma Prieta Lumber Company in 1902, claimed that the lumber from Hopkins' land was the last timber processed at the mill at Loma Prieta and newspapers support this statement. Yet the relative proximity of the timber to the millpond makes it seem strange that railroad spurs were required to deliver it. Why not just drag the logs directly to the pond? In both cases, skid roads were used for at least some of the distance to bring the logs to the flatcars. The obvious answer is that the cars were not delivering the logs to the millpond but rather sending the logs elsewhere. During his interviews in the 1960s, Woods Mattingley claimed that the logs were taken to Watsonville where a mill with a capacity of cutting 50,000 board feet of lumber daily was located. This was precisely the capacity of the former Game Cock mill, which was owned by Hopkins and had been operating adjacent to Buzzard Lagoon at around this time. Did Hopkins move the mill to Watsonville? While I continue to believe that the logs were processed at Loma Prieta, the evidence is inconclusive.[276]

D. A. Rider Company incorporated

On May 7, 1898, Dickamon Rider reincorporated D. A. Rider & Son as the D. A. Rider Company. The directors of the company were all members of the Rider family, with Dickamon serving alongside his sons, Homer and Frank, and his daughters, Jessie M. Pease and Cordelia E. Rider. The company was incorporated to better provide for the entire family and to mark its transformation from a lumber company to a real estate firm. The certification of the articles was only filed at the County Clerk's office on August 25, 1900, suggesting the firm may have waited until after it finished its logging operation above Corralitos Creek.[277]

Agreement between F. A. Hihn Company, Timothy Hopkins, and Loma Prieta Lumber Company regarding Tracts 8 and 9 in the Augmentation

On October 31, 1898, an agreement was reached between the Loma Prieta Lumber Company, on the first part; Timothy Hopkins of San Francisco, on the second part; and the F. A. Hihn Company of Santa Cruz, on the third part. It stated:

> *The party of the first part is the owner of a certain tract of land known as Lot No. 9 located within a tract of land known as the Rancho Soquel Augmentation, while the party of the second part is the owner of a certain tract of land known as Lot No. 8 in the said Rancho, and that the party of the third part is the owner of that certain tract of land known as Lot No. 10 of the said Rancho plus that certain tract of land known as Lot No. 2 of the said Rancho.*
>
> *Because of the decree made by District Judge Samuel Bell McKee concerning the partition of the Soquel Augmentation Rancho made in September of 1864, that neither of the parties of the first part or the second part can deny the F. A. Hihn Company a right-of-way across their lands in order to reach the nearest highway. Therefore, the party of the third part shall be deemed to have the right to construct, operate, use and maintain, and may construct, operate, use and maintain the wagon road, or any part thereof, and for the term of six years next ensuing may construct, operate, use and maintain on such wagon road a railroad from the point at or near said point of beginning, and extending thence southerly to the Loma Prieta Railroad.*

In other words, Hopkins and the Loma Prieta Lumber Company agreed to allow the Hihn Company to erect a wagon road down Bridge Creek and across Aptos Creek in order for it to connect its Tracts 2 and 10. In the agreement, the road's route is methodically laid out, a summary of which will be given here. The road would begin 60 feet west of the southeastern

The Turn of the Screw 1898

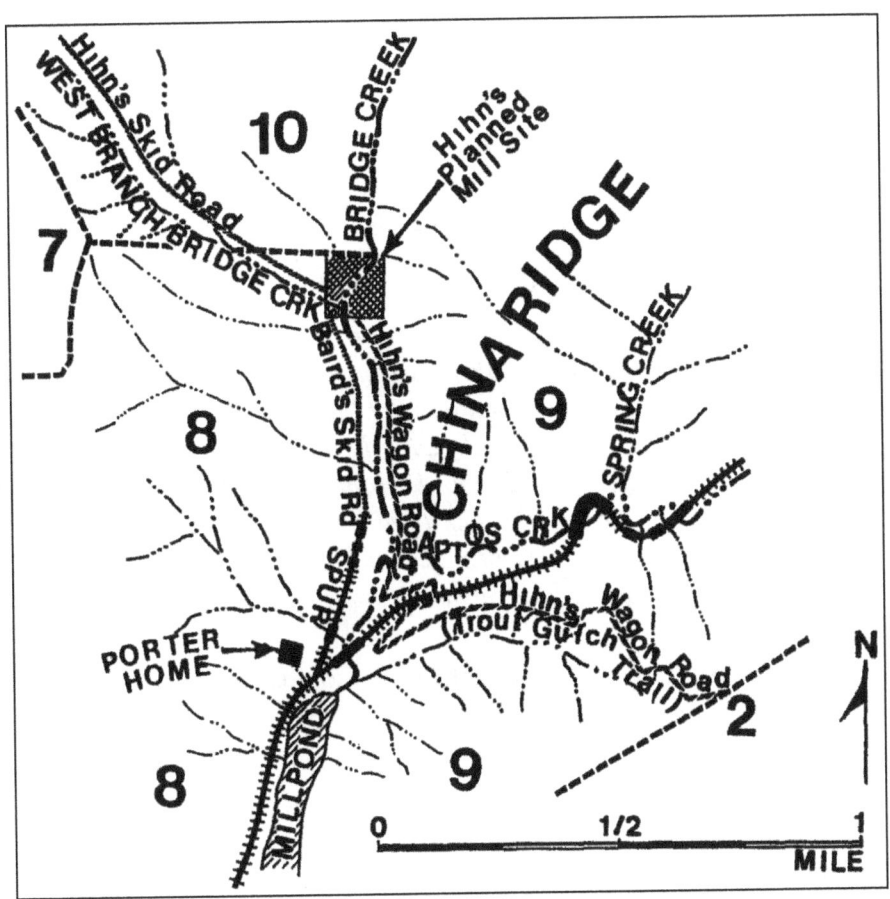

FIGURE 7.4 PROPOSED SITE OF HIHN'S MILL ON BRIDGE CREEK

corner of Tract 10 on the west bank of Bridge Creek. It would then continue south for a short distance until crossing the creek in order to avoid William Baird's skid road. The road would go on for 3,389 feet until it reached the Loma Prieta Branch slightly northeast of the village of Loma Prieta. At this point, it would turn sharply east for a short distance, paralleling the railroad before crossing it at an established point where an existing road had been constructed. This existing road is today's Trout Gulch Trail and continued in an easterly direction into Tract 2 and beyond to Aptos. The Hihn Company agreed to relocate or remove any structures that were in the path of the wagon road at its expense.

Another aspect of this agreement granted the Hihn Company permission to construct a mill on Hopkins' and the Loma Prieta Lumber Company's land:

> *It was also agreed by the parties of the first and second parts that the F.A. Hihn Company, for and during a term of six years may occupy, possess and use, for a millpond, a mill and a yard, and for other purposes, a parcel of land being a part of Lot No. 8 and Lot No. 9, and being bounded on the north by Lot No. 10; on the west by the agreed upon wagon roads; on the south by a line running east and west and distant 600 feet south from the south boundary of Lot No. 10; and on the east by a line running parallel with the wagon road line 170 feet easterly therefrom. The F. A. Hihn Company agreed to pay the owners of Lot No. 8 and Lot No. 9 rent for use of the land at an annual rate which shall yield eight per cent on the assessed value of the land while it is occupied or used.*

Furthermore, Hopkins allowed the Hihn Company to build a skid road through a corner of his property adjacent to the west branch of Bridge Creek. In exchange for all these allowances, the Hihn Company agreed not to interfere with any logging activity conducted by Hopkins within Tract 8 or build a railroad spur with the intention of connecting it to the Loma Prieta Branch. Naturally, the Hihn Company was also responsible for any damage its operations intentionally or unintentionally caused to property downstream of the mill.

The agreement was signed by Hopkins in his own right and signed by him a second time in his capacity as president of the Loma Prieta Lumber Company. August Hihn, who was president of the F. A. Hihn Company at the time, signed on behalf of his firm.

Land transfer from Timothy Hopkins to the Southern Pacific Railroad concerning Tract 8 in the Augmentation

On January 31, 1899, Timothy Hopkins sold the Southern Pacific Railroad's easement through Tract 8 in the Augmentation to the railroad company. The property included a 100-foot-wide right-of-way from the southern boundary of the Augmentation north to the railroad bridge across Aptos Creek into the village of Loma Prieta (the boundary of the Loma Prieta Lumber Company's Tract 9), a distance of about 1.5 miles. It also included approximately 800 feet of the railroad's spur line at Molino across Aptos Creek to the mill at Loma Prieta. The total area of transfer encompassed 18.887 acres. The deed was filed on March 25.[278]

Land transfers from the Loma Prieta Lumber Company to the Southern Pacific Railroad concerning land in Tract 9 in the Augmentation

Only three days after Timothy Hopkins transferred the railroad easement through his land to the Southern Pacific Railroad, on February 3, 1899 he also transferred the easements through the Loma Prieta Lumber Company's property to the railroad. In the first deed that he signed, Hopkins transferred 15,150 square feet of land in Tract 9 of the Augmentation to the railroad. This section included the right-of-way from Aptos Creek to the mill at Loma Prieta and encompassed the entirety of the company's lumber yard including all three of its spurs. In the second deed, Hopkins transferred the right-of-way of the Loma Prieta Branch from the bridge over Aptos Creek south of the village of Loma Prieta to the end-of-track at the bottom of Bassett Gulch, a distance of 3.38 miles. As with the previous transfer, this land was all located within Tract 9 and was filed on March 25.

With these two transfers and the one of January 31, the Southern Pacific Railroad came into conditional ownership of the entire 7.08-mile-long Loma Prieta Branch from Aptos to the end-of-track. The right-of-way throughout the line was 100 feet wide, as measured from the center of the track, and ownership included the right to install telegraph and telephone lines as necessary, and granted full water usage rights to the railroad. However, the deeds also included reversion clauses that compelled the railroad to return the land to the Loma Prieta Lumber Company if it ever abandoned the Loma Prieta Branch.

It is unclear why the railroad wanted more direct control over the land through which its railroad passed. With operations wrapping up along the branch, this transfer makes even less sense. Could it be further evidence that the railroad planned to build the proposed tunnel to Hinckley Gulch? That would certainly explain the need for telegraph and telephone lines, which would be necessary for communicating with the distant outpost on Hinckley Creek. But why were water rights included? Was it simply to provide water for trains operating along the branch or was there some other reason?[279]

Storm damages railroad line north of Loma Prieta

On March 24, 1899, the *Evening Sentinel* reported that "two bridges on the Loma Prieta R. R. have been washed out. There are also several slides on the road." Two weeks later, on April 8, *The Mountain Echo* elaborated:

> *The Loma Prieta Railroad was so seriously damaged last month during a big storm that it is said that the portion above the sawmill in Loma Prieta will not be reopened for traffic, the amount of timber left being not sufficient to warrant the heavy expense of reopening repairs. The road is now being reopened from Aptos Station to the Mill.*

In fact, the route being repaired was that to the village of Loma Prieta, which the *Evening Sentinel* noted reopened on April 8. However, *The Mountain Echo* was incorrect in stating that there was insufficient timber to keep the line operating beyond the village. Enough timber still existed along Aptos Creek to keep the full branch to the 1,000-foot elevation point open through the summer of 1901. Indeed, an annotated Southern Pacific Railroad List of Officers, Agencies and Stations shows that regular freight and passenger service was still available to Monte Vista until November 20, 1899, meaning that the extension track did not shut down until some point after that date.[280]

Santa Cruz Lumber Company dissolves

On May 11, 1899, the *Surf* announced the dissolution of the Santa Cruz Lumber Company, jointly owned by the Loma Prieta Lumber Company and the F. A. Hihn Company. The newspaper said:

Imitators of Solomon

The Loma Prieta Company and the F. A. Hihn Company Severing Associations

Great Corporation Hew to the Line Let the Chips Fall Where They May—A Simple Problem in Division Solved

Years ago—but not so many that they cannot be recalled—four concerns competed for the lumber trade of Santa Cruz and vicinity. That competition is the life of trade, has passed into a proverb, but the truth of the adage was not verified in this instance.

Although each of the competing parties had access to fine bodies of timber and the milling outfits in this city were of superior capacity yet with the keenest of competition and lowest of prices trade languished and profits—there were none.

The natural outcome of such a situation in these days would be a lumber trust, with higher prices and fewer mills, but somehow the lumber deals of this locality were not built that way, and months passed in vain efforts to get together on any sort of agreement.

Meanwhile, the Loma Prieta Company and the F. A. Hihn Company made common cause, with mills and yards on Washington street, and Cunningham and the Grovers consolidated at the foot of Pacific Avenue. The result is written in the insolvency records of the Courts.

Finally the day came for the Loma Prieta and the Hihn Companies to dissolve.

They are doing it now. Dissolving amicably and equitably with saws, axes and cleavers. Doing it after the teachings of Solomon, reputed to be the wisest man of the world.

It is an old story of how Solomon proposed to settle the dispute over the possession of an infant by severing it through the center of its anatomy with a sword and giving to each claimant half a kid.

But the story has not been forgotten and so when the Loma Prieta and the Hihn corporations came to the point of a separation, instead of buying or selling the buildings which were partnership property, they reverted to primitive methods and simply split them in twain.

It is a great show, worth walking down Washington street to see. The planing mill sawed in two from peak to sills, barns, sheds and other buildings similarly severed.

Machinery, tools and traps have been through the same segregating process. It is said that when the tools will not divide in whole numbers they are also cut up, one party, for instance, taking the handle of a shovel and the other the blade.

As good luck would have it for the town the F. A. Hihn Company own the land on which these partnership improvements were located, otherwise the Loma Prieta Company in order to secure their share on division might resort to excavating and removing the earth and thus leave a big hole in the heart of Santa Cruz.

It is a great object lesson these corporations are giving the public upon the partition of partnership property. What is the use of a "give or take" proposition when the matter can be settled with a saw?[281]

Mills open for the season

The last season of full operations at the mill at Loma Prieta began on May 13, 1899. The *Evening Sentinel* reported that 250 men were employed at the mill and that the facility had an output of 50,000 board feet of lumber per day. Meanwhile, Timothy Hopkins' mill beside Buzzard Lagoon far above Corralitos Creek, which opened in early June, was cutting a similar amount of lumber per day.[282]

Lucius Sanborn dies

Lucius Sanborn was one of the most active businessmen in Santa Cruz County throughout his life, and certainly the most active among his three brothers. He joined in many business ventures, often with Charles Ford. And while he was rarely mentioned in the context of the Watsonville Mill & Lumber Company or the Loma Prieta Lumber Company, he was an original investor in and board member of both. At the time of his death on September 10, 1899, he was half of the firm of Vanderhurst, Sanborn & Company of Salinas. He was survived by his wife, a son, and a daughter.[283]

The Great Summit Fire

Fires were a constant source of devastation in the Santa Cruz Mountains throughout the lumber age, but no fire had more of a long-term impact on Santa Cruz County than the disastrous Summit fire of October 8, 1899. Not only did it effectively put an end to the Loma Prieta German Colony and stalled the wine industry on the Summit for decades, it also led to Josephine McCrackin's campaign to protect the redwoods from further decimation. It was fortunate that McCrackin was there to witness the devastation firsthand, but equally important was the fact that several of her friends were also there, including author Ambrose Bierce, poet Herman Scheffauer, and photographer Andrew P. Hill, the latter of whom became famous for his artistic portrayals of the Santa Cruz redwoods following the disaster.

A long-form article in *The Wide World Magazine* published in August 1900 and written by Professor C. F. Holder of Pasadena entitled "How a Forest Fire Was Extinguished With Wine" tells in detail the events of the fire, with first person accounts of what occurred on October 8:

> *California is so vast, and has so many industries, that it is not at all singular that many curious things happen which are not heralded the world over. One of the largest and most important industries of the State is wine, and the vineyards can be seen in the vicinity of many towns, the vast acres of green all through the summer presenting an attractive picture. In the autumn, after the picking, the branches are cut away and burned, and the vineyards present the appearance of a forest of stumps, black and monotonous....*
>
> *During 1899 a dry season made fire particularly prevalent*

in California, and thousands of acres of forest were burned out, owing to careless campers and sheepherders who believe that a forest destroyed makes good fodder the next year for the sheep. Thus it is to these ignorant Basques, and some equally ignorant and wilful Americans, that the destruction of some of the finest forests in California is due. The great redwood trees in the Santa Cruz Mountains are of especial interest, and they too were threatened, the flames eating their way across the mountains from the sea, cutting a wide and deadly path, and leaving only blackened and smoking stumps to tell the story. The trees of this range are among the wonders of the world.

The fire which swept over the Santa Cruz Mountains on October 8th, 1899, was especially destructive, and to reduce it to subjection the entire mountain community came to the front. Many acts of heroism were performed, for information regarding which the writer is indebted to Mrs. Josephine Clifford McCrackin, a Californian author, who was entirely burnt out and upon whose vineyard grew some of the grapes whose juice later on did good service in saving the Meyer winery. I am also indebted to Mr. E. E. Meyer....

The fire, it was believed, was deliberately caused on the other side of the mountain by some irresponsible and even criminal individual, who merely wished to burn some brush. A high wind, however, blew the flames forward, and in a short time a vast area was a raging sea of fire.

The moment it was seen that it was going to threaten life and property the men of the mountains turned out en masse. *Some of them were on horseback, others in teams, with all the appliances at hand for fighting fire on a large scale. The men hurried to the threatened ranches. At two o'clock in the morning Mr. Meyer and his son were battling with the flames on the adjoining ranch of the McCrackins, and also on Dr. Goldmann's place; but the flames swept over the fifty-acres timber tract, destroying the trees, burning the ranch-house and the forest cottage at the McCrackin estate, and driving the little band of fighters before them.*

It was now seen that the Meyer house was threatened, and

the weary men accordingly turned their attention to it. They had been fighting fire on the Goldmann place, and had been driven back on the McCrackin ranch. The fire at three o'clock in the morning was destroying the ranch-house, and running down to lick up fifty acres of timber-land before six. So it may be imagined that the band of workers were well-nigh exhausted before they turned their attention to the Meyer place. Mrs. McCrackin, who, almost surrounded by fire, was a witness to all the scenes described, says: 'How utterly exhausted the men were after performing almost incredible feats of bravery it is impossible to say in words; only those who passed through such a furnace of blinding fire and stifling smoke can possibly understand and appreciate their condition.'

The writer regrets that all the brave men who formed the little army beaten back by the advancing wall of flame cannot be mentioned. There were at least fifty, not to speak of women and children. They had seen tens of thousands of dollars in valuable vineyards go up in smoke during the night, and had witnessed priceless trees centuries old drop before the invader. They had likewise watched orchards worth thousands, which had been years in maturing, melt away like thin air. Among these heroes were Frank and Louis Matty, sons of Mr. A. Matty, who was among the wealthiest landowners in the vicinity. These gentlemen loaded all their waggons with tools and implements which might be of service in fighting the fire, and started to assist their friends and neighbours. With them were Messrs. Robert Borella, George Robishott, James Feely, Albert Morrell, Fred Smith, and Pow King, together with Messrs. McKinney, Humferville, Montgomery, Wilson, Shane, Hoops, and other ranchers who are shown in the accompanying photograph. These brought with them the Frenchmen working on their vineyards—M. Patin and others. 'There were also men from Alma, then miles to the west of us,' said McCrackin; 'besides men from Soquel, ten miles to the south of us, who had left their own places to help beat back the common enemy.'

The roar of the flames was now so loud that men could

not make themselves heard a yard or two away. The heavens were illuminated, and vast columns of smoke rose so high that they were seen fifty miles distant. There was not a fire-engine for a great number of miles around, and no appliances for fighting flames except the small hose used at the ranch. The men began to fear that the women would soon be surrounded, while the latter were in an agony of fear lest their husbands, brothers, and friends should fall victim to the waves of flames that seemed to come roaring on in every direction, licking up the trees. And the trees falling added to the horrors of the scene. The battle at Mare Vista was under the leadership of Mr. Meyer and his son, and no force was ever led with better strategy. A few men happened to be on the ground when the fire swept upon the ranch. Ying, the Chinese cook, proved himself possessed of no little forethought. Without orders he had collected all the vessels which would hold water, and at once an amateur fire brigade was formed, composed of the heroic wife of the owner and some guests. The grounds were literally mined with water pipes, and from these water was passed in buckets by the little brigade, who devoted their energies to wetting the verdure and ground, and trying to keep the flames from a ravine filled with trees, near at hand, which wound around the wine-cellars.

A fierce wind was now blowing, and the flames shot into the canyon like a fiery serpent and ate their way through it with incredible velocity. In a few minutes the building was surrounded with a crescent of fire. The sight at this time was altogether terrible. Great tongues of flame shot into the air, enveloping large trees and setting them ablaze at once. It was almost impossible to face the conflagration, and those who did had narrow escapes from death. The winery was evidently doomed. Trees blazing from top to bottom had plunged across the gulch, bridging it with flame, and the building was threatened on every side. Mr. Meyer had long before this placed men at the water-hose, of which there were two, and for some time this seemed successful, and the men kept the fire away from the main building, although facing a fiery furnace in the effort.

But a new danger soon became apparent. On the west was a small canyon, into which the flames were seen eating their way with resistless force. They came on with a roar, licking up the largest trees, encircling and devouring groups of beautiful madrones, giant oaks centuries old, and then sped on in the direction of the house itself, following the drive-way. The house was surrounded, but saved by the fire-fighters, partly by the heroism of Mr. Frank Matty and others, who crawled through the brush, up the Soquel Creek Canyon, and with a bucket brigade fought off the flames.

This done, the Chinese cook and his assistants ran to the winery, which was now threatened with destruction, the wind blowing a gale from the north. It was about noon, and many of the men had been battling with the fire from the early hours of the previous morning, and were therefore nearly exhausted. The sun was red in the sky, and seemed to add to the terrors of the situation by its burning heat. Men faltered and almost lost their reason, and the deeds accomplished by every fire-fighter in the little mountain brigade if witnessed in a city would have made each man a famous and much-chronicled hero.

While the fire was at its worst Mrs. Meyer, fearing for her husband and son, approached the spot as near as she could to call them away. She found Mr. Meyer and Albert Morrell fighting the fire literally in a seething pit of pumice, into which the flames had found their way below the winery. They were directing a stream into the red-hot vat, while above them, in a window surrounded by flame, stood Emil Meyer, making it possible for them to work by turning a second stream of water on their own persons. It was said afterwards that had the young man faltered or been driven back the others would have been roasted alive.

The situation at this time was highly exciting and dramatic. Men were rushing from point to point, some falling exhausted, whilst others were screaming orders which could be only faintly heard above the roar of the flames. Suddenly a fierce gust sent a cloud of embers upon the roof of the scale-house, and in a moment the cupola bust into a blaze. A shout gave the warning. There was no ladder at hand, but one of the men, named George Roeshot, who had fallen from the blazing McCrackin cottage early in the morning, made a running leap for the roof, and finally, after almost fatally injuring himself, he succeeded in keeping his hold. He then crawled slowly upward, facing the intense heat, and smothered the blaze with water-soaked blankets which were sent up to him.

Small buildings and outhouses now began to catch fire from the terrible heat, and the men took their axes and tore down whatever they could. They were engaged in this when a cry of warning came. The pall-like cloud, which had hung over the north end of the winery buildings, suddenly blew aside, and they saw the gasoline-house smoking. In it were stored about one hundred gallons of gasoline, which, if it exploded, might as well have been dynamite, as it would have destroyed every person in the vicinity. Emil Meyer was on the top of the winery roof, facing sure death if the house caught, and shouts of warning were given which rose above the roar of the flame. At first he did not understand what was meant, but finally learned that the key of the gasoline-house was wanted—and he alone knew where it was. There was not a moment to lose. He could not come down quick enough, and so he shouted a message to the Chinese cook, who quickly produced the key.

It was necessary to break the connecting pipe between the gasoline-house and the winery, and Albert Morrell climbed up to the engine floor and attempted to break it, but failed. Emil Meyer heard his call and swung himself down. Then, single-handed, he broke off an iron pipe which, it was said later, two men could not have bent under ordinary circumstances. This and the fact that they had reached the roof of the gasoline-house and had broken the connection enabled them to stop the fire there. But the end was not yet, and a new danger threatened, which all but took even their courage away, and resulted in the final effort with wine as a fire-extinguisher!

The fine old trees of the estate were falling in every direction, when suddenly the wind began to drive the flames in the direction of those trees which surrounded the water-tank, *from which the men were obtaining their supply. The trees about this tank were so large that Mr. Meyer believed that they would actually resist the flames. But nothing could stand before the whirlwind of fire. A huge fir caught, blazed upward like a gigantic rocket, struggled vainly for a short time, and then fell with a terrible roar directly upon the tank, crushing in its side, breaking or choking the pipe, and stopping the supply-flow of water. It was impossible to go near the spot, and hope nearly fled from the brave band. They faced the disaster a few seconds in utter dismay. Men with buckets and hose; men singed and blistered; men ready and willing to work, but suddenly deprived of water, while the flames, like living things, came creeping ever onward.*

It was now that the resources—the genius—of Mr. Meyer as a fire-fighter were displayed. Attaching the hose unhesitatingly to the big wine-vats, he shouted, 'Man the wine-pumps!' The flames were almost licking the western wall; the heat was so intense from the surrounding blazing trees that the building was afire in several places, and simultaneously flames burst from the top of the roof near the ventilators. Also from the tower of the open storehouse, and two places on the side; while another blaze appeared at a corner of the building. It was like spontaneous combustion. The very air seemed on fire. But the men soon had a hose on the wine-vat near the south-west door, and, with a shout, manned the pump, while another gang manned a second pump, and the hose was run out upon the roof. There were now one hose of water and two of claret. It was a sight to make Bacchus shed tears—this seeming waste of ruby-red glorious wine that was played upon the devouring flames.

What would the effect be? Probably not one man there had ever heard of wine being used in this way. And yet Dr. Goldmann, the physician of the vicinity, knew that wine exposed to heat would produce carbonic acid, which would smother fire. Besides, Mr. Meyer knew the same thing, and it did not take him a moment to decide whether he should or should not pump his valuable wine on the mighty conflagra-

tion. *The result was altogether remarkable. The wine seemed to kill the flames or smother them down. Merrily rang the clank of the pumps; and by tapping vat after vat, and pumping no less than* four thousand gallons *of wine, the flames on the winery were finally subdued, and by noon this extraordinary victory was won.*

In a communication to the writer Mr. Meyer stated that part of the wine used was young—hardly through fermentation, in fact; and it contained about 1 per cent. of sugar and was still warm. It was pumped through a thin hose; these are facts which will probably interest those to whom wine as a fire-extinguisher is a total novelty.

The men now devoted themselves to fighting the fire away from the house; and it was soon evident that there was actual danger to life. Some of the heroes of the wine-hose were missing; the terrible ordeal had been too much for them. Since two o'clock in the morning every man had been fighting fire, with no food and no rest. Emil Meyer fell fainting across the threshold of his home, and it was found that his clothes were literally burnt from his body. George Roshott was unable to reach the house, and was found lying senseless in the yard. Frank Matty shouted that his brother had been overtaken by the fire; and a brave band of volunteers started in search of him. He was found lying exhausted where he had fallen, badly burnt, but still alive.

If the men performed prodigies of valour, what shall be said of the women who lived in these beautiful homes? They too did their share in fighting the flames. One instance of remarkable pluck deserves particular attention—that of Miss Inez Goldmann, the sixteen-year-old daughter of the doctor. Before daybreak the flames were eating their way about her home; and from a point of vantage she could see that the Meyer estate was threatened. She also saw the flames approaching the stable in which were six valuable horses, and knowing that all the men were fighting fire on her father's and the McCrackin estates, she determined to make the attempt to save them herself. Alone, and unaided, she started through the brush, which here and there was smoking and blazing. She plunged through thickets where she was liable to be cut off by the fire, and at last she reached the stable. With the roar of flames high above her on the mountains sounding in her ears, she rushed into the stable and led out the terrified animals. Miss Goldmann then took them to a place of safety, while the flames were yet crackling and roaring about the big trees which surrounded her.

She had rescued all the horses, and was dragging out the harness, when she saw that the fire had been driven around, and was now menacing her own unprotected and beautiful home—the 'Villa Bergstett.' So rapidly did the fire run up the ravines, that on attempting to beat a retreat she found herself completely surrounded by a river of flame. But help was coming; the fire-fighters were now marching on to the Meyer estate, and at the stable they found the fair heroine standing guard by the valuable property she had saved.

All that night the little band patrolled the place, taking turns in sleeping, as the mountains were still burning, and, of course, the workers never knew when the wind might shift and blow the flames back again. Fortunately there were other reservoirs near the house which were full, and from these water was taken with which to fight the flying embers, which were still a grave danger. For three or four whole days the demon of fire swept on, carrying away everything before it, and eating a portion of the very heart out of the famous Santa Cruz Mountains....

In a letter to the writer [A. P. Hill] gives an idea of how rapidly the enormous redwood trees, 200ft. high, were destroyed. He says: 'One night I watched the fire creeping along the ridge near the summit of Loma Prieta. Presently it entered a thickly-wooded place on the mountain, composed of pine, redwood, spruce, and fir. Some of the redwood trees were about 200ft. in height. I could see a great blaze at the base of the trees that seemed like a furnace. Then, one after the other, they were simply enveloped from base to tip with flame, which leaped upwards with a velocity so great that it seemed unable to stop when it reached the top of the tree. Then, with one great bound, it continued, leaving tree and earth far behind, and exploding high in mid-air, lighting up the country for miles around.'

Mr. Hill was on the foothills with his bicycle and camera when suddenly he found that the atmosphere was thick with smoke. He says: 'I realized that the forest fire in the Santa Cruz Mountains, which we had noticed the night before, had now assumed rather alarming proportions. That night people walked to the western outskirts of the town to view the grand spectacle of miles of blazing fire above them; and on the following day the smoke had become so dense in the valley that the outlines of houses and trees could hardly be discerned only one block distant. That night the fire had spread so extensively that single large trees could be distinguished, as the blaze seemed to shoot up the trunk and rapidly spread through all the branches. The following morning I decided to take the early train to Santa Cruz and step off at Wright's, high up in the mountains, where I had many friends, and could perhaps be of some help. The conductor told me that precautionary measures had been taken in case the fire should at any place or time cross the track or attack one of the tunnels of the railroad. He also said that a force of thirty men had been on the train the day before, and this day, Saturday, fifty men had been taken on at San Jose. I was further told that so far the fire had not crossed the Los Gatos River, and for that reason, when we reached Wright's, I found a far clearer atmosphere than we had in San Jose, lying to the north of this celebrated mountain trout-stream.

'As none of my friends were at the station I mounted my wheel and proceeded leisurely to climb farther up by slow degrees. The day was sultry—unusually so for an October day; but when I came within sight of Loma Prieta I saw volumes of smoke rolling out towards the valley from a fire that was running riot on the south slope of what is called the Cattermole Ridge, or North Ridge. And although I knew that there were miles between it and me, I did not like the gusts of hot air which a fitful breeze wafted in my direction, and I was glad to think

there were miles of land and a stream of water between that great fire and myself. It was pleasant, too, to think of the cool, shady veranda, with a breath of fresh air from Monterey Bay, which would greet me at my friend Meyer's place; and I felt not at all unfriendly toward the huge casks and vats of his winery, where I knew wine-making was going on, and where I expected to drink deeply of the new-pressed "must," which some people, with degenerate taste, I own, prefer to the wine proper.

'For days after the great fire had died down the sturdy youngsters who live in these mountains could go out and catch by hand foxes, quail, wild cats, and jack rabbits, whose feet were so burned from the ashes and coals that they could not run away from their pursuers; and where the fire had swept along the road the carcasses and corpses of wood-rats, foxes, and cotton-tail rabbits were found bestrewing it, with half-charred birds of all kinds among them.

'That was the great fire of whose near approach there was no thought on the night of Saturday, 7th of October, and which, fanned through the night by a sudden terrific gale from the north, had destroyed many homes before midday on Sunday, and which will long be remembered by spectators and participants, as well as the sufferers themselves, to whom, in many cases, there remained absolutely nothing save the ruins of the old home amid the devastated forests, orchards, and vineyards.'

Following the disaster, McCrackin was inspired to ensure that such destruction, natural or man-made, did not destroy the redwood forests wholesale. In an article published in the *Sentinel* on March 7, 1900, she wrote of the plight of the giants that were destroyed. It attracted the attention of nature-lovers everywhere, leading her to found the Sempervirens Club of California the next year. The following year, California Redwood Park—today's Big Basin Redwoods State Park—was established as the first California state park intended specifically to protect *Sequoia sempervirens*.

Meanwhile, although the main thrust of the fire was halted at Mare Vista, tendrils of it continued to the west, eventually reaching the hamlet of Burrell. There, it wrought destruction on the Arbor Villa resort and

Lyman Burrell's old Mountain Home resort. The schoolhouse survived. To the east, the fire raged uncontrolled, burning many of the homes of the Loma Prieta German Colony including Herman's Resort and Lomita Ranch. Across the Summit, most families rebuilt their homes, but most of the resorts were not rebuilt and the Summit region more generally declined as a destination afterwards.[284]

Grover & Company's mortgage for Tract 7 in the Augmentation forecloses

Although Grover & Company had absorbed Cunningham & Company and finally joined the Santa Cruz Lumber Company, it was not enough to save the company. The lumber company was simply too far in debt. Creditors came knocking to reclaim their debts in January 1899 and the Santa Cruz Superior Court repeatedly delayed declaring the company insolvent. On April 21, the court ordered Grover & Company to pay $991.12 to the court for fees. It also allowed this payment to be deferred repeatedly. Meanwhile, creditors were becoming upset that their debt remained unpaid. On May 20, a list of creditors with their claims in descending order was published in the *Evening Sentinel*. Yet still the company held on, forcing the Santa Cruz Bank of Savings & Loan to finally file to foreclose the mortgage it held on Grover's Tract 7 in the Augmentation on October 30. It hoped to recoup a debt owed to it totalling $7,500 that was still left outstanding from the original loan of $25,000. The total area of the property encompassed 1,098 acres. Over the next five years, the bank sold 304 acres along the tract's south end, most of which soon returned to the bank through foreclosures.[285]

Loma Prieta Lumber Company mills shut down for the season

The annual shut-down of the Loma Prieta Lumber Company's mills on Aptos Creek on November 20, 1899 marked the end of an era for the Augmentation. Shortly afterwards, Warren Porter decided to permanently move his family back to Watsonville, where he could more actively pursue his nascent political career and become more directly involved in his other business ventures. In January 1900, he became co-owner alongside Arthur

The Turn of the Screw   1899

R. Wilson of Oakland of the Granite Rock Company, which owned an aggregate quarry outside of Aromas. Shortly afterwards, in February, Porter became a member of a state legislation committee for public schools. And on March 12, he became the president of the Pajaro Valley Bank and the Pajaro Valley Savings and Loan Society. In September, Porter received a special honor when he was named an elector in the November 1900 presidential election of William McKinley, the first person ever chosen from the residents of Santa Cruz County.

When the mills shut down for the season, the Southern Pacific Railroad used the opportunity to end formal service along the rapidly deteriorating Loma Prieta Branch beyond Bridge Creek. The railroad station at Monte Vista was abandoned and the station itself was removed from timetables and agency books, with railroad service only provided as required. Meanwhile, passenger service to the village of Loma Prieta was still permitted but was no longer scheduled. As a result, service became inconsistent, especially during the winter months when the mills were closed. Freight may have adhered to a schedule during subsequent lumber seasons, but outside of that time, rolling stock was only brought in or taken out upon request.

With no more passenger service to Monte Vista, there was no longer a need to retain the recreation facilities such as the dance hall and saloon. The buildings were likely disassembled and loaded onto flatcars, after which they were either scrapped or sent elsewhere. Other buildings may have been dismantled too since the logging operations at Monte Vista were quickly wrapping up. Today, all that remains for hikers to find at the site of Monte Vista are the remains of the railroad bed in several places and the occasional scrap of metal.

Southern Pacific likely retained the track to Monte Vista in the unlikely chance that it decided to build the tunnel to Hinckley Gulch. Initially, cruisers gave a glowing report regarding the potential of such a railroad route. They stated that the gulch contained at least 90,000,000 board feet of potential lumber on the Loma Prieta Lumber Company's land. Furthermore, they reported that a log loading station built at the 1,000-foot elevation point, where the proposed tunnel would exit, would be an ideal location. Logs from higher up the hillsides could be pulled down, while logs below the landing could be pulled up. All the logs could then be cut at the mill at

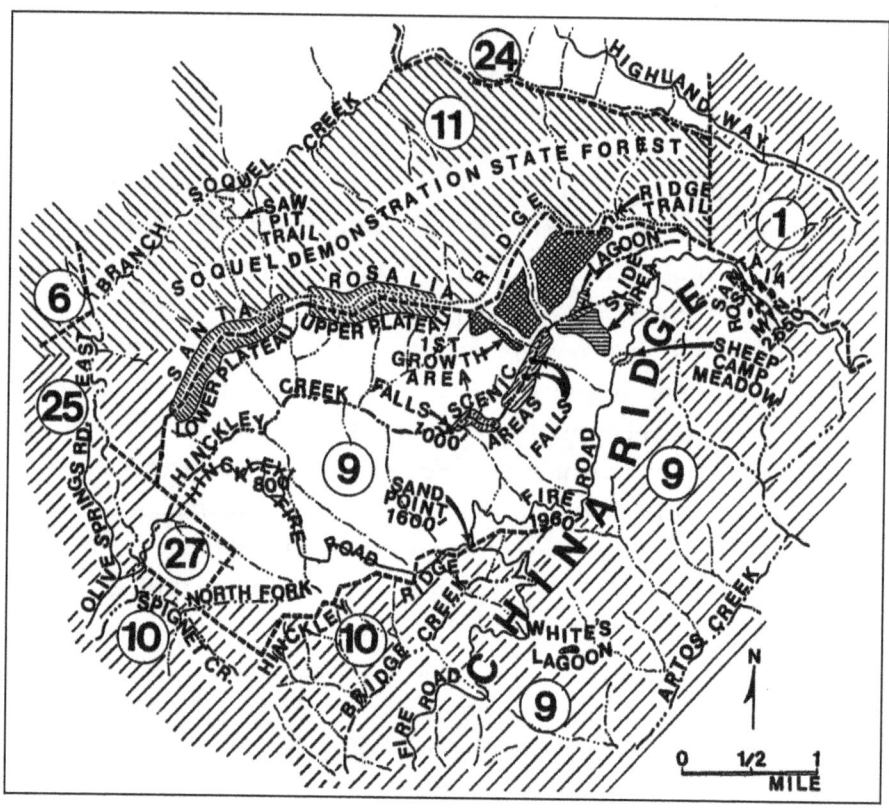

FIGURE 7.5 UPPER HINCKLEY CREEK HIGHLIGHTING AREAS OF INTEREST

Loma Prieta, thereby avoiding the need for building a mill far up Hinckley Gulch, where a long and arduous dirt road would have to pass through Olive Springs and Soquel before reaching the railroad at Capitola.

The Loma Prieta Lumber Company wholeheartedly encouraged this plan. However, the disastrous rain storm in March, which briefly knocked the existing track out of commission, gave the railroad company pause. Over the year, more information came in that put a damper on the proposed extension of the Loma Prieta Branch. A second survey found that the hill below the 1,000-foot elevation point was too rugged to allow workers to effectively pull logs to the proposed landing site. The gulch was narrow, twisting, and steep, with sheer drop-offs to the creek below. The creek featured waterfalls, some 30 feet high, and rapids, while many of the feeder creeks also had sudden drops in elevation. In other words, the timber at the lower end of the gulch would have to be logged separately, either at a nearby mill or by hauling the logs over Hinckley Ridge. Following this second round of reports delivered in early 1900, Southern Pacific decided against building the tunnel. The company reasoned that there would not be a sufficient amount of timber above the proposed landing site to justify the high cost of building the tunnel.

Faced with no other option, the lumber company prepared to wrap up its operations on Aptos Creek and relocate the mill to the bottom of Hinckley Gulch. Its backup plan to haul logs cut from the lower half of the gulch over Hinckley Ridge and down Bridge Creek through the F. A. Hihn Company's land proved infeasible. The Hihn Company was already using the skid road down Bridge Creek to haul out logs and two rival operations using the same route would only lead to problems. The only solution was to bring all of the logs from both the upper and lower parts of Hinckley Gulch down to a new mill at the bottom of the gulch. It was an unenviable task and one that the company delayed for two more years.[286]

John Porter dies

On February 13, 1900, John Porter died in Watsonville. At the time of his death, he was the last one remaining of the original investors and directors of the Loma Prieta Lumber Company, as well as the earlier Watsonville Mill & Lumber Company. His son, Warren, remained an investor and secretary of the Loma Prieta company.[287]

D. A. Rider Company mill begins its last run

After harvesting timber above Corralitos Creek for nearly thirty years, Dickamon Rider and his D. A. Rider Company began its final milling season in the second week of March 1900. The mill was abandoned at the end of the season but moved in 1902 when the Rider Company took up a timber-cutting contract with the McAbee brothers of Boulder Creek, who wished to harvest timber along Pescadero Creek in San Mateo County. Dickamon died at the age of 71 on July 4, 1904 and was buried in Watsonville. Five days later, his family sold all of the company's milling equipment to the McAbees and all but Homer Rider ended their involvement in the local lumber industry.[288]

James Dougherty dies

Five months after John Porter's death, one of his business partners, James Dougherty, passed away as well. The younger brother of William Dougherty, the founder of the Santa Clara Valley Mill & Lumber Company, James died of lip cancer on July 27, 1900. James had succeeded his brother as president of the Santa Clara firm in 1894, following William's death, and also served as a director for the Loma Prieta company, for which business he also worked as a logging contractor alongside William Baird. His and Porter's death left control of the Loma Prieta Lumber Company entirely in the hands of A. C. Bassett and Timothy Hopkins, two wealthy and influential men with no firsthand experience in operating lumber mills. Time proved their deficiencies.[289]

Collis Huntington dies

A death of national importance occurred two weeks after James Dougherty's passing. On August 13, 1900, Collis Huntington, the last surviving member of the Southern Pacific Railroad's 'Big Four,' died of a heart attack at his summer home, Camp Pine Knot, in the Adirondacks of New York State. The death of Huntington put the presidency of and control over the railroad up in the air for it to be eventually caught by the Union Pacific Railroad's chairman and director, Edward Henry Harriman in 1901.[290]

Logging ends along Aptos Creek

On December 6, 1900, the *Evening Sentinel* revealed that the Loma Prieta Lumber Company's primary mill on Aptos Creek would be moved to Hinckley Gulch in the near future. Hints of this move had appeared earlier with plans announced for an extension railroad to the gulch in 1896 and a contract to install telegraph lines to a location within the gulch in July 1900. Even after the move, though, some lingering operations would continue for several years at the old mill site. The article reads:

> *The Loma Prieta mill, which has been in existence for about sixteen years, is to be moved to Hinkley gulch, two miles from the present location. The moving of the mill does not mean the desertion of Loma Prieta, for there will be enough work left in the way of wood cutting to keep a force of men occupied for four years. The best record of the Loma Prieta mill is a run of three months with an average of 72,000 feet a day. In Hinkley gulch the new mill will have a capacity of about 30,000 feet a day, less than the present mill. The railroad will not be extended to Hinkley gulch, so that the lumber will have to be hauled to Capitola by teams for shipment by rail. A shingle mill is to be built in Spignet gulch by the Loma Prieta Co.*

With all of the logs now presumably within the immediate vicinity of the mill and millpond, it is likely that the Southern Pacific Railroad ended its on-demand service to Monte Vista and up Bridge Creek around this time. The village of Loma Prieta would remain the official final stop on the Loma Prieta Branch for nearly thirty more years.[291]

Mill at Loma Prieta begins its last season

With the main focus of the Loma Prieta Lumber Company shifting to Hinckley Gulch, the old mill on Aptos Creek was left in spring 1901 with a considerably reduced capacity to process the remaining logs left from the late 1900 harvest and from earlier years. Part of the original mill including the main structure was left behind but most of the machinery was moved, so the small mill crews had only limited resources to work with to process the remaining logs. These logs came from the last harvested sections of the Bridge Creek acreage in Tract 9 and Hopkins' land in Tract 8 in the Augmentation, as well as from other places where they had been discarded over the previous 15 years. Most were low quality, which is why they had previously been ignored. The majority of the logs were cut into splitstuff and cordwood in order to not damage the mill's saws, although a small amount was still turned into marketable lumber.

Loma Prieta Lumber Company moves its offices to San Francisco and Capitola

The directorial power of Timothy Hopkins over the affairs of the Loma Prieta Lumber Company became abundantly clear on April 13, 1901, when it was announced in the *Sentinel*:

> *TO WHOM IT MAY CONCERN:—NOTICE IS hereby given that the Loma Prieta Lumber Company, a corporation duly incorporated under the laws of the State of California and having its principal place of business at Loma Prieta, Santa Cruz County, State of California, intends to change and remove its principal place of business from said Loma Prieta, County of Santa Cruz, to the City and County of San Francisco, State of California.*
>
> *By order of the Board of Directors, Timothy Hopkins, President.*
>
> *W. R. Porter, Secretary.*

This change was inevitable once Hopkins gained control over the company since he lived and worked primarily in San Francisco and had to commute to Santa Cruz for regular board meetings. The removal of the mill from Loma Prieta, in effect leading to the village's rapid abandonment, certainly was a factor as well. However, Hopkins also never particularly liked Santa Cruz County. He commented in the *Surf* on the same day that he announced the relocation of the company's offices that "in former visits Santa Cruz had seemed to him the dullest of dull towns."

The closure of the company's offices in Loma Prieta also meant that a new local office had to be established somewhere nearby. In late 1899, a site was selected outside Capitola named Opal on land leased from the F. A. Hihn Company. The closure of the offices at Loma Prieta had the unanticipated result of prompting Warren Porter to resign his position as secretary of the Loma Prieta Lumber Company. Only a few months afterwards, Porter was appointed by the governor of California to the board of directors of the state's prisons, succeeding Daniel E. Hays.[292]

Loma Prieta post office closes

With the end of large-scale milling on Aptos Creek, the village of Loma Prieta began to lose many of its inhabitants. Cabins were boarded up and the company store shut down, its contents sent to Opal. With Warren Porter's move back to Watsonville, the officers' cabins were left vacant and the local branch office moved to Opal. Meanwhile, the reduction of railroad traffic to the village and the elimination of traffic beyond it meant that picnickers were no longer visiting the area. On October 31, 1901, the Loma Prieta post office shut its doors permanently, signaling end-of-life for the locale. Soon the village would become a virtual ghost town, hosting only a small group of hardy lumbermen working to process the remaining material left by the relocated mill. The Southern Pacific Railroad did not entirely abandon its station, but the occasional arrival of a train was more a gesture than a necessity.[293]

Loma Prieta School closes

At the end of the 1901-1902 school year in early June 1902, the Loma Prieta School closed permanently for want of students. On June 7, the Superintendent of Schools ordered that the Loma Prieta School District be declared lapsed and the territory annexed to adjacent school districts. Most of the area was added to a new Olive Springs School District in April 1903, with the remainder annexed to the Valencia School District. The old schoolhouse building, including its furniture, books, and other amenities, was moved to Olive Springs to resume its intended function in the new location.[294]

Southern Pacific Railroad abandons track beyond the village of Loma Prieta

On June 30, 1902, the Southern Pacific Railroad officially de-registered the Loma Prieta Branch beyond the 5.0-mile marker, the site of the original Monte Vista mill. The railroad had retained this stretch beyond Loma Prieta Station in order to harvest the uncut timber near the top of Spring

Creek, which had been left standing so as not to contaminate the drinking water for the nearby village. With the reduced population now living around Loma Prieta, other sources of water could be used to supply workers and this remaining timber could be cut.

At some point in the years immediately after the extension's abandonment, logging crews ventured up Spring Creek to retrieve the uncut trees. Since the Spring Creek spur had long since been removed, they logged the gulch from the top down, stationing donkey engines along the top of the ridge between Spring and Aptos Creeks. As the upper trees were cut and turned into logs, they were pulled to the ridgetop and then lowered to railroad cars using cables. Crews collected the logs near the former site of the first Monte Vista.

While there is no documentation verifying the preceding information, during my exploratory hikes I found a number of indications that logs had been pulled from lower elevations in the gulch up to the top of the ridge, not in the direction of the original spur line into Spring Creek Gulch. The logs had either been taken to be cut into splitstuff at the remnant mill at Loma Prieta or were hauled to the larger mill at Watsonville for cutting into lumber. All remaining tracks beyond Loma Prieta were erased from company records on June 30, 1907 and were probably removed around the same time.

Today, the area beyond where the switchback up to China Ridge begins in The Forest of Nisene Marks State Park appears startlingly different from what it would have looked like in the late 1880s and 1890s. Intrepid explorers will likely struggle to find anything left of the railroad right-of-way beyond Marijuana Gulch. This is because Mother Nature left an impression on the area dating all the way back to the 1906 earthquake. The months prior to the earthquake were unusually wet, which only made slide activity more likely when the earthquake actually struck on April 18 of that year. An article in the *Surf* published on October 20, 1906 gives an impression of the changes that this area experienced because of the quake:

> On a fishing trip early in the summer, Branch Wallace of Glen Haven district, with his brothers-in-law, Geo. Ayers and Sam Scott, came across the earthquake's trail, and it was as his guest and under his guidance that the writer a

few weeks later visited the locality. It was a daybreak start from the Wallace residence, with team up and over the new Capitola Park grade to the end of the road on the crest of the ridge that separates Bates creek, a tributary of the Soquel, from the easterly fork of the Aptos....

The team is left on the summit and the downfall began over a fairly good forest trail, which leads ultimately to the abandoned mill site. From the sawmill a railroad ran up the canyon about three miles, on which the logs and wood were hauled. This road, long since abandoned, has passed into the picturesque period. Fresh forest growths have hid the stumps and covered most of the scars made in the landscape by the axeman and the fire fiend, and the Aptos creek is one of the most beautiful brooks, as well as one of the best fishing streams in the county.

Gradually the growth of shrub and vine encroaches upon the former railroad right of way, until only a trail is passable, and then overhanging alders and wild berry vines clasp the entire way, and for a considerable distance a passage is tunneled through, half bent, or on hands and knees. Winter rains have brought down slides, and in places Alpine climbing must be resorted to. The creek murmurs and meanders gracefully a hundred feet below, and one misstep, or one sliding rock, or one breaking bush, can land you by its side in a twinkling.

A few fishers and hunters are lured up this canyon, but the thirst of exploration is really the only sufficient incentive.

Shortly after leaving the mill site, a trestle crosses the creek on a curve, at a bend in the stream, making what surgeons would call a "compound" crossing, the creek flowing easterly and again westerly under the trestle. The railroad then hugged the westerly bank of the creek about two thirds of the way up to Monte Vista. There was another trestle crossing about thirty feet above the stream, and here is where the earthquake commenced to do things. This trestle and bridge is a total wreck. Timbers snapped off, iron rods twisted like green withes, and the bridge span dropped into the bed of the brook.

From here onward, the rent or split in the mountain that

caused the disaster at Hinckley Gulch and did so much damage in the Eureka Canyon is plainly visible. For half a mile the westerly bank for a height in places of two hundred feet is stripped bare and looks like the shining side of an avalanche.

There is no more railroad track to be seen, except scattered ties lying in and alongside the stream.

The timber left here was not heavy, but the few scattered pines and madrones were tumbled over and tossed about and sent plunging headlong towards the bottom of the canyon.

In places the right, or easterly bank, appears undisturbed. At others the jar evidently brought both banks together and formed dams in the bed of the creek. The first of these is perhaps thirty feet high and about thirty feet wide on the top. It stopped the flow of water entirely for a few days, but now the stream has made an outlet and as time goes on will develop a series of beautiful cascades and pools. This pond is about fifty yards in length.

Where this pond ends another dam begins. Not as high, nor as wide, but the backwater or pond extends a longer distance.

By the time this is passed, we have reached the site of what was once called Monte Vista, where the canyon spreads out, giving glimpses of the Highland orchards and vineyards and the stream forks.

At this point a third dam. It is impossible for a stranger to estimate accurately, but it would appear that the bed of the stream for some distance had probably been raised from twenty to thirty feet by the debris. In the open space here there is a huge moraine, not unlike the one on Deer creek, although not as deep. This came down the westerly fork of the stream, which it chokes and fills and clogs and dams with varying degrees of depth and density for two miles. (This estimate of distance we took from a hunter met at this point who was familiar with the locality. Trudging and climbing over it under an August sun, it seemed fully twice these figures.)

Up here, known to a few hunters and woodsmen, was a body of water covering between two and three acres called "White's" lagoon. It is dry. Its bottom was cracked by the

> *earthquake as a kettle might be. Augmented by the hunters, our party of seven sat at midday on a promentory* [sic] *fully forty feet above the former bed of the creek and quietly surveyed the work of thirty seconds, which had completely transformed the face of Nature in this locality.*
> *A little to the left was a huge clump of bushes, with wonderfully broad leaves for a bush. Ah! ha: Not a bush, but the top of a great maple tree, roots, trunk and branches all down below, imbedded in the oozy earth, its more slender branches and topmost twigs visible. Closer inspection showed that all the apparent shrubbery in sight was simply tops of trees. As at Deer creek, the camera fails to catch any adequate conception. It is beyond the scope of any lens; it is beyond the range of the physical vision. It is only the eye of the imagination aided by a full view of the locality that can comprehend the magnitude and majesty of the instantaneous movement which wrought these results. A marvelous manifestation of that invisible Power which existed before even the mountains were brought forth, and which endures world without end.*

While the earthquake certainly left a major impression on the extension tracks of the Loma Prieta Branch, further damage was caused by the storm of 1955, which led to a realignment of Aptos Creek north of its confluence with Whites Lagoon Gulch's stream. The United States Geologic Survey created maps of the area that show this rerouting of the creek between the 1955 and 1968 maps, The site of the second Monte Vista is a victim of this realignment. A debris pile between an unnamed seasonal creek—the former route of Aptos Creek—and the present flow of Aptos Creek south of Five Finger Falls is all that remains of the once expansive site of the mill camp.

Beyond Five Finger Falls, virtually nothing exists of the right-of-way leading some historians to doubt it ever extended beyond Monte Vista. However, when I first explored this area in 1978, the railroad bed was still easily identified right down to the location of trestles. In fact, finding abandoned trestle pieces between the 1,000-foot and 1,200-foot elevations helped me accurately determine where the railroad passed. This was before I was given a copy of Southern Pacific's letter that confirmed that the line extended beyond Monte

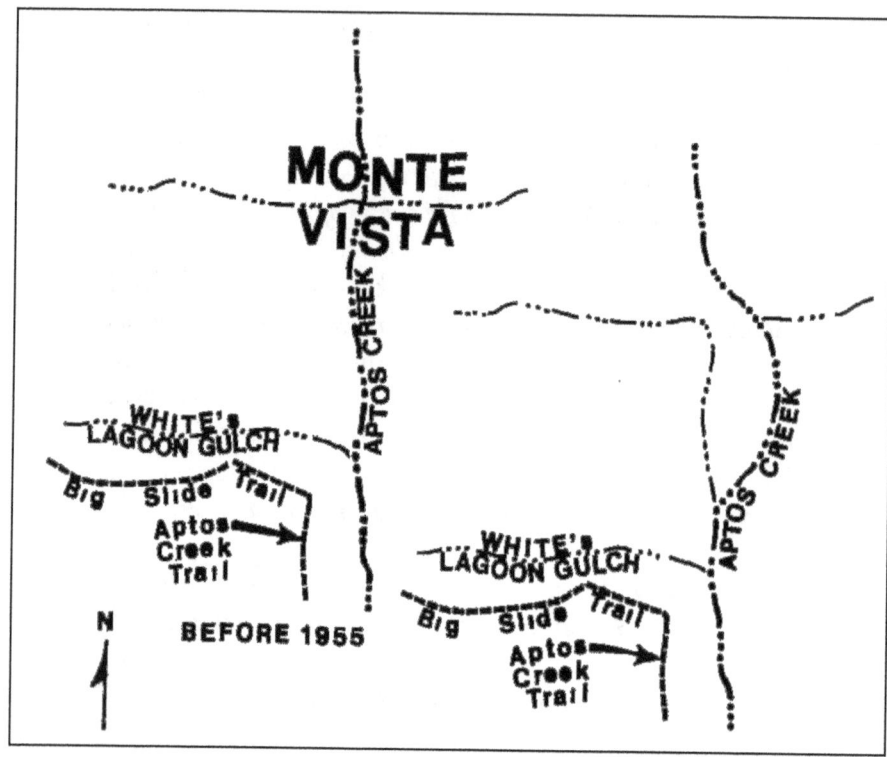

FIGURE 7.6 REROUTING OF APTOS CREEK CAUSED BY THE STORM OF 1955

Vista. As a responsible investigator working in a state park, I left the parts lying along the creek for the next person to discover.

For the next three years, I would travel this last mile of right-of-way in order to reach the canyon's upper gulches, always putting off documenting them or taking pictures. After all, the line had survived some 92+ years in spite of the best that Mother Nature could throw at it. It never occurred to me that two "storms of the century" would occur within a period of four years. The first occurred on the night of January 4, 1982, a storm of such intensity that most of the railroad bed beyond Monte Vista was washed away. This was also the storm that caused the massive landslide between Marijuana Gulch and White's Lagoon Gulch south of Monte Vista. Two smaller storms followed in February and March, compounding the damage. The second major storm occurred in February 1986, which removed the last evidence that a railroad bed existed beyond Five Finger Falls.

Today, little evidence remains of the railroad right-of-way or the Loma Prieta Lumber Company's presence north of Marijuana Gulch and the Big Slide Area. The Aptos Creek trail cuts through the slide area at a higher elevation than the original railroad grade and the path to Five Finger Falls is difficult and often closed due to maintenance. No formal trail now continues beyond the falls and exploring for evidence of the railroad in this area is dangerous and likely a fruitless endeavor.[295]

Ronald G. Powell's story
of the later lumber operations in the Augmentation
and its transformation into The Forest of Nisene Marks
State Park and the Soquel Demonstration State Forest
is concluded in

The Shadow of Loma Prieta

Available soon from Zayante Publishing

NOTES

1 Harrison, 371; Rowland, 167; *Sentinel*, 07/04/1868, 2:6.
2 *Sentinel*, 09/07/1884, 3:5.
3 Clark, 134; Farquhar, 77-78, 81n17; Koch, 123; Patten; Santa Cruz County, Book of Agreements No. 1, and Book of Deeds 8:28; *Sentinel*, 11/22/1964, 4A (full page), 6/4/1967, 6:2-5, and 3/16/1986, B4:2-6; *Surf*, 11/2/1886, 1:2.
4 Clark, 92-93; Hamman, 114; *Mountain Echo*, various articles, 12/31/1881 to 11/25/1882.
5 Hamman, 3-7; Robertson, *Encyclopedia*, 214, 241; *Sentinel*, 01/06/1866, 2:2.
6 *Sentinel*, 02/10/1866, 2:3.
7 Payne, "Resorts in the Summit Road Area," 2; Young, 81.
8 *Sentinel*, 06/22/1867, 2:1.
9 Hamman, 4-5; Robertson, 228; *Sentinel*, 01/11/1868, 4:1.
10 Santa Cruz County, Book of Agreements 1:274 and Book of Deeds 12: 474 and 13:140.
11 Clark, 57-58; *Pajaronian*, 07/29/1869, 2:1, 2:5.
12 *Pajaronian*, 26/08/1869, 2:4; *Sentinel*, 08/14/1869, 1:1.
13 *Pajaronian*, 09/02/1869, 3:2.
14 *Sentinel*, 09/04/1869, 2:4, 2:6.
15 *Sentinel*, 10/16/1869, 2:4.
16 *Sentinel*, 10/16/1869, 2:2-3.
17 *Sentinel*, 04/24/1869, 3:2, 06/26/1869, 2:2, 10/30/1869, 2:6, and 05/20/1871, 2:4.
18 *Pajaronian*, 11/4/1869, 2:4.
19 *Pajaronian*, 11/4/1869, 2:3.
20 *Pajaronian*, 12/23/1869, 2:1.
21 *Pajaronian*, 12/30/1869, 2:1.
22 Payne, "Education in the Summit Road Area," 1.
23 *Sentinel*, 01/29/1870, 4:1.

Notes

24 *Pajaronian*, 02/03/1870, 2:1, 3:2-3.
25 Hamman, 7.
26 *Pajaronian*, 3/24/1870, 2:1, 2:3.
27 Hamman, 7, 9.
28 Robertson, 100; *San Francisco Examiner*, 05/31/1870, 1:2.
29 Payne, "Felling the Giants," 5; Young, 20-23.
30 Book of Agreements No. 1, 381; Voter Registration Records, 8/30/1869.
31 Rowland, 170-171.
32 *Bennington Banner*, 07/30/1904, 1:4; *Sentinel*, 01/17/1874, 3:2; *Surf*, 11/09/1888, 2:1.
33 *Sentinel*, 05/13/1871, 2:1.
34 *Pajaronian*, 04/07/1870, 2:1.
35 *Sentinel*, 10/28/1871, 3:1.
36 *Sentinel*, 01/27/1872, 1:5.
37 Clark, 236-241; Young, 27-31.
38 *Sentinel*, 03/30/1872, 3:2.
39 *Sentinel*, 04/06/1872, 3:1; *Pajaronian*, 04/11/1872, 2:1.
40 *Sentinel*, 04/27/1872, 3:2. See also *The Tragedy of Martina Castro*, 359-365.
41 *Sentinel*, 05/11/1872, 3:1.
42 Book of Deeds No. 15, 224.
43 Adler, 21-23; Book of Deeds No. 16, 33.
44 *Pajaronian*, 08/01/1872, 2:2.
45 *Sentinel*, 08/31/1872, 2:2.
46 Book of Deeds No. 15, 361.
47 *Pajaronian*, 09/19/1872, 2:2; *Sentinel*, 09/07/1872, 2:1.
48 Hamman, 12; *Sentinel*, 09/07/1872, 2:1.
49 *Sentinel*, 11/09/1872, 2:3-4.
50 *Sentinel*, 11/23/1872, 2:3, 12/21/1872, 3:1, 01/11/1873, 3:4, and 03/08/1873, 2:1.
51 *Sentinel*, 05/24/1873, 4:1-2.
52 Santa Cruz Railroad Company, Articles of Incorporation (Santa Cruz Museum of Art and History).
53 Carruth, 308.
54 Payne, "Felling the Giants," 5; Young, 21.
55 *Sentinel*, 3/7/1874, 2:1, 2:3.
56 *Sentinel*, 04/18/1874, 3:4-5.

Notes

57 *Sentinel,* 06/06/1874, 3:2.
58 *Sentinel,* 6/13/1874, 2:5.
59 *Mountain Echoes,* various articles; Young, 57-58.
60 Book of Deeds No. 18, 449.
61 *Sentinel,* 09/12/1874, 2:2.
62 *Sentinel,* 10/17/1874, 3:1, 10/24/1874, 3:3, and 10/31/1874, 3:4.
63 *Sentinel,* 11/21/1874, 3:2.
64 *Sentinel,* 11/28/1874, 3:3.
65 *Sentinel,* 12/12/1874, 3:2-3.
66 Book of Deeds No. 18, 449; Clark, 75; *Mountain Echoes,* various articles; Payne, "Felling the Giants," 6; *Surf,* 10/23/1889, 3:1; Young, 25.
67 *San Francisco Examiner,* 03/31/1875, 1:6, and 04/28/1875, 1:6.
68 *Sentinel,* 3/20/1875, 4:5.
69 *Sentinel,* 5/1/1875, 3:3, and 5/15/1875, 2:2, 2:4.
70 *Sentinel,* 5/22/1875, 1:6-9.
71 Clark, 356; Hihn Record Book, Vol. 5, 12; "Map showing disputed lines in the Rancho Soquel Augmentation for the case of Frederick A. Hihn v. Loma Prieta Lumber Company, from surveys made by R. R. McLeod and A. T. Herrmann" (September 1891).
72 Hamman, 309; *Sentinel,* 6/12/1875, 3:2, 4, 6/19/1875, 3:5, and 7/24/1875, 3:3.
73 *Mountain Echoes,* various articles; Payne, "Felling the Giants," 6; Young, 57-58.
74 Clark, 134; Koch, 123; *Sentinel,* 11/22/1964, 4A (full page), 6/4/1967, 6:2-5, and 3/16/1986, B4:2-6; *Surf,* 11/2/1886, 1:2.
75 Harrison, 327.
76 Hamman, 95-96; *Oakland Tribune,* 03/27/1876, 3:7; *Sentinel,* 6/17/1876, 2:2, and 7/1/1876, 3:3.
77 Hamman, 18-20; *Sentinel,* 6/17/1876, 3:5.
78 *Sentinel,* 7/15/1876, 2:3.
79 *Sentinel,* 8/5/1876, 2:3, 3:2-3.
80 Dillon; *Pajaronian,* 8/15/1878, 1:3; *Sentinel,* 5/11/1872, 3:1.
81 *Pajaronian,* 12/7/1876, 2:1.
82 Clark, 143, 172; Hamman, 96.
83 Book of Deeds No. 20, 572; *Petaluma Weekly Argus,* 02/16/1877, 3:2; *Weekly Sentinel,* 01/06/1877, 1:9.
84 Clark, 219; *Sentinel,* 08/10/1878, 2:4.
85 Clark, 204; *Surf,* 5/31/1904, 5:1; USGS Laurel Quadrangle, 7.5 Minute Series

Notes

(Topographic) (1955, revised 1968); Wright, 1880.
86 Book of Deeds No. 25, 406.
87 Book of Deeds No. 24, 588.
88 *Sentinel*, 12/15/1877, 3:4.
89 *Pacific Bee*, 03/11/1878, 5:6-7.
90 Book of Deeds No. 25, 406.
91 *Mountain Echoes*, various articles; Young, 57-58.
92 Payne, "Felling the Giants," 5; Young, 21-22.
93 Clark, 134; Koch, 123; *Sentinel*, 11/22/1964, 4A (full page), 6/4/1967, 6:2-5, and 3/16/1986, B4:2-6; *Surf*, 11/2/1886, 1:2.
94 Clark, 251, 338; Dillon; *Pajaronian*, 8/15/1878, 1:3; *Sentinel*, 05/11/1872, 3:1, 08/28/1880, 3:4, and 7/8/1888, 1:4.
95 Book of Deeds No. 29, 371 and Book of Deeds No. 29, 40.
96 Book of Deeds No. 28, 139.
97 Hamman, 25; *Weekly Sentinel*, 08/02/1879, 2:2.
98 *Sentinel*, 7/19/1879, 3:5.
99 Hamman, 96; *Weekly Sentinel*, 09/06/1879, 3:6.
100 Book of Deeds No. 26, 579.
101 Pajaro Valley Historical Association, unrecorded records; *Sentinel*, 05/17/1880, 3:1.
102 Payne, "Stagecoach Days in the Mountains," 12-13; and Young, 4-5, 37, 42-43.
103 Lewis.
104 Book of Deeds No. 34, 582.
105 Clark, 312; Hihn Record Book Vol. 3, 51.
106 Book of Deeds No. 26, page 634. *See also* Payne, "Josephine Clifford McCrackin."
107 Hamman, 25-26; *Sentinel*, 03/05/1881, 3:3, 04/16/1881, 3:3, 04/23/1881, 3:2, and 05/14/1881, 3:4
108 *Bennington Banner*, 07/30/1904, 1:4; Clark, 279; *Sentinel*, 04/09/1886, 4:2.
109 Book of Agreements No. 2, 361-366; Devereaux, 43-45; Hamman, 39.
110 Book of Deeds, unknown number.
111 Book of Agreements No. 2, 424; Deveraux, 46.
112 Book of Deeds, unknown number; *Evening Sentinel*, 02/08/1899, 3:2; *Sentinel*, 10/08/1881, 2:4; *Surf*, 1/31/1891, 3:3.
113 Book of Deeds No. 32, 344.
114 Book of Deeds, unknown number; Holder, 340-342; Perry; Young, 60-66, 69-78.
115 Hamman, 39; Marks Family; *Pacific Bee*, 07/15/1882, 5:1; Stoodley, personal files.

Notes

116 Book of Agreements, unknown number.
117 Book of Deeds No. 34, 294.
118 Southern Pacific, "Loma Prieta Branch."
119 Book of Deeds No. 34, 401.
120 Book of Deeds No. 34, 403; Wright, "Map of Santa Cruz County."
121 Hamman, 26.
122 Clark, 172; *Mountain Echoes*, various articles; Young, 53, 57-58.
123 Aiken.
124 Book of Deeds, unknown number.
125 Book of Deeds, unknown number.
126 Book of Deeds, unknown number; Wright, "Map of Santa Cruz County"; USGS Los Gatos Quadrangle (1919, revisited 1942).
127 Hamman, 39-43; *Record–Union*, 05/08/1883, 3:3; Stoodley, personal files.
128 Hamman, 58; *Surf*, 06/20/1883, 3:3.
129 Book of Agreements, unknown number.
130 Hamman, 43; Stoodley, personal files; *Surf*, 08/22/1883, 2:2-3, and 09/18/1883, 3:2-3.
131 Book of Deeds, unknown number.
132 Hamman, 30, 43.
133 Hamman, 43; *Pacific Bee*, 12/08/1883, 5:6.
134 Stoodley, oral history; *Surf*, 11/20/1883, 3:1.
135 Book of Deeds, unknown number.
136 *Surf*, 01/05/1884, 2:2.
137 Book of Deeds, unknown number; Wright, "Map of Santa Cruz County"; USGS Los Gatos Quadrangle (1919, revised 1942).
138 *San Francisco Examiner*, 03/07/1884, 4:2.
139 *Surf*, 05/13/1885, 3:2, and 10/20/1906, 1:3.
140 Clark, 180.
141 *Sentinel*, 07/18/1884, 2:1-2.
142 *Surf*, 09/06/1884, 2:1, and 09/10/1884, 3:4.
143 *Sentinel*, 10/16/1884, 2:1.
144 *Sentinel*, 06/12/1885, 2:2.
145 *Sentinel*, 05/06/1885, 2:3.
146 *Sentinel*, 05/14/1885, 2:2.
147 Clark, 364-365; *Sentinel*, 05/21/1881, 2:2, and 12/03/1881, 3:2.

Notes

148 *Surf*, 06/15/1885, 3:1.
149 *Sentinel*, 07/17/1885, 2:3.
150 *Surf*, 07/31/1885, 3:3, and 06/05/1887, 3:4.
151 *Surf*, 10/27/1885, 3:2.
152 Payne, 137; *Sentinel*, 11/28/1939, 8:7-8; *Surf*, 07/16/1889, 2:2; Young, 60, 83-84.
153 Clark, 182.
154 *Stockton Mail*, 04/07/1886, 2:3.
155 *Sentinel*, 04/11/1886, 5:2, and 05/02/1886, 3:4; *Surf*, 05/31/1886, 1:3-4, and 10/20/1886, 3:3.
156 Book of Deeds, unknown number; Wright, "Map of Santa Cruz County"; USGS Los Gatos Quadrangle (1919, revised 1942).
157 *Surf*, 10/20/1886, 3:3.
158 *Surf*, 11/02/1886, 1:2, and 11/04/1886, 3:3.
159 *Surf*, 11/29/1886, 3:2; Hamman, 58.
160 Southern Pacific, List of Officers (1887).
161 *Surf*, 03/01/1887, 3:3, and 01/16/1887, 3:3.
162 *Surf*, 04/12/1887, 3:2.
163 *Surf*, 05/06/1887, 3:4, and 06/05/1887, 2:2, 3:4.
164 *Sentinel*, 07/10/1887, 3:1.
165 Hamman, 101-102; *Oakland Tribune*, 05/24/1887, 3:7; *San Bernardino Daily Courier*, 03/23/1887, 2:4; *Surf*, 06/28/1887, 3:1.
166 *Surf*, 07/30/1887, 3:5
167 *Surf*, 09/01/887, 2:1.
168 *Surf*, 10/05/1887, 3:2.
169 *Los Angeles Herald*, 10/22/1887, 1:1.
170 Clark, 341.
171 Hamman, 48-54; Harrison, 193; *Surf*, 05/26/1890, 3:1; Mattingley.
172 *Surf*, 05/14/1888, 5:1.
173 *Sentinel*, 05/16/1888, 2:1.
174 *Surf*, 05/18/1888, 5:2.
175 *Surf*, 05/26/1888, 5:5.
176 *Surf*, 07/03/1888, 5:2.
177 *Oakland Tribune*, 07/15/1888, 1:6.
178 *Surf*, 08/15/1888, 3:5.
179 *Surf*, 08/23/1888, 3:6.

Notes

180 *Surf*, 09/12/1888, 2:2.
181 *Surf*, 10/08/1888, 3:3-4.
182 *Surf*, 10/17/1888, 3:4.
183 *Sentinel*, 03/19/1889, 3:2.
184 *Surf*, 02/05/1889, 3:5.
185 *Surf*, 02/18/1889, 1:3, and 10/15/1891, 3:1; *Sentinel*, 06/19/1894, 1:6; *Bennington Banner*, 07/30/1904, 1:4; *Fort Bragg Advocate and News*, 05/17/1893, 3:3; *San Francisco Call*, 05/30/1891, 8:7.
186 *Surf*, 02/18/1889, 3:5.
187 Clark, 147; *Sentinel*, 05/20/1891, 3:3; *Surf*, 03/20/1889, 3:3.
188 *Surf*, 03/21/1889, 3:5.
189 *Surf*, 04/03/1889, 3:5.
190 *Sentinel*, 05/07/1889, 3:5.
191 *Surf*, 05/15/1889, 3:4.
192 *Surf*, 06/05/1889, 3:4.
193 *Surf*, 07/19/1889, 3:4.
194 *Surf*, 08/24/1889, 3:4.
195 *Surf*, 08/30/1889, 2:2.
196 *Surf*, 09/27/1889, 3:4.
197 *Surf*, 11/08/1889, 3:5.
198 *Surf*, 11/20/1889, 3:5.
199 *Surf*, 12/14/1889, 1:4.
200 *Surf*, 12/27/1889, 3:4.
201 *Surf*, 01/13/1890, 1:2.
202 *Surf*, 01/21/1890, 3:4.
203 *Surf*, 02/18/1890, 3:5.
204 *Surf*, 02/19/1890, 4:2.
205 *Surf*, 02/20/1890, 3:2.
206 *Surf*, 02/27/1890, 1:4.
207 *Surf*, 05/26/1890, 2:2.
208 *Surf*, 06/11/1890, 3:3-4.
209 *Surf*, 06/24/1890, 3:5.
210 *Surf*, 04/30/1890, 3:1.
211 *Surf*, 09/02/1890, 3:2.

Notes

212 *Surf*, 09/08/1890, 1:4.
213 *Surf*, 10/20/1890, 1:3.
214 *Surf*, 11/10/1897, 1:3.
215 *Surf*, 11/17/1890, 3:4.
216 *Surf*, 11/26/1890, 3:2.
217 *Surf*, 12/06/1890, 3:4.
218 Mattingley.
219 *Surf*, 03/26/1891, 3:2.
220 *San Francisco Chronicle*, 06/03/1891, 10:3; *Surf*, 06/04/1891, 3:3.
221 *Surf*, 05/18/1891, 1:4.
222 *Surf*, 05/21/1891, 3:2.
223 *Surf*, 05/26/1891, 1:4.
224 *Surf*, 06/03/1891, 3:4.
225 *Surf*, 06/17/1891, 3:4.
226 *Surf*, 06/25/1891, 3:4.
227 *Boston Globe*, 07/31/1891, 1:8, and 03/05/1892, 1:5-6; *San Francisco Chronicle*, 07/26/1891, 11:1-2.
228 *Surf*, 07/27/1891, 2:1, 3:5, and 07/28/1891, 3:3.
229 *Surf*, 08/08/1891, 6:5.
230 *Pajaronian*, 01/14/1892, 3:3; *Surf*, 01/29/1892, 3:5.
231 *Surf*, 03/25/1892, 3:4.
232 *Surf*, 03/26/1892, 7:3.
233 *Surf*, 04/09/1892, 3:5.
234 *Surf*, 04/16/1892, 3:5.
235 *Surf*, 04/30/1892, 1:2.
236 *Sentinel*, 03/12/1892, 4:4; *Surf*, 01/23/1892, 7:3, and 05/17/1892, 3:1.
237 *Surf*, 06/09/1892, 8:3.
238 Southern Pacific, Coast Division Time Table No. 1.
239 Hamman, 62.
240 *Surf*, 02/28/1893, 2:3.
241 Clark, 364.
242 *Sentinel*, 04/26/1893, 3:4.
243 *Sentinel*, 05/04/1893, 2:3.
244 Carruth, 365, 367.

Notes

245 *Sentinel*, 05/09/1893, 2:3.
246 *Sentinel*, 05/19/1893, 3:2.
247 *Sentinel*, 06/01/1893, 3:2.
248 *San Francisco Call*, 06/21/1893, 1:1-4.
249 *Sentinel*, 05/20/1893, 3:3, 08/10/1893, 3:1, and 09/20/1893, 3:1.
250 *Surf*, 08/25/1893, 3:2.
251 *Sentinel*, 12/06/1893, 1:8.
252 *Sentinel*, 12/06/1893, 1:8.
253 *Sentinel*, 12/12/1893, 1:8.
254 *Sentinel*, 12/17/1893, 3:3.
255 *Sentinel*, 12/31/1893, 3:3.
256 *Sentinel*, 01/10/1894, 3:2.
257 *Sentinel*, 01/18/1894, 3:2.
258 *Sentinel*, 02/01/1894, 3:4; *Surf*, 02/01/1894, 3:2.
259 *Sentinel*, 02/10/1894, 3:3; *Surf*, 02/10/1894, 3:3.
260 *Surf*, 11/10/1897, 1:3.
261 *Sentinel*, 03/20/1894, 2:1.
262 *Surf*, 04/26/1894, 3:1.
263 *Sentinel*, 03/10/1893, 3:1, and 08/30/1894, 3:1.
264 Clark, 42.
265 Clark, 364-365; *Sentinel*, 04/04/1895, 3:1; *Surf*, 04/13/1895, 4:3, 04/20/1895, 7:2, 05/24/1895, 4:3, and 11/16/1905, 1:3.
266 *Sentinel*, 08/16/1895, 3:1.
267 *Surf*, 04/29/1897, 1:1.
268 *Surf*, 01/10/1896, 1:2.
269 *Surf*, 01/10/1896, 1:2, and 11/10/1897, 1:3.
270 *Evening Sentinel*, 08/29/1896, 3:1; *Sentinel*, 07/14/1896, 1:1-2, 07/19/1896, 3:2, and 09/27/1896, 3:2.
271 *Surf*, 01/18/1897, 1:1-2.
272 *Surf*, 11/10/1897, 1:3.
273 *Sentinel*, 06/19/1897, 1:6.
274 *Surf*, 06/09/1897, 1:1, and 12/08/1900, 4:4-5.
275 *Surf*, 11/10/1897, 1:3-4.
276 Stoodley, personal files.

Notes

277 *Evening Sentinel*, 08/27/1900, 3:1; *Sacramento Record–Union*, 05/12/1898, 7:5; *Surf*, 05/07/1898, 4:6.

278 *Sentinel*, 03/26/1899, 3:4.

279 *Sentinel*, 03/26/1899, 3:4.

280 *Evening Sentinel*, 04/11/1899, 3:1, and 04/24/1899, 4:2; *Mountain Echo*, 04/08/1899; Southern Pacific Officers Book, 1899.

281 *Surf*, 05/11/1899, 2:1-2.

282 *Evening Sentinel*, 05/10/1899, 3:1.

283 *Surf*, 09/11/1899, 4:4.

284 Holder, 339-348.

285 *Evening Sentinel*, 04/21/1899, 3:4, and 05/20/1899, 3:1; *Sentinel*, 10/31/1899, 3:1; *Surf*, 02/09/1899, 4:3.

286 *Evening Sentinel*, 01/27/1900, 3:1, and 09/07/1900, 2:1; Mattingley; *Sentinel*, 03/16/1900, 3:1; *Surf*, 02/08/1900, 4:2.

287 *Surf*, 02/14/1900, 1:2.

288 *Evening Sentinel*, 05/06/1902, 3:1, and 09/08/1904, 1:2-3; *Sentinel*, 03/02/1900, 3:1, and 07/10/1904, 3:6; *Surf*, 07/06/1904, 2:2.

289 *Sentinel*, 07/29/1900, 3:3.

290 *Standard Union*, 08/14/1900, 1:6-7.

291 *Evening Sentinel*, 12/06/1900, 3:2; *Surf*, 07/25/1900, 4:2.

292 *Evening Sentinel*, 05/09/1901, 2:5; *Sentinel*, 04/13/1901, 2:5; Southern Pacific, Coast Division Timetable No. 17; *Surf*, 04/13/1901, 1:2, 06/11/1901, 1:1-3, 06/12/1901, 3:5, and 06/15/1901, 4:4.

293 Clark, 182.

294 *Evening Sentinel*, 04/07/1903, 1:5; *Sentinel*, 06/07/1902, 4:1.

295 Mattingley; *Surf*, 10/20/1906, 1:1-4.

Select Bibliography

Newspaper articles are cited in full within the endnotes and not included in the list below. The following newspapers have had their titles simplified: *Santa Cruz Evening Sentinel* (*Evening Sentinel*), *Santa Cruz Weekly Sentinel* and *The Santa Cruz Sentinel* (*Sentinel*), *Santa Cruz Surf* (*Surf*), and *The Watsonville Pajaronian* (*Pajaronian*).

Adler, Jacob. *Claus Spreckels: The Sugar King in Hawaii*. Honolulu: University of Hawaii Press, 1966.
Aiken, Charles. Personal files. Harold Lee collection.
Aptos Library. Miscellaneous articles and records.
Carruth, Gorton. *Encyclopedia of American Facts and Dates*. Eighth edition. New York, NY: Harper & Row, 1987.
Clark, Donald Thomas. *Santa Cruz County Place Names: A Geographical Dictionary*. Scotts Valley, CA: Kestrel Press, 2008.
Dillon, Brian Dervin. *Archaeological and Historical Survey of the Soquel Demonstration State Forest, Santa Cruz County, California*. Sacramento, CA: Department of Forestry and Fire Protection, 1992.
Farquhar, Francis P. *History of the Sierra Nevada*. Berkeley, CA: University of California Press, 2007.
Hamman, Rick. *California Central Coast Railways*. Second edition. Santa Cruz, CA: Otter B Books, 2002.
Harrison, Edward Sanford. *History of Santa Cruz County, California*. San Francisco: Pacific Press Publishing, 1892.
Hihn, Frederick August. Miscellaneous records. Santa Cruz, CA: University of California, Santa Cruz, McHenry Library Map Room.

Bibliography

Holder, C. F. "How a Forest Fire Was Extinguished With Wine," *The Wide World Magazine* 5:28 (August 1900).

Koch, Margaret. *Santa Cruz County: Parade of the Past.* Santa Cruz, CA: Western Tanager Press, 1973.

Lewis, Betty. Papers (1985). Watsonville, CA: Pajaro Valley Historical Association.

Marks Family. Personal files. Sandy Lydon collection.

Mattingley, Bernard Woods. Personal files (1965).

Moungovan, Thomas O. *Logging with Ox Teams: An Epoch in Ingenuity.* Logging in Mendocino County (Monograph No. 1). Revised edition. Ukiah, CA: Mendocino County Historical Society, 1968.

Pajaro Valley Historical Association. Miscellaneous records and articles.

Patten, Phyllis B. *Oh! That Reminds Me.* Felton, CA: Big Trees Press, 1969.

Payne, Stephen Michael. "A Howling Wilderness: Education in the Summit Road Area." Santa Cruz, CA: Public Libraries Local History, 1978. https://history.santacruzpl.org/omeka/files/original/9c-4699c3e0dca921585f65bf6c910d51.pdf

---. "A Howling Wilderness: Felling the Giants." Santa Cruz, CA: Public Libraries Local History, 1978. https://history.santacruzpl.org/omeka/files/original/f0f7b73030ae88a086557746ff3a80b7.pdf

---. "A Howling Wilderness: Josephine Clifford McCrackin." Santa Cruz, CA: Public Libraries Local History, 1978. https://history.santacruzpl.org/omeka/files/original/de4337b248b822827bd7ef7177555b47.pdf

---. "A Howling Wilderness: Resorts in the Summit Road Area." Santa Cruz, CA: Public Libraries Local History, 1978. https://history.santacruzpl.org/omeka/files/original/55f9821c8ec7c80251c1884a1ccf3461.pdf

---. "A Howling Wilderness: Stagecoach Days in the Mountains." Santa Cruz, CA: Public Libraries Local History, 1978. https://history.santacruzpl.org/omeka/files/original/de80b293391129d-77d1e511db1db9234.pdf

---. "A Howling Wilderness: The Summit Road Area – Santa Cruz Mountains." Santa Cruz, CA: Public Libraries Local History, 1978. https://history.santacruzpl.org/omeka/files/original/99a1eb8a-2f5a58b44d9235f2c2aa7f12.pdf

Perry, E. D. Plat of Lands of the Estate of E. E. Meyer, being part of Lot

Bibliography

24 of the Rancho Soquel Augmentation. 1919.
Robertson, Donald B. *Encyclopedia of Western Railroad History*. Volume IV: California. Caldwell, ID: Caxton Printers, 1998.
Rowland, Leon. *Santa Cruz: The Early Years*. Santa Cruz, CA: Paper Vision Press, 1980.
Santa Cruz County Records Office. Miscellaneous records.
Santa Cruz Railroad Company. Articles of Incorporation. Santa Cruz Museum of Art & History collection.
Southern Pacific Railroad. Coast Division Employee Time Table No. 1 (07/01/1892).
---. Coast Division Employee Time Table No. 17 (04/09/1899).
---. List of Officers, Agencies and Stations. 1887.
---. List of Officers, Agencies and Stations. 1899. Courtesy Lynn D. Farrar Collection, Central Pacific Railroad Photographic History Museum.
---. "Loma Prieta Branch, Aptos, Loma Prieta: A Map of Real Estate and Right-of-Way Properties through Santa Cruz County, California." 1916.
Stanger, Frank M. Sawmills in the Redwoods: Logging on the San Francisco Peninsula, 1849–1967. San Mateo, CA: San Mateo County Historical Association, 1967.
Stoodley, Albretto. "The Loma Prieta Lumber Company and Santa Cruz in the Early Twentieth Century." Oral history. Interviewed by Elizabeth Spedding Calciano. Santa Cruz: University of California, Santa Cruz, McHenry Library, 1964. https://escholarship.org/uc/item/8pq1n4qt
---. Personal files. Sandy Lydon collection.
Wright, Thomas W., and Charles Herrmann. "Map of part of the boundary between Santa Clara and Santa Cruz Counties, jointly surveyed by order of the respective Board of Supervisors." Santa Clara County, 1880.
Wright, Thomas W., M. V. Bennett, and L. B. Healy. "Map of Santa Cruz County." 1881.
Young, John V. *Ghost Towns of the Santa Cruz Mountains*. Expanded edition. Santa Cruz, CA: Western Tanager Press, 1984.

Glossary of Logging Terms

after cut: *see* back cut

anchor cable: a short line that is used to tie down a donkey engine in order to prevent it from tipping over or pulling itself towards an exceptionally heavy load of logs that it is bringing in.

ass: any of a genus of animals resembling horses but having longer ears and a shorter mane, as the common wild ass of Africa. Donkeys and burrows are domesticated asses. *See also* mule

axe: any of a type of handheld tool with a blade on one end and a handle on the other used in felling timber and producing lumber and other wood products.

against the log: when a skid road or logging road reaches an area where the log train faces an uphill climb. When oxen are involved and the climb is exceptionally steep, the road is generally lengthened in order to ease the burden on the team. If the incline is too steep for the animals, an alternate solution is found, such as utilizing a donkey engine.

back cut (*also* after cut, felling cut): in felling timber, the final cut that is put in a tree after the undercut has been completed.

back line: when using a donkey engine, a cable that is much lighter than the main line and is used to pull the main line into the forest where logs are waiting to be brought in. To do this, the back line is pulled to the logs, wrapped around a stump, and brought back and tied to the main line. The back line is then pulled in, in the process pulling out the main line to the logs. This technique allows an area to be cleared of logs while eliminating the need to move the donkey engine.

bailing wire: a material used in bundling shingles. *See also* hay rope

Glossary of Logging Terms

band rig: a type of headrig that featured a bandsaw revolving around two large wheels.

bandsaw: a toothed steel belt mounted on a band rig.

barber chair: a tree that splits the trunk when falling, leaving the split portion on the stump instead of breaking through cleanly to the undercut.

barker: (1) *see* peeler; (2) *see* peeling bar

barking bar: *see* peeling bar

barley: a cereal grass with dense bearded spikes of flowers, each made up of three single-seeded spikelets. The grain, after processing, is used as a feed for animals.

barley mill: a place where barley grain is processed into feed for animals.

barn shake: a split or sawn wood product used primarily on the roofs of buildings such as barns.

barrel: the drum on a donkey engine around which the main and back lines are wound. An axel runs through the middle of the barrel allowing it to rotate, while flanges at the ends of the barrel can be used to hold the lines in place.

becket hook (*also* swamp hook): a large, all-purpose open hook that is attached to the end of a line or chain used in animal skidding. The hook has a link and a very sharp point at the head that can dig into a log or stump. It can be pulled free easily when the need for its use ends, but with great danger to the men working nearby because of the tension between the hook and the animal.

block: a shingle bolt, used following the invention of a machine capable of tapering shingles.

board foot: a unit of measurement for lumber equal to a board measuring one-foot square and one-inch thick. It is a simple yet confusing term to many, especially when a total as large as 638,589,000 board feet is referenced. Where did such a large figure originate? It is the total approximate amount of lumber produced within Rancho Soquel Augmentation by Joel Bates, Grover & Company, Timothy Hopkins, the Loma Prieta Lumber Company, Frederick Hihn, and the Monterey Bay Redwood Company. This number was estimated in 1916 by the A. W. Elam Company and does not reflect the abandonment of up to twenty-five percent of viable lumber by these companies or lumber produced after this date. The reason for the substantial loss is because competition between firms led to companies ignoring or leaving on the forest floor trees with higher amounts of white sapwood, which was less desirable in construction.

How much lumber is 638-million board feet? According to California State Park officials, this amount of lumber, if loaded onto flatcars, would stretch a distance of 152 miles. An early-day mathematician versed in the production of cordwood from standing trees stated: "if all the trees on just Carmel Fallon's Tract 9 were felled, cut into cordwood, then piled upon the space once occupied by the forest, every foot of ground denuded would be covered to a depth of eight feet."

boat: a tree trunk that is about twelve feet long and hollowed out in the center in order to store tools and equipment. In log trains, the boat is attached to the last log and dragged with the rest of the train.

bridle: two lengths of chain, each three to four feet long, connecting the wheelers to the first log in a train. The bridle is tied together at one end with a ring attached to the oxen's yoke and at the other end with a dog hook that is driven into the sides of the log. The bridle prohibits the log from shearing from side to side. If the first several logs in a train are large with the biggest placed first, several bridles may be required. The lighter logs following are fastened together with a single bridle.

broad axe: a broad-headed axe that has a beveled blade on one side with an offset handle. It is used in hewing crossties and squaring off bridge timbers.

broom boy: usually a young boy who sweeps away dust, chips, rocks, and fallen branches from a skid road being used by a log train.

buck: to cut trees into logs.

bucked logs (*also* felled logs): logs cut up in the woods.

bucker (*also* crosscutter): a person who cuts felled trees into log lengths. The bucker received their instructions from the camp boss, who stated the rules, such as where to cut the tree in the vicinity of

Glossary of Logging Terms

the branches, at the crooked sections, etc. Buckers usually worked alone, where they could set their own pace and potentially accomplish more in the long run. This method was largely restricted to the redwood forests south of San Francisco, where the coast redwoods had a smaller average diameter when compared to the Mendocino, Humboldt, and Del Norte redwoods.

bull: a reliable ox that is used to skid logs; also used to refer to anything mean, big, strong, etc.

bull buck: *see* chopping boss

bull bucker: *see* chopping boss

bull chain: a heavy chain that is wrapped around a log and acts like a brake when skidding logs down a steep hill with animals. Its purpose is to prevent logs from running into the animals pulling them.

bull donkey: *see* donkey engine

bull driver: someone who drives a team of oxen using a goad or prod. He is one of the highest paid men in a logging crew and for good reason. He must know how to handle his oxen—not an easy task. While his team pulls a log train, it is not what he says to the animals, but how well he says it that makes the team work together. The bull driver uses a goad to both train and control his animals while pulling a log train. *See also* bull whacker

bull logging: the skidding of logs using a team of oxen. The earliest known use of oxen on the Central Coast of California was in the vicinity of the Albion River in Mendocino County in the 1850s. At that time, the logs were cut into short lengths and rolled, not skidded, to the landing.

bull puncher: *see* bull whacker

bull team: a team of six to eight yoke of oxen

bull whacker (*also* bull puncher): someone who drives a team of oxen using a bull whip. Generally, a whip is easier on animals compared to a goad or prod. *See also* bull driver

bull wheel: a belt-driven geared wheel that rotates a log during the process of squaring a log; the largest toothed gear wheel on a donkey engine.

bull whip: a type of whip with a long braided handle that is about six feet long with at least three straps at the end that snap loudly when the whip is flicked. Since the thick hide of oxen means that they do not feel the whip when it hits them, the sound serves as the motivating factor that leads them to react to the whacker's commands.

burn off: to burn off the slash wood (the branches and bark from the fallen redwood tree) and undergrowth in early spring before the forest has a chance to dry out. This allows the oxen teams and logging donkeys to get into an area and remove logs. It also makes the job of road builders easier. Any material that is not burned away between the logs and the roadway or along the road's right-of-way becomes the job of the swamper crew.

burro: Spanish word for donkey. A small pack animal common throughout the Southwestern United States. *See also* mule

butt: the bottom of a tree; the stump end of a log.

butt cut (*also* butt log): the bottom log in a felled tree; the cut that severs the bottom log from other logs above it.

butt the skid: to dislocate a log that serves as a part of a skid road, usually requiring it to be replaced.

cant: (1) to turn a log or make it lean to one side; (2) the side of a squared log removed by the headrig's saw that is as long and wide as the log.

cant hook (*also* canting hook): a large hook five feet or more in length with a sharp point on one end that was used to turn, roll over, or lean small logs against something. *See also* peavey

canting hook: *see* cant hook

capstan donkey: the earliest version of the vertical spool donkey engine. The first practical donkey engine was built by Dolbeer, a seafaring man turned logger and founder of Dolbeer & Carson, an early day logging outfit located in Eureka, California. Dolbeer adapted the ship's capstan (an apparatus around which cables are wound for hoisting anchors and consisting of an upright, spool-shaped cylinder that is turned on an inner shaft by machinery, animal power, or by hand) to use in logging, using one small upright cylinder to drive a vertical spool through a set of gears. Manila rope was used at first to haul logs, the line being taken back to the woods by a line horse. It was several years before wire cable replaced rope. A capstan donkey used rope or cable that was about 150 to 200 feet

Glossary of Logging Terms

in length. It brought logs only to the edge of the skid road where bulls could reach them easily. It was some time before loggers developed the method of roading, or moving the logs down the skid road totally by steam power.

capstan spool: the spool that draws rope or cable in or out of a donkey engine. The first capstan spool used on Dolbeer's donkey engine did not start the line on the spool. The line was instead dragged to the logs and then the other end was wound several times around the spool before the source of power turned the spool, thereby pulling the logs in.

carriage: a flat platform upon which a log is tied to allow it to pass beneath a headrig's saw. After each pass, a cant is removed. *See also* ratchet

carriage setter: a person working under a sawyer who operates a dial on a carriage that controls the size of the board that the headrig's saw will cut.

chaser: *see* log chaser

checker axe: an axe with a wide blade that is used to split a large block of wood.

choker: a heavy wire about 40 feet long that has a hook on one end and an eye on the other. When a log needs moving, a choker is put around it and then attached to the donkey engine. As the log is pulled in, the wire tightens around the log.

chokerman (*also* choker setter): a person who places the choker around a log. Unless instructed otherwise, the worker used their own judgment to place the choker. Historically, this position was the second lowest on a logging crew, just above whistle punk.

choker setter: *see* chokerman

chopper: (1) a person who produced cordwood from felled trees or logs. *See also* piece worker; (2) an alternative name for a faller.

chopping board: the springboard upon which fallers stand.

chopping boss (*also* bull buck, bull bucker, *and* head chopper): the foreman of a crew of fallers and buckers.

chopping platform: a staging used instead of a springboard that provides a working place when felling a large tree. Platforms were most commonly used in Northern California.

Glossary of Logging Terms

circular saw: a disk-shaped saw with teeth around the edge that is rotated at a high speed. In order to cut logs of large diameters, two circular saws are used, one mounted on top of the log and another beneath it with each rotating in opposite directions.

clear cut: (1) an area in which all of the standing timber has been removed; (2) to remove all standing timber from an area. Clear cutting old-growth redwoods was standard practice in the Santa Cruz Mountains due primarily to its rugged terrain.

clear log (*also* clear wood): the place on a felled redwood with the least number of knots; typically found in the upper half of the tree.

clear wood: *see* clear log

clevis (*also* shackle): a U-shaped piece of iron with holes bored through the ends. When two chains need connecting, such as when dragging logs, an iron pin is inserted through one end, through the chains, and then through the other end. The pin is then secured in place using a cotter pin.

coast redwood (*Sequoia sempervirens*): a species of evergreen common in the Coast Range of California from Big Sur to the Oregon border. It is distinct from the heavier but shorter giant redwoods (*Sequoiadendron giganteum*) of the Sierra Nevada.

collar (*also* yoke): a piece of timber averaging about five feet long, two feet high, and eight inches thick that joined together two oxen.

commands for bull teams: there were four common commands used to verbally control a team of oxen. These were "GO" for starting a team moving, "GEE" for turning a team right, "HAW" for turning it left, and "WHOA" for bringing a team to a halt.

compound geared donkey: a donkey engine with a gear for low speed and a second direct gear for higher speeds. The yarding drum was geared for power to haul heavy loads. Meanwhile, the haul back drum was geared for speed allowing the back line with attached main line to be returned back to the donkey in a hurry.

cordwood: a type of splitstuff that functions as a fuel source. Before petroleum took over as the primary fuel source used by Americans, cordwood satisfied most energy needs. Houses were heated with cordwood, laundries in San Francisco required it for heating water,

Glossary of Logging Terms

and paper mills in Soquel and Corralitos, the California Powder Works in Santa Cruz, and fruit driers in Watsonville used enormous amounts of it in their operations.

In Santa Cruz County, the biggest users of cordwood were lime kilns. The production of lime was a major industry in the early days. Lime was used in making mortar for construction and needed two main ingredients to be produced: limestone and the fuel necessary to head it. The forests around lime kilns provided the necessary fuel.

Thousands of cords of redwood, Douglas fir, tan oak, madrone, laurel, and other hardwoods were burned. At night, the sky was aglow with the light of kiln fires. The Cowell Lime & Cement Company consumed nearly every standing tree within hauling distance of its kilns, including most of the land in Henry Cowell Redwoods State Park as well as the University of California, Santa Cruz, campus.

corral posts: a type of splitstuff that was intended for use as posts in livestock corrals, often cut to customer specifications. Corral posts were usually wider in diameter and taller than fence posts.

cotter pin: a split iron pin that can be wedged into a hole to fit parts tightly together.

crack-a-jack donkey: a light yarding donkey engine with a large bull wheel that drives two narrow drums placed side by side on a common shaft. It differs from the more common yarding donkey, which places one drum behind the other and requires two shafts.

crosscut: a type of saw that is used for felling and bucking by hand.

crosscutter: *see* bucker

cross skids: small wooden poles laid perpendicular to a road and set no more than five feet apart to create a skid road. Cross skids often had shallow saddles carved into them in order to help guide logs to the center of the road.

crosstie: *see* railroad tie

cruise: (1) a timber inventory; (2) to estimate the quantity and quality of standing timber in a given area. A cruise by a cruiser and their crew is always conducted before logging begins in an area. The potential

Glossary of Logging Terms

yield of an area depends on the quality of logs and the company's preferred thickness of slabs and sapwood.

cruiser: a timber estimator; a person who cruises a forest to estimate the potential lumber yield of an area.

cure (*also* tan): to convert a cow hide into leather by soaking it in tannic acid.

cutting crew: *see* felling crew

deckman: *see* log deckman

dog: (*also* timber dog) (1) to secure a log for movement in order to prevent it from rolling, either while being transported or on a ratchet or carriage while being sawed; (2) a device used to dog a log

dog hook: a short, curved metal stake that has an eye on one end and is driven into a log and tied to another log using a chain. *See also* bridle

dog tripper: a person who knocks dog hooks out of logs at landings after a log is dogged to a location.

dogger: (1) a person who drives dog hooks into logs and stumps; (2) a person who ties a log onto a carriage after it has been pulled from a millpond.

donkey: (1) a domesticated ass, *see* mule; (2) *see* donkey engine

donkey driver: *see* donkey puncher

donkey engine (*also* bull donkey, donkey, steam donkey, steam engine): originally applied to a small steam engine of less than one horse power; later used to refer to any wood-burning boiler that sits on a log or metal platform and releases steam to control a series of gears, brakes, and levers, which in turn control one or more drums, each with a cable wound around it. The drum and its cable are controlled like winches or hoists that can be used to pull a log, or a train of logs, over the ground. The cable (one for each drum) can also hoist logs through the air from ridge top to ridge top or from one side to the other. Dean McCulloch in his book *Woods Words: A Comprehensive Dictionary of Logging Terms*, defines a donkey as "an endless variety of steam, gas, diesel, or electric power plants, plus drums to hold wire rope, all used to haul logs from the woods, to load at landings, move equipment, rig up trees, and in the old days, to lower cars down inclines."

Donkeys are referred to in many ways: by their use, as skidder,

Glossary of Logging Terms

loader, roader, etc.; by the number of drums: two-drum, three-drum; by other characteristics: simple, compound, two-speed; by the size of cylinders, which varied from 6¼' x 10' loaders to 16' x 20' roaders; by such names as 'crack-a-jack,' 'flyer,' 'duplex': or when they don't work, by the worst mess of profanity ever heard. At the height of their glory, twenty-six different types of donkey engines were built in the Pacific Northwest by one firm alone. In 1913, the Willamette Iron Works in one 49-day period built 51 donkeys, all sold before they left the plant to fill rush orders. The most common makes were Seattle, Portland, and Tacoma, named after iron works in those cities; and Washington, Willamette, Vulcan, and others, named for the company that built them.

donkey engineer: a person who operates the controls of a donkey engine under the direction of the log deckman.

donkey pounder: *see* donkey puncher

donkey puncher: a person in charge of a donkey engine who usually sits at the controls after instructing crews on which logs to prepare for movement.

double drum donkey: a yarding donkey engine with two drums, one for the back line and the other for the heavier main line. This was the most popular and the largest type of donkey engine used in Santa Cruz County from the early 1890s into the twentieth century.

Douglas fir (*Pseudotsuga menziesii var. menziesii*): a species of evergreen conifer widespread in the Coast Range of California. When logging first began in the Santa Cruz Mountains, the abundance of Coast Redwood made Douglas fir appear almost nonexistent.

dump man: a person who unloads material from mules at a landing.

duplex flyer donkey: a donkey engine capable of operating a double slackline logging rig. It has two sets of engines that are powered from the same boiler. One engine operates the drum with the skyline, while the other operates the drums that have the back-, main-, and strawlines.

duplex loader donkey: a donkey engine with two loading lines, each on a separate drum operated by separate boilers that allow each line to be operated independently of the other. These engines are capable of running in either direction.

edger: a machine with a number of saws, each controlled by a lever that cuts a cant into boards of predetermined widths. *See also* trimmerman

edger man (*also* gang edger): a person who operates an edger.

faller: a person who fells timber.

falling axe: a type of axe with two blades and a 30- to 48-inch-long handle that is used for cutting springboard slots or cutting notches into trees in preparation for a saw. One side of the axe can be used for taking snips out of a tree, while the other removes the snip. The handle was offset to prevent hands from being skinned during cutting. The falling axe can be quite versatile and its style varies according to personal preference.

feed bag: a canvas sack containing grain that is tied around the neck of a pack animal and over its nose in order to provide it with food.

fell: to chop down a tree.

felled logs: *see* bucked

feller: *see* faller

felling: cutting down trees.

felling crew (*also* cutting crew): a group of people who fell timber.

felling cut: *see* back cut

felling saw: a crosscut saw used to fell a tree.

fence post: a type of splitstuff made from heartwood. Usually split into one of two standard sizes: 3" x 4" x 6.5' or 4" x 5" x 7'. A Grade No. 1 post was free of knots and sapwood, while a Grade No. 2 post was allowed some knots and a small amount of sapwood. Grade No. 2 posts were made from the butt ends of trees and were often very irregular in shape but were more durable than Grade No. 1 posts.

fit chain: a chain with a fit hook on each end that is connected to a ring under the center of a lead yoke of oxen and then connected to the rings of the trailing yokes. The chain ensures that a team of oxen works together.

fit hook: a hook closed by a ring that could be pounded shut to close it or pounded loose to open it.

flyer donkey: any type of fast, powerful donkey engine. *See also* double flyer donkey

Glossary of Logging Terms

froe: a straight blade about ten inches long with a single sharp edge and a handle set at a right angle to the blade used to split shingles and shakes from shingle and shake bolts.

gang edger: *see* edger man

gang mill: a sawmill with a headrig that consists of a number of saws, each operating up and down, that is capable of producing in a single cut one more cant than there are saws.

gang saw: a saw used in a gang mill.

gate saw: *see* sash saw

glut: a type of wedge made of seasoned live oak measuring between 18 and 30 inches used in tie making or to raise a log if it is caught on a skid.

goad stick: a small pole usually made of oak or laurel that is about six feet long, an inch in diameter at one end, and half an inch at the other, with a sharp nail driven into the tip that is used to prick oxen. How much a goad stick was used depended on the bull puncher—some used it sparingly, others chose to be crueller.

go-devil: a type of axe with a blunt blade on one side and a hammer on the other used for splitting logs and driving wedges during back cut operations.

grade: a classification system used in assessing the amount of sapwood present in posts and shakes.

grape stake: a type of splitstuff made from heartwood that is free of sapwood and knots. The standard measurement was 2" x 2" with a variable length and a sharp, hand-cut point at one end.

grease boy (*also* grease dauber, swabber, water boy): a person who greases the cross skids in front of an oxen team traveling down a skid road in order to help the logs skid easier. Grease is used only when water is not available. If a section is too steep, the grease boy sands the cross skids instead of greasing them, increasing friction and slowing the descent of the logs. If the logs become unruly, a suglar is called.

grease dauber: *see* grease boy

guides: *see* line rollers

gypsy drum: a stationary drum attached to a shaft of a donkey engine that allows a donkey engine to be moved in any direction. Most early donkey engines performed their work using this type of drum. In later

Glossary of Logging Terms

years, gypsy drums were reserved primarily for handling strawlines.

hames bells: a set of approximately five bells that hang from the collar of a lead horse in a team in order to notify approaching teams of its presence.

hand axe: a type of axe with a 24-inch handle used in sharpening grape stakes and trimming rough posts. *See also* piece worker

hand faller: a person who fells timber using a crosscut saw.

hay rope: a strong rope made from a hay or grass. Replaced with bailing wire.

head chopper: *see* chopping boss

head faller: the senior-most position in a felling crew.

headrig: a device to which a saw or saws are attached in order to square logs and remove slabs and cants. A headrig can have any combination of band, circular, or vertical saws. In larger mills, multiple headrigs may operate independently, each with its own boiler to provide steam power.

heartwood: the high-quality wood at the center of a tree that has been felled.

hew: to shape a piece of wood with an axe. *See also* broad axe

hung tree: a cut tree that has become lodged in an adjacent tree while falling. It is difficult and often dangerous to detach such trees.

Hudson Bay axe: a small and light axe with a wide cutting face that is used by cruisers for removing brush from a path. This type of axe is not used for heavy work.

jack: a movable, metal device used by lumberjacks in the lumberyard to move piles of stacked and sorted lumber from one location to another.

jackass: a male donkey.

jackscrew: a piece of heavy pipe of variable length with a set of gears that allowed for the pipe to be manually or mechanically lengthened along a screw. At one end, a metal plate or dish was mounted for stability, while on the other end a toothed head or dog with a sharp point was installed. The head or dog was placed against a log and the gears were then rotated using a jack to increase the length of the screw, allowing the device to move a large log using the lifting power of forty men.

Historically, this was probably the most valuable piece of equip-

Glossary of Logging Terms

ment in the logging world. Jackscrews were used in all phases of logging. When a log needed moving, such as from the place where it fell to a nearby skid road, two men each with a jackscrew would set to work. The first man would place his jack beside the log at one end, quickly raising it off the ground and moving it towards the skid road. The second man, after the log again rested completely on the ground, would place his jack at the other end of the log and repeat the procedure. Likewise, if a log became displaced in a log train, a pair of jackscrews used by the suglar and a grease boy could quickly correct the problem.

Until certain safety devices were built into the jackscrew, it was a very dangerous piece of equipment to use. To correct for this, several notches were added to the jack around the handle. If the jack was jarred or began to slip, a pin would fall into a notch, locking the jack in place and stopping the log from rolling backward or the handle from spinning freely. A spinning handle could easily maim a worker and sometimes led to death. A locked jackscrew could also be left in place to allow for a crew to work a log or place more jacks for further stability while preparing it for a move.

jay-hawking: the removing of two rings of bark from a young tan oak tree by a peeler.

jerk line: a long rope attached to the lead horses in order to control them while driving a wagon heavy laden with lumber.

jointing: to remove the rough edge from a shingle or other splitstuff. *See also* sawyer, trimmer

landing: (1) typically a flat area where logs are prepared for skidding; (2) an area where mules are unloaded of material collected from the forest by a dump man and are fed and cared for.

latigo leather: a type of leather used to tie a load of forest material onto the saddle of a mule. The Spanish word *latigo* means whip, cord, strap, or lash. When loading a mule, the packer cuts a side of leather into strips of appropriate size and length as needed.

lay out: to set down a mat made of brush and limbs to serve as a bed for a redwood tree in order to limit damage to the trunk when it falls.

leader: the first two oxen in a bull team, responsible for steering a train.

Glossary of Logging Terms

They are specially trained to respond to voice commands from a bull puncher.

line rollers (*also* guides): free-rolling hardwood poles that a log sits atop allowing it to be more easily moved into place before it is dogged to a carriage.

load: *see* log train

loader: (1) a person who loads logs; (2) any kind of donkey engine used for loading logs onto a conveyance.

log chaser (*also* tree chaser): a person or child who spots a log or logs as it is pulled by a donkey engine from one location to another to ensure that it does not get hung up en route. Part of the job included hooking the main line or choker onto the log or logs and ensuring that the chokers remained in place as the log was moved.

log deckman: a person responsible for pulling logs from a millpond into a sawmill and ensuring that the log is properly positioned and securely attached to a carriage prior to sawing. *See also* donkey engineer

log dogger: a person who dogs a log onto a carriage under the direction of a log deckman.

log pond: *see* millpond

log slip: the wood planks that a log is pulled across when it is hauled from a millpond into a sawmill.

log sniper: a person who rounds off the front end of a log for easier skidding. *See also* snipe *and* sniping axe

log train: a series of logs aligned back to front and connected together using heavy chains with dogs driven into each log and the front log attached to a team of oxen or a donkey engine so that the logs can travel down a skid road from one location to another. Usually, logs in a train are arranged in order of weight or size, with the heaviest or largest at the front.

logger: any person who worked in a forest to perform logging-related tasks.

logging donkey engine: *see* donkey engine

lumber grades: a scale for rating the quality of lumber, based on knots per foot, cracks, kinks, and warp.

lumberjack: a person who sorts lumber by grade and size in a yard and then stacks them using jacks.

Glossary of Logging Terms

main line: a heavy cable of up to 1.25 miles in length and ⅝" in diameter that serves as a donkey engine's primary line. Usually operates in tandem with a back line.

mill fireman: a person responsible for maintaining the fires in a mill's boilers, usually using sawdust, slabs, and/or scantlings.

mill race: (1) a current of water that drives a mill wheel; (2) the channel through which water runs to a mill wheel.

millpond (*also* log pond): a body of water created through the damming of a creek beside a sawmill so that logs can be sorted, soaked, and stored before being pulled into a sawmill for processing. The soaking of logs is necessary in order to keep the headrig's saw from overheating during cutting.

millwright: (1) a person who designs, builds, or installs mills or mill machinery; (2) a person who installs, maintains, or repairs the shafting, belting, and other machinery in a mill.

monitor: a raft used to move logs within a millpond or to retrieve sinker logs.

muley guide: a bearing used to hold a straight saw blade in place in a headrig, allowing multiple blades to move independently.

mule: the offspring of a horse and a donkey, especially a mare and a jackass. Mules are almost always sterile. *See also* ass

mule train: a train consisting of a packer, a saddle horse, and five mules, used to haul smaller log trains and splitstuff.

near side: the rightmost, forward-facing side of a log train.

near wheel: in a lumber wagon, the horse located on the left side nearest the driver.

off bearer: the person responsible for removing the cants or boards from a carriage.

off side: the leftmost, forward-facing side of a log train

ox (*rarely* bullock): a male cow that was castrated at maturity, weighing between 1,400 and 1,800 pounds, used to transport logs in bull teams. The most popular breed of cattle used for ox in the Santa Cruz Mountains was the Bridle Durham, although these were frequently crossbred with Ayshire and other draft breeds.

packer (*also* weaver): (1) a person who packs trimmed shingles into bundles for shipment; (2) a person who loads material gathered in a forest

Glossary of Logging Terms

on the back of a mule.

parbuckling: *see* rolling logs

peavey: a heavy handled tool with a spiked point and a free-swinging hook that is used in the rolling of logs. The peavey was an improvement on the cant hook, with a heavier and longer handle and an iron brad in the handle that was sharp and would stick into a log.

peel: to remove the bark of a redwood tree, thus making it easier to saw in a forest. Logs also have to be peeled before they can enter a sawmill to keep the saws clean and in working condition.

peeler (*also* barker, spudder): a person who removes bark from a tree using a peeling bar.

peeling bar (*also* barking bar, spud): a long steel bar that is used to peel bark from a tree. The bar came in two main versions: a four- to five-foot-long bar made of common steel about an inch wide with a steel tip sharpened to a razor point on one side, used primarily on redwood trees; and a long bar of steel, widened at the end like a screwdriver, used primarily on tan oak trees. Redwood trees would be peeled after being felled, while tan oak trees could be peeled while standing or felled.

picket: a versatile type of splitstuff measuring between 2" x 3" and 3" x 3" and of variable length that can be used as fence posts, survey markers, stakes, or any use requiring a wood post with a sharp end.

piece maker (*also* piece worker): a person who manufactured splitstuff in the forest using only hand tools.

piece worker: *see* piece maker

pike pole: a pole at least ten feet long with a three-inch spike on one end that is used to move logs in a millpond.

planing mill: a post-production mill in which rough lumber is dressed and finished by being passed through planers or edgers. For example, a rough-hewn 2" x 4" board can be planed into a smooth board measuring 1¾" x 3¾". Planing mills also produce commercial products such as doorjambs, window casings, doors, deck lumber, etc.

pole axe: an axe measuring between 26" and 36" with only a single blade, which is used to trim branches from a felled tree. The other side of the blade is flat and can be used to drive pickets, pegs, spikes, etc.

Glossary of Logging Terms

punk: *see* whistle punk

railroad tie (*also* crosstie): a type of wood product intended for use on ballast beds to support rails, measuring on average for standard-gauge tracks 8" or 9" wide by 7" high by 8' long, although they can be longer for switches, sidings, spurs, and other railroad features, sometimes reaching up to 16' in length. Because of their weight and dimensions, railroad ties are only manufactured in a sawmill. Some sawmills also produce narrow-gauge ties of variable dimensions, but all narrow-gauge railroads that operated within Santa Cruz County either brought in railroad ties from outside or used cordwood as a more cost-effective replacement.

raker: a chisel-pointed tooth on a crosscut saw that alternates with and is slightly longer than the side-sharpened tooth. Rakers break the shaving loose and curl it up into the gullet, where it is carried out of the cut, thus preventing binding.

ratchet: a sturdy frame that holds a log in place as it passes beneath a headrig's saw. After each pass, a cant is removed. *See also* carriage

ratchet setter: a person who is responsible for setting the thickness of boards.

ride side: the side of a log on which it will settle as it is pulled along a skid road. In most cases, the ride side is the heavier side of a log, which also usually indicates which side will sit above the water once the log is dumped into a millpond. The people who assemble log trains are responsible for determining the ride sides of the logs to ensure that they do not twist and turn or fall off the road while being pulled. The ride side was sometimes shaved slightly to maintain better stability over skids. *See also* snipe

rigging slinger: a person who oversees the operation of a suspended rigging system and directs the movement of logs across the system.

ring-a-tree: to remove portions or an entire section of bark around a redwood or tan oak tree in order to make sawing easier. Typically done using a peeling bar.

ring of bark: the bark removed in a single piece from a tan oak tree, rolled and usually no more than four feet in length in order to properly be attached to a donkey or mule.

road: *see* skid road

Glossary of Logging Terms

road donkey (*also* road engine, roader): a large type of donkey engine with a large drum capacity for the main line, sometimes up to 10,000 feet of ⅝" cable, used to haul logs from a yarding donkey to within reach of a swing donkey, which usually carried logs to a landing. Road donkeys were not used in Santa Cruz County but could be found elsewhere in the Santa Cruz Mountains.

road engine: *see* road donkey

roader: *see* road donkey

rolling logs: the process of moving logs to a specific place, usually with the assistance of an animal, jackscrew, or donkey engine. When using the latter, logs are either rolled using a becket or swamp hook attached directly to the log with a cable, or the log is parbuckled by wrapping cable around the top of a log several times depending on the distance the log needs to be rolled and then pulling the cable in, slowly rolling it toward the donkey.

rough lock: (1) a metal shoe that was locked onto the wheels of a wagon to stop it from accidentally slipping on a steep grade; (2) a heavy circular chain, usually with a trip link, that can be dropped by a suglar in front of the first log in a log train in order to slow the speed of the logs as they go down a steep grade. At the bottom of the grade, the trip link is released and the chain removed from under the log, although it often has to be dug out with a shovel. *See also* suglar

saddle horse: the horse upon which a packer rides when leading a team of mules.

sap: the viscous liquid that circulates through a tree delivering water, food, and nutrients to its living tissue.

sapwood: the living wood in a tree that increases the size of the tree over time. When sapwood dies, it becomes heartwood, which in a redwood tree produces the highest quality lumber.

sash saw (*also* gate saw): an early type of saw that is held in a frame and driven by a steam engine.

sawn shake: a type of shake that is produced in a mill using automated equipment. *See also* shake

saws: any of a variety of one-sided toothed metal blades used to fell trees. In the Santa Cruz Mountains, most saws were eight to ten feet long,

Glossary of Logging Terms

although trees over ten feet in diameter required longer saws. The two major brands of saws in use in the 1860s through to the early 1900s were Simonds and Disston.

Saws used by fallers had side-by-side cutting teeth with a notched tooth called a raker that cleaned the grove of sawdust on the back pull. The saw's handles were usually simple pegs attached to metal loops, just long enough for both of a man's hands to hold.

Buckers used a saw with four cutting teeth in a row separated by a raker. Usually, the saw had an enclosed loop handle on one end while the handle on the other end was mounted to the top of the saw and set back slightly from the end.

Usually when fallers bought new saws, they would remove the handles and replace them with personal handles that better fit their hands. If they usually worked with the same companion, both fallers would install preferred handles. The handles would pass down from one saw to the next. If a shorter saw was required for jobs such as cutting branches from a felled log or cutting smaller oak or madrone trees, a faller would carefully break a longer saw to turn it into a one-person saw.

sawyer: a person in charge of all operations within a mill, from selecting a log in a millpond to delivering it to the edger. A sawyer also controls a carriage's speed and direction. In shingle mills, a sawyer is responsible for cutting shingles and sometimes jointing shingles as well, although this task was delegated to a trimmerman in larger mills. A sawyer has authority over the donkey engineer, log deckman, carriage setter, and ratchet setter.

scantlings: the edgings from the cants after being run through the edger. Scantlings end up in the same pile as the slabs and sawdust, all headed for the fires that keep the boilers producing the steam to run the headrig.

score: to hack a felled log with an axe before hewing it.

scoring axe: a type of axe used to score a felled log before squaring it with a broad axe.

screw jack: *see* jackscrew

shackle: *see* clevis

Glossary of Logging Terms

shake: a type of wood product used to roof buildings that originally measured ¼" thick, 36" long, and as wide as the shake bolt it is cut from. Split shakes produced in the forest are cut using a froe and have to be hauled by mules equipped with specially modified saddles. Sawn shakes produced in a mill can be cut thinner and trimmed to more exact sizes. Shakes are graded as either No. 1 or No. 2. No. 1 shakes are made entirely of heartwood, while No. 2 shakes have a narrow strip of sapwood on one edge, not exceeding 1" in width.

shake bolt: a type of splitstuff comprised of a block of heartwood from a redwood tree measuring 36" long, from which shakes are produced. Owing to the relatively small size of shake bolts, timber cut in the forest and intended for use as shakes is formed into 72" sticks before being loaded on mules. Upon reaching the mill, these are unloaded and cut in half to create shake bolts.

shake mill: a small sawmill focused almost exclusively on producing sawn shakes using automated or semi-automated equipment. The Loma Prieta Lumber Company used a shake mill in Hinckley Gulch from 1900 to 1906.

shingle: a type of wood product used to cover the roofs of buildings, usually measuring ¼" thick, 16" long, and as wide as the bolt it is cut from. Shingles usually are tapered on one end, which means all shingles are sawn. Higher quality machines are able to cut shingles from ⅜" to 7/16". Shingles produced in the forest are cut using a portable machine and carried out by mules with modified saddles.

shingle block: *see* shingle bolt

shingle bolt (*also* shingle block): a type of splitstuff comprised of a block of heartwood measuring 18" from which shingles are cut. A froe is used to produce a ¼" thick board, after which a machine smooths and tapers the shingle. Owing to the small size of shingle bolts, timber cut in the forest and intended for use as shingles is formed into 54" sticks before being loaded on mules. Upon reaching the mill, these are unloaded and cut in thirds to create shingle bolts.

shingle mill: a small sawmill focused almost exclusively on producing shingles using an automated cutting and tapering machine.

simplex donkey: a type of donkey engine that does not have a set of gears

Glossary of Logging Terms

but rather has a pinion connected to a crankshaft.

single drum yarding donkey: an early type of donkey engine with only one drum and no attached mainline or back line. *See also* capstan spool

sinker log: a log that is too heavy to float in a millpond, sinking to the bottom as soon or shortly after it is deposited. A sinker log is usually a green log that contains enough moisture to counteract its natural buoyancy. The log will remain at the bottom of the millpond until the mill shuts down and the pond is drained, at which point it will be gathered and processed. Since water preserves the quality of timber, it will produce lumber or splitstuff of the same quality as it would have had it not sunk. If a potential sinker log is detected before it is deposited in a millpond, workers may tie it to other logs to keep it afloat until it can be brought into the sawmill. Sinker logs can also sometimes be fished out of a pond without draining it.

skid road: a road usually with horizontal wooden skids at regular intervals across which logs are dragged to a millpond or landing. One of the earliest known skid roads was built by Henry Yesler in 1852 to skid logs from the woods to his mill on the Seattle waterfront. Along the road near the mill, several businesses arose to cater to the needs of the workers, including a company store, saloons, and whorehouses. It was likely for this reason that this section of road and others like it across the United States became known as skid row. It can be argued that skid roads through industrial towns were no more or less disagreeable than any other road in such a place, but the name stuck and later was transferred to any seedy neighborhood in a city.

The Mendocino County Historical Society released a report entitled "Logging with Ox Teams—An Epoch in Ingenuity," which outlines the importance of skid roads to logging:

> *skid roads were not put in for the entire length of the haul, but only where needed. Often at the head of a very steep gulch, they would have a yarding team of oxen waiting. The team would pull the first log to a point where it would not go over the side by itself. After the first log was in place, they would bring up the next log, placing it end to end*

with the first. With a third log they would bump the second log into the first, but not hard enough to push the three over the side. When the entire load was made up and tied together, they placed the yarding team next to the log train while placing a hook into the center log. With a nudge, the entire log train would go over the side while the hook would automatically disengage itself.

When the logs reached the bottom of the gulch, hopefully they would be bunched together end to end alongside the main skid road. Here they had placed skids opposite to the logs and parallel to the skid road's skids. These temporary skids were used to skid the logs up onto the road. Because the logs were probably bunched together, this made it easy to get them up onto the skid road.... If once on the road...the chain connecting the logs was stretched tight between them, it would be difficult, if not impossible, for the oxen to start the load down the road.

To eliminate this problem, jack screws were used. The suglar and the waterboy knowledgeable in the use of the tool would begin with the lead log, placing a jack screw on each side of the log about a quarter of the way back, then lifting the log with it slanting towards the rear. If this operation was not sufficient to move the first log back towards the second, they would use the peavey with its long iron spike in the end. The peavey would be used as a bar at the front end of the log as they attempted to nudge it back towards the second log. Using the peavey would generally move the log back about eight to ten inches. This entire operation would be repeated until the distance between the first and second log was satisfactory. The identical operation would be performed on the second log, but its movement back would not be as much. With the proper distance between the two logs achieved, the operation, if necessary, was performed on the third log to make sure that the spacing between the first three logs was proper. As each log was raised, the waterboy would throw an ample supply of water under it. With proper spacing achieved

Glossary of Logging Terms

between the logs and water applied to the skids, the water boy took up his station alongside the log train, then as the bull puncher gave the command to go, he would begin to put lubricant in front of each log while the broom boy kept the road clear of obstacles. Once the log train was underway, unless there was an obstruction in the road, the team was not stopped until the next landing was reached.

skyline yarding donkey: a type of donkey engine with four separate drums: one for overhead (skyline) operation, one for the main line, one for the bank line, and one for the strawline.

slab: the outer four sections of a log that are removed in order to square the log before cutting it into lumber. Slabs are only cut at a sawmill and are generally not discarded, but rather sold as cheap fencing or for use on roads. Slabs produced at the Loma Prieta Lumber Company mill on Hinckley Gulch were sold to the O'Neill Brothers & Callahan Paper Mill in Soquel to be pulped and turned into dark paper used by butchers to wrap meat.

sled: the platform, typically composed of two heavy redwood logs bolted to smaller cross timbers, upon which a donkey engine's boiler, gears, controls, and operator sit.

sled runners: the two heavy redwood logs that form the main frame of a donkey engine's sled.

snag: a dead standing tree that is dangerous to fell because of loose bark, limbs, or tops. A snag also becomes a torch when an area is ignited to burn the underbrush.

snipe: a bevel hewed across the front end of each log before it is placed in a log train in order to prevent the log from catching on skids and pulling them out. A snipe was usually cut at a 45 degree angle.

sniper: a person who bevels the front end of a log using a sniping axe before the log is joined to a log train. When not sniping, a sniper usually assists the peelers in removing limbs from felled trees using a sniping axe.

sniping axe: a type of axe with blades of at least eight inches on each side of the head. It is used to cut snipes into the front of logs before

Glossary of Logging Terms

attaching them to a log train.

snubbing post: a rounded post stuck in the ground to which an ox is attached. An attached ox can be goaded into circling the post until its rope is tightly wrapped around the snubbing post. Sufficiently snubbed to the post, the ox can be handled by a worker in any way that is needed, such as replacing shoes or treating a wound.

split products: *see* splitstuff

split shake: *see* shake

splitstuff: a broad term that may refer to any type of small, rough timber products, specifically ones that can be cut in a forest outside of a mill. Various types of splitstuff include shakes bolts, shingle bolts, sticks, grape stakes, pickets, fence posts, corral posts, and even cordwood.

In the early years of logging in the Santa Cruz Mountains, the production of splitstuff was big business. This was because the rugged terrain made removal of felled trees from many areas either impossible or too expensive to make a profit. Production of this rough-cut material in the forest required little investment for the piece makers who produced it. Generally, splitstuff can be produced with only a saw, wedges, a sledgehammer, and a lot of muscle power. Splitstuff was typically removed from the forest using mules with specially modified saddles, which restricted the size and weight of the material that was produced.

splitter: a person who produces cordwood from logs.

springboard: a wood board measuring 2" x 6" by whatever length is necessary, balanced upon two short wood blocks that are inserted into notches cut into a redwood tree. Standing on a springboard allows a faller to reach the part of a tree that is easier to cut, generally above burls or a flared base. Sometimes, multiple boards are used, especially for larger trees where more movement by the feller may be necessary.

spud: *see* peeling bar

spudder: *see* barker

steam donkey: *see* donkey engine

steam engine: *see* donkey engine

stick: a type of splitstuff measuring at least 4' long made of heartwood that

Glossary of Logging Terms

can be turned into either shake bolts or shingle bolts.

strawline: a short line used to move a donkey engine or other items short distances.

stump: the section of a tree that is left in the ground after a tree has been felled.

suglar: a person who uses a rough lock to ensure that the logs in a log train do not overtake the ox team. Suglars also help string the chains on the logs and connect couplings.

swabber: *see* grease boy

swamp: to clean out brush by chopping and clearing, as in preparing a road.

swamp hook: *see* becket hook

swamper: a person who cleans out brush in order to get to a felling area. When a swamper is not clearing an area, they use their axe to help peelers remove branches from felled trees.

swamping axe: a type of axe with a wide double-bitted blade that is used by a swamper to clear out brush.

swing donkey: a type of donkey engine used to swing logs from one spot to another or from one donkey engine to another.

tan: *see* cure

tan oak bark: the bark of the tan oak tree that contains the tannic acid used in the curing of cow hide to make leather.

tandem drum donkey: a type of donkey engine with two drums, one for the main line and one for the back line. Usually, the drum for the main line is in front of the second drum. These donkey engines were highly versatile and could be used in yarding, loading, roading, and lowering equipment down inclines.

tannery: a place where cow hide is cured in order to make leather.

tannic acid: a yellowish, astringent substance derived from the bark of the tan oak tree that is used in the curing of cow hides to produce leather.

timber dog: *see* dog

Tommy Moore: a large metal block or pulley sometimes weighing several hundred pounds used in conjunction with a choker line to maneuver logs around obstacles. Although it was invented by Henry Hoeck, the device was not patented. A blacksmith named Tommy Moore perfected the block and marketed it heavily under his own name.

Glossary of Logging Terms

tracks: wood or metal rails upon which a carriage carried logs to and from a saw.

trail maker: a person who prepares paths for mules to travel into and out of a forest.

trailer wagon: a small trailer attached to a wagon that carries lumber.

train: *see* log train

tree chaser: *see* log chaser

trimmer: a machine that turns boards or splitstuff cut on an edger machine into uniform lengths by removing broken ends, bark, and large knots.

trimmerman: a person who operates a trimmer and is responsible for sizing boards and cutting them to the correct lengths. *See also* sawyer

triple drum donkey: a type of donkey engine with three drums, two for main lines and one for a back line. These were used only in Northern California and the Pacific Northwest.

two-speed donkey: a type of yarding donkey with either direct or compound gears. It has a low gear for starting and pulling heavy loads, and a high gear for rapid travel once a load is underway. The high gear can also be used to send the main line out into a forest quickly via the back line.

underbrush: the brush growing on the forest floor.

undercut: the first cut made in felling a redwood tree that determines the direction that the tree will fall.

undercutter: (1) an expert faller who has the job of making undercuts on trees. The task of felling the tree was then left to less experienced fallers; (2) a tool used to support the back of a crosscut saw when making an undercut. Often an axe is used if an undercutter is not available.

water boy: *see* grease boy

weaver: *see* packer

wedge: a metal tool shaped like a V that measures ¾" wide along its edge, 3" on its backside, and up to 16" in length, used in the felling of trees and for cutting splitstuff.

wheeler: the last yoke of oxen in a team, specially trained to hold back the first log in a log train.

whistle punk: a young person who conveys messages between the rigging slinger or chokerman to the donkey engineer when logs are being

Glossary of Logging Terms

yarded. This is often the starting job in a logging crew, but not the least important. If a whistle punk makes a mistake, serious injury or death can result.

widowmaker: a large dead branch, heavy piece of bark, or top of a tree that can fall unexpectedly on a faller causing injury or death.

yard: to move a log from one place to another using a donkey engine.

yarding donkey: a type of donkey engine used to move a log from its stump to a landing where a larger engine can take over.

yoke: (1) *see* collar; (2) a pair of oxen connected together by a collar.

INDEX

Amesti, Jose, 61
Anchorage, The, 35-36
Anthony, Elihu, 15, 34
Aptos, 22, 42, 87, 93-94, 99, 106, 108, 131, 133, 136, 138-139, 157-158, 160-166, 169-170, 173, 176-177, 191, 192-194, 214, 274, 327
Aptos Falls, 197, 223, 235-236, 238, 415-417
Aptos Hotel, 95-97, 109
Aptos mill, *see* Valencia Creek mill
Arbor Villa, 202-203, 403
Averill, Volney, 36, 126
Averon (family), 6, 152
Baird, Bill, 213, 218, 287, 295, 298, 302, 303, 309, 322, 326, 382
Bank of Watsonville, 49, 125-126, 156, 255, 301
Bassett, A. C., 92, 130-131, 139-140, 151-152, 156, 176, 190, 195-196, 239-240, 241, 299, 304, 305-308, 320-321, 330, 339, 380, 408
Bernal (family), 97-98
Betsy Jane (F. A. Hihn Company), 221

Betsy Jane (Santa Cruz Railroad), 84-85, 170, 174
Big Basin Redwoods State Park, *see* California Redwood Park
Bishop, Thomas, 136, 139-140, 192, 207, 330
Blackburn, Harriet, 292
Bockius, Godfrey M., 49, 156
Brown, John Bernard, 3-4, 111-113, 137-138, 152
Brown, Williamson & Company, 4, 100, 111
Burrell (town), 144, 202, 403
Burrell, Birney, 201
Burrell, Lyman J., 11, 123, 129, 141, 404
Burrell School, 28, 202
Buzzard Lagoon, 131, 157, 178, 363-364, 385, 392
Cahoon, Benjamin, 23
Caldwell, Caleb, 120-121
California Coast Railroad, 12
California Redwood Park (Big Basin), 403
California Southern Railroad, 28, 29
Capitola, 15, 50, 111, 262, 267, 410

Index

Castro, María Martina, x, xiii, 98, 106, 201
Castro, Rafael, 41, 61
Chase (family and company), 31, 49, 115
Chinese, 48, 88, 99, 106, 157, 165, 172, 187, 209, 396-398
Comstock (family and mills), 88-92, 109-110, 120-121, 139
Corralitos (town), 3, 190, 258
Corralitos Creek, 3-4, 32, 61, 100, 131-132, 223-224, 355, 364, 371-372
Corralitos Lumber Company, 32-33, 123, 131
Crocker, Charles Frederick, 306-307
Crocker, Charles, 13, 151, 164, 190, 197, 245
Cummings, Charles Osgood, 15-17, 30, 33, 37, 104-105
Cunningham & Company, 32, 349, 356, 368-369, 370
D. A. Rider & Son, 131-132, 364, 371-372, 385, 407-408
Dougherty (family), 8, 132, 134-138, 156-157, 174-176, 196, 226, 287, 295, 302, 303, 309, 355, 408
Dudgeon, Edwin, 157
Edgemont, 35
Ellis, Enoch, 126
Elsmore, Luther, 6-8
Ercanbrack, C. K., 17-18
Eureka Canyon, *see* Corralitos Creek

Eureka Mill Company, 100
F. A. Hihn Company, 267-268, 318-320, 321, 349-350, 359, 379-381, 386-388, 390-392
Fallon (family), 103, 106-108, 110-111, 113-115, 126, 132-138, 153, 154, 156, 177-180, 201
Five Finger Falls, *see* Aptos Falls
Flume Mill, 83, 99
Ford, Charles E., 4-5, 12, 49, 100, 111-113, 134-135, 176, 200, 207, 224, 301
Game Cock mill, 223-224, 226, 256, 321-322, 326, 355, 363-364, 385
Goldman, Edmund, 146-148, 394-395, 399-401
Grover (family and company), 5-8, 13, 31-32, 41, 43-44, 100, 103, 115-117, 141, 152-153, 215-217, 241, 245, 349, 356, 363, 368-369, 370, 372-381, 391, 404
Grover, Cunningham & Company, *see* Grover (family and company)
Hacker, John C., 157, 225-226
Halstead, James L., 4, 111
Heaton (family), 83, 110-111, 113-115
Herman's Place, 146
Highland Center, 11-12, 106
Highland, see Laurel
Hihn, Frederick A., 8-21, 27, 29-30, 33-34, 37, 39-40, 44-45, 47-50, 64, 76-77, 84, 93, 97-

99, 103-106, 111, 113, 115, 118-120, 122, 126, 129-131, 135-136, 138-139, 153, 160-162, 163, 173, 188-189, 194, 199-200, 258-262, 267-268, 337, 369, 371
Hihn Railroad Grade, 258-262
Hihn's Sulphur Springs, 104, 118-120, 262
Hinckley (family and mill), 39, 66, 111, 365
Hinckley Creek mill (Loma Prieta Lumber Company), 65, 77, 366, 382, 405-406, 408-409
Hinckley Creek tunnel proposal, 366-368, 371, 382, 390
Hite, Henry, 123, 140
Hopkins, Mark, xii, 13, 113, 178
Hopkins, Mary (*née* Sherwood), xii, 178-180, 199, 214, 316-318, 322-323
Hopkins, Timothy (*né* Nolan), xii, 177-180, 199, 317, 322-323, 330, 339, 344, 368, 370, 380, 381-390, 408, 410
Hotel Bohemia, 201-202
Hotel de Redwoods, 39, 126, 128
Hotel Miltonmont, 12
How, James, 13
Hoy, Jones, 3
Huntington, Collis, 13, 197, 306, 320-321, 408
Knox, W. F., 157, 164-165, 174, 187, 197
Lassen, Peter, 61-62

Laurel, 105-106, 126-128, 154-156, 262
Laurel Creek mill, 71
Linscott, James, 6, 100, 176
logging (practice), 53-81
Loma Prieta Branch, 180-188, 197, 221-223, 229-241, 292-295, 328, 329, 350-355, 366-368, 390, 389-390, 405, 411-417
Loma Prieta German colony, 141-148, 393-404
Loma Prieta Lumber Company, 60, 65, 77, 80, 174, 184, 191, 192, 195-199, 200, 204-209, 214, 215, 221, 223, 225, 228, 235-236, 240, 245-247, 249-253, 254-255, 295, 304, 322, 323, 329-330, 339, 344, 349-355, 356-359, 368, 381, 386-388, 389-392, 404-407, 408-417
Loma Prieta Post Office, 188, 207, 411
Loma Prieta Railroad, 151-152, 153, 157-160, 163-173, 174-175, 180
Loma Prieta School, 208, 256, 411
Lomita Ranch, 404
Loomis, Fred, 113
Mangels, Claus, 41, 176
Mare Vista, 142-144, 396, 403
Mark's Place, 146
McCrackin, Josephine, 129, 143, 201, 393-403
McKiernan, Charles "Mountain Charlie," 103, 115, 154

Index

Meyer, Ernst Emil, 141-145, 394-403
Molino mill (Pacific Improvement Company), 76, 184-188, 195, 199, 204, 209, 215, 381, 385
Monte Paraiso, 129, 201
Monte Vista mill (1884-1887), 69, 71, 163-168, 180-184, 192, 195-199, 200, 209-211, 214, 223, 224
Monte Vista mill (1887-1900), 199, 223, 235-241, 352-355, 363, 366, 381, 390, 405, 409, 411-416
Monterey Bay Redwood Company, 60, 71
Montgomery (family), 109-110, 395
Morrell, Albert, 156
Morrell, Brad, 83, 99, 115, 121, 154, 156
Morrell, Hiram, 92, 156
Mountain Home, 201-202, 404
Mountain School, 23
Nichols, Benjamin, 15, 85, 108-109
Nichols Iron & Magnesia Springs, 108-109
Olive, Charles Wesley, 32, 41
Olive Springs, 71, 365-366
Opal, 80, 410-411
Pacific Improvement Company, 76, 130, 136, 151, 154, 164-165, 199, 207-208
Pajaro mill, 214, 224, 254
Panic of 1873, 48-49
Panic of 1893, 334-335
Parker, Charles H., 83-84, 110-111, 157

Partridge, Mr., 157, 169, 171, 174, 181, 187, 197
Patchen, 34-37
Porter, Benjamin, 15, 47-48, 100, 103, 120-121, 141
Porter, George, 103, 120-121, 141
Porter, John, 15, 49, 125, 132-138, 156-157, 176, 200, 344, 407
Porter, Warren Reynolds, 125-126, 176, 207-208, 251, 338-339, 404-405, 410-411
railroad debate, 8-10, 11, 19-27, 29-30, 33, 37, 44-45, 46
Ramsey Gulch mill, see Game Cock mill
Rancho Aptos, 41, 61, 97, 153, 176
Rancho Soquel Augmentation, *see* Shoquel Augmentation
Rancho Soquel, x, 15, 120, 121, 135, 259-260
Ricardo Gulch, 98
Rider, Dickamon Allen, 32-33, 131-132, 256-257, 407-408
Sanborn, Alvin, 5, 12, 111, 137-138, 139-140, 152, 156, 176, 191
Sanborn, Lucius, 4-5, 111, 200, 207, 392
Sanborn, Newman, 4, 5, 111
Santa Clara & Pajaro Valley Railroad, 12-13
Santa Cruz & Watsonville Railroad, 34, 42-43, 47
Santa Cruz Lumber Company, 349-350, 379-381, 390-392

Santa Cruz Railroad, 47-48, 49, 50, 84-88, 93-97, 98-99, 101-102, 103-104, 121-122, 129-131
Schultheis, John, 126-128
Shoquel Augmentation, x-xii, 6-7, 15, 39, 90-91, 106-108, 112, 117, 135-136, 138, 179, 198, 217, 228, 299, 318-320, 366, 386
Sinclair, Pruett, 3
Skyland, 11-12, 106, 144
smallpox, 156
Smith, Nicholas T., 139-140, 151, 156, 176, 255, 304, 339
Soquel, x, 14-15, 21-23, 24, 25, 38-39, 84, 88, 93, 96, 106, 122, 125, 216, 259, 262, 377, 406
Soquel Turnpike, 12, 34, 37, 38-39, 89-92, 109-110, 126-128, 226-229
Soquel wharf, 116
South Pacific Coast Railroad, 100-101, 103, 105-106, 121-123, 124-125, 130-131, 135, 160, 165, 224-225, 329
Southern Pacific Railroad, 11, 12-13, 22, 28, 30-31, 44-47, 92, 130-131, 135-136, 138, 139-140, 151-152, 154, 157-160, 164-165, 169-170, 173-174, 177-180, 197, 204-205, 207, 221-223, 224-225, 229-241, 258, 260, 292-295, 305-308, 318, 320-321, 353, 363, 366-368, 371, 382, 388-390, 405-407, 409, 411-412
Spignet Gulch mill (Hihn), 76, 226-229
Spignet Gulch mill (Loma Prieta Lumber Company), 409
Spreckels, Claus, 41-42, 47-48, 95-97, 99, 103, 153, 169, 176
Stanford, Leland, 13, 37, 46-47, 197, 338
Summit Hotel, 113
Taylor, James, 31, 269
Trout, Emmanuel T., 98
Trout Gulch mill, 97-98, 160-162, 191
Valencia Creek mill, 64, 71, 97-98, 191, 192, 199-200, 211-215, 218-221, 224, 243, 245-247, 249, 267, 320, 338, 339, 356, 359-360
Valencia Post Office, 332, 340, 360
Valencia School, 200, 244, 247, 268, 271, 282, 285, 290, 292, 316, 341, 360, 411
Villa Bergstedt, 148, 401
Waterman, Frederick H., 43-44, 83, 111, 126, 157
Watsonville, x, 3, 4, 9-11, 12, 19-29, 43-45, 49, 77, 84, 85-87, 99, 103-105, 164, 176, 254, 301, 330, 385, 404
Watsonville mill, 254
Watsonville Mill & Lumber Company, 111-113, 123, 132-138, 151, 152, 157-158, 160, 163, 164, 174, 177, 188-189, 192, 194, 196-197, 214, 223, 322
Wilcutt, Joseph Lewis, 151
Williamson, William, 4, 111
Willows, The, 203-204

Ronald Gabriel Powell was an electrical engineer and local researcher from Los Altos, California. He received his engineering degree from Cogswell Polytechnic Institute in San Francisco in 1953. For most of his career, he worked at Lockheed's Missile Systems division, Rytheon, and GTE Sylvania. He retired in the late 1970s and started exploring and photographing The Forest of Nisene Marks. Around 1990, he began writing his long history of Rancho Soquel Augmentation and later donated his research to the McHenry Library at the University of California, Santa Cruz. Powell died on September 11, 2010 at the age of 79.

Derek R. Whaley is a historian, librarian, and former resident of Felton, California. He earned a doctorate in history from the University of Canterbury in 2018. He began researching Santa Cruz County history in 2011 and continues to do so from overseas. He has worked at the Santa Cruz Beach Boardwalk and The Tech Museum of Innovation, volunteered at the San Lorenzo Valley Museum and Santa Cruz Museum of Art & History, and is well-known for his Santa Cruz Trains book series and website. He currently lives in Aotearoa New Zealand.

www.ingramcontent.com/pod-product-compliance
Lightning Source LLC
Chambersburg PA
CBHW021138160426
43194CB00007B/616